ACROSS OCEANS OF LAW

Global and Insurgent Legalities

ACROSS OCEANS OF LAW

The *Komagata Maru* and Jurisdiction in the Time of Empire

| RENISA MAWANI |

Duke University Press   Durham and London   2018

Printed in the United States of America on acid-free paper ∞
Cover and text designed by Courtney Leigh Baker.
Typeset in Garamond Premier Pro by Graphic Composition, Inc., Bogart, GA.

Library of Congress Cataloging-in-Publication Data
Names: Mawani, Renisa, [date] author.
Title: Across oceans of law : the Komagata Maru and
jurisdiction in the time of empire / Renisa Mawani.
Description: Durham : Duke University Press, 2018.
| Includes bibliographical references and index.
Identifiers: LCCN 2018008234 (print) | LCCN 2018012234 (ebook) |
ISBN 9780822372127 (ebook) |
ISBN 9780822370277 (hardcover : alk. paper) |
ISBN 9780822370352 (pbk. : alk. paper)
Subjects: LCSH: Komagatamaru (Ship) | Guradita Siçngha,
1859–1954. | Law of the sea—History—20th century.
Classification: LCC KZA1145 (ebook) | : LCC KZA 1145 .M258 2018 (print)
| DDC 341.4/5—dc23
LC record available at https://lccn.loc.gov/2018008234

Duke University Press gratefully acknowledges the support of the
Peter Wall Institute for Advanced Studies at the University of British
Columbia, which provided funds toward the publication of this book.

Cover art: *Komagatu Maru leaving Vancouver*. Photograph by Leonard Frank. Courtesy of
the Vancouver Public Library, 16639.

For the future ... Lialah   Sayeed   Safiya   Zia

Contents

Illustrations

Acknowledgments

In *Labyrinths*, Borges writes that "a book is not an isolated being: it is a relationship, an axis of innumerable relationships." Though his reflections gesture to the intimacies and interactions between author, reader, and text, they aptly describe the "innumerable relationships" that inspire, nourish, and sustain the process of writing a book, from which I have benefited, and for which I am grateful.

A number of institutions have generously supported my research, including a Hampton Research Grant from the University of British Columbia (UBC) and a Standard Research Grant from the Social Sciences and Humanities Research Council for Canada (SSHRC). The Dean of Arts Faculty Research Award and a one-year residency as a Wall Scholar at the Peter Wall Institute for Advanced Study (UBC) gave me the rare gift of time so I could think, write, and ultimately, finish the monograph. I am especially grateful to the Peter Wall Institute for providing a vibrant intellectual space where interdisciplinarity is curated, stimulated, and nurtured. Thanks to the other Wall Scholars in my cohort and to the program staff—especially Emma MacEntee—for making my year in residence so formative and memorable.

In the eight years I have been researching and writing, I have received overwhelming generosity from family, friends, colleagues, and strangers. The archival research for this project took place in cities located across several oceans, in Vancouver, Ottawa, London, Glasgow, and Delhi. This undertaking would not have been possible without the assistance of many people. Sanjeev Routray found documents in Delhi that have since become a central focus of this book, and Prabhsharanbir Singh assisted with translations from Gurmukhi to English. Over the years, I have learned so much from my ongoing discussions with each of them. Nilum Panesar, whom I did not know at the time, sent articles and images as unsolicited gifts. Darren Pacione located key texts when I needed them most, and Radhika Singha facilitated the permissions process at a critical time in the book's completion. Parvinder Dhaliwal and Gurdip Singh translated several archival documents and discussed them with me in detail. For their assistance and patience, I am indebted to the archivists and staff at the British Library, Asian and African Studies Reading Room (London); Caird Library (Greenwich); Glasgow City Archives; City of Vancouver Archives; Guildhall Library (London); Library and Archives Canada (Ottawa); UBC Special Collections; and Vancouver Public Library. Melanie Hardbattle at Simon Fraser University's Rare Books and Special Collections and Jaya Ravindran at the National Archives of India (Delhi) deserve special mention.

Many friends and interlocutors asked critical questions and offered feedback that shaped the final product in innumerable ways. Many thanks to Antoinette Burton, Denise Ferreira da Silva, Eve Darian-Smith, Jonathan Goldberg-Hiller, Thomas Kemple, Kunal Parker, Cliff Pereira, Mitra Sharafi, Nandita Sharma, Radhika Singha, Chris Tomlins, and Anand Yang.

Over the past few years, the *Komagata Maru* has become a topic of resurgent interest among historians, community researchers, artists, and others. I am grateful to Hugh Johnston for discussing his legal sources with me and to Rita Dhamoon for inviting me to collaborate on a workshop to mark the centenary of the ship's arrival to British Columbia. Thanks to all the participants at this event, especially Satwinder Bains and Davina Bhandar, who were co-organizers and more recently collaborators. Radhika Mongia's work has been an inspiration throughout, and I'm pleased we could be together to experience the centenary celebrations in Victoria, Patiala, and Chandigarh. There is now a new generation of historians who, through community engagement and public history, are reinterpreting the role of the ship and documenting the many contributions of South Asians in early Vancouver. I am especially thankful to Naveen Girn and Milan Singh. The website and digital archive they helped to create—*Komagata Maru: Continuing the Journey*—has become a vital resource for researchers. The many events they have organized, along with their recent podcasts, speak to the importance of community-based research and the need to reach a wider audience.

Many friends and colleagues have offered comments, suggestions, and various forms of support. Special thanks to Neel Ahuja, Phanuel Antwi, Suchetana Chattopadhyay, Shaunnagh Dorsett, Stacy Douglas, Peter Fitzpatrick, Julian Go, Ayesha Hameed, Mark Harris, Iza Hussin, Stephanie Jones, Riyad Khoya, Michelle McKinley, John McLaren, Minelle Mahtani, Bruce Miller, Stewart Motha, Adele Perry, David Sealy, Bernhard Siegert, Irina Spector-Marks, Juanita Sundberg, Alka Tandon, Mariana Valverde, Danny Vickers, Geoffrey Winthrop-Young, and Nurfadzila Yahaya. Leopold Lambert drew all of the initial maps with great care. His work has inspired me to do more with visual archives. Many friends also took time to read and comment on draft chapters at various stages: Bonar Buffam, Antoinette Burton, Eve Darian-Smith, Jon Goldberg-Hiller, Anna Jurkevics, Chris Tomlins, and Anand Yang. Tom Kemple read the penultimate version and provided constructive feedback gently, as only he could. My deepest gratitude goes to Antoinette Burton for her ongoing guidance, mentorship, and friendship and for pushing me to clarify everything, always. She models brilliance and generosity as a way of being in the academy. Her example is a rare gift.

My current and former students have been a continual source of insight, community, and camaraderie, even after moving on to pursue their own interests and careers. In particular, Elizabeth Bruch, Bonar Buffam, Sherry Dilley, Shelly Ikebuchi, Leah Keegahn, Stefano Pantelone, Pooja Parmar, Sanjeev Routray, and Tanvi Sirari have helped to create a stimulating intellectual environment that remains even after many of them have left. I am also grateful to students in my graduate and undergraduate classes who indulged me with such patience, as I wove ships and oceans into our discussions of law, history, and social theory.

In addition to those already mentioned, many colleagues at UBC have provided encouragement, enthusiasm, and much more. As successive department heads, Francesco Duina and Sean Lauer produced and sustained a collegial environment and always made space for interdisciplinary work. Rumee Ahmed, Ayesha Chaudhry, Dawn Currie, Gillian Creese, Sneja Gunew, Stephen Guy-Bray, Chris Lee, Becki Ross, Mark Vessey, Rima Wilkes, and Henry Yu have been terrific colleagues, and in some cases, collaborators.

At Duke University Press, Courtney Berger has been an exemplary editor. Long before I could, she saw something coherent in the many disparate strands that have now become this book. She pushed me to refine my arguments from the very start, to work harder to realize the ambitions of this project, but also restrained me when it was time to move on. Sandra Korn, Jessica Ryan, and the marketing team have been wonderful in moving the production process forward. Paul Betz cleaned up my prose and Roberta Engleman compiled the index. I am especially thankful to the three readers—Clare Anderson, Gaurav Desai, and Isabel Hofmeyr—no longer anonymous, who provided such rigorous and detailed feedback at different stages. Their comments challenged me to clarify key ideas and interventions and their enthusiasm was deeply appreciated. Catherine Hall and Michael Watson at Cambridge University Press deserve special mention for believing in this project in its early stages and for devoting time and resources to it.

Parts of this work have been presented at Boston University, Cambridge University, Carleton University, University of Kent, Northwestern University, Panjab University, Punjabi University, Queen Mary University, Ross Street

Gurdwara, Simon Fraser University, the University of Alberta, the University of British Columbia (Allard School of Law, Chan Centre, Green College, Peter Wall Institute, and the Institute for Gender, Race, Sexuality, and Social Justice), the University of Chicago, the University of Hawai'i, the University of Leiden, the University of North Carolina at Chapel Hill, the University of Portland, the University of Toronto, the University of Victoria, York University, and the Vancouver Museum. Many thanks to those who invited me to speak and made arrangements for my visits, and to the audiences for questions and comments on works-in-progress.

Various sections of chapters 4 and 5 have been published in earlier forms in the following journals and books and are reworked and reprinted with permission here: "Specters of Indigeneity in British Indian Migration, 1914," *Law and Society Review* 46, no. 2 (2012): 369–403; "Law and Migration across the Pacific: Narrating the *Komagata Maru* Outside and Beyond the Nation," in *Within and Without the Nation: Canada's History as Transnational History*, edited by Adele Perry, Karen Dubinsky, and Henry Yu (Toronto: University of Toronto Press, 2015), 253–75; "Sovereignties in Dispute: The Komagata Maru and Spectral Indigeneities, 1914," in *Legal Histories of the British Empire: Laws, Engagements, Legacies,* edited by Shaunnagh Dorsett and John McLaren (New York: Routledge, 2014), 107–23; "Criminal Accusation as Colonial Rule: The Case of Gurdit Singh," in *Accusation: Creating Criminals,* edited by George Pavlich and Matthew Unger (Vancouver: University of British Columbia Press, 2016), 73–99.

Throughout and always, my family has been an ongoing and unconditional source of love, support, and guidance. My parents, Najmudin and Zarin, have reminded me of what matters most and why. My father-in-law, Nizar, asked me weekly how my writing was going but never when I would finish. Rosy, Sarah, Shezmin, and Sadru Madhani gave me good company and a place to stay during my regular research trips to London. My brother, Ash, sister-in-law, Ashifa, and nephew, Zia, as they work through the unimaginable pain of losing a child and a younger sibling, have humbled me with their astonishing strength and courage. Safiya, I know, is always with us. The elders in my family—aunts, uncles, and cousins—have taught me that the past endures and animates us often in unexpected and inexplicable ways. My nieces and nephews help me believe that the future can be otherwise.

Without Riaz, my life partner, best friend, and soul mate, nothing would be possible. Through the joys and struggles of parenting, the demands of competing careers, and amid the unexpected and immeasurable grief of loss, our love has endured and deepened. Between our discussions of commerce, shipping, and time, our mutual commitments to family and community, and his insistence on living generously and with humility, Riaz reminds me of how much I still have to learn. Our children, Lialah and Sayeed, have inspired me from the very start. The conceptual framing for this project developed out of a world map filled in and colored by my daughter, Lialah, who was seven at the time. The map, with all of its misspellings, has remained on our kitchen table for the past five years as a kind of lesson plan, reminding me not only that oceans make up most of the earth, but that they are generative spaces that connect rather than divide, and are important to think with. Without her cartographic curiosities, this book would have been very different. Over the many years I have been researching and writing, Sayeed has been an attentive listener, critical commentator, and invaluable interlocutor. He has indulged my interests in ships and oceans and has invited Gurdit Singh to join our family. As Lialah and Sayeed have grown into kind and beautiful souls, their talents, aspirations, and many accomplishments have been a source of strength and motivation, reminding me of the unlimited power that ensues when determination meets imagination. With love and gratitude I dedicate this book to them and to the future.

Currents and Countercurrents of Law and Radicalism

Steam has brought India into regular and rapid communication with Europe, has connected its chief ports with those of the whole south-eastern ocean, and has revindicated it from the isolated position which was the prime law of its stagnation. The day is not far distant when, by a combination of railways and steam vessels, the distance between England and India, measured by time, will be shortened to eight days, and when that once fabulous country will thus be actually annexed to the Western world.—KARL MARX, "The Future Results of British Rule in India," 1853

We, Indians, boast that we are enjoying our rights and religion. The Western tyrants, Eastern slaves, and some Indians say that every nation has a right to prevent natives of other countries from entering their dominions. We ask whether the earth is the property of anyone's father? God has created things for the enjoyment of mankind, it is open to anyone to derive benefit from it.—DALJIT SINGH (Secretary to Gurdit Singh), "Manuscript on the *S.S. Komagata Maru*," c. 1914

In February 1914, Baba Gurdit Singh, a fifty-five-year-old "native of the Amritsar district" in Punjab and a purported rubber planter in Malaya, issued a "Proclamation to Indians."[1] Directed primarily at his Sikh countrymen, this was not an announcement, as its title suggests, but an urgent appeal for private investors. "Awake Oh Indian brothers, the night has passed. Why are all you stars (sons) of Sat Guru (God) sound asleep. Negligence has ruined us: we should destroy negligence now and should jointly and wisely do the work."[2] The "work" to which he so passionately referred was maritime trade and commerce. Since moving to Malaya in the 1880s, and after working in various industries,

Singh established himself as a successful railway contractor. However, his current proposal took an entirely different tack. It turned from land to sea, seeking sponsors to fund a new commercial venture, the Sri Guru Nanak Steamship Company. At first glance, Singh's proposal seemed carefully and deliberately planned out. He would charter a steamship and cross the Pacific. If this initial voyage proved successful, he would purchase the vessel and then three more. His fleet of four ships would eventually travel the Indian, Atlantic, and Pacific Oceans, carrying Indian passengers and commodities from Bombay to Brazil and Calcutta to Canada, placing India at the center of maritime worlds. The Guru Nanak Steamship Company, Singh promised, would yield high financial rewards. It "will increase the money of share-holders with profits," he urged, while expanding India's role in global trade.[3] "Improve yourselves and your nation. Do not continue in sound sleep." Buy shares in the Guru Nanak Steamship Company "and sell to others also."[4] For Gurdit Singh, the illustrious history of Indian shipping was not the past but the future.[5] More than railways, it was steam vessels that opened a pathway to freedom from British imperial rule.

The Guru Nanak Steamship Company, as Singh envisioned it, would someday become a global commercial enterprise. But it also held political objectives that were equally significant. Given the growing legal restrictions imposed on Indian mobility by the white settler colonies of Natal, Australia, Canada, and the United States, and the role of steamship companies in extending maritime surveillance and expanding immigration controls, Singh's proposal was both timely and urgent. His firm would ensure the unobstructed journey of Indian migrants and travelers from the subcontinent outward. If the steamship company's "offices are everywhere, and its steamers travel (round the world)," Singh reasoned, "then the Gurmukh (Sikhs) can travel everywhere and no one can stop them."[6] Become traders and "merchants and derive benefit," he cajoled. Relinquish "all differences, for now is the time to work." Though Singh encouraged all his countrymen to unite in the interests of a common economic and political goal, it was the triumph of Sikhs that was foremost on his mind. "The flag of Guru Nanak shall fly (on our ship), and all the world shall see it, and we shall be reckoned among nations."[7] Notwithstanding his ambitions and assurances, Singh's plan was missing a key element. At the time of his proclamation, he did not yet have a vessel. It was not until one month later, and after several failed attempts, that he successfully chartered the SS *Komagata Maru*, a British-built and Japanese-owned steamship (see fig. I.1). In an unprecedented voyage that departed from Hong Kong in early April, and stopped briefly to recruit passengers in Shanghai, Moji, and Yokohama, Singh transported 376 Punjabi

FIGURE I.I. Gurdit Singh is pictured here in a white suit, waving binoculars, on the upper deck of the *Komagata Maru*. The photo was taken sometime after the ship landed in Vancouver Harbour (c. May 1914). (Photo courtesy of Vancouver Public Library, Accession number 136, Canadian Photo Company)

migrants across the Pacific to Vancouver. Those aboard were mainly Sikhs and adult men. However, there were some Hindu and Muslim passengers, two women and three children, including Gurdit Singh's six-year-old son, Balwant.[8]

Despite the grand objectives he conveyed to potential investors, Singh's steamship company was no more than a pipedream. There were no ships, shareholders, or profits, only scandal and insurmountable debt. The *Komagata Maru* did not fly the Guru Nanak flag but a Japanese one. Its passage to Vancouver was the first and last under Gurdit Singh's command. Though his company was not "reckoned among nations," as Singh had hoped, his audacious plan to charter and launch a ship along the Pacific drew the attention of colonial authorities and anticolonials from various parts of the British Empire and beyond. The steamer's passage unleashed a series of repressive laws—in Canada, India, and elsewhere—that expanded and fortified legal restrictions on Indian mobility. Canada's newly revised immigration legislation, which barred most of

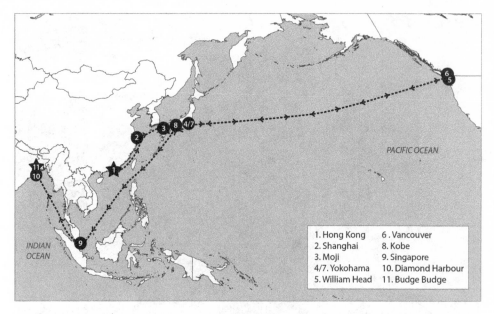

MAP I.I. The outbound and return voyages of the *Komagata Maru,* April–September 1914.

the *Komagata Maru* passengers from entering the Dominion, was not repealed until 1947, when India gained independence from Britain.[9]

In June 1914, four months after Gurdit Singh made his announcement, Bhag Singh and Husain Rahim issued their own call for financial support, this time from Vancouver. On 23 May 1914, after a long and arduous six weeks at sea, the *Komagata Maru* finally landed at Vancouver Harbour (see map I.1). But only twenty passengers were allowed to disembark.[10] The others, including Singh, were detained aboard the ship, where they would remain for two months in deplorable conditions and with limited supplies of food and water. In 1913, the British Columbia Court of Appeal had struck down the continuous journey provision, which effectively barred the entry of Indians to Canada. Almost immediately, the Dominion government began revising the regulation and passed a new order-in-council while the *Komagata Maru* was at sea.[11] The ship was in serious trouble, and those ashore knew it. If the "Proclamation to Indians" penned by Singh was directed at Sikhs, the second appeal was cast more widely. "Oh brave Indian people, you may have seen and heard that the Guru Nanak Company's steamer *Komagata Maru,* whose arrival has been expected and awaited for a long time, reached Vancouver," Bhag Singh and Husain Rahim wrote.[12] The ship was moored in the harbor, proximate to the shoreline and within clear sight of onlookers. Though it was clearly located within Canadian waters, "Immigration authorities have not given any decision about her," the two men charged, "and no Indians (residing in America) can see the passengers." Local police were judiciously guarding the vessel "on every side" as it lay anchored "on the sea." Security was so tight, "not even the passengers' [legal] Counsel is allowed an interview."[13]

As a British subject, Gurdit Singh, like many of his contemporaries, insisted on a legal right to travel throughout the British Empire. By chartering a ship and commanding its transpacific passage, however, he asserted an unparalleled legal and political claim to the sea. From the early seventeenth century onward, European maritime empires—especially the Portuguese, Dutch, and later British— engaged in lively debate on the racial and legal status of the high seas. The publication of Hugo Grotius's *Mare Liberum* in 1609 afforded these deliberations a newfound significance.[14] Here, the Dutch jurist concluded that the high seas were the "free sea," a common space that was beyond national and imperial claims to sovereignty. In drawing this conclusion, Grotius imposed an elemental and juridical distinction between land and sea, a divide that has since featured prominently in European thought, most visibly evidenced in maps of world regions.[15] Importantly, this distinction remains foundational to international and maritime law today. Notwithstanding its designation as "free," the high seas, from Grotius onward, were highly regulated.[16] Britain's ascendency as a maritime empire was achieved through a *juridification of the sea*, advanced in legislation, treaties, agreements, and in legal restrictions imposed on ships, passengers, and cargos. By the early twentieth century, as the *Komagata Maru* crossed the Pacific, the freedom of the sea remained a freedom of trade and travel accessible only to European men.[17] Gurdit Singh's aspirations to begin a commercial steamship company, to revive India's vibrant history of maritime trade, and to circumvent immigration prohibitions imposed by the white Dominions thus imperiled Britain's global, imperial, and racial order in significant ways. Ultimately, what Grotius called the "free sea" demanded the subjection and unfreedom of countless non-Europeans: slaves, indentured laborers, and so-called free migrants.

By many accounts, the *Komagata Maru's* voyage was a dismal failure. The ship never completed its journey as planned. The Guru Nanak Steamship Company was halted even before it began. However, the vessel's outbound voyage from Hong Kong, its two-month confinement in Vancouver, and its arrival outside Calcutta inspired new forms and intensities of Indian radicalism. "The blood of Indians is raging at the injustice," Bhag Singh and Husain Rahim claimed, as the passengers remained detained aboard the ship. "There is great excitement among the Indians resident in Canada, and we will never accept defeat at the hands of the Immigration authorities. We will never allow the 376 passengers to return to their country. We are ready to fight up to the walls of Vancouver, Ottawa and London," they pledged.[18] "The whole world is anxiously waiting to see how the fate of the *Komagata Maru* is decided; because the decision about her fate will make a mark in the history of the world."[19] Over the course of its protracted voyage, the vessel came to symbolize the disruptive and subversive force of Indian anticolonialism. For Gurdit Singh, the steamer's journey offered clear evidence of untapped maritime opportunities. To others, it signaled the potency and possibility of religious unity and solidarity, especially in struggles against British rule. It "was a wonderful sight when the ship sailed," Bhag Singh and Husain Rahim recounted from those in Hong Kong, "regimental bands, soldiers and several regimental companies were present" to send the vessel on its transpacific passage. The "different communities in India were always quarrelling with each other on religious points, and they hated each other," the men explained. But these divisions became less prominent as Indians departed the subcontinent in ever-greater numbers. "Cries of Sat Sri Akal and Ali Ali"—Sikh and Muslim appeals to the Almighty's omnipotence—"were raised when the ship set sail." This mutual respect and camaraderie flourished at sea with a "Sikh place of worship on one side of the *Komagata Maru* and a Muhammadan [*sic*] place of worship on the other."[20] The steamer's future, Bhag Singh and Husain Rahim vowed, "will not be the decision of the fate of 376 passengers only, but will be the decision of the fate of 33 crores of Indians."[21]

Across Oceans of Law asks what is at stake, historically and conceptually, when histories of Indian migration are situated within maritime worlds. Specifically, the book considers how immigration restrictions and Indian radicalism, which have now become familiar narratives, take on different contours when the ship and the sea are foregrounded and analyzed as key juridical forms. How might a shift from land to sea open additional vantage points from which to examine changing itineraries of British and colonial law and anticolonial contest? In what ways does a maritime view of Indian travel and migration invite a wider and more capacious geography to track racial, legal, and political struggles over mobility, movement, and imperial control? If the world of the ship inaugurated new global regimes of time, as I suggest in this book, how did these operate as critical registers of colonial and racial governance and as sites of opposition? Inspired by ocean and maritime studies, but expanding beyond their area studies focus, this book traces the currents and countercurrents of British and colonial law and Indian radicalism along multiple ocean arenas.[22] Redirecting the optics from land to sea, and placing the Pacific, Atlantic, and Indian Oceans into much-needed conversation, the book foregrounds the spatial and temporal

FIGURE I.2. The SS *Komagata Maru* anchored in Vancouver Harbour. The detained passengers pictured here are looking from the ship to the shoreline. (Photo courtesy of City of Vancouver Archives)

coordinates that joined seemingly disparate histories and geographies of the British Empire: through circulating and shared legalities that connected the Dominions, colonies, and territories; in shifting intensities of racial, colonial, and legal violence that constrained the past, present, and future of mobility; and in transoceanic repertoires of anticolonial critique that challenged the empire's underlying racial, spatial, and temporal divides, including land/sea, east/west, and subject/citizen. By centering the world of the ship and bringing oceans into sharper view, the book places motion at the heart of colonial legal history.

To draw multiple oceans into a single analytic field and to underscore the geographical and historical connections integral to empire, *Across Oceans of Law*, as should now be clear, centers on the 1914 journey of the *Komagata Maru* (see fig. I.2). Though the ship crossed the Pacific and Indian Oceans and most of its passengers never disembarked, its voyage has been written largely as a history of landfall, territoriality, and national sovereignty. The existing historiography has typically centered on Canada, though scholars are increasingly interested in the ship's arrival in India.[23] Moving away from prevailing narratives of departure and entry, I follow the ship through time and space, retelling its passage as a global, maritime, and legal history. Repositioning the sea, and drawing historically and conceptually on its expansive, continuous, and ceaseless mobility, the book invites a wider set of historiographical discussions on oceans and ships as legal forms, the overlapping and entangled currents of British and colonial law and anticolonial contest, and disputes over time and jurisdiction that these maritime mobilities engendered. Tracking the movements of a single ship allows me to consider these broader themes while retaining analytic precision through the specificities at hand, including the struggles waged by Gurdit Singh and his seafaring contemporaries against colonial and imperial legalities.

To trace the *Komagata Maru*'s literal passage along the Pacific and Indian Oceans as well as the memories it evoked of Atlantic worlds, the book draws on what I term "oceans as method."[24] I expand on this approach further on. But for now, let me say that oceans—as vast, dynamic, and ungovernable forces—reorient histories of Indian migration in several important ways. First, by drawing attention to the peripatetic movements of vessels, laws, and people, oceans offer novel techniques for writing colonial legal history. Second, as sites of ongoing and ceaseless change, the sea emphasizes motion as central to imperial and colonial politics. Indian travelers, migrants, and radicals, including Gurdit Singh, viewed the empire through moving global vistas, in which land and sea featured as interconnected spaces of anticolonial struggle. Finally, oceans point to alternative histories of race. Racial regimes of power were not static, mutable, or fixed in land and territory alone. Rather, they were the potent effects of maritime circulations and collisions that generated changing forms and intensities of (anti)colonial violence, opposition, and struggle.[25] When viewed oceanically, the *Komagata Maru*'s passage vividly demonstrates the jurisdictional workings of race as a foundational structure of colonial and imperial command, one that demarcated people, differentiated populations, and divided seas from continental regions.[26]

From the late nineteenth to early twentieth centuries, the period that forms the primary focus of this book, the British Empire was imagined as a vast and interconnected space, but one that was racially and politically unequal. Its farflung jurisdictions, including the Dominions (Canada, New Zealand, Australia, and South Africa), colonies (Hong Kong and India), and territories (the Straits Settlements) were not discrete or separate polities but were integrated through a coordinated network of railways and steamships that joined land to sea, albeit unevenly. In his 1853 writings in the *New York Tribune*, Marx viewed the shrinking distance between England and India to be a sign of technological progress and imperial triumph, as the first epigraph above suggests.[27] In earlier historical moments, the moving ship featured as a key symbol of Britain's maritime prowess. Imperial power worked "at the level of the engine, the size and shape of the ship" and was projected through navigational technologies that required new registers of global time.[28] By the turn of the century, the compressed spatial and temporal distance between England and the colonies, combined with greater interoceanic traffic between Asia and the so-called New World, opened new anticolonial networks and solidarities that were cast as global and racial exigencies. The *Komagata Maru*'s landing in Vancouver produced a set of urgent questions on the legal standing of the sea, the racial, territorial, and temporal bounds of imperial jurisdictions, and the rights of British subjects to move through aqueous and terrestrial regions. Its voyage brought the empire's distinctions between land and sea and its territorial ambiguities and temporal asymmetries directly into clear sight.

As a railway contractor and supposed rubber planter, Gurdit Singh was by no means an experienced mariner, but he was also no stranger to the sea. In 1885, at the age of twenty-five, he left India to accompany his father and elder brother to Malaya and Singapore. Over the next two and a half decades, he traveled between the subcontinent and the Straits Settlements, crossing the Eastern Indian Ocean at least twice.[29] By the turn of the century, Singh was part of an expanding and highly mobile network of Indian radicals, including anarchists and revolutionaries, whose travels took them along ocean regions and to port cities around the globe.[30] Just as steam opened new opportunities for England, as Marx noted, it invited additional possibilities for anticolonialism and radicalism. For Singh, the empire's greatest strength was also its ultimate weakness. The sea, as he viewed it, held enormous potential for commerce, trade, and political contest. Recall that the *Komagata Maru*'s voyage was to gauge the viability of the Guru Nanak Steamship Company while also challenging Canada's immigration restrictions. Though the ship's passage did not achieve the objectives that Singh intended, it dramatically reshaped the legal regimes imposed and enforced by colonial authorities in Canada, Hong Kong, and India, while shifting the pitch, tenor, and arena of anticolonial politics.

In January 1915, the *Register*, an Adelaide daily and the first newspaper in South Australia, remarked on the vessel's historical significance as follows. The "sensationalist voyage of the *Komagata Maru*, will some day be regarded as one of the landmarks in the history of the Empire," the paper declared.[31] To be sure, the ship's detention and deportation became a topic of vigorous debate among colonial authorities and a rallying point for Indian radicals. Its voyage conveyed the expansive, global, and seafaring visions of Indian travelers, whose struggles for freedom from British imperial rule were not tied to territoriality alone, but were waged on a planetary scale. Is the *"earth* the property of anyone's father?" Daljit Singh—Gurdit Singh's secretary—asked his readers, as the *Komagata*

Maru awaited its fate in Vancouver Harbour.[32] Today, more than one hundred years later, the ship's transoceanic voyage and its global significance continue to be overshadowed by historical accounts that privilege land/territory and region/nation, thereby diminishing the seaborne itineraries and oceanic imaginaries of Indian radicals. In the remainder of the introduction, I elaborate on the historiographical significance of narrating the *Komagata Maru*'s journey as a global and maritime legal history and the conceptual stakes of using oceans as method to do so. Although the ship's 1914 voyage is a central focus of the book, it might also be read as a critical porthole through which to explore larger questions on the so-called free sea and the circulations of law that its putative freedom demanded. The racial and legal status of oceans emerged as a site of contest in the seventeenth century, became a topic of renewed struggle in the early to mid-twentieth century, and remain very much with us today. In the contemporary moment, memories of the *Komagata Maru* are echoed in the precarious, failed, and tragic journeys of other migrants aboard open boats, and in the ongoing juridification of the "free sea," most evidenced in the Mediterranean.

Maritime Chartings

The *Komagata Maru*'s voyage was part of a much longer historical trajectory of maritime travel that accelerated in the late nineteenth century with the rise of steam, and carried sojourners and migrants from India to East and South Africa, Japan, Hong Kong, China, Canada, the United States, and often back to India.[33] Indian travelers did not follow a smooth or linear trajectory of departure, arrival, and domicile, as immigration histories often suggest. When viewed from the sea, the routes of traders, migrants, pilgrims, and radicals emerge as circuitous and multidirectional, punctuated by stops that were scheduled and fortuitous, and shaped by changing legal regimes that engendered opportunities to forge anticolonial networks along the way.[34] The maritime voyages of Indian travelers joined the eastern and western Indian Oceans to the Pacific, and in some cases, the Atlantic. Their itineraries connected the subcontinent to distant regions in and beyond the British Empire, while placing India within a dynamic, expanding, and racially charged imperial world. When read oceanically, the *Komagata Maru*'s voyage challenges the nationalist and territorial focus of Indian migration histories, while presenting new spatial-temporal accounts of colonial, imperial, and racial power that coalesce in the ship and its movements along the sea.

The transoceanic itineraries of Indian travelers are vividly materialized in the lives of the vessels that transported them across the globe. The steamer that came to be known as the *Komagata Maru* had a long and illustrious history that included Atlantic, Pacific, and Indian Ocean crossings, voyages along the Mediterranean, and later the South China Sea. Built in 1890 for the German Hansa Line, the ship was initially named the *Stubbenhuk* and in 1894 renamed the *Sicilia*. For the first twenty-three years of its life, it carried European settlers and sojourners from ports of call in continental Europe and along the Mediterranean, across the North Atlantic to the eastern seaboard, and to the regions now known as Canada and the United States. Montreal and Ellis Island were two of its regular stops.[35] The famous Connell and Company, located in Glasgow on the Clyde River shipyards, constructed the steel screw schooner. Connell's ships—including the *Stubbenhuk/Sicilia*, which transported Europeans from the "Old World" to the "New"—were firmly embedded in circuits of global capital that joined settler colonialism to longer histories of colonial and racial violence. Connell was well known for its high-quality vessels, especially those constructed for the Indian indenture trade.[36] Long after the abolition of slavery, company-built ships transported women and men from the subcontinent to Britain's Caribbean sugar plantations.[37] In their transoceanic crossings, the firm's ships facilitated the large-scale dispossession of indigenous peoples and the exploitation of Indian indentured laborers, all under the shadow of transatlantic slavery.[38]

In 1913, the *Sicilia* was sold to a small Japanese firm and renamed the *Komakata Maru*.[39] Soon after, it began a regular route transporting coal to various ports along the South China Sea. The following year, accompanied by a Japanese captain, crew, and flag, and with Gurdit Singh in command, the ship crossed the Pacific Ocean. Two months later, it traveled in the opposite direction, along the Pacific and Indian Oceans to Calcutta, carrying those passengers who were refused permission to disembark in Vancouver. For Singh and many others who were domiciled outside the subcontinent—in some cases for decades—the ship's deportation to India was deracinating. For all, it was violent. On 29 September 1914, shortly after the ship landed at Budge Budge, approximately thirty kilometers south of Calcutta, a struggle ensued between passengers and Bengal police, leaving at least twenty-six people dead and many more injured.[40] Gurdit Singh successfully fled authorities and became a fugitive. For seven years, he traveled west, north, and circuitously across India, eventually surrendering himself to police in Punjab. The *Komagata Maru*'s 1914 voyage expanded the global circuits of colonial and racial dispossession that so clearly marked its previous lives. Though the vessel never entered the Atlantic in 1914, its voyage recalled longer maritime histories of transatlantic slavery and fugitivity.

The *Komagata Maru* was British-built and Japanese-owned and was chartered by a British subject originally from Punjab, who spent most of his adult life traveling between Malaya and Singapore. Despite the ship's transoceanic itineraries—both literal and figurative—its voyage continues to be recalled in terms of immigration controls, Dominion sovereignty, and white nationalism.[41] Even today, the ship's journey is written through a narrative of arrival that is presumed to mark an apogee in Canada's long history of racial exclusion.[42] As important as these histories are in foregrounding the repressive politics of racial governance in white settler colonies, they obscure and even foreclose the ship's wider colonial, imperial, and global significance. The *Komagata Maru*'s passage across the Pacific, its detention in Vancouver, its deportation to India, and the violence at Budge Budge unleashed a series of repressive laws while also galvanizing a transnational anticolonial politics that figured prominently in struggles for Indian independence. Given the vessel's actual route from Hong Kong to Vancouver, Singapore to Calcutta, and the ripples and waves it generated in other regions of the empire, its implications and effects cannot be sufficiently explained through the coordinates of metropole/colony, center/periphery, or national/transnational. Rather, the moving ship—as one of the empire's most vital agents and expressions of imperial power—demands a methodological orientation that foregrounds the sea as an expansive and contested racial and juridical space.[43]

The past two decades have witnessed a proliferation of scholarship that seeks to address the historical dynamics of migration and mobility on a global scale. These interventions have emerged from a number of related fields: global and imperial history, historical anthropology, and transnational, feminist, colonial, and postcolonial studies.[44] In particular, imperial and world historians have developed exciting innovations and approaches to address the transnational and global movements of peoples, ideas, and commodities that made up imperial worlds.[45] Tony Ballantyne's pathbreaking "webs of empire" invites a rethinking of colonial and imperial circulations beyond the well-trodden tracks of metropole and colony. The web metaphor, as he describes it, places emphasis on the "horizontal" connections between Britain's colonial territories. In so doing, it seeks to address the problems of linearity and unidirectionality in transnational and imperial history.[46] Webs signal imperial regimes as expansive, durable, delicate, and vulnerable, conveying "the double nature of the imperial system." Webs, like empires, were "fragile (prone to crises where important threads are broken or structural nodes destroyed), yet also dynamic, being constantly remade and reconfigured through concerted thought and effort." For Ballantyne, "empires were not just structures, but processes as well."[47] More recently,

Thomas Metcalf has adopted and elaborated Ballantyne's "webs" to emphasize India's political and legal significance in the Indian Ocean arena and the British Empire, more generally. India "was more than just one of the many colonial 'knots' that may be said to constitute that web," Metcalf contends.[48] It was "a nodal point from which people, ideas, goods, and institutions—everything that enables an empire to exist—radiated outward."[49]

To be sure, the transnational and global turn, as evidenced in the work of imperial and world historians, has made concerted efforts to unsettle the analytic dominance of the nation. Yet, transnationalism, as its appellation suggests, remains tied to borders and territories, even as it explores movements between and across them. As compelling as this literature is in pluralizing and expanding our understandings of global migrations, it inadvertently centers land and territoriality. Transnational approaches seldom problematize oceans as prominent sites of global mobilities in their own right.[50] When oceans are the primary subjects of analysis, they are often identified as distinct and/or exceptional sites of inquiry, under the banner of ocean and maritime studies, rather than transnational or global history. Even in these specialized fields, as geographer Philip Steinberg observes, territoriality persists and prevails. The sea is commonly "reduced to a surface, a space of connections that merely unifies the societies on its borders."[51] Ocean arenas are typically viewed as spaces *linked* by connections and "not the actual oceanic space *of* connections."[52] Though some historians have recently extended transnational and global frames to account for oceans, others continue to privilege surrounding littorals over aqueous regions. In Metcalf's "imperial connections," for example, the Indian Ocean is not an *actual* site of movement, mobility, or legality.[53]

Beginning with land and territory, what transnational approaches cannot fully grasp is the ubiquity of movement, especially the dynamics of motion against motion. Imperial circulations took place on surfaces that were fluid, mobile, and constantly in flux. The mobilities that constituted colonial and imperial worlds followed multiple directions—horizontal, vertical, and circuitous—unfolded on divergent scales and in many dimensions. Their effects were not always straightforward, intended, or predictable, even if they were far-reaching. Transnational histories, as some critics have noted, typically foreground certain movements over others. For Isabel Hofmeyr, the transnational turn has followed mobilities from north to south and back, implying that global migrations of peoples, ideas, and commodities began in Europe and expanded outward.[54] In their own ways, Ballantyne and Metcalf usefully problematize this unidirectionality of colonial migrations and the putative significance of Europe by emphasizing the horizontal itineraries of imperial mobility. But webs continue to imply a center from which movements were generated and extended. Perhaps more importantly, the horizontal connections foregrounded by the web metaphor do not sufficiently account for the vertical relations and hierarchies imposed on imperial jurisdictions and their respective populations. India and the Dominions, to draw but one example, were ordered legally, geographically, and temporally along distinct registers of racial and civilizational superiority and inferiority. This positioning was key to imperial structures and arrangements and conjured very specific meanings within imperial imaginaries.

The emphasis on land, territory, and nation is especially pronounced in the fields of law and legal studies, including legal history.[55] Law, save for international law, is commonly understood to be an institution, a myriad of regulations, and a set of cultural practices hinged to the territorial and political boundaries of imperial, national, and sovereign polities.[56] The "modern legal political imagination," Paul Halliday writes, "is sustained by an illusion of neat boundaries containing internally coherent identities, each dealing with the others as theoretical equals in an international 'order.'" For Halliday, this artifice "is as much a product of our geographical visions" as it is our political and legal ones. "Our minds color in the whole of each space called a nation-state with a single crayon. We don't use pastels, overlap tints, or paint outside the lines."[57] More recently, world historians have sought to disrupt this territorial boundedness in a number of ways. Conceptualizing law as a global and flexible set of institutional and cultural processes, Lauren Benton uses a "multi-centric" approach to capture the intersecting legal orders in early imperial worlds.[58] Echoing Ballantyne, Metcalf, and others, Kerry Ward turns to "nodes and networks" to track the overlapping legalities that marked the "Indian Ocean grid."[59] Yet despite their innovations, familiar spatial representations of land and sea abound. "Our metaphors fail us," Halliday writes. "However much we blur the lines and overlap the patches, two dimensions won't do."[60] The circuitous movements and punctured itineraries of Indian migrants and travelers, including Gurdit Singh, and the currents and countercurrents of law and radicalism that seagoing vessels put into motion, demand a set of analytic tools that transcend the limits of the nation and of terra firma.

To reposition oceans as global sites of law and legality, transnational approaches require some recalibration. In conventional accounts of imperial history and colonial legality, oceans recur as empty voids that are unremarked or situated beyond law, order, and authority.[61] In Grotius's writings, for instance, territorial borders could be legibly inscribed on land, but never on the expansive and moving surfaces of the seas. Though the sea was not lawless in his account, it was beyond imperial claims to property and sovereignty.[62] In *The Nomos of the Earth*, Carl Schmitt, a German jurist, Nazi sympathizer, and influential twentieth-century thinker, characterized the inauguration of modern law through a line in the soil. This line, he insisted, gave a material foundation to European juridical orders, one that continues to inform legal regimes today.[63] But the line that has featured so prominently in Schmitt's thinking, and in legal studies more generally, is firmly and unmistakably embedded in a terracentric order.[64] Moving from land to sea opens additional perspectives on British and colonial law as well as imperial power. A shift from fixed and bounded territories to expansive and undulating oceans exceeds the borders of national and imperial polities, providing an alternative view which foregrounds the interconnections of land and sea. As juridical spaces, oceans highlight the overlapping and intersecting histories of colonial, legal, and racial violence and point to new forms of globality, legality, and sovereignty that are not easily discerned from land alone. But to fully understand the "free sea" as an international legal order requires a maritime charting that traces the routes and itineraries of moving ships. After all, it was seagoing vessels that transformed oceans into legal spaces by inaugurating the freedom of the sea as the basis of an international order in the first place.[65] As juridical formations themselves, ships were deeply embedded in wider structures of European conquest, territorial expansion, and resource/labor extraction as my brief discussion of Connell and Company suggests, and as I elaborate throughout the book. Ships operated as key technologies of British imperial rule, initiating and sharpening structures of colonial, racial, and legal subjection that circulated between land and sea, while also engendering anticolonialism, radicalism, and other expressions of power that directly challenged British dominance.[66]

The *Komagata Maru*'s passage, as my opening pages make clear, engendered a large-scale international response that extended beyond its Pacific and Indian Ocean itineraries. The ship's movements, and its detention and deportation, were regularly reported in newspapers and periodicals published in Australia, Canada, the United States, Japan, India, Singapore, and South, East, and West Africa.[67] This transimperial coverage generated indignation, critique, and support from onlookers, and spirited comment from Indians on the subcontinent and across the diaspora. Years later, critics continued to remark on the ship's enduring political and legal effects. For some commentators, the *Komagata Maru*'s deportation and the violence at Budge Budge incited conditions for "revolution and mutiny in India."[68] By positioning East against West, the voyage also signaled a wider set of racial and geopolitical conflicts. "Remember, India is part of Asia," cautioned *Indian Opinion*, Mohandas K. Gandhi's weekly Natal periodical. A "coalition of China and Japan against England would mean practically the whole of the East against the whole of the West—white versus black and yellow." This pan-Asian uprising, onlookers maintained, was already fomenting "within the cabins" of the Japanese steamer, and under Gurdit Singh's command.[69]

Given that the ship's voyage incited fears of radicalism and revolution, colonial and imperial administrators in Ottawa, Vancouver, London, Delhi, Tokyo, Hong Kong, and Singapore initiated a series of urgent deliberations on possible legal and political interventions. Telegrams and letters were dispatched and received on a daily basis. Reports were written and circulated. Laws were debated and enacted. As authorities contemplated the *Komagata Maru*'s return route, they initiated a shared repertoire of immigration controls and security measures that gained traction through concerns of unrestrained Indian mobility along a racially imperiled sea.[70] The Dominions, as is now well known, were the first to introduce coercive immigration regulations in the interests of protecting a "white Australia" and a "white Canada," respectively.[71] When viewed oceanically, however, these repressive and prohibitory legal regimes rematerialize in ways that were not specific to the white Dominions alone. In September 1914, following the outbreak of World War I, amid escalating fears of anticolonialism abroad, and in anticipation of the *Komagata Maru*'s arrival in Calcutta, the Indian colonial government passed the Foreigners Ordinance and the Ingress into India Ordinance. These regulations were to assist Indian authorities in restricting the maritime movements and reentry of foreigners and nationals alike.[72] When these juridical developments are repositioned and analyzed from the sea, legal statutes and vernaculars become increasingly untethered from national boundaries and sovereign polities. Instead, they emerge as circulating expressions of law, order, and authority that traveled via ship and connected the Dominions, colonies, and territories to the metropole and beyond. Viewed from contiguous oceans rather than divided continents, immigration exclusions appear as part of a broader set of juridical procedures aimed at maintaining racial, territorial, and temporal divisions across the British Empire while at the same time connecting land/sea and East/West, divisions that distinguished India and other parts of Asia from Europe and the "New World."

As a global and transoceanic event, the *Komagata Maru*'s journey joined seemingly distinct histories, regions, and legalities into a racially uneven whole. Approaching the ship as a juridical form and situating it within longer legal and political debates over the "free sea" brings additional constellations of colonial, racial, and imperial power to the fore. In the sections to follow, I outline the analytic and methodological import of using oceans, race, and time as conceptual and navigational devices in rewriting the *Komagata Maru*'s journey as a global and maritime legal history.

Oceans as Method

In 1850, in a short comment published in the *Neue Rheinische Zeitung Revue*, Marx and Engels remarked on how colonial and capitalist expansion to North America was changing the economic and political significance of the world's ocean regions. "A coastline which stretches across thirty degrees of latitude, one of the most beautiful and fertile in the world and hitherto more or less unpopulated," they observed, "is now being visibly transformed into a rich, civilized land thickly populated by men of all races, from the Yankee to the Chinese, from the Negro to the Indian and Malay, from the Creole and Mestizo to the European." Gold from California "is pouring in torrents over America and the Asiatic coast of the Pacific and is drawing the reluctant barbarian peoples into world trade, into the civilized world," they wrote.[73] For Marx and Engels, gold was to dramatically alter the place of the Pacific, both in terms of global markets and world history. Nineteenth-century maritime travel, they predicted, would unleash a civilizing force on "the reluctant barbarian peoples," particularly Asiatics who crossed oceans in search of new riches and opportunities for trade. "The Pacific Ocean will then play the role the Atlantic Ocean is playing now, and the role that the Mediterranean played in the days of classical antiquity and in the middle ages," they anticipated. If the Pacific was to become "the great water highway of world communications," the Atlantic Ocean would eventually "sink to the level of a great lake such as the Mediterranean is to-day."[74] The observations made by Marx and Engels may have been prescient in some respects, but they were off the mark in others. By the early twentieth century, maritime travel along the Pacific became the locus of imperial surveillance and control, as evidenced by the *Komagata Maru*'s unsuccessful voyage and the demise of Gurdit Singh's steamship company.

The maritime cartography of world regions as Marx and Engels narrated it, was premised on a double erasure. They say nothing of indigenous peoples or of the Indian Ocean arena. Just as Europeans never arrived on empty lands, they also did not sail on vacant seas. European mariners and empires inserted themselves into existing social, religious, and trade networks that were established through indigenous, Asian, and Muslim seafaring technologies, including knowledges of monsoon winds.[75] Their portrayal of the Pacific, Atlantic, and Mediterranean expresses a Eurocentric and developmentalist teleology that characterizes their work writ large.[76] Yet, the problems of maritime periodization and division are not specific to them alone. Rather, Marx and Engels's observations are symptomatic of broader methodological shortcomings that prevail and persist in historical accounts of European expansion.[77] In 1872, the famous Scottish scientist James Croll criticized the imposition of maritime boundaries as follows. We often "speak of parts, or geographical divisions, of one great ocean, such as the Atlantic and Pacific as if they were separate oceans."[78] Little has changed. Borders remain as persistent today in ocean studies and in maritime history as they were in the nineteenth century when Marx, Engels, and Croll were writing.[79] Let me briefly explain.

In his magisterial study, *The Black Atlantic*, Paul Gilroy deploys the Atlantic Ocean as analytic ballast through which to overcome what he terms the "narrow nationalism" of English historiography.[80] For Gilroy, the Atlantic is not solely an empirical site or a geographical designation but an analytic concept that foregrounds "a system of cultural exchanges" that centers slavery as foundational to European modernity.[81] *The Black Atlantic* extends and elaborates the earlier work of historians Marcus Rediker and Peter Linebaugh. In their account, the Atlantic features as a continuous historical network of institutional confinement and conviviality, one that engendered flourishing ideas of freedom, liberty, and equality.[82] The Atlantic, in Gilroy's formulation, is "one single, complex unit of analysis" that triangulates West Africa, Europe, and the Americas through the capture, transport, and enslavement of Africans, producing "an explicitly transnational and intercultural perspective."[83] In his analysis, the Atlantic features as an exceptional site of racial subjection and black subjectivity. By privileging this aqueous region, Gilroy distinguishes it from other oceans and their attendant histories of imperial, colonial, and racial violence.[84] Though many have remarked critically on the limitations of Gilroy's analytic framework, few have pushed beyond his geographical frame. In *The Red Atlantic*, Jace Weaver extends Gilroy's arguments to account for the transoceanic mobilities of indigenous peoples. In his chronology of the modern world, the Atlantic was as red as it was black.[85] Even in Weaver's compelling account, the Atlantic remains a distinct maritime space, one that is divisible from the Indian and Pacific Ocean regions.

Though conspicuously absent in Marx and Engel's maritime cartography, the Indian Ocean has also been a site of considerable scholarship. As many scholars have demonstrated, the eastern and western arenas have long histories of trade, commerce, and interethnic encounters among Arabs, Africans, Indians, and Chinese, and between Muslim and non-Muslim worlds.[86] These are rich and densely connected regions that predate European contact by centuries. Prior to the age of steam, Indian Ocean travelers sailed on vessels that were highly dependent on the weather. The directional currents of the seas, which were produced by changing seasons and monsoon winds, carried ships between and across continental divides. By the nineteenth century, the rise of steam accelerated the frequency and speed of travel, and inaugurated different human relationships with land and sea.[87] Curiously, these technological shifts and changes have drawn little attention in Indian Ocean studies. Much of the existing scholarship, as Sugata Bose explains, focuses on premodern and early modern crossings via sail. Yet, the movements of people, ideas, commodities, and legalities have continued throughout the nineteenth and twentieth centuries and well into the present day.[88] "The Indian Ocean was global long before the Atlantic," Sunil Amrith observes.[89] Though nestled between the Atlantic and Pacific, it is rarely connected to these oceans, either historically or analytically.

More recently, scholars have shifted their attention to the long-neglected Pacific. Influenced by Atlantic studies, while emphasizing the Pacific's own particularity, many have echoed the enthusiasm of Marx and Engels, describing this region as a newly prominent arena of global movement, circulation, and exchange.[90] Notwithstanding characterizations of its presumed newness, the Pacific has been the site of indigenous mobilities for millennia. Pacific peoples developed seafaring technologies to navigate, cross, and map the seas long before Europeans left their shores.[91] In his groundbreaking essay "Our Sea of Islands," Epeli Hau'ofa describes the Pacific of his ancestors as "a large world in which peoples and cultures moved and mingled, unhindered by boundaries of the kind erected much later by imperial powers."[92] The vast Pacific opened pathways of migration that connected Asia to the Americas and invited new itineraries and possibilities for self-determination. Given these layered narratives of indigenous and Asian mobilities, the Pacific is often described in terms of overlapping, intersecting, and plural histories. There are "multicoloured Pacifics— brown, black, white, and yellow," David Armitage and Alison Bashford argue.[93] The Pacific is thought to designate "a whole globe in a way that other oceans do not."[94]

Despite the vitality and vibrancy of ocean and maritime studies, the field's analytic potential is limited and even constrained by the geographical divides of the cartographer's map. Indigenous and nonindigenous scholars have long criticized the prevailing historical periodizations and spatial divisions imposed onto ocean arenas. The land/sea distinction that was brought into being through the movement of ships, and which became foundational to European maps and to international law, did not register in the same way, if at all, in indigenous and non-European cosmologies. These are part of a European modernism that continues to hold significant consequences for contemporary geopolitics.

"Nineteenth-century imperialism," Hauʻofa argues, "erected boundaries that led to the contraction of Oceania, transforming a once boundless world into the Pacific Island states and territories that we know today."[95] Damon Salesa insists, "all seas are connected, and there are no neat limits."[96] For Karen Wigen, a "colossal fragment like the Pacific Ocean is not big enough to contain most ocean themes." Rather, "the skeins of maritime connections—whether in the realm of idiom and ideas, diasporic dispersals, imperial projections, scientific linkages, or strategies of resistance," she contends, "quickly transcend the confines of a single ocean."[97] Colonial authorities and Indian travelers in the British imperial world did not see oceans as divided or detached either spatially or temporally. By the early twentieth century, Canadian, British, and Indian authorities expressed apprehensions about the increased transoceanic traffic that connected East and West via the Pacific and Indian Oceans.[98] Importantly, indigenous peoples and colonial subjects did not abide by the lines of imperial maps. Sojourners and migrants—including Gurdit Singh and Husain Rahim—looked out to the Pacific, Atlantic, and Indian Oceans as overlapping and intersecting in a number of ways: in the physical contiguities of riverine and oceanic waterways, through shared colonial histories, and as sites of racial and imperial control. Remember, it was Singh's own turn, from land and rail to sea and ships that inspired his anticolonial agenda and his struggles against British rule.

To trace the circulations of colonial law and Indian radicalism and to draw connections between the seemingly discrepant histories and geographies of the Pacific, Atlantic, and Indian Oceans, this book draws on oceans and currents as its guiding methodology.[99] "Ocean currents exercise a very important influence not only on climate but also on commerce," wrote one source in 1893. "The seas join the nations they divide."[100] Though movement is constantly occurring but not often visible on land, oceans bear the ocular, audible, and palpable marks of motion and change.[101] Currents, as oceanographers and others argue, are made up of vertical, horizontal, and circuitous movements that mark the surface of the sea and also its subterranean depths. Currents are not singular or unidirectional but heterogeneous and plural. They connect the ocean regions that have long been divided in European thought. Surface currents, crosscurrents, undercurrents, and rip currents move in multiple directions, with changing velocities and intensities depending on season, temperature, and climate.[102] Precisely because of their active and powerful force, "the sea never stops moving."[103] Historically, currents were as influential in determining the sea routes of sailing vessels, as they were in directing the passage of steamships. The "sailing-ship navigator's principal aim when remote from the land," one source explained, "is to proceed along that much desired track where a fair wind and favorable current will probably be experienced."[104] Recast and reworked in analytic terms, currents foreground mobility and change as central features in colonial legal history. Currents do not have a readily identifiable beginning, a fixed or static center, or a clear end. Animated by multiple movements and countermovements, they join distant coordinates, in both space and time. Through their lively physical properties, currents speak compellingly to the limitations of other transnational and imperial frames, including webs. Currents exist in several registers at once. They follow multiple trajectories, exhibit changing dimensions, and thus offer alternative metaphors and additional ways to chart the discrepant mobilities of colonial and imperial worlds.

Across Oceans of Law draws on oceans as both metaphor and materiality to trace the legal overlaps between ocean arenas and the movements of colonial law and Indian radicalism that connected them.[105] For some readers, my turn to the "free sea" and to multiple oceans might appear too broad, potentially obscuring the rich and particular histories of world regions. That is a fair charge. To temper these risks, the book traces the figurative and literal passage of a single ship. If the Pacific and Indian Oceans formed the actual sites of the *Komagata Maru*'s crossing, the Atlantic appeared with a patterned regularity in its 1914 voyage, echoing other times and places, and profoundly shaping struggles over the ship, its passengers, and their futures. Much like currents, the movements of law and radicalism were not uniform, linear, or straightforward as the case of Gurdit Singh suggests. Legal prohibitions and anticolonial formations zig-zagged, crisscrossed, and joined ocean regions along diverse routes, in multiple directions, and in shifting conceptions of past, present, and future. Tracing the itinerary of one ship, through the materiality and metaphoricity of oceans, helps to reposition the Pacific, Atlantic, and Indian Oceans as overlapping and indivisible, despite their geographical locations and their presumed shifts in historical prominence and global significance.

Ocean currents are intimately connected to ships through technology and legality.[106] The "breadth, depth, length and velocity" of currents have always been central to the design, construction, and direction of seagoing vessels, observed one source in the *Chambers's Journal of Popular Literature, Science and Arts.*[107] Depending on the time of year, currents carried ships more easily across some seas than others. By the sixteenth century, with advances in shipbuilding and navigation, seagoing vessels were no longer confined to single ocean regions.[108] Their movements and itineraries became transoceanic, joining continents, changing the earth's contours, and opening new possibilities for movement, expropriation, and resettlement. In 1850, just as steamships were making their debut on the world stage, transforming and eventually routinizing the movements of people and commodities, Marx and Engels commented on the tightly braided histories of oceans, ships, and imperial expansion: "It may be said that the world has only become round since the necessity has arisen for this global steam shipping."[109] Irrespective of "how many companies go bankrupt, the steamships—which are doubling the Atlantic traffic, opening up the Pacific, connecting up Australia, New Zealand, Singapore and China with America and are reducing the journey around the world to four months—the steamships will remain."[110] If ships were vital to colonial, capitalist, and territorial expansion, we must remember that they were equally significant to expanding regimes of colonial law and global time.

For some European thinkers, as I have noted above, oceans were seen as empty voids that were situated beyond conviviality, legality, and authority.[111] As Carl Schmitt declared from his bird's-eye view of the *nomos* of the earth: "On the waves, there is nothing but waves."[112] Yet the shipbound lives of Indian lascars who traveled on European vessels from the eighteenth century onward suggest a very different account of the sea. The ships that crisscrossed the world's oceans engendered vibrant conditions for intimacy, solidarity, and racial and political contest. From the decks of the ship, maritime worlds appear as concentrated sites of sociality that were highly structured through law and time. As ships lost view of land, they became vulnerable to disorder, instability, and even mutiny. For that reason, captains kept order on their ships by means of rigid timetables that organized day and night and through the law of the sea, which they enforced with impunity. The "laws of the land have no hold on the water," declared Captain Chillingworth of the *Ibis* in Amitav Ghosh's novel, *Sea of Poppies*. "There is another law, and you should know that on this vessel, I am its sole maker."[113] To retain sovereign command over their ships, captains organized their crews through regional, religious, and caste distinctions that preceded and animated modern forms of racial governance.[114] Ships were colonial-legal laboratories where racial labor hierarchies, rules of order, and regimes of violence were projected, implemented, disputed, and eventually extended to land.[115] Viewed from the ship, oceans appear as socially vibrant though highly regulated spaces. These maritime activities disrupt Schmitt's characterization of vacant and empty seas.

In the domain of early maritime law, oceans and ships were often inseparable. Before European contact, the Maritime Code of Melaka was the most comprehensive maritime legal regime in the Eastern Indian Ocean arena. This was not a law of the sea, as commentators have noted, but a law that governed the sea through rules of navigation, the safety of vessels, and the transport of goods.[116] Oceans and ships as legal forms became further entangled through European expansion. Though the seas were beyond the claims of imperial sovereigns, as Grotius made clear, moving ships were regarded as pieces "of quasi-territory" that enabled sovereigns to advance jurisdictional claims to sea lanes and ocean regions.[117] By displaying the flags and colors of their sponsors, vessels represented the authority of the powers that financed them.[118] Moreover, flags conveyed messages of law, order, and authority in the instability and uncertainty of aqueous worlds. But ships were never only representations of law. They were vital to the *actual* movements of law and legality across the seas and in ways that connected imperial territories. "The physical circulation of legal papers, case notes and correspondence via shipping and transportation," Kerry Ward explains, "was essential in the implementation of imperial law."[119] Ships were crucial to the transoceanic expansion of colonialism and capitalism as Marx and Engels noted, but featured just as prominently in Britannia's efforts to rule the waves.

Despite being powerful symbols of law and sources of legality, moving ships proved to be difficult targets of imperial and legal control. In the late nineteenth and early twentieth centuries, as I discuss briefly in the opening pages above, imperial authorities expressed heightened concerns regarding Indian travelers, traders, and migrants who many alleged were voyaging in greater numbers across the Pacific.[120] Contra Marx, the shortened geographical and temporal distances facilitated by steam only augmented and intensified these fears. As Indian radicalism and anticolonialism were reputed to be flourishing within port cities, officials were increasingly troubled by the lengthy periods that passengers spent at sea. The middle passage, as scholars of the Black Atlantic have argued, unfolded *between* territories and temporalities and was therefore not only a site of extreme violence but also a dangerous space-time of mutiny and revolt.[121] Concerns of Indian men traveling by ship echoed these fears and produced others. By the time the *Komagata Maru* commenced its 1914 voyage, imperial authorities alleged that seditious materials including pamphlets and periodicals were circulating on steamers that journeyed from India to Hong Kong, China, Japan, and eventually North America. Radical ideas and anti-British sentiments were believed to be in ferment aboard the *Komagata Maru* as it journeyed to Vancouver Harbour and especially on the ship's voyage to India. Gurdit Singh and his associates allegedly gave talks and lectures to incite passengers to revolt against British rule. Thus, for colonial and imperial authorities, the transoceanic passage was a perilous transition zone where Indian passengers were transformed from "migrants" to "revolutionaries" that escaped law's reach. Escalating fears of maritime radicalism only bolstered ongoing initiatives to prohibit Indian migration from India to Canada.

Oceans invite novel insights and perspectives through which to rethink the global movements and effects of British and colonial law. In European thought, the free sea was an international space that was situated beyond national, territorial, and sovereign control. Yet it was governed by multiple, competing, and overlapping sources of legal authority, though not always successfully. To highlight the plurality and "patchwork" of legalities on land, some scholars have shifted their attention from sovereignty to jurisdiction.[122] In its broadest sense, jurisdiction refers to the inauguration and enunciation of law, "that there is law," and that law speaks on its own behalf, authorizing itself through competing and overlapping legal forms.[123] Unlike sovereignty, which assumes a coherent and homogeneous unity of legal and political authority, jurisdiction points to the multiplicity and heterogeneity of law. The British common law, as some have noted, was polyvocal from the very start. It was composed of multiple and overlapping legalities, most notably ecclesiastic, criminal, and admiralty law.[124] It was in the colonies, as Shaunnagh Dorsett and Shaun McVeigh argue, that fragmented legal jurisdictions were especially pronounced. "It is through jurisdiction that the authority of the common and imperial laws have been asserted," they explain, and "through questions of jurisdiction that the settlement of the colonies has been effected."[125]

The "free sea" assists in foregrounding the plurality and polycentricity of European juridical orders. Between the fifteenth and sixteenth centuries, "mapping, navigation, and astronomy," which were vital to imperial expansion, transoceanic navigation, and the world of the ship produced overlapping jurisdictions and divided authorities.[126] Contests over where laws intersected, which ones were most applicable, and which were to prevail featured prominently in maritime disputes and disagreements. Grotius's *Mare Liberum*, for instance, was a formal response to a maritime contest between the Dutch and the Portuguese in the Straits of Singapore.[127] Though oceans could not be legally occupied, Grotius readily agreed that sovereign and imperial polities did make overlapping and opposing claims to strategic waterways, thereby extending their territorial control from land to sea and vice versa.[128] As these few examples suggest, and as I elaborate throughout the book, oceans were by no means empty spaces. Rather, they were key sites of racial, colonial, and legal struggle to which the movements of ships proved crucial.

To be sure, jurisdiction is much more than a territorial concept. In the British Empire, questions of jurisdiction often centered on the racial and legal status of people, populations, and territories, dividing Dominion/colony, native/foreigner, citizen/subject, and slave/free.[129] Regimes of racial superiority and inferiority were not only terrestrial, as the maritime orders of transatlantic slavery remind us. It was aboard ships—on deck and in the hold—that distinctions between human/inhuman and slave/free were produced, debated, and violently enacted.[130] Rethinking jurisdiction through maritime worlds emphasizes the spatial and temporal force of racial power. If race has a geography that is inscribed "into continental divides, national localities, and geographic regions," oceans point to its expansive and alternative histories by emphasizing the polyvocality, mobility, and mutability of racial orders.[131] Modern conceptions of race emerged in part from maritime worlds, through regional, religious, and racial hierarchies that were mobilized by captains to govern crews and (human) cargos, and expanded through the circuitous routes of moving ships. Race operated jurisdictionally as a structuring element of the British Empire, one that demarcated the status and hierarchy of oceans, territories, and colonial populations. But racial power, however potent in force, was always open to fierce struggle, including opposition and appropriation. As colonial authorities and Indian migrants traveled across the seas, they borrowed, deployed, and disputed conceptions of racial superiority and inferiority in innovative ways. Regimes of race acquired their legibility and potency through seaborne hierarchies of slavery, forced labor, and caste that circulated and collided with other racial orders.[132] The *Komagata Maru*'s passengers and supporters drew from alternative geographies and histories to mobilize racial and temporal grammars of globality, indigeneity, and "imperial citizenship" through which to demand inclusion within the wider imperial polity.[133] The contiguity of oceans that I propose in this book draws these multiple geographies, histories, and temporalities of race into a broader and more capacious analytic frame, while currents reveal their changing intensity, velocity, and mutability.

When situated in the Pacific, Atlantic, and Indian Oceans, and read through the force of currents and countercurrents, the *Komagata Maru*'s journey brings into sharper focus the imperial circulations through which the British Empire aspired to rule land, sea, and littoral, and how these mobile legalities were disputed by the counter-movements and anticolonial imaginaries of Indian travelers. Ocean currents, as I envision them, offer a productive method through which to explore the plurality, globality, and connectivity of colonial, legal, and racial histories that continue to be written as differentiated and divided.[134] But prioritizing maritime worlds offers even more. Repositioning the sea in colonial legal history directs necessary attention from land and territoriality to time and temporality. Britain's status as a maritime empire, as I explain in the following section, was achieved not only through a projected mastery over space but also in the inauguration of a global and universal time. Greenwich Mean Time introduced the formation of new registers of imperial power and additional repertoires of anticolonial contest that arose from the sea and from shipping.

Nautical Time

One of the most enduring consequences of European imperial expansion was the reconfiguration of space and time.[135] European empires, scholars have noted, held a distinctly spatial imaginary. They projected their sovereign claims and extended their legal and political control geographically and territorially.[136] But Europe's growing dominance over land and sea was achieved also through the production and imposition of global time. Maritime navigation, which led to latitude and longitude and their enactment as a universal grid, proved especially crucial.[137] From the fifteenth century onward, with advances in marine technology and the so-called discovery of the Americas, ships, people, and laws traveled with growing frequency and regularity across the seas and farther inland through ports of call. These transoceanic movements—which facilitated the transport of European settlers, slaves, indentured laborers, and migrants, and the circulations of law and order they made possible—were instrumental in founding a new global, spatial, and temporal order. Latitude and longitude repositioned the earth as four interrelated quadrants: north/south and east/west. By the 1880s, when Greenwich became the world's prime meridian, these spatial and temporal grids that long ordered the cartographer's map, placed Britain at the center of earth. Global time newly became a clear expression of the empire's "universalizing will."[138]

Across Oceans of Law tracks the circulations of British and colonial law and Indian radicalism through imperial registers of time as well as the more conventional coordinates of space. Struggles over global time have generated considerable scholarly attention of late.[139] In studies of globalization and empire, histories of a standardized and universal time have typically focused on the railway and the telegraph. Train timetables and telegraph cables, so the argument goes, expanded and extended European demands for temporal uniformity and consistency.[140] "In the opalescent history of time coordination," writes Peter Galison, "clocks trapped nerve transmissions and reaction times, structured work places and guided astronomy. *But the two scale-changing domains of material time centered on the railroad and the map.*"[141] By the mid-nineteenth century, as railway travel became more widely accessible in Europe and North America, travelers were required to "calculate their way through a thicket of times kept on different [train] lines."[142] Though railway companies in England began standardizing time, they did not yet coordinate train schedules. As long as traffic between cities remained intermittent, the "patchwork of varying local times" posed little problem. But as railway travel increased in frequency, so too did the need for temporal synchronicity.[143]

Focused on the mid-nineteenth to early twentieth centuries, these accounts of global time, as fascinating as they are, come far too late. Perhaps more importantly, the railway, with its emphasis on continental travel, obscures the role of the sea, thereby directing attention away from key maritime developments. The rise of a universal time commenced with the transoceanic movements of ships and was only later extended to land.[144] As vessels traveled from coastal regions to the high seas with growing regularity, they demanded navigational practices that could more accurately measure space *through* time. Timekeeping was central to maritime navigation for a number of reasons: to determine the horizontal distances between different points in space and to assess the vertical span from the surface to the depths of the sea. To ensure the efficiency of their voyages and the safety of their cargos and crews, captains depended on temporal measures including winds, tides, and currents, as well as the changing position of the moon and stars.[145] Early ship logs reveal that shipmasters and crews were acutely aware of clock time long before industrialization.[146] Over the course of several centuries, the world of the ship produced a complex system of time reckoning: "the watch" and hourglass, time balls, nautical almanacs, and eventually the chronometer.[147]

Longitude was not merely a set of lines inscribed vertically across continents and oceans. Rather, it was *a measure of time* that was used to determine a ship's position at sea.[148] The quest for longitude, which began in the sixteenth century, was not formalized until the eighteenth century. But once it was, longitude helped to establish a new European global order. Though Britain arrived late to contests over maritime imperial expansion, the empire featured prominently in the rise of nautical time. King Charles II founded the Royal Observatory, Greenwich, in 1675. By the 1760s, it became the reference point for European shipping as naval almanacs were increasingly synchronized to Greenwich.[149] At the close of the eighteenth-century, as maritime navigation advanced, marine chronometers were also calibrated to Greenwich Mean Time (GMT).[150] The quest for longitude, and the standardized measurement of time that it demanded, became one modality through which Britain aspired to consolidate its distant Dominions, colonies, and territories and to rule the "free seas" that connected them. European conceptions of time—as nautical, legal, and global—were not natural or objective measures but were potent expressions of imperial power.

Ocean currents offer a rich set of analytic tools through which to consider the global and imperial significance of global time. "For most of us," recalled one correspondent, writing for *Harper's Monthly Magazine*, "the sea has only two dimensions. It is the restless, glittering surface we see from the shore or from a ship."[151] But oceans exist in four dimensions, this source continued. These are measured through depth, width, length, and time. "We have become accustomed . . . to regard the currents of the ocean as separate, and independent of one another," James Croll explained. "The true way of viewing the matter . . . is to regard the various currents merely as members of one grand system of circulation" that connected multiple oceans and seas.[152] In 1884 at the Prime Meridian Conference, Britain advanced a single, homogeneous, and linear time that was eventually to encompass the entire globe. Greenwich Mean Time, which had long been vital to the world of the ship, became "time zero" on land.[153] Thus, it was through the ship, and not the train, that a uniform time was inaugurated and extended from sea to continental regions. By the late nineteenth century, the earth was newly united through currents of time that engendered "one grand system of circulation," and with Britain at its center.[154]

Like space, time also operated territorially as a register of colonial, racial, and imperial control. As a system of measurement, time was considered by missionaries, settlers, and authorities to be a marker of order, efficiency, and much more. In imperial jurisdictions, missionaries viewed time as clear evidence of racial civility and progress. Through the introduction of bells, timetables, and later clocks, many sought to impose European time onto indigenous and colonial populations.[155] For British colonists who were sent to settle distant colonial outposts, a shared sense of time allowed them to remain in touch with a wider European community. Time created a mutual "sense of connectedness," joining familiar and unfamiliar geographies across vast distances.[156] When taken together, what longitude, clocks, and timetables make clear is that European conceptions of time were neither objective nor inevitable. Time was one of the many ways by which Britain projected its presumed racial, cultural, and civilizational superiority over its Dominions, colonies, and territories.[157] The empire's efforts to impose a homogeneous time—through ships, trains, and telegraphs—were justified through reason, rationality, and efficiency. Writing of colonial India, Dipesh Chakrabarty points to the stakes of this spatial, temporal, and global reordering. Britain's presumed superiority, projected via global time, was further expanded through universal history. Imperial temporalities of past, present, and future overwrote the plurality of Indian theologies, laws, and customs, and in so doing, eroded—albeit not entirely—the histories and chronologies of many diverse and heterogeneous communities.[158]

Despite the quest for a global and unified time, multiple temporalities continued to thrive across the British Empire and beyond. Much like the patchwork of local railway times, this heterogeneity created problems for the quotidian practices of colonial administration. In Britain's Dominions, colonies and territories, time was routinely displayed through public clocks and central towers.[159] Clock time held a material and symbolic power that organized colonial bureaucracies, whether offices were open or closed, and when they operated at full speed. However, these official registers of time did not often influence the lives of colonial subjects. Writing against the idea of an "empty homogenous time," Partha Chatterjee argues that these formulations of time, which have been dominant in postcolonial studies, reflect abstractions and not lived realities. The empty homogeneous time that has been repeatedly evoked by critics of empire, he contends, is not an inhabited or lived time but one that is thought and projected.[160] Beginning with ships and maps, and expanding through clocks and trains, Britain aimed to extend a global and chronological time over its colonial subjects and territories. But imperial authorities, as Chatterjee reminds us, were routinely confronted by the heterogeneity of lived times that were inspired by religious, spiritual, and alternative cosmologies. Despite Britain's efforts to mechanize, quantify, and expand time through longitude and in the circuits of British and colonial laws, the lived time of colonial subjects, like Gurdit Singh and Husain Rahim, regularly defied imperial control.[161] Notwithstanding the best efforts of colonial bureaucrats and missionaries, time and space remained uneven, disjointed, and fiercely disputed across imperial divides.

If ships inaugurated a global and universal time, British and colonial laws helped to expand and consolidate it. Legal documents, court sittings, and the use of time as punishment reinforced the authority and legitimacy of clock and calendar time.[162] British authorities sought to unite its distant and disparate territories through the expansion of global time and in the extension of British and colonial law. However, the Dominions, protectorates, and colonies continued to produce their own legalities and temporalities.[163] The Dominions, including Canada, cast themselves as "young" and self-governing colonies. India, by contrast, was seen to be an ancient place, but one that had no history of its own making. These jurisdictions, with their competing racial, territorial, and temporal markers, demanded distinct forms of order, authority, and legality. But even the British common law did not represent a universal, cohesive, or coherent unity. Rather, it was composed of a "patchwork" of legalities and temporalities that made up a larger colonial and imperial system.[164] Thus, British and colonial laws were marked by rules and procedures that produced discrepant temporalities that did not always correspond to Greenwich Mean Time. Drawing its power from "time immemorial" and from a plurality of legal sources of authority, the common law did not follow a direct temporal line.[165] Rather, it oscillated between the weight of the past as archived in precedent and the uncertainty and openness of a future that it tried to anticipate.[166] The common law drew its power from a composite of sources—ecclesiastic, criminal, and admiralty law—each with its own corresponding temporal rhythms. Despite Britain's efforts to consolidate and synchronize time, the British common law was temporally disjointed, potentially disrupting the linear chronology that the empire sought to impose upon its distant territories. The Dominions, colonies, and territories eventually became part of a global empire, but they were situated in vertical hierarchies and uneven topographies that remained racially, temporally, and geographically disparate.

In many ways, the *Komagata Maru*'s journey ruptured Britain's claims to temporal and spatial uniformity by bringing the multiplicity of time, the heterogeneity of law, and the racial asymmetries of empire vividly to the fore. Struggles over the ship were routinely framed as problems of space and time: where were Indians allowed to settle? Could they travel and trade on the "free sea"? Were they ready to join the imperial polity? As an aspiring seafarer, Gurdit Singh was well attuned to the importance of a global and standardized time, especially its significance for maritime navigation. However, his anticolonial imaginaries were inspired by and deeply grounded in other cosmologies, including Sikhism and Sikh nationalism, which did not easily follow the prescriptions and demands of British legality, temporality, and authority.[167] Importantly, for Singh, the fractured and dynamic times inherent within the British common law opened further opportunities for anticolonial struggle. If the ungovernability of the sea invited renewed plans for maritime commerce and additional aspirations for freedom, it was law's splitting between past and future that presented novel legal and political occasions to challenge British imperial rule. As I discuss further on, time became a site of struggle that was disputed, appropriated, and reinvented by Indian migrants and travelers aboard the *Komagata Maru* and beyond.

Oceans, more so than land, draw our attention to regimes of global time, circulations of law, and to the growing threats of Indian radicalism that flourished in maritime worlds. When the contiguity of oceans—which was divided by Marx and Engels and sutured by Croll—is considered both historically and conceptually through moving ships that produced the "free sea," it presents new and innovative ways of rethinking race, time, and law beyond national, regional, and transnational registers. Keeping these themes at hand, the following section returns to the voyage of the *Komagata Maru* and outlines the specific chapters that constitute this book.

Navigations

Across Oceans of Law is deliberately wide-ranging, drawing from historical debates on the freedom of the seas, scholarly engagements with law/jurisdiction, race/empire, time/temporality, and historical developments surrounding maritime law and navigation. The five chapters that form the core of this book are organized along a loose chronology of the *Komagata Maru*'s passage. Each foregrounds a different segment of the ship's journey and is narrated through a specific legal artifact, concept, or figure: the sea, the ship, the manifest, the indigenous, and the fugitive. Each draws on historical records and documents collected from seven years of research in multiple archives and libraries in Canada (Ottawa and Vancouver), India (Delhi), and Britain (London and Glasgow). The discussion that follows is engaged as much with conceptual and historiographical debates as it is with the facticity of the ship's voyage. It is through close readings and historical detail, I contend, that the analytic potential of oceans as method is most fully realized.

Oceans, as I argue throughout, have not featured prominently in law and legal studies.[168] To begin sketching a colonial and legal history of the sea, I turn to two prominent European thinkers and their respective works, already introduced above: Hugo Grotius, whose *Mare Liberum* was published in 1609, and Carl Schmitt, whose *Land and Sea* and *The Nomos of the Earth* were published more than three centuries later.[169] Whereas Grotius precedes the *Komagata Maru*'s 1914 voyage, Schmitt follows it. Read together, they draw attention to the Dutch, British, and American Empires and may therefore seem a curious historical and conceptual starting point for my analysis. What makes Grotius and Schmitt especially useful is that they were writing at key moments of European imperial and maritime expansion: in the seventeenth century, with the rise of "free trade" in the East Indies, and in the mid-twentieth century, during and after World War II. Their arguments remain significant today, perhaps even more so than when their respective works were first published. To provide an oceanic frame through which to retell the *Komagata Maru*'s voyage, chapter 1 places these texts into conversation. More specifically, I read them alongside each other and also against the maritime aspirations and legal struggles of Gurdit Singh and Husain Rahim. Grotius and Schmitt wrote compellingly, albeit differently, on the free sea. Each highlighted the elemental distinctions of land and sea as vital to the juridical status of oceans at particular moments in European imperial history. Unlike other commentators on their work, I approach their writings not as theoretical accounts of the so-called free sea or the emergence of an international legal order, but as competing histories of maritime legalities that still need to be provincialized.[170] The *Komagata Maru*'s voyage, as I suggest throughout, directly challenged the freedom of the sea and, for this reason, became a global, legal, and racial exigency. Through their oceanic travels, Gurdit Singh and Husain Rahim produced their own anticolonial cartographies that were inspired by the past and future of Indian seafaring and which disrupted the land/sea divide inaugurated and imposed by European thinkers.

The moving ship, as Grotius and others noted, featured prominently in the juridification of the sea. Following these arguments, chapter 2 situates the *Komagata Maru*'s passage within another set of maritime histories. Focused on the vessel as a juridical form, I build on and elaborate my arguments regarding the racial and legal status of the sea. Here, I extend Gilroy's suggestive remarks on the role of the ship.[171] Whereas Gilroy emphasizes the *representation* of slave ships in Atlantic worlds, I focus on the *materiality* of one specific vessel that journeyed literally and figuratively through multiple ocean regions. Despite the voluminous literature on the *Komagata Maru*'s journey, there has been remarkably little discussion of the ship itself. This chapter situates the vessel in time and space and follows its routes across the Mediterranean Sea and the Atlantic, Pacific, and Indian Oceans. Its hundreds of voyages—under new names, different owners, and across multiple ocean regions—produced the sea as a legal space while implicating the ship in wider circuits of colonial, imperial, and racial terror, including transatlantic slavery, Indian indenture, and indigenous dispossession. These histories of ocean crossings and racial violence, I contend, were conjoined in the vessel's corporeality and in the status of the ship as legal person.

Chapter 3 moves from a broader discussion of the sea and the ship as juridical entities and tracks the *Komagata Maru*'s arrival and detention in Vancouver Harbour. In this chapter, I present a detailed reading of the Immigration Board hearing and the legal case—*Re Munshi Singh*—that was initiated by Husain Rahim and other members of the shore committee and heard by the British Columbia Court of Appeal. Drawing on discussions of race, territoriality, and temporality, the court unanimously rejected the passenger's claims to enter the Dominion. Though the legal proceedings were centered on questions of racial subjecthood and admissibility, they were animated by the ship's manifest and by competing jurisdictional claims over land, sea, and coastal regions. Ultimately, the court fortified Canada's legal and political sovereignty in three ways. First, by emphasizing the Dominion's right to control its territorial waters. Second, by insisting that "Hindoos" were "Asiatics" and thus barred entry. Finally, by evoking indigenous peoples as the original inhabitants of Canada, and therefore the Dominion's primary responsibility. Effacing questions of indigenous dispossession and settler colonialism altogether, the Court of Appeal recast Canada's relations with its indigenous inhabitants from the past to the future. In so doing, the court deployed indigeneity as a way to reinscribe Dominion sovereignty against the presumed threat of Asiatic migration.

To develop my claim that the free sea was a racial and legal space marked by overlapping histories of colonial and racial dispossession, chapters 4 and 5 turn to indigeneity and transatlantic slavery, respectively. Focused on English-language newspapers and periodicals published in South Africa, Canada, and India, chapter 4 charts the transoceanic responses to the *Komagata Maru*'s failed journey. The ship's detention in Vancouver and its eventual deportation to Calcutta galvanized a global anticolonial vernacular in which indigeneity featured prominently. To date, studies of Indian radicalism have focused primarily on the Ghadrs.[172] In chapter 4, I present an alternative genealogy of Indian radicalism, one that engages with maritime mobilities and British and colonial law through wider racial and subaltern claims to inclusion, equality, and justice. To challenge the sovereignty of the white Dominions, some Indian dissidents and radicals emphasized the territorial dispossession of indigenous peoples in Canada, South Africa, Australia, and elsewhere. Contests over the *Komagata Maru*, I argue, were waged through transoceanic vernaculars that reorganized, and in some cases fortified, racial taxonomies and hierarchies that differentiated "indigenous" from "migrant." The ship's supporters evoked indigeneity and "imperial citizenship" as challenges to global time and universal history, but often with unintended and objectionable effects.

Chapter 5 returns to the maritime movements and aspirations of Gurdit Singh and follows him farther inland. Notwithstanding his vital role in planning, executing, and commanding the *Komagata Maru*'s journey from Hong Kong to Vancouver, Singh remains an enigmatic figure. Very little attention has been given to his peripatetic movements between India and the Straits Settlements and to his struggles against British imperial rule.[173] Attentive to his travels across the Indian and Pacific Oceans and following his fugitive sojourns in India, chapter 5 emphasizes the analytic and historical import of viewing oceanic regions as overlapping and interconnected, both geographically and temporally. Drawing on the concept of fugitivity, this chapter focuses on Gurdit Singh's English-language memoirs: *Voyage of the Komagatamaru: Or India's Slavery Abroad*. By fashioning himself as a legal subject, Singh drew a set of intersecting lines that marked the historical, territorial, and juridical overlaps between the Pacific, Indian, and Atlantic Oceans. Through an expansive maritime and global imaginary, he initiated a remarkable and convincing critique of transatlantic slavery, Indian indentured labor, and immigration prohibitions.[174] Singh's repudiation of British imperial authority and the violence that underpinned it, I argue, was made possible through his own maritime itinerancy and his sojourns across the subcontinent. Rejecting a linear, teleological, and global time, Singh's writings echo the rhythm of the sea and present a disjointed temporality of law, justice, and freedom. The splitting of time that was inherent within British legality allowed him to condemn its past while remaining open to a future in which justice might someday be possible. Ultimately, Gurdit Singh's anticolonial imaginaries were animated by his claims to the free sea. Maritime commerce, trade, and travel were vital to India's future, he urged, a point he made lucidly in his "Proclamation to Indians," with which I begin this book.

The epilogue returns to the conceptual and methodological stakes and revisits the analytic and historical significance of oceans as method. Struggles over the free sea, as I argue in chapter 1, had a long and protracted history in European thought. As the *Komagata Maru*'s passage illustrates, the free sea was also a site of anticolonial and racial contest over the legality of oceans and maritime spaces. The ship's 1914 voyage affords one snapshot of these struggles. But there are many others. The epilogue moves from histories of Indian migration along the Pacific and Indian Oceans to the Mediterranean, Europe's primeval sea, a region that was crossed regularly by the *Sicilia*. Debates over the free sea are as critical today as they were historically. The West's current "crisis of migration," as evidenced in Mediterranean crossings from North Africa and the Middle East to Europe, remains a racial contest over life/death and past/present/future. As juridical forms, oceans and ships continue to be vital to these racial and legal struggles and in ways that echo the *Komagata Maru*'s voyage and its purportedly despotic Sikh commander. Today, Europe has recast the free sea as an expanding and contracting juridical space that sits beyond the jurisdiction of individual nation-states. Its elasticity has inaugurated a new international legal and political order in which migrant lives remain expendable and where racial violence is enacted with impunity against black and brown bodies. When positioned in these contemporary exigencies, the *Komagata Maru*'s voyage and the itineraries and imaginaries of Gurdit Singh and Husain Rahim remind us that the sea has long been a site of legal, political, and racial contest and a space well worth fighting for.

The Free Sea: A Juridical Space

Modern steamship traffic and cheap passages have brought the Asiatic into contact with the new continents that are being peopled. —JOHN COWEN, "Race Prejudice," 1910

The visions of men are widened by travel and contact with the citizens of a free country will infuse a spirit of independence and foster yearning for freedom in the minds of the emasculated subjects of alien rule. —GURDIT SINGH, *Voyage of the Komagatamaru,* 1928

Gurdit Singh's turn to the sea was preceded by a much longer history of Indian maritime travel. From the seventeenth century onward, thousands of men left the subcontinent as lascars working on vessels that expanded the commercial, political, and legal reach of the East India Company and subsequently the British Crown.[1] Indian seafarers, G. Balachandran writes, were among the first global workers. They "manned decks on the world's ships, and crewed engine rooms, saloons, cabins, and galleys." Though many were drawn to oceans as sites of freedom and adventure, they "inhabited a world deeply marked by race which determined what they could do, how much they could be paid, and how they could be treated."[2] To be sure, British vessels were ordered and regulated through rigid hierarchies of race, caste, and religion. With increased maritime traffic, imperial control expanded from the ship outward, creating planetary divisions between land and sea and inaugurating new spatial, temporal, and civilizational orders.[3] This juridification of the sea did not deter Indian travelers, however. In the last decades of the nineteenth century, advances in steam technology offered unprecedented opportunities to Indians and other "Asiatics." It was no longer only lascars and seafarers who crossed the seas, but also merchants, soldiers, and laborers. Ordinary men (and women), including the *Komagata Maru* passengers, sought opportunities to see and experience the world, though not often in conditions of their own choosing.[4] Others pursued maritime routes to escape from British imperial rule. By the early twentieth century, colonial authorities and their supporters feared that "cheap passages" would avail the seas and open the "new continents" to "Asiatic" peoples.[5] And they did.

The *Komagata Maru* was not the only ship to carry Indian migrants and travelers to Canada's west coast. Many real and imagined journeys preceded it.[6] In 1913, Canadian authorities received news of an Indian merchant in Seattle who had plans to hire a steamer to transport his countrymen from India to Vancouver.[7] But the report was unfounded. One year later, these fears were materialized with the *Komagata Maru's* arrival along British Columbia's coast. This was the only vessel to be chartered and commanded by a British/Indian subject and the first to be turned away from Canadian waters. The ship's ingress, which coalesced with wider speculations on the dangers of Indian seafaring, spawned two interrelated concerns. One centered on the presumed maritime ambitions of Indian men who many feared were newly asserting their rights to mobility as British subjects. The other revitalized European debates on the freedom of the sea. Increased outbound migration from the subcontinent to the white Dominions was met with greater restrictions, prohibitions, and increased surveillance. These contests over transoceanic travel produced a renewed interest in the racial and legal status of the seas: were they open or closed and for whom?

Until the early twentieth century, Indian migration to Canada was relatively insignificant. From 1905 onward, rates of outbound passage increased slowly and steadily.[8] Like their counterparts in Australia and Natal, Canadian officials responded with calls for tighter immigration laws. Efforts to control Dominion borders were tightly bound up with maritime governance.[9] In 1908, fearing a sharp rise in ocean travel from India to Canada's Pacific coast, the Dominion government passed the continuous journey regulation. Written without explicit reference to race or nationality, the law required all prospective immigrants to make a direct journey from their place of birth or naturalization to their port of entry.[10] In its objectives and in practice, the law was openly and unabashedly aimed at excluding Indian migrants. To ensure its successful enforcement, Canadian officials halted the Calcutta-Vancouver route almost entirely. They also instructed steamship companies not to grant passage to Indian travelers seeking to leave the subcontinent or from ports of call in East and Southeast Asia.[11] In so doing, Dominion authorities transformed a seemingly race-neutral law into one with markedly racial effects. Between 1908 and 1914, following several

FIGURE I.I. Five men standing outside the Immigration Detention Center, Victoria, November 1913. The photo was taken after the British Columbia Court of Appeal's hearing of *Re Thirty-Nine Hindus,* a case that challenged the validity of the continuous journey provision one year before the *Komagata Maru's* arrival. Husain Rahim, who helped initiate the legal action, is pictured fourth from left. (Photo courtesy of Simon Fraser University Library Special Collections and Rare Books, Kohaly Collection)

successful legal challenges, the Dominion revised and reenacted the continuous journey provision, adding further restrictions on the seabound passage of Indians and other "Asiatics."[12] Together, these prohibitions extended Canadian jurisdiction outward, from land and littoral into the Pacific and Indian Oceans.

Though Gurdit Singh's efforts to charter the *Komagata Maru* and lay claims to the sea were unprecedented, it is important to note that his maritime ambitions were established upon and shaped by the struggles of many others. One of the first and most significant challenges to the Dominion's continuous journey provision came from Husain Rahim (see fig. 1.1). Rahim arrived in Vancouver in 1909 and immediately began initiating legal measures aimed at defying the Dominion government. In 1914, he quickly rose to prominence as the leader of the "shore committee."[13] Composed of fifteen men—mostly, but not only, Sikhs from Punjab—the group accumulated a considerable sum of money to assist Gurdit Singh and the other passengers to disembark. Their campaign began with an appeal for financing, issued by Husain Rahim and Bhag Singh, and which I discuss in the introduction. Although these men eventually assumed the *Komagata Maru*'s charter, their efforts to secure the vessel's disembarkation was ineffective and even disastrous.

On account of his own discontinuous itineraries and his ongoing legal troubles, Rahim was deeply sympathetic to those aboard the ship. To begin, his journey from India to Canada did not follow a continuous or direct route. Rather, Rahim left the subcontinent in 1895, ten years after Gurdit Singh, and lived in Kobe for over a decade. Though the two men resided in different ports—in Malaya/Singapore and Kobe, respectively—and though they came from distinct regions in India, their travels followed similar patterns, animated by commercial aspirations, itinerant movements, and legal restrictions. Because of Rahim's "great capacity for business," particularly his experience in the cotton trade, he was recruited as a working partner in a newly established Kobe firm owned by Jamshedi Manekji Nanporia, a Bombay Parsi.[14] Seven years later, when Nanporia left Kobe and returned home for a brief visit, Rahim allegedly "made a huge speculative business and incurred heavy responsibilities." He "paid up the firm's dues and left Japan under the [Muslim] name of H. Rahim partly to avoid Jamshedi and partly to avoid further prosecution." He then boarded a steamer and "bolted" to Hawai'i.[15] On 28 December 1909, after residing in Honolulu for nearly two years, Rahim embarked on another ship, the SS *Moana*. This time, he landed in Vancouver, where the vessel made its regular stop en route from Sydney.[16]

By the early twentieth century, seaborne Indian men raised questions and generated suspicions among colonial and imperial agents. In Rahim's case, his seemingly fraudulent business practices combined with his mutable religious identities and his multiple aliases incited concerns for authorities in India, Canada, and the United States. "There has been a certain amount of distrust in the Hindu colony with respect to Rahim," wrote William Hopkinson, the Dominion's immigration inspector in Vancouver. Hopkinson assumed a key role in the *Komagata Maru*'s detention and deportation, and was eventually assassinated for his involvement.[17] "No one has yet been able to ascertain his village address in India," he reported, "and many suspect that he is not a Mahomedan [*sic*], as he claims, but is a Hindu and comes from the province of Bambay [*sic*]."[18] Rahim's arrival in Vancouver would only incite further speculation: Was he Hindu or Muslim? Did he come from Bombay or elsewhere? By some accounts, he was a revolutionary from Bengal. By others, he was a trader from Gujarat, a princely state in the northwest region of the subcontinent that was widely known for its merchant and seafaring classes.[19] According to J. W. Mattoon, the superintendent of Bombay Police, Rahim's given name was "Changan Khairaj Varma," though many knew him as "Changan Lal." He was a forty-six-year-old Hindu from the "Lohana Bania" caste and a "native of Porbander State in Kathiawar."[20] When Rahim fled Kobe for Hawai'i, he carried with him "a large sum of money," which he allegedly stole from Nanporia's firm.[21] In Honolulu, he became "the owner of considerable property."[22] But following his arrival in Vancouver, Rahim's commercial interests quickly turned political. The legal actions he waged on behalf of his countrymen in British Columbia and those not yet arrived, would hold far-reaching consequences, radically altering the fate of the *Komagata Maru* passengers and the futures of hundreds of others seeking passage from India to Canada. It was these political and legal disputes that set the conditions for the *Komagata Maru*'s unsuccessful journey and transformed Gurdit Singh into a supposedly dangerous radical.

The *Komagata Maru* was the first and last ship to carry a full complement of Indian passengers into Canadian waters. However, the global conflicts it engendered over the freedom of the sea were not new. Questions regarding the racial and legal status of oceans emerged in the early seventeenth century, coinciding with the travels of Indian lascars, and growing out of European inter-imperial struggles over "free trade" in the East Indies. These discussions were formalized in 1609, with Hugo Grotius's *Mare Liberum,* which centered on a maritime dispute in the Straits of Singapore. This well-traveled waterway was a meeting point between the Pacific and Indian Oceans and a region that featured prominently in the race for European control.[23] More than three hundred years later, the *Komagata Maru* would pass through those very same waters as Gurdit Singh sought to disembark at Singapore.

To be clear, these seventeenth-century debates on the "free sea" were never referenced directly by colonial authorities or by Indian passengers for that matter. In telling a maritime and legal history, however, I situate the *Komagata Maru*'s voyage—including the threats it posed through Indian seafaring, commerce, and mobility—in these longer racial and juridical contests over oceans and ships. Given nineteenth-century advances in steam technology and the growing accessibility of maritime travel, observers in Canada, London, India, and elsewhere queried whether the sea, which was free for European navigation and commerce, now included "Asiatics." Repositioning the *Komagata Maru*'s voyage as a conflict over oceans, rather than a contest over arrival and immigration, foregrounds the vessel and its passage as a disputed site of law, order, and authority. Struggles over the ship, I suggest, were not limited to national or territorial borders but also expanded Dominion and imperial jurisdiction unevenly into the sea. British imperial control over oceans and maritime worlds increasingly took the form of intersecting and overlapping global lines, as evidenced in navigation, longitude, and global time. These impositions generated new spatial, temporal, and legal orders, which were vociferously challenged by Indian travelers and equally by an aspiring white Canada.

Using oceans as method, this chapter situates the *Komagata Maru*'s voyage in a longer history of the free sea. Specifically, I juxtapose European and non-European chronologies of oceans as juridical spaces and, in so doing, present a set of competing accounts of their racial and legal significance. Part one begins with Grotius, whose writings on "The Free Sea" established the land/sea divide as an elemental and legal distinction, one that grounded a new global European order in maritime imperial legality. In part two, I move to the work of Carl Schmitt. Though Schmitt was not writing until the 1940s, long after the *Komagata Maru*'s voyage was completed and forgotten, his discussion of "firm land" and "free sea" as elemental, juridical, and geopolitical, offers an important historical critique of British maritime power and a useful counterpoint to Grotius. Here, I expand and elaborate on Schmitt's spatial *nomos* through a discussion of global time. In the final section, I return to Husain Rahim. Through his personal experiences of seaborne travel, Rahim viewed oceans as sites of increased regulation and surveillance but also as lucrative spaces of trade, commerce, and freedom. The legal and political challenges he waged against the Dominion government were informed by a counter-*nomos* of the earth, one that he envisaged from the decks of the *Moana,* and one that sutured land/sea, space/time, and east/west.[24] These planetary visions also shaped and animated the anticolonial imaginaries of Gurdit Singh. Seaborne travel, Singh urged, "fostered [a] yearning for freedom in the minds of the emasculated subjects of alien rule."[25] Oceanic struggles, especially the elemental, juridical, and racial distinctions they inscribed between aqueous and terrestrial spaces, established a legal architecture for the *Komagata Maru*'s failed journey and spawned a global and transoceanic vernacular of anticolonial critique.

Land/Sea

European debates on the legal status of the high seas—whether they were open or closed, held in common, or under imperial control—did not originate in Europe or the colonies. For Grotius, they grew out of European struggles over trade, commerce, and maritime control that centered on moving ships, cargos, and strategic waterways in Southeast Asia.[26] In his early twenties at the time, the young jurist and humanist was commissioned by the Dutch East India Company (VOC) to consider a maritime dispute that would have far-reaching historical, political, and legal consequences: could oceans, like land, be subject to proprietary claims or were the seas to be held in common by all? These questions emerged from the capture of a ship. On 25 February 1603, three Dutch vessels surrounded and attacked the *Santa Catarina,* a Portuguese-flagged carrack.[27] The Portuguese officers and its polyglot crew—including Arab, Turkish, and Indian men—departed Macao and were en route to Goa along the Straits of Singapore, when the assault took place. Portugal declared the attack to be illegal as the shipping channel, authorities claimed, was under its sovereign control.[28] The carrack, which was traveling with a larger fleet of ships, turned out to be a treasure trove. It carried a handsome cargo of raw silks, damask cottons, porcelain, and other high-value items.[29] Though Jakob van Heemskerk, the commander of the Dutch fleet, was not formally authorized to attack, either by the company that employed him or by the VOC, he did so opportunistically and on his own accord.[30] The seizure of the *Santa Catarina* initiated a series of legal questions on the competing jurisdictions of imperial control and the dividing line between legitimate and illegitimate commercial activities at sea.[31] The results of the case held far-reaching consequences: the VOC profited enormously from the ship's cargo; van Heemskerk was promoted to admiral; and most significantly, the *Santa Catarina* established a basis for international law, one that entrenched Grotius's land/sea distinction.

Mare Liberum (*The Free Sea*) was first published anonymously in 1609. The initial manuscript was pithy, comprising merely sixty-six pages.[32] The text drew directly from a much lengthier chapter in *De Jure Praedae* or *Commentary on the Law of Prize and Booty,* a monograph that Grotius drafted between September 1604 and November 1606, shortly after the Dutch Admiralty Board reached its decision.[33] But the *Commentary* remained undiscovered and unpublished until the nineteenth century. Though *Mare Liberum* represented merely a fragment of Grotius's thinking, it was the only piece of writing to enter European deliberations on the legal status of the sea. For years, the Portuguese had waged egregious acts of hostility against the Dutch and their indigenous trading partners, Grotius argued. By preventing peaceful maritime trade, Portugal was violating the Hollanders' natural rights to commerce. Accordingly, explicit permission to attack the *Santa Catarina* was not required. Jakob van Heemskerk's actions were sanctioned by natural law, Grotius reasoned, and the carrack's seizure was a just and lawful act of retaliation in a time of war.[34] Perhaps not surprisingly, Grotius's arguments were closely aligned with those of the

Admiralty Board. Privateering was the final recourse for van Heemskerk and his officers, the court concluded. It was a necessary act of reprisal aimed at securing Dutch commercial undertakings in the East Indies.[35]

Unbeknownst to Grotius, his writings on the freedom of trade and navigation would become foundational to international law. Though he focused on the Hollanders' right to maritime commerce, *Mare Liberum* was received as an important meditation on the legal standing of the sea.[36] The seizure of the *Santa Catarina* drew considerable attention from European sovereigns and jurists. Though the attack was not unusual for the period in question, so huge a prize was atypical. Even Grotius remarked wondrously on the vessel's cargo: "When the prize ... was recently put up for sale, who did not marvel at the wealth revealed? Who was not struck with amazement? Who did not feel that the auction in progress was practically the sale of a royal property, rather than of a fortune privately owned?"[37] The Straits of Singapore was a key maritime thoroughfare that featured prominently in European imperial expansion. Portugal realized this early on.[38] The Dutch later recognized the importance of the straits—and Britain long thereafter. Following the issuance of a royal charter to the East India Company in 1600, Britain's interest focused largely on India. It was not until the early decades of the nineteenth century, particularly after Singapore was "founded" in 1819, that British administrators became increasingly aware of the financial and political opportunities in Southeast Asia.[39] The case of the *Santa Catarina* underscored the lucrative prospects of European commerce and control in the region.[40] The sale of the ship's cargo totaled half of the VOC's capital base and was more than double the value of the British East India Company.[41]

The attack on the *Santa Catarina* and Grotius's assessment of it did not, by themselves, inaugurate an inter-imperial debate on *imperium* (jurisdiction) and *dominium* (property) over the seas. Rather, they extended and amplified these discussions in important ways. As Britain sought to protect its coastal fisheries from the encroachment of other European powers, most notably the Dutch, debates on the legal status of the seas were already under way in England and Scotland.[42] The seizure of the *Santa Catarina* raised additional queries. Was the Dutch capture of a Portuguese vessel legal? Did the Portuguese have a sovereign right to claim the waters on which its ships traveled? If so, was this assertion based on first arrival, use, custom, or natural law? What was the legal and political status of indigenous rulers in the Straits Settlements? These were just some of the issues that Grotius was asked to address.[43] Though *Mare Liberum*'s message was clear—the sea was free from occupation and possession—its format was not. The text was written and published long after the Admiralty Court reached its decision. Therefore, Grotius's writings were never intended to serve as a legal brief or rejoinder in the case. In fact, *Mare Liberum* references the *Santa Catarina* case only obliquely and indirectly. The carrack's seizure and its aftermath were more fully elaborated and discussed in the *Commentary*. How then might we read Grotius's intervention? For Martine van Ittersum the slim book is "half theory, half apology." In her reading, the text offers a retrospective explanation, rationalization, and defense of van Heemskerk's actions, one that inadvertently established a law of the sea, additional forms of Dutch colonial rule, and a new European legal order.[44]

Conventional interpretations of *Mare Liberum* have typically highlighted Grotius's ideas on natural law and the law of nations. In these well-known accounts, Grotius is positioned alongside two other "founding fathers," most notably Francisco de Vitoria and Alberico Gentili.[45] But *Mare Liberum* might also be read as an aesthetic meditation on the high seas, one that was informed by an elemental-turned-legal distinction between land and sea. For Grotius, it was the physico-material properties of oceans—their expansiveness, and ceaseless change—that rendered them to be juridically different from terra firma. Though Grotius's writings were intended to be a treatise on global commerce and not a legal reflection on the high seas, the two were inseparable. "It is axiomatic," writes K. N. Chaudhuri, "that the technology of shipping and the art of navigation must attain a certain level of development before men are able to sail safely and carry goods across the open sea."[46] The high seas and the vessels that crossed them were vital to Europe's aspirations to dominate the earth, economically, legally, and racially. The movement of ships enabled European empires to violently appropriate indigenous lands, waterways, and natural resources through what many have termed "free trade." Oceans were viewed as "maritime highways," and vessels brought "Asian emporia" closer to Europe.[47]

In advancing his arguments on the Hollanders' right to commerce, Grotius drew a clear and foundational dividing line between land and sea. It was their elemental differences, he argued, that determined legal questions of occupation and possession. Whereas land was solid and easily divisible, owned, and conquered, the sea was liquid, ephemeral, and expansive. Unlike "parts of the earth [that] do not cohere" and are already partitioned, he opined, "all the sea properly so-called coheres and is one and continuous . . . Therefore the limit of lands is in the air and sea, the limit of the entire sea is only the air."[48] By conceiving of oceans as *actual* but uncontainable spaces, Grotius offered an alternative view of the earth, one that emphasized the sea and repositioned imperial sovereignty accordingly. Land—including islands, sand, and rock—did "not physically limit the sea," he explained, but was limited by it.[49] Oceans were more comparable to the ephemerality of other earthly substances such as air than they were to the solidity of land. For Grotius, air was common "for a double reason": it could not be possessed and it "oweth a common use to men." If air and sea were analogous, he explained, then "the element of the sea is common to all, to wit, so infinite that it cannot be possessed and applied to all uses, whether we respect navigation or fishing."[50]

Grotius's view was that God gave all things to humankind. However, some gifts of nature, particularly land, were more amenable to division than others. Just as *Mare Liberum* set the foundation for an international law of the sea, it also forged a rationale for Europe's conquest of the Americas, as evidenced in the writings of John Locke and others.[51] It was through lines in the soil that land was transformed into a commodity to be owned, occupied, and sold. "And the ground, which had hitherto been a common possession like the sunlight and the air, the careful surveyor now marked out with a long-drawn boundary," Grotius wrote.[52] If the fixity and immovability of land meant that it could be measured and parceled, the sea was a different matter altogether. "The sea therefore is in the number of those things which are not in merchandise and trading, that is to say, which cannot be made proper.... The people of a country might possess a river as included within their bounds, but so could they not the sea."[53] Ultimately, it was their elemental differences that distinguished the solidity of land and the limitlessness of the sea in legal and political terms. Given that "*the sea is incomprehensible,* no less than the air, it can be added to the goods of no nation," Grotius explained.[54] Inscrutability featured prominently in his arguments on oceanic freedom.

Though *Mare Liberum* was commissioned as an official response to a maritime dispute between Portugal and the United Provinces, it carried serious implications for Britain's ascent as a maritime empire. British authorities feared that the Hollanders' recent aggressions might avail additional opportunities for Dutch ships to enter English coastal waters.[55] Not surprisingly, *Mare Liberum* incited a vigorous response from scholars and jurists in Scotland and England, respectively.[56] Grotius received two rejoinders, one from William Welwod, professor of mathematics and civil law at the University of St. Andrews, and another from English jurist John Selden. In 1590, Welwod wrote the first comprehensive text on maritime law. Selden further developed and expanded several of his insights and arguments.[57] Though they held distinct views, both began with a mutual premise that the sea was not free. Rather, it was a closed space— *mare clausum*—that was subject to imperial control. According to Welwod, who penned the only response to which Grotius replied, the sea was a site of restraint.[58] Drawing his authority from Genesis, he recalled God's command to Adam and Eve: "subdue the earth, and rule over the fish." The mastery over land and fish, Welwod maintained, could only be possible "by a subduing of the waters also."[59] In advancing their arguments, neither Welwod nor Selden distinguished land from sea. In fact, Welwod castigated Grotius for asserting this division in the first place. Oceans did not exist as a two-dimensional or undifferentiated whole, he urged. Through fishing, trade, and transportation "the waters became divisible … requiring a partition in like manner with the earth." Even by "the law of nations," Welwod continued, "the sea is divided into distinct realms" much "like the dry land," that distinguished coastal waters from the high seas.[60] Though Selden was clearly influenced by Welwod's thinking and writing, he advanced his own arguments on a closed sea. British imperial rule extended over land *and* sea, he claimed. "The King of Great Britain is Lord of the Sea flowing about as an irreparable and perpetual Attendant of the British Empire."[61] Despite their divergent views, Welwod and Selden agreed that land and sea made up an interconnected and indivisible imperial whole.

One of the most forceful aspects of Welwod's critique was aimed at Grotius's elemental claims. Oceans could not be free to all, just because they were moving and infinite. That the sea was flowing was an incontrovertible truth, Welwod observed. Oceans were "liquid, fluid, and unstable in the particles thereof." Notwithstanding its expansiveness, however, the sea retained "prescribed bounds" that were established through new scientific technologies, most notably the compass:[62]

> God, who is both the distributor and first author of the division and distinction of both land and sea, hath given an understanding heart to man for the same effect as well as for all other necessary actions wherein he hath to employ himself, so that to a very wonder God hath diversely informed men *by the helps of the compass,* counting of courses, sounding, and other ways to find forth and to design *finitum in infinito* so far as is expedient for the certain reach and bounds of seas properly pertaining to any prince or people.[63]

Whereas Grotius characterized oceans as vast and incomprehensible, Welwod rendered them knowable and thus governable. God bestowed man with the will and the intellect to devise technologies that would allow him to navigate, traverse, and eventually master the waves, he urged. By the eighteenth century, maritime navigation became another site of inter-imperial contest and an additional register of imperial control, a point I consider more fully in the next section.

In his reply to Welwod, Grotius reiterated the elemental distinctions between land and sea as natural and therefore, indisputable. Possession is "a holding fast of a physical thing," he retorted.[64] "Now nothing can be apprehended unless limited corporally." Thus, liquids must "be limited by something else" and "liquids cannot be possessed except by means of that whereby they are limited." Though Grotius acknowledged that some fluids were finite and could be contained, "as wine is possessed by means of a vessel, [and] rivers by means of their banks," the sea, he argued, was *an unlimited liquid* [that] *is not to be possessed*."[65] Several pages later, Grotius clarified that the freedom of the sea was not solely an outcome of its expansiveness. The "proximate reason why the sea cannot be possessed is neither its fluid nature nor its 'continually flowing to and fro' (which Welwod brings up against himself in vain)." It is because of "*its incomprehensibility the same as in the case of the air*."[66] Yet, Grotius acquiesced to Welwod's insistence on the advances of scientific innovation. The sea, he conceded, could be known through "assisting instruments, such as the nautical compass, the astrolabe, etc." Oceans "can be distinguished" into coastal waters and the high seas, he continued, and "there is a certain use for this distinction, both in matters which the intellect performs *per se,* such as geographical observation, and in matters which the intellect performs with the aid of the will, to which contracts of men should be referred."[67] However, to know and measure the sea, he maintained, did not equate with possession. If "the drawing of a line" was "sufficient for occupation," Grotius charged, "the astronomers should be said to be the possessors of the heaven and the geometers of the earth."[68] Scientific and technological developments surely facilitated greater accuracy in navigation, but for Grotius this did not translate into a closed sea.

Following its publication, *Mare Liberum* engendered spirited debate, especially among British thinkers. Disputes over the text have continued to persist, albeit along different lines. One of Grotius's most provocative and contentious twentieth-century commentators was an international lawyer named Charles Henry Alexandrowicz. Grotius's thinking on maritime trade and navigation, Alexandrowicz argued, was supposedly informed by primary research that he conducted at the VOC Archives.[69] It was by analyzing documents and folios that Grotius apparently recognized Asian maritime histories of the Indian Ocean arena.[70] *Mare clausum,* according to Alexandrowicz, was far more prevalent in seventeenth-century European legal and political thought than *mare liberum.* Thus, Grotius's ideas on the free sea must have been influenced by Indian Ocean histories, especially the commercial practices and customs of Arab and Chinese seafarers. "According to these traditions," Alexandrowicz explained, "the high sea had been, since time immemorial, considered a free international highway."[71] It was a vibrant place of movement, mobility, and interethnic trade, a history that Gurdit Singh sought to recover through his own maritime aspirations.

As compelling as these arguments are, scholars have questioned their veracity. The documents that Grotius received, read, and considered in writing *Mare Liberum* came directly from VOC authorities and not from his own archival research.[72] Thus, in formulating his arguments regarding the free sea, Grotius relied on official legal texts, including the affidavits of ship officers, sailors, and seafarers. The most important of these was the testimony of van Heemskerk.[73] Critics maintain that Grotius was not versed in Asian seafaring customs at all, but was focused entirely on Dutch maritime rule.[74] Dutch claims to order and authority in the Indian Ocean arena were informed, shaped, and enforced through patterns of trade and commerce. Thus, it was the movement of European ships and not Asian ones that informed Grotius's conceptions of land, sea, and sovereignty.

To be sure, Grotius did acknowledge the authority of Asian rulers. However, he had less knowledge of Southeast Asia, and was better informed of colonial expansion elsewhere, including Spain's violent efforts to colonize the Americas.[75] The School of Salamanca was especially influential to his thinking. Grotius was particularly inspired by the work of Francisco de Vitoria, whose writings on Indians in the Americas enabled him to compare colonization in the "New World" with what was happening in the East Indies. European traders in Southeast Asia, unlike their counterparts in the Americas, did not command territorial rights through *terra nullius* or occupation.[76] Given that Dutch interests were centered on commercial maritime trade and not on large-scale European settlement, authorities were forced to recognize the presence of indigenous rulers.[77] For some, Grotius's attentiveness to Asian sovereigns served as evidence of his humanitarianism and his tacit opposition to Dutch colonial rule. However, others remain rightly cynical, suggesting that Grotius did not oppose colonization but merely presented another version, one that foregrounded law and sea.[78] The Hollanders, Peter Borschberg explains, "did not claim or impose a monopoly in the same manner as the Portuguese and Spaniards, i.e., on the basis of discovery, first occupation or donation." Rather, for Grotius the Dutch "secured their monopoly *legally* through mutual consent."[79] But mutual consent operated as a misnomer in practice. The VOC used suspected breaches of treaty to extend their political and economic control and to justify their use of force.[80] "Free trade" in the East Indies, Grotius claimed, necessitated the active defense of indigenous rulers, a condition that demanded violence, as evidenced by the seizure of the *Santa Catarina*.[81] *Mare Liberum* was written as a treatise on free trade that afforded a legal status to the sea. In so doing, it set the juridical groundwork for more than three centuries of Dutch rule in Southeast Asia.[82] Yet Grotius's influence reached even further. His emphasis on the elemental as juridical established the foundation for a land/sea divide that formed the basis of international law historically and endures into the present day. The juridico-political distinctions between land and sea remain elemental, and are therefore largely unquestioned and unproblematized.

Grotius's interest in maritime worlds shaped and influenced his views of sovereignty. He was well aware that Dutch control over the Indian Ocean region was exercised through partial rule.[83] This view marked a radical departure from many of his predecessors and contemporaries. Though Grotius agreed with Jean Bodin that sovereignty was indivisible, he offered several important exceptions.[84] To begin, the VOC's efforts to govern the Indian Ocean were advanced through a loosely connected set of jurisdictional claims in which Dutch power was layered on top of indigenous sovereignties.[85] More importantly, Grotius argued that sovereignty at sea was divisible, as the Dutch case illustrated.[86] Thus, he readily acknowledged that imperial sovereigns could (and did) make jurisdictional claims to the high seas, a position he advanced most clearly in response to Welwod. "Purposely have we refrained from treating of the dominium (*imperium*) and jurisdiction of the sea, because that question has no connection with ownership (*dominium*)."[87] Jurisdiction was to be distinguished between that "which is competent to each in common and that which is competent to each one properly speaking."[88] Princes and their people "can punish pirates and others, who commit delicts on the sea against the law of nations," Grotius explained. As "jurisdiction over a person is competent without taking account of the place," the prince can also "make law for the maritime actions of his subjects, judge these acts, even impose tribute, but also do this for his allies, if this has been agreed to by treaty."[89] The sea was common to all but remained subject to multiple and overlapping jurisdictional claims. By the early twentieth century, it would be Britain, the Dominions, and British/Indian subjects fighting over maritime access and control in the Pacific Ocean region.

The sea has long been conceived "as a void between societies," a "nonterritory," an untamable space that resists "filling."[90] Given Grotius's emphasis on the immeasurable and infinite properties of oceans, it may be appealing to read *Mare Liberum* as promoting this myth of the empty sea. However, to do so would be a mistake. For Grotius, the free sea was expansive and limitless, but it was never vacant or beyond law. To begin, he acknowledged the rich histories of Asian maritime trade and the authority of indigenous rulers. Furthermore, Grotius drew extensively on Greek and Roman legal and literary sources and was deeply influenced by a history of the Mediterranean. The Romans, he explained, saw themselves as holding a right to *control* the Mediterranean Sea though not to *possess* it.[91] European jurisdiction over the high seas was cast through multiple legalities as evidenced in international treaties, agreements, and naval practices.[92] Moving ships inscribed their own lines of authority, dividing oceans into coastal waters and the high seas, each with a distinct and corresponding legal status. Vessels at sea did not mark ownership, but their regular passages materialized the assertions of their sponsors and supporters.[93] Recall that for Grotius jurisdiction was not occupation: "Even if any navigator could be said to have obtained possession of the sea or any part of it (which is by no means so because he who navigates does not stand on the sea, does not hold the sea, 'does not hold fast,' but rather 'is even held fast')." With "the departure of the ship, possession likewise would straightway cease."[94]

In her innovative reading of Grotius and Gentili, Lauren Benton concludes that these early legal thinkers shared much in common. Oceans, in their respective views, were not sites of lawlessness. Nor were they empty spaces to be filled by international law. For both Grotius and Gentili, oceans were marked by overlapping and competing legalities in which ships featured prominently. In Benton's account, seagoing vessels were "islands of law" where captains and admirals exerted their authority as lawmakers and law enforcers, and where flags and colors represented specific national and imperial interests.[95] The VOC's ships, as Kerry Ward describes them, were "seaborne colonies where the exercise of Company authority was absolute."[96] But moving vessels extended jurisdiction in other ways. As juridical forms, ships produced the foundational and legal distinction between land as fixed and sea as fluid. Moreover, ships were "colonial laboratories," places of confinement and conviviality where legal idioms, practices, and forms of violence were not only enforced, but also deliberated, disputed, and often extended to terra firma.[97] What came to be known as "law" emerged from protracted voyages and in the quotidian folds of seafaring life, as Grotius intimated. European men in great imperial cities were not the ones to create a new global order as the myth of international law suggests.[98] Rather, in Grotius's formulation, the sea was a site of intersecting and overlapping jurisdictions that were polyvocal and plural.[99] As moving targets, ships were never just "islands of law." They were legal forms that were integral to imperial expansion. They connected distant places and reinvented and expanded the contours of law, while constituting the sea as a legal domain.

From the seventeenth century onward, as Europe's coordinates and concentrations of maritime power shifted, and as Britain gained its status as an empire of the sea, oceans remained legally charged sites of imperial contest. One of the British Empire's greatest ideological foundations, David Armitage argues, was its oscillation between *mare liberum* and *mare clausum*.[100] Though Britain sought to control the high seas in a number of ways—with navigation acts and agreements, and through the compass and the chronometer—the empire continued to insist on the freedom of the sea. The economic and political gains of the free sea were especially evident in the transatlantic slave trade and in the production and circulation of plantation commodities.[101] Perhaps ironically, the itineraries of British ships inaugurated a new era of oceanic freedom, one that could only be possible through Britannia's efforts to rule the waves.

The elemental and juridical distinction between land and sea that featured so prominently in Grotius's thinking was reinscribed and extended through other maritime orders. By the eighteenth century, the fluctuating status of the open and closed sea was stabilized and reinforced with the inscription of new global lines, most evident in the search and codification of longitude. Tracing these inscriptions, as I do in the following section, requires a historical and geographical shift from Grotius, Southeast Asia, and the VOC to Carl Schmitt and the so-called New World. Against Schmitt's contention that a new juridical and global order could only be established on "firm land," I argue that the aqueous world of the ship inaugurated a *nomos* of the earth that was centered on the sea, and was as temporal as it was spatial. By the early twentieth century, the free sea became a site of increased surveillance and regulation, not only by Britain but also by Canada and the United States. It was precisely this maritime imperial and racial order that the continuous journey provision sought to protect and that Husain Rahim and Gurdit Singh aspired to challenge through their respective legal struggles over transoceanic Indian mobility.

Global (Time) Lines

The land/sea divide that Grotius outlined in *Mare Liberum,* resurfaced in the mid-twentieth century in the writings of Carl Schmitt.[102] A Nazi sympathizer and collaborator, Schmitt was known as the "crown jurist of the Third Reich," and for good reason. Under the Nazi regime, he received several prestigious honors. He was appointed to the Union of Nationalist-Socialist Jurists and named professor of jurisprudence at the University of Berlin.[103] Whereas Grotius was a humanist, Schmitt was a highly conservative and controversial thinker. His ideas were widely circulated in the Weimar and Nazi eras and have gained renewed prominence today.[104] Though he was a deep admirer and advocate of European global supremacy, he was also a staunch critic of the British Empire, a view that often places him in strange company today. "Many of Schmitt's arguments," Antony Anghie points out, "bear a striking resemblance to the arguments made by post-colonial and Third World scholars, regarding the character and geopolitics of international law."[105] Schmitt's political and legal thought offers important reflections and competing chronologies of changing imperial orders. Grotius and Schmitt may share a common juridico-political vernacular in which the "free sea" figures prominently, but they used this concept dissimilarly and to distinct legal and geopolitical ends.

In *Land and Sea,* a short book written for his young daughter Anima that would serve as a critical precursor to *The* Nomos *of the Earth,* Schmitt argued that the struggle for world dominance grew from the elemental distinctions by which the planet was divided and organized.[106] The elements, in his account, were not equally or evenly arranged. For Schmitt, the sea was not a vibrant juridico-political space, as it was for Grotius. Rather, oceans served as a subdued backdrop that only accentuated the fixity of land and the terrestrial order of modern law. "Among the four traditional elements," Schmitt wrote, "the earth is the element that is prescribed for humans and that most strongly defines the human."[107] While he associated the sea with European dominance, most clearly exemplified in British maritime power, it was land that granted a material foundation to European international law. The aqueous worlds of Asian, indigenous, and European commerce that featured so prominently in Grotius's writings was lost to a Eurocentric and terracentric Schmitt. Given his preoccupations with terra firma and his refusal to think seriously about the sea, Schmitt had other blind spots. Though it was the moving vessel that facilitated circumnavigation, produced imperialist distinctions of land/sea, and enabled Europe's efforts to conquer the Americas, the ship—like the sea—proved largely inconsequential in Schmitt's "world-historical meditation."[108]

The seizure of the *Santa Catarina* took place in 1603. *Mare Liberum* was published anonymously in 1609. In Schmitt's chronology, however, this periodization of the free sea came far too late. It was in 1492, he insisted, after Columbus "discovered" the Americas that "a 'new world' actually emerged." From that moment onward, the earth was no longer what it had been in the physical or metaphysical sense, Schmitt argued. With European imperial expansion, "the structure of all traditional concepts of the *center* and the *age* of the earth had to change."[109] Global "lines were drawn to divide and distribute" the new continents, and a different European cartography was established.[110] Schmitt described this planetary order as *nomos.* The Greek term translates as "norm" and "right," but *nomos* also "means both 'to divide' and 'to pasture.'"[111] As a juridico-political concept, *nomos* was already rooted in land: "All pre-global orders were essentially *terrestrial* even if they encompassed sea powers and thalasocracies," Schmitt wrote.[112] Thus, the sea featured obliquely in his analysis. Schmitt described the *nomos* as "a concrete spatial order."[113] Significantly, his preoccupation with land foreclosed any possibility that the *nomos* could also be an oceanic and temporal order.

Long-distance sea travel was vital to the economic and political success of Europe's competing empires. Just as ships were crucial to European expansion via "free trade" in Southeast Asia, as my discussion thus far suggests, seagoing vessels were equally significant to territorial appropriation, indigenous dispossession, and European resettlement in the Americas.[114] People, commodities, ideas, and laws were transported across oceans via ship, processes that Grotius recognized and Schmitt largely ignored. Each of them highlighted the ocean's aqueous properties as elemental qualities that distinguished it from land. In Schmitt's account, however, land and sea were not elemental in the scientific sense; they were materially and juridically produced.[115] If soil "manifests firm lines" through fences, enclosures, and walls, he explained, "the *sea* knows no such apparent unity of space and law, of order and orientation." Fields cannot be planted at sea "and firm lines cannot be engraved." Vessels "that sail across the sea leave no trace."[116] While Grotius perceived the sea as a legal domain that was peopled by Arab, Chinese, and European traders, Schmitt portrayed it as empty. Land appropriations, he claimed, were at the center of all juridical orders and were the "primeval act in the founding of law."[117] Unlike "firm land," which could be parceled, divided, and cultivated, the free sea "has no *character,* in the original sense of the word," he wrote. Character "comes from the Greek *charassein,* meaning to engrave, to scratch, to imprint."[118] For Schmitt, the open sea had "no limits, no boundaries, no consecrated sites, no sacred orientations, no law and no property. . . . 'On the waves, there is nothing but waves.'"[119] Though Schmitt agreed with Grotius on the legal status of the sea, he criticized his predecessor for failing to address the question of land. Grotius was well aware of Spain's conquest of the Americas, Schmitt charged, but he said nothing of the "European appropriation of non-European territory."[120] Interestingly, in his commentary on Grotius and in his discussion of the "New World," Schmitt made no mention of indigenous peoples. Like the free sea, "firm land" was also empty, awaiting Europeans to arrive, claim, and settle it.

Schmitt was clearly a geographical thinker. Space, as many have noted, was foundational to his account of a changing global and imperial order.[121] The "first authentic spatial revolution" in world history and in historical consciousness occurred "in the epoch of the discovery of America and the first circumnavigation of the earth," he claimed.[122] As soon as the earth "emerged as a real globe—not just sensed as myth, but apprehensible as fact and measurable as space," he elaborated, "there arose a wholly new and hitherto unimaginable problem: the spatial ordering of the earth in terms of international law."[123] Though this new order uneasily subsumed land and sea, Schmitt's own narrative commenced only with land. Whether one begins a discussion of the global juridical order terrestrially or oceanically is not insignificant. Rather, these starting points determine the legal histories of empire and conceptions of sovereignty to follow. Repositioning the sea in Schmitt's *nomos,* for example, raises questions regarding his characterization of European imperial dominance. Efforts to measure and circumnavigate the earth were only achievable through the unpredictable and ungovernable sea.[124] The so-called age of discovery was not an era of undisputed European expansion and control, as Schmitt portrayed it. Rather, it was a time of heightened danger, volatility, and uncertainty, in which shipwrecks were all too commonplace.[125] Through the fury of the sea, ships were regularly confronted by the violence of nature on an unprecedented scale. The ocean "signifies nature in a different sense than the continent," Schmitt remarked. "The sea is more unfamiliar and hostile."[126] Before the invention of the chronometer, European vessels were regularly imperiled by common errors in navigation. Miscalculations of a ship's location carried severe consequences including delays, shortages of food and water, disease, desperation, and death. Any of these could open possibilities for mutiny and revolt.[127] As captains and navigators had yet to develop an accurate way to measure their naval coordinates, ships voyaged on well-traveled routes, making them vulnerable to theft, seizure, and piracy.[128] The *Santa Catarina* is a vivid case in point. Yet, these maritime vulnerabilities were lost on Schmitt, whose *nomos* of the earth commenced with land and ignored the sea.

The reorganization of space and time was one of the most significant and enduring effects of European struggles for global dominance.[129] The cartographic practices of European empires that resulted in maps, atlases, and almanacs produced a modern "imaginative geography" that remains fiercely contested today.[130] Imperial regimes drew lines, inscribed borders, created idioms of property, and made claims to sovereignty. In so doing, they divided the world into knowable fragments that could be charted, owned, and occupied.[131] Despite the histories and geographies of European triumph recalled by Grotius, Schmitt, and others, global lines were never imposed on empty lands or vacant seas. Rather, they were always layered atop indigenous sovereignties. Columbus's ostensible "discovery" was not a discovery at all. What he termed the "New World" was only new for Europeans. The Americas were not a space of "free *land*" open to European settlement, as Schmitt claimed.[132] These were places long inhabited by indigenous peoples whose histories were as terrestrial as they were oceanic.[133] Claims of discovery, and the global lines they engendered, facilitated a long, violent, and ongoing process of colonial deracination and indigenous dispossession.[134] As devastating as these developments were, European claims to sovereignty and territoriality were never processes of land acquisition alone. Control over the earth was asserted through Europe's spatial *and* temporal projections over "firm land" *and* "free sea."

A fundamental difference in the free sea, as conceived by Grotius and Schmitt, centers on the role of the ship. In writing *Mare Liberum,* Grotius directed his attention to Dutch and Portuguese vessels, beginning with the *Santa Catarina.* Thus, he was attentive to the plural legalities of maritime worlds, including their key differences from terrestrial orders. The polycentricity of maritime worlds dramatically shaped his conceptions of sovereignty.[135] Schmitt, by contrast, expressed little interest in ships. Though he wrote briefly and sporadically of seagoing vessels, he was far more concerned with their contrast to house and land. For Schmitt, the antithesis between land/sea and house/ship was also a contest of East/West, a geopolitical distinction that he identified but left largely unproblematized. The lines that separated East from West did not exist in some natural, neutral, or objective register. These distinctions were produced through shipping and in the quest for longitude, with effects that were territorial, temporal, and racial. Whereas East was defined through land, West, as embodied first by Europe and then North America, was associated with the sea. What "we call today the Orient," Schmitt observed, "is a contiguous mass of land-based countries: Russia, China, India. . . . And what we call the Occident today is the hemisphere surrounded by the great oceans; the Atlantic and Pacific."[136] This division of the earth along elemental, juridical, and civilizational registers coalesced in the existential and legal distinctions between ship and house. "The ship or sea vessel lies at the center of man's maritime existence, in the same way that the house lays [*sic*] at the center of terrestrial existence," Schmitt explained. But only one of these—the house—represented a true juridical order: "the fundamental institution of law, *dominium* or property, receives its name from *domus,* house." Whereas "terrestrial life revolves around the house . . . maritime life revolves around the ship which one must navigate."[137] In Schmitt's assessment, the ship was not a symbol, expression, or materialization of law, as it was for Grotius. If the house was a spatial expression of European property, the ship was "a technical vehicle," a "necessary instrument for man's domination over nature."[138]

Schmitt paid little attention to the ship. Yet, he underlined the role of the compass. Seafaring instruments like the compass, he argued, dramatically altered Europe's relationship to space. Recall, this was a point of contention in the *mare liberum/mare clausum* debate. In Welwod's rejoinder to Grotius, the legal status of the sea was inseparable from questions of navigation. Though the sea was an infinite and limitless expanse, it was divided by a set of global lines that ran north/south and east/west, through latitude and longitude respectively.[139]

Writing in the mid-twentieth century, Schmitt would have been well aware of the rapid advances in maritime technology. But in his chronology, it was only the compass that featured as "a nautical achievement."[140] The compass, Schmitt claimed, transformed human relationships with land and sea, bringing "the most distant terrains of all the oceans ... into contact with one another, so that the globe expands."[141] By lauding the compass, however, he overlooked another maritime innovation—the chronometer—an invention that truly "perfected" Europe's relationship with terrestrial and aqueous spaces. It was the clock and not the compass that offered greater precision in naval measurement, thus rendering the sea to be progressively less elemental and increasingly spatial and temporal.[142] Through the precision of the chronometer, longitude could be determined with greater accuracy, the earth could be mapped with reliability, and East/West became seemingly objective coordinates that naturalized geographical, temporal, and civilizational orders.

Schmitt was highly critical of Britain's maritime prowess. It was "the English who finally overtook everyone, vanquished all rivals, and attained a world domination erected upon the domination of the oceans," he charged.[143] Britain's rise to maritime supremacy was not solely the result of its physical mastery over the sea. Rather, the power of the British Empire lay in its ability to maintain transoceanic connections across vast distances, through shipping lines, undersea telegraph cables, and in the regularized circulation of vessels and documents.[144] To achieve maritime control and to establish relations between its far-flung colonies, Dominions, and territories, Britain needed to ensure the safety of its ships at sea. However, this was a challenging task. Latitude had a natural midpoint: the equator. As a result, seafarers had little difficulty determining their North/South positions. But the dividing line between East and West, a distinction that Schmitt naturalized and took for granted, proved to be a far greater problem. For centuries, Europeans were in search of greater precision in determining a ship's coordinates at sea. From the sixteenth century onward, the Spanish and Dutch committed large sums of money to facilitate this undertaking, a quest that Britain joined much later.[145] But it was not until 1707, when the fleet of British admiral Sir Cloudsley Shovell returned from a battle in Gibraltar and crashed into the Scilly Islands, that longitude became a matter of imperial and national concern. After losing four ships and almost two thousand men, British authorities realized the urgency of navigational accuracy.[146]

The imperial bureaucracy moved very slowly. On 29 April 1714, the British Parliament received a petition calling for a "Reward for the Discovery of Longitude." Writing on behalf of merchants and sea captains, the petitioners explained the importance of the matter: "whereas it is known, that nothing can be either at home or abroad, more for the common Benefit of Trade and Navigation, than the Discovery of the Longitude at Sea which has been so long desired in vain, and for want of which so many Ships and Men have been lost." On 9 July 1714, Britain finally passed An Act for Providing a Publik Reward for such Person or Persons as Shall Discover the Longitude at Sea. The ability to measure longitude precisely and accurately was officially recognized to be "of particular Advantage to the Trade of *Great Britain,* and very much for the Honour of this Kingdom."[147] The newly invented instrument was to be tested across the Atlantic, the act specified, "over the Ocean, from *Great Britain* to any such Port in the *West Indies.*"[148] Accuracy in measurement would enable Britain to master the seas with greater certainty, regularity, and security. The safety and security of vessels was especially critical for the Atlantic transport of African slaves. This may be why the West Indies became the referent point for gauging the chronometer's exactitude.[149]

Longitude is commonly described as a cartographic practice aimed at calculating the distance between two or more spatial coordinates. For Schmitt, the earth's East-West divide was clearly a terrestrial and spatial one. When viewed from the sea, however, longitude emerges as a key marker of time, one necessary for the safe and effective navigation of ships.[150] The format of early logbooks suggests that captains and seafarers were acutely concerned with timekeeping on long voyages.[151] Time was necessary for maritime navigation, but ships were also organized and ruled through a highly structured timetable called the "watch." Crews were divided into two groups, each alternating four-hour shifts that were measured by an hourglass and logged accordingly.[152] Maritime worlds produced a complex system of temporal procedures that were finally deemed accurate with the invention of the chronometer. To establish a vessel's position at sea, captains and crews required an instrument that could measure temporal simultaneity; the time at their current location and that of a reference point. A navigator who could establish both concurrently could calculate a ship's longitude by taking the difference of the two coordinates and multiplying it by fifteen degrees.[153] As European empires recognized the financial and political possibilities of long-distance sea travel, maritime supremacy depended not only on the compass but also on the chronometer.

When Schmitt's *nomos* of the earth is reoriented toward the sea, it can no longer be contained within a terrestrial or spatial order. As my discussion of navigation and the chronometer suggests, the *nomos* of the earth was also temporal. The world of the ship, as the search for longitude makes clear, was at the forefront of an expanding regime of European time. It was through shipboard time and eventually Greenwich Mean Time that Britain's efforts to measure the seas and rule the waves became possible.[154] When the Longitude Act was first passed, no one believed that a clock with such accuracy would ever be invented. As Sir Isaac Newton put it, "there have been several projects" aimed at "determining the longitude at sea." Most have been "true in the theory but difficult to execute" in practice.[155] More than a century earlier, Grotius characterized the "vigorous motion of the sea, as the untamed instinct in wild beasts." It was the ocean's perpetual movements, he claimed, that made its possession and occupation impossible.[156] The very materiality of oceans—their changing temperatures, moving currents, and dynamic forces—posed a significant challenge to technological innovation and human mastery. The invention of the chronometer took John Harrison, an accomplished English clockmaker, nearly fifty years to complete. Harrison created four versions—H1, H2, H3, and H4. In 1763, H4 was tested aboard a ship en route to Barbados. But it was not until almost a decade later, in 1772, that Harrison's latest chronometer, the H5, was successfully tested at sea. The following year, he was finally awarded the prize for longitude.[157]

By the eighteenth century, Britain aspired to rule the seas not only through space but also time. Though timekeeping and longitude did not facilitate British *possession* over the seas, Harrison's chronometer empowered Britain to consolidate and integrate its empire into a composite whole, producing new forms of order, authority, and control in the process. The Royal Observatory in Paris was opened in 1667. The Royal Observatory in Greenwich was established in 1675. Both served as critical reference points for ships at sea.[158] With the publication of Britain's *Nautical Almanac* starting in 1767, English vessels began to calculate their longitude almost entirely in reference to Greenwich. By the 1880s, to retain consistency with the world of shipping, Greenwich became the unofficial choice of prime meridian.[159] For Schmitt, the rise of Greenwich was an entirely political act. That "the prime meridian of the earth's cartographic grid is still the one that runs through Greenwich is neither purely objective and neutral nor purely coincidental," he charged; "it was the result of a [European] rivalry between prime meridians."[160] Schmitt described Greenwich as an enduring sign and "symbol of the former English domination of the sea and the world"[161] Though he never characterized it as such, Greenwich offers a persistent reminder of the role of the ship in Britain's ascendency as a global imperial power.

By the 1880s, at the high–water mark of the British Empire, the new status of Greenwich as prime meridian was extended from sea to land and from ship to house.[162] Though the sea played a minor role in Schmitt's *nomos,* for others, it was vital to an emerging European international order. In 1884, at the Prime

Meridian Conference held in Washington, D.C., Sanford Fleming, the Irish-born engineer-in-chief of the Canadian Pacific Railway, made a persuasive case for a global and shared universal time. Disparate times across cities, nations, and continents, he explained, produced conditions for travel that were unwieldy and confusing. He proposed an international set of temporal coordinates that he believed would eventually help to integrate the far reaches of the earth. In a well-known essay, "Uniform Non-Local Time (Terrestrial Time)," he articulated his vision as follows. "The question to which I propose to direct attention is not limited to any particular country or continent," he maintained. "It is a question which in different degrees concerns all nations," though it is "of greatest importance to the populations of great continental countries, advanced or advancing in civilization."[163] In Fleming's view, accurate timekeeping did not impact all countries or empires equally. It was far less significant for Britain—a small island nation that Schmitt described first as a "whale-fish" and then a ship—than it was for the "New World" countries of Canada and the United States with their expansive landmass.[164] The problem of time, Fleming urged, was especially acute in long-distance sea travel:

> Suppose we take the case of a person traveling from London to India. He starts with Greenwich time, but he scarcely leaves the shores of England, when he finds his watch wrong. Paris time is used for the journey until that of Rome becomes the standard. At Brindisi, there is another change. Up the Mediterranean, ship's time is used. At Alexandria, Egyptian time is the standard. At Suez, ship's time is resumed, and continues with daily changes until India is reached. Arriving at Bombay the traveler will find two standards employed, local time and railway time, the latter being that of Madras. If he has not altered his watch since he left England he will find it some five hours slow.[165]

Maritime travel from the metropole to Britain's "jewel in the crown" brought the heterogeneity of time—as oceanic, terrestrial, and island time—into a confusing, chaotic, and incoherent whole.

Fleming, whose expertise was in railroad engineering, subtitled his essay "Terrestrial Time." Yet, the ship and the sea animated his temporal order in significant ways. To begin with, Fleming's conception of time was profoundly influenced by the "watch." When vessels were at sea, the "day is divided" into watches he explained. This was the "most convenient scheme for daily routines at sea" and "would perhaps prove useful" on land as well, he opined.[166] In addition to this interest in shipboard timetables, Fleming was fascinated by the ways in which moving vessels calibrated their spatial coordinates. For more than a century, ship time in Britain and around the world was adjusted to the Greenwich observatory. It became the point from which over 70 percent of the world's shipping had come to set its course.[167] By 1884, with the Prime Meridian conference and under Fleming's influence, the empire "*export[ed]* British time as a commodity to an entire globe."[168]

Whereas Schmitt ignored the role of the ship and viewed the *nomos* of the earth in terms of terra firma, Fleming prioritized time as an order and orientation that emerged from the sea and extended to land.[169] Indeed, Fleming had great aspirations for uniform time. He embraced it as a modernizing force that would ensure greater global and imperial efficiency through homogeneity and synchronicity. "Every connecting steamline, indeed every communication on the face of the earth would be worked by the same standard, viz., 'terrestrial time,'" he urged. Each traveler, wearing a "good watch, would carry with him the precise time that he would find employed everywhere." Under Fleming's scheme, "*Post meridian* would never be mistaken for *ante meridian*. Railway and steamboat timetables would be simplified and rendered more intelligible."[170] This newly synchronized temporal order would ensure that no one would ever miss a train as Fleming had done once before.[171] Significantly, terrestrial time was to be modeled on the same "standard for geographical reckoning" as ships.[172] Uniform time, Fleming believed, was a concern for all countries. However, it was of "greater importance to the colonial Empire of Great Britain." The empire was made up of "settlements and stations in nearly every meridian around the entire globe," and encompassed "vast territories to be occupied by civilized inhabitants in both hemispheres," he maintained.[173] Thus, global time would help to amalgamate land and sea into an integrated imperial whole.

As uniform time extended outward from oceans, it became part of a temporal, spatial, and juridical order. On 14 May 1880, the *Times* of London published a letter from the "Clerk to the Justices." Writing in a tenor of great urgency, the correspondent explained that while "Greenwich time is now kept almost throughout England," it "appears that Greenwich time is not legal time." The article raised a pressing question that had yet to receive sufficient attention: what was the relation between law and time, and more specifically, which time was to prevail within British law? The question of legal time, the correspondent implored, was a matter that "often arises in our criminal courts." Yet, it "has hitherto escaped a proper decision and discussion." Can "some new M.P. take up this point and endeavour to get an Act" passed so that "Greenwich time [would become] legal time!"[174] On 2 August 1880, Britain passed the Definition of Time Act. The act was intended to "remove doubts as to the meaning of Expressions relative to Time occurring in Acts of Parliament, deeds, and other legal instruments." All references to time in Parliament and in the courts would refer to Greenwich mean time in England and Scotland, and to Dublin mean time in Ireland.[175] At the apogee of imperial control, the official status of Greenwich as prime meridian became the "crowning symbol" of Britain, reinforcing its self-proclaimed power to "measure, regulate, and delimit the uneven temporalities of global modernity."[176] The inauguration of Greenwich as the international reference point for global time emerged directly from the moving ship.

Fleming's grand plan for a uniform terrestrial time was clearly inspired by maritime worlds and by transoceanic travel. However, he was not in favor of unrestricted seaborne movement. Like many of his imperial counterparts, Fleming warned that increased ocean traffic, particularly from east to west, would present serious problems for the empire's racial and civilizational order. "Lines of telegraph and steam communications are girdling the earth, and all countries are being drawn into one neighborhood," he observed. But these were not positive developments. "When men of all races, in all lands are thus brought face to face, what will they find?" Fleming asked. "They will find a great many nations measuring the day by two sets of subdivisions as if they had recently emerged from barbarism and had not yet learned to count higher than twelve." Fleming's immediate concern was the division of the day into two twelve-hour halves. If this system was adopted, he warned, people "will find the hands of the various clocks pointing in all conceivable directions. They will find at the same moment some men reckoning that they live in different hours, others in different days."[177] But Fleming's remarks also gestured to growing concerns about maritime travel from Asia, including India. As time was slowly becoming unified, Britain's imperial geography became further divided. The *nomos* of the earth—as a spatial, temporal, and juridical order—did not integrate the earth as Schmitt had predicted. It produced cleavages, asymmetries, and inequalities along racial, national, and civilizational lines, which demanded further scrutiny and regulation.[178] Drawing on spatial, temporal, and maritime imaginaries that were informed and animated by longer histories of Indian seafaring, Husain Rahim and Gurdit Singh vigorously challenged these racial and imperial visions of the sea and the earth. It is to these imaginaries, which set the conditions for the *Komagata Maru*'s voyage, that I now turn.

A Counter-*Nomos* of the Earth

In *Mare Liberum,* Grotius characterized oceans to be *res nullius* or common property. But if the sea was held in common by all, then theoretically, no one could be legally barred from crossing or trading.[179] Although Grotius was attentive to the presence of Asian traders and to the sovereign claims of indigenous rulers, the rights of non-European seafarers did not enter his writings, at least not explicitly. The English subtitle of *Mare Liberum* was "A Disputation Concerning the Right Which the Hollanders Ought to Have to the Indian Merchandise for Trading."[180] Nowhere did Grotius consider the rights of indigenous and/or Asian rulers to set their own course for maritime commerce, or to refuse European encroachment in their territorial waters. Thus, the freedom of the sea, as Grotius conceived it, was a freedom enjoyed by European men. Under natural law, it was the natural right of European sovereigns to send vessels to partake in trade.[181] Though India had a long history of maritime commerce with Arabs, Africans, and Chinese seafarers, one that preceded the arrival of Europeans by centuries, the freedom of the seas was not extended to them. Instead, they were at the service of European vessels, including the *Santa Catarina,* where they were assigned subordinate positions often below deck, and which were organized through hierarchies of race, caste, and region.[182]

In non-European chronologies of maritime commerce, the sea featured as a collective, shared, and contested space. Arab, Chinese, and Indian vessels crisscrossed the eastern and western Indian Oceans, trading goods, establishing commercial routes, and developing lasting social and religious networks.[183] In 1912, Radhakumud Mookerji, a professor of Indian history at the National Council of Education in Bengal, documented some aspects of this rich history, especially as it pertained to India.[184] In his widely read *Indian Shipping: A History of the Sea-Borne Trade and Maritime Activity of the Indians from the Earliest Times,* Mookerji compiled the first "coherent survey of Indian navigation from earliest times down to the end of the Moghul period."[185] This "handsomely printed volume" detailed India's illustrious past of maritime commerce, particularly its influence along Indian Ocean worlds. In Mookerji's account, India "began seaborne trade with the very beginning of recorded time."[186] The subcontinent's shipbuilding technologies and its oceanic commerce were so far advanced that they drew the attention and admiration of many prominent Europeans, including Marco Polo and fifteenth-century Genoese and Venetian merchants.[187] For over twenty centuries, India's strategic position along the eastern and western Indian Oceans meant that shipping became "one of the great national industries." Over the course of this long history, Mookerji declared, India established trade relations with "every quarter of the globe," including Asia, Europe, Africa, Australia, and America.[188] Maritime trade and commerce "was undoubtedly one of the triumphs of Indian civilization." It was "the chief means by which ... civilization asserted itself and influenced other alien civilizations."[189]

India's eminent maritime past, as Mookerji recalled it, was the outcome of several key developments. These included unrivaled sophistication in early ship design and construction, as well as a lengthy record of Indian labor at sea. By the eighteenth century, as lascars had long been employed on Portuguese ships and increasingly on British ones, Bombay was reputed to be a prominent center for shipbuilding. The Parsis, originally from Surat, dominated maritime construction in the western port city.[190] Between 1736 and 1821, Lowji Nuserwanji Wadia and his sons built 159 ships.[191] These vessels were constructed from solid teak and were styled on a mix of European and Indian influences. Calcutta and Chittagong, along the northeast corner of the subcontinent, also became important cities for maritime design and construction, and drew equal interest from European traders.[192] However, Bengal's ports were not deep enough for ocean-going vessels and therefore did not achieve the same global status as Bombay.[193]

Like shipping, maritime labor also extended India's reach across the seas. Lascars, who initially worked on Portuguese vessels like the *Santa Catarina* in the seventeenth century, became integral sources of labor on British ships.[194] By the nineteenth century, as Britain's status as a maritime power expanded, Mookerji lamented, India's prominence on the seas diminished. Imperial administrators actively curtailed Indian shipping: first, by imposing restrictions on the movement of Indian vessels, and second, by finding ways to limit the routes and itineraries of Indian sailors. Colonial officials in Asian ports reprimanded owners and captains of Indian-owned boats for overcrowded and unsanitary conditions.[195] By the 1890s, British officials in London initiated discussions on how best to restrict the mobility of Indian lascars and seafarers, proposing regulations that would confine them to prescribed latitudes, for example.[196] For Mookerji, Britain's efforts to expand its legal and political control across the sea dramatically altered the prospects and possibilities for Indian shipping. "India is now without this most important organ of national life," he wrote regretfully. "There can hardly be conceived a more serious obstacle in the path of her industrial development than this almost complete extinction of her shipping and shipbuilding."[197] By the early twentieth century, British and European ships came to replace Indian vessels, which for centuries had transported passengers along the Western and Eastern Indian Ocean regions. "Our entire passenger traffic is in the hands of foreign shippers," Mookerji charged.[198] But this "lost industry that rendered such a brilliant service in the past," could still be revived, he claimed assuredly.[199] Mookerji was not alone in his maritime ambitions and aspirations. For Husain Rahim and Gurdit Singh, seaborne travel and trade were key not only to India's economic and political progress but also to freedom from British imperial rule.

Early twentieth-century Indian migration, as I suggest at the outset of this chapter, was preceded by much longer patterns of maritime mobility. Lascars, merchants, pilgrims, and soldiers traveled with regularity "along the Silk Road, across the Indian Ocean and the China Sea."[200] During the age of sail, few Indian and Chinese seafarers ventured into the Pacific. Its winds and currents made the ocean difficult to navigate, especially toward the Americas.[201] With the rise of steam, however, Indians began traveling greater distances, pursuing new Pacific and Atlantic itineraries, establishing communities in London, East Africa, and East and Southeast Asia, and expanding their geographical imaginaries of the earth.[202] Until the late nineteenth century, these maritime worlds were fluid, mobile, and relatively unconstrained. Between the time that Gurdit Singh left for Singapore and Malaya, in 1885, and when Husain Rahim departed for Kobe a decade later, the Indian and Pacific Oceans were becoming progressively restricted. For British and Canadian authorities, the mobility of "Asiatics" explicitly threatened the racial and legal standing of the free sea, necessitating new forms of racial surveillance and maritime control.[203] Despite growing levels of scrutiny, especially along the Pacific, Indians continued to travel. Many journeyed to China and Japan, which were known to be hospitable to Indian merchants, former soldiers, and even radicals.[204] Others voyaged to East and South Africa. Though the numbers of Indians landing in North American port cities remained relatively insignificant by comparison to rates of migration elsewhere, British authorities collaborated with Dominion officials and later with the Indian colonial state and introduced additional restrictions on travel.[205] Investigations into the transpacific movements of Indian nationals began in the first few years of the twentieth century. By the close of the first decade, British authorities were collecting and sharing information with administrators in Canada and the United States, and implementing plans to deport those alleged to be troublesome.[206] It was precisely this oscillation, between *mare liberum* and *mare clausum* that Husain Rahim experienced firsthand.

When Rahim arrived in Vancouver, following his voyage from Honolulu, he had no intentions of staying. In December 1909, he boarded the *Moana* as a tourist, with a first-class ticket to Montreal via the Canadian Pacific Railway.[207] As the *Moana* called at Vancouver, after its six-week journey at sea, Rahim was immediately barred from disembarking. "The Immigration officer put some questions to me and asked if I had Two Hundred Dollars," he recalled.[208] These legal requirements only heightened his curiosity. What "kind of enchanted land this must be," where "Hindus were refused entry" and a tourist who purchased a "first-class railway fare to Montreal should not even be allowed to stretch his legs upon the shore, a performance always longed for by voyagers after the confinement of a long sea voyage."[209] Knowing "nothing whatsoever about the immigration act," he vowed to pursue legal action. "Next morning I threatened the officers of the ship that a suit would be filed on the owners of the SS *Moana* for booking me to Montreal and not seeing that I was allowed to reach my destination." Rahim's threats proved effective. He was permitted to disembark in Vancouver and to board his train for Montreal. After reaching the eastern seaboard, he was to take a steamer to England.[210] But Rahim never crossed the Atlantic as intended. Nine months later, when he returned to Vancouver with plans to open a small business, William Hopkinson arrested him. Once again, Rahim faced deportation to India; once more he was allowed to remain in Canada.[211]

Rahim's arrival on the *Moana* marked the beginning of a series of protracted legal struggles that centered on the seaborne mobility of Indian migrants, including their rights to enter Britain's most northerly Dominion. After arriving in Vancouver for the second time, Rahim was caught in a series of legal dilemmas of his own. In March 1911 and then again in November of the same year, he was charged under Canada's continuous journey regulation. Both times, he successfully challenged the law and was immediately released. The Dominion government initially passed the continuous journey regulation in 1908 and then revised it shortly after Rahim's arrival in Vancouver. Immigration officials sought to apply the provision retroactively against Rahim, a maneuver that the court disallowed.[212] In 1913, following his own legal victories, Rahim secured J. Edward Bird as legal counsel in the *Thirty-Nine Hindus* case. This time, due to inconsistencies in wording, the British Columbia Court of Appeal struck down the continuous journey regulation once again. Given these positive outcomes, Rahim continued to fight the Dominion so that Indian women would be permitted to land and so his countrymen could vote in local elections.[213] "Having proved successful in his own case," Rahim "took up the cases of other Hindus, and became a source of great annoyance to the Immigration Department," one source complained. He was described to be "a leader" in "the agitation against the Immigration laws," and assumed "a prominent part in stirring up discontent in the Hindu community."[214] Despite the uncertainties of his identity, another official called him a "renegade Muslim."[215] But Rahim would be most feared and celebrated for his political and legal campaign in support of the *Komagata Maru*. His collaborations with Gurdit Singh, Bhag Singh, and other members of the shore committee generated considerable attention across the British Empire, catalyzing a transoceanic, heterogeneous, and uneven network of anticolonial engagement that connected Canada, India, and South Africa, united the subcontinent and diaspora, and generated fears of rebellion and revolution. For Rahim and his counterparts, the *Komagata Maru* would change their fate and fortunes forever. Their efforts to secure the vessel's monthly charter from Gurdit Singh resulted in a series of financial losses that became the subject of a government investigation, but for which they were never compensated.[216]

In a column he wrote for the *Hindustanee,* an English-language newspaper he founded in Vancouver in 1914, Rahim documented the hardening of territorial borders across land and sea. His periodical was active between January and June 1914, each month featuring its own separate issue. Three of these—April, May, and June—contained sections of a column titled "Canada as a Hindu Saw it," which Rahim penned from his own experiences on the *Moana.* Importantly, his writings coincided and directly overlapped with Gurdit Singh efforts to plan and execute the voyage of the *Komagata Maru.* The April to June issues, including his own lengthy column, were refracted through the ship's departure from Hong Kong and its arrival and detention in Vancouver Harbour. Over this three-month period, the *Hindustanee* included a range of contributors and covered an array of topics. Some detailed disputes over Indian labor, others featured advertisements regarding upcoming celebrations that were of interest to Vancouver's Sikh and Punjabi communities, still others openly condemned Canada's immigration prohibitions. Like many Indian periodicals of the time, authorities in the Dominion and the subcontinent described the *Hindustanee* as "seditious." Colonial administrators closely monitored its circulation and banned its entry into India.

Written retrospectively, Rahim's column traced his own struggles with Canadian immigration officials, beginning with his arrival at the Pacific littoral in 1909. Composed in multiple temporalities at once, he documented the tightening of borders along Canada's west coast. Though Rahim was writing in the present, he imagined himself in the past, standing on the decks of the *Moana* and looking out from the sea to the future. By inverting the gaze of land/sea and house/ship, Rahim was well positioned to reflect on the terminus and its surrounding waters. Vancouver, as he described it, was a polyglot port. Its racial heterogeneity was evident not only in the people on ship and ashore but also in the many vessels anchored in the harbor. Together, these shipping lines and their sponsors displayed a vibrant globality that joined East and West, Orient and Occident. Steamers from the "Canadian-Australian, Canadian-Mexican, C.P.R. Empress Line, Blue Funnel, Osaka Shosen, Nippon Yusen Naisha, Andrew Weir, [and] German Kosmos" sat side by side in Canadian waters, he observed. These ships connected Vancouver to "various destinations in different parts of

FIGURE 1.2. The *Komagata Maru* in Vancouver's busy port, 1914. Vancouver Harbour is bounded by Stanley Park, on one side, and the North Shore Mountains, on the other. In 1909, Rahim would have encountered this view, which he described as breathtaking. (Photo courtesy of City of Vancouver Archives)

the world."[217] Though the extent and scale of maritime circulations surely impressed Rahim, it was the landscape that he found most spectacular (see fig. 1.2). Canada "is a land of bewitching scenery with glorious forests, snow-clad mountain ranges, magnificent rivers, rivulets, and springs, hills, [and] harbours." It seemed to be a bountiful place, one especially well suited to agriculture and settlement. Complete with its "bewildering magnitude, and with its wild flowers and a rich virgin soil," Canada "can afford to the settlers a sustenance as a mother country would comparatively to a newborn babe."[218] While he was ashore, Rahim remarked on seeing several Chinese and Japanese men. Their presence challenged prevailing impressions that Vancouver was a white city and Canada a white country. As disruptive as his reflections were, Rahim's cartography continued to echo European accounts of empty lands, as expressed in maps, travel books, and in the writings of jurists and intellectuals, including Schmitt.

Rahim said nothing of the Coast Salish peoples—the Squamish, Musqueam, and Tsleil-Waututh—who inhabited the land and waterways for millennia, a glaring omission I return to below.

Over the six months that Rahim edited the *Hindustanee,* he was deeply immersed in legal and political struggles of various kinds. As the leader of the shore committee, he worked assiduously on behalf of Gurdit Singh and the *Komagata Maru* passengers so they might be permitted entry.[219] Rahim had followed this path before, in his own legal struggles against the continuous journey regulation and less directly in *Re Thirty-Nine Hindus.* He had no reason to assume that this occasion might be any different, or that the passengers would lose their case. To represent Gurdit Singh and the passengers, Rahim again recruited J. Edward Bird. He was well known to the Punjabi community, assisting them in legal dealings with trade, commerce, and immigration, most notably in the *Thirty-Nine Hindus* case. Appointing Bird would ensure that those who were called to appear before the Immigration Board and the British Columbia Court of Appeal would have appropriate legal counsel, a representative who knew the law and had successfully defended other Indians against it. As legal developments unfolded, Rahim used his monthly periodical to condemn Canada's responses to Indian migration and to elicit financial and political support for the legal proceedings at hand. However, his column, "Canada as a Hindu Saw it," was about the *Komagata Maru*'s voyage and much more. Here, Rahim offered his readers—both far and near—strategic advice on how best to reach the Pacific littoral in an era of increased maritime surveillance. In so doing, he sketched a counter-*nomos* of the earth, one that encouraged seabound itineraries and transcontinental travels from India outward, while undermining the land/sea divide that was foundational to Grotius, Schmitt, and to European international law.

In the first line of *Land and Sea,* Schmitt characterizes the human to be "a land-being, a land-dweller" who "stands and walks and moves upon the firmly grounded earth."[220] However, non-Europeans, including Indian seafarers, who drew their livelihoods and identities from the sea, "seldom share the landsman's image of it," as K. N. Chaudhuri explains. "They know that for man the sea is a hostile environment, but that its predictable dangers can be partially mastered with a seaworthy vessel."[221] Imagining himself on the decks of the *Moana,* Rahim began his reflections of Vancouver and Canada not with land but with sea. Oceans, he insisted, offered Indian migrants, sojourners, and travelers necessary economic and political opportunities through which to witness and experience the world firsthand. As such, he strongly encouraged his readers to leave the subcontinent for North America, giving them calculated directions on how best to proceed and without being apprehended. "The principal connection and the method of transportation between Asia and America . . . is inter-oceanic over the Pacific," he noted. The vast distance "between Asia and North America" is "being materially reduced, as the C.P.R. White Liners, the magnificent Empress boats, have rendered the accessibility of Japan from North America and vice versa in 10 days and Hong Kong can be reached in 15 days from Vancouver."[222] The Pacific Ocean, Rahim agreed, held great promise for "Asiatics." In "the awakening of Asia . . . Japan has taken the lead, China is making rapid strides onward, and India is shaking off British strangulation." The modern steamship, he continued, precipitated an "awakening" that would surely increase circulation and exchange between East and West, while opening new opportunities for anticolonial struggles.[223]

This "inter-ocean traffic in merchandise and passengers between Asia and America," Rahim cautioned, was "engaging the attention of the people of the countries lying on both sides of the Pacific Ocean."[224] Canadian, British, and Indian officials were deliberating new ways to curtail the seaborne mobility of Indian travelers. Instructions have been "surreptitiously given to the offices of steamship companies in India" who are prohibited from booking Indian passengers "except under certain most exceptional conditions, when sanctioned by Indian authorities," he cautioned.[225] Britannia's efforts to rule the waves did not assuage or discourage him, however. In light of this expanding scrutiny, Rahim proposed alternative itineraries. "The two largest oceans of this globe, the Pacific on the west and the Atlantic on the east coast, surround the North American continent," he explained. The continent has a "tremendous coast line of 24,500 miles."[226] The eastern and western coasts, as Rahim described them, were joined through a coordinated network of steamships and railways. "A flood of time tables, leaflets, guides, descriptive pamphlets, beautifully illustrated and richly bound literature, are published and gratuitously offered by the steamship and railroad agencies to offer the virtues of their respective routes." But "this desirable advertising matter, which is of great mutual benefit to the tourist and the railroad and steamship companies," Rahim lamented, "hardly ever finds its way into India."[227] Through ongoing collaborations between the "home authorities and Colonial government, the government of India has checked all tours and travels of the Hindustanee, outward from India to Europe, Australia, Canada, South Africa, and America, which cynically claim to be white man's countries."[228] Although Indian migrants and sojourners left the subcontinent, many were denied entry on their arrival in the Dominions. His own case, especially when juxtaposed against the *Komagata Maru*'s detention in Vancouver Harbour, dramatically illustrated the harmful effects of prohibitory legislation. But Rahim remained steadfast. Indian travelers could evade surveillance simply by redirecting their routes, he maintained. "Instead of asking the reader to come from the Pacific to the Mainland," Rahim instructed, "I want him to look up to the Atlantic, which connects the American continent with the Old World and Africa, the side from which Columbus entered this hemisphere in 1492, conferring a world's boon to the Old World denizens."[229] In Rahim's estimation, traveling west rather than east allowed Indian travelers to follow the well-worn tracks of European settlers. In so doing, it also enabled them to evade maritime surveillance, including the continuous journey regulation.[230]

Rahim was well aware of the ways in which European powers had divided the earth using the lines of latitude and longitude. These imaginary grids carried real material effects, inaugurating new conceptions of space and time that repositioned Britain at the center of the world, while rearranging the earth racially and civilizationally along east/west and north/south. But Indians could marshal these global lines to their clear advantage, Rahim advised. From the 1880s onward, with the advocacy of figures like Sanford Fleming, conceptions of global time integrated the earth in unprecedented ways. This process was never straightforward, synchronized, or entirely successful in eroding the chronologies and temporalities of indigenous peoples and colonial subjects. For Rahim, however, this new global temporal order opened additional prospects for transoceanic mobility. To "the people of India," he quipped, "the North American continent is on the antipodes." When "it is night in North America it is morning in India and vice versa. At every daybreak India is *one date ahead of America in the chronicle of time*."[231] If a passenger "travelled eastward, say from Calcutta, he would move across America from the Pacific to the Atlantic, and then back to India." But "if he moved westward he would move across the Atlantic and cross America to the Pacific," a route that would also lead him to India.[232] The global time lines that were calibrated from Greenwich ensured that the journey from west to east was more efficient than the typical voyage from east to west. "Access to Canada by the Trans-Atlantic route is of importance to Hindustanees," Rahim insisted.[233] Those who traveled to North America via the Atlantic could experience places of great historical significance, such as "Egypt, Italy, France, [and] Europe, including England." But crossing the Atlantic was much faster, he maintained. It gave "an advantage of nearly one week in time over the Pacific course."[234] Land and sea were interconnected through coordinated steamship and train schedules. Atlantic ports were joined "to the mainland by railways," he remarked, allowing "passengers to reach the slope of the Pacific Coast without a break in their journey."[235]

Rahim's maritime cartography, as fascinating as it is, disrupted some imaginative European geographies and reified others. To begin, he convincingly challenged claims of Vancouver as a white city and Canada as a "white man's country."[236] Attentive to the coordinated movements of ships and trains, and reversing the direction of travel, he began to undermine the imperialist divides between land and sea, on the one hand, and East and West, on the other. For Rahim, these were not elemental or juridical distinctions, as they were for Grotius and Schmitt, but inherently racial and colonial ones. However, Rahim's counter-*nomos* said as much in what was present as it did through what was absent. Though he remarked on the cosmopolitan ships and on Chinese and Japanese businesses, his descriptions of the city obfuscated the uninterrupted presence of the Coast Salish peoples. By characterizing Vancouver to be a sublime domain of nature, Rahim reproduced European and Canadian myths of empty lands. His counter-*nomos* made no mention of the long and violent histories of indigenous dispossession that were integral to the terminus and its polyglot port. In 1886, the City of Vancouver was incorporated on the unceded territories of the Musqueam, Squamish, and Tsleil-Waututh peoples, communities that have never surrendered their land through conquest or treaty. Notwithstanding the city's many efforts to displace them, through forced removals and razings, the Coast Salish have remained resilient, maintaining their legal and political claims to the land and its surrounding waters.[237] The Musqueam paddled their canoes to greet all vessels that landed in the Salish Sea. They likely received the *Moana* in 1909, the *Komagata Maru* in 1914, and the hundreds of ships that arrived in the intervening years.[238] Yet, indigenous peoples remain conspicuously absent from Rahim's maritime account. His counter-*nomos* was marked by other significant omissions. In reiterating that the Mediterranean was Europe's primeval sea, Rahim repeated triumphalist histories of European maritime supremacy, thereby foregrounding the "Greeks, Romans, Arabs, and Spaniards" as setting "the foundation of the modern economic history of Europe."[239] Though Rahim mentioned the "great Atlantic," he said nothing of the Chinese, African, Arab, or Indian seafarers who traveled and traded in the Indian Ocean arena, creating the histories of Indian seafaring and maritime commerce that Mookerji recalled in his book, and which would inspire Gurdit Singh to conceive of the Guru Nanak Steamship Company and charter the *Komagata Maru*.

DESPITE ITS MANY GAPS, omissions, and absences, Rahim's counter-*nomos* of the earth was aimed at challenging European, British, and Dominion accounts of the free sea. His conceptual map emphasized the overlaps and interconnections between shipping routes and railway tracks, suggesting that oceans and continents were not easily divisible by land and sea, as European cartographies suggested, but were integrated into a contiguous and uneven planetary whole. Rahim's view of oceans was informed by his own maritime journeys from India to Kobe, Kobe to Honolulu, and Honolulu to Vancouver. It was aboard the *Moana*—where he imagined himself standing as he wrote for the *Hindustanee*—that he aspired to find alternative sea routes and itineraries of anticolonial opposition. Ultimately, the moving ship afforded Indian travelers like Rahim a seaborne perspective that was necessary to dispute the elemental, juridical, and racial distinctions of "firm land"/"free sea," East/West, and Orient/Occident, divides that had long been established in European thought.

In *The* Nomos *of the Earth,* Schmitt argued that anticolonialism lacked "the capacity" to produce a new world order.[240] A new *nomos* of the earth, he insisted, could only be envisaged and imposed from within Europe, when German airpower finally surpassed British maritime control. Though Schmitt's Eurocentric and terracentric worldviews ignored indigenous peoples and colonial subjects, it is important to remember that they never relinquished the earth to European control. Ancestral place-names, migratory routes, rights, and responsibilities continued to mark territories and waterways. Oceans did not divide continents, nor were they a passive backdrop to terra firma. The sea connected peoples and places; it was as much the past as it was the future.[241] Proposing a counter-*nomos* of the earth, Rahim's column, "Canada as a Hindu Saw it," disordered the lines of the cartographer's map. The order and orientation that he envisioned was preceded by an illustrious history of Indian shipping and animated by an emergent maritime anticolonialism. By reversing the circuits of seaborne travel, from west to east, instead of east to west, Rahim challenged the spatial and temporal lines imposed on the Pacific and Atlantic Oceans. In so doing, he identified new directions and itineraries to circumvent colonial and racial divides. Looking out from the ship, Rahim underscored the vitality of the free sea, not only as a lucrative source of commerce and capital as it had been for European travelers and traders, but also as a necessary pathway to global mobility and to Indian freedom. Ultimately, the legal and political struggles that Rahim initiated against the Dominion government would set the legal groundwork for the *Komagata Maru*'s arrival and its forced removal.

In the following chapter, I reflect on the land/sea distinction in further detail, and from another angle. My focus shifts from the racial and legal status of the sea to the racial and legal standing of the ship. Under the common law and admiralty law, vessels were regarded as distinct juridical forms. They were afforded the status of legal persons and ascribed specific rights and responsibilities at sea. Though the common law and admiralty law were established and developed through the land/sea distinction that featured so prominently in the writings of Grotius and Schmitt, the moving ship problematized these juridical divides in important ways. In its previous lives, as the *Stubbenhuk* and the *Sicilia,* the ship that would eventually become the *Komagata Maru* made hundreds of voyages, along the Mediterranean Sea and the North Atlantic, Pacific, and Indian Oceans, joining ostensibly disparate ocean regions and their respective histories of colonial and racial violence. It is to the racial and legal status of the ship that I now turn.

The Ship as Legal Person

A ship is not a slave. You must make her easy in a seaway, you must never forget that you owe her the fullest share of your thought, of your skill, of your self-love. If you remember that obligation, naturally and without effort, as if it were an instinctive feeling of your inner life, she will sail, stay, run for you as long as she is able, or, like a sea-bird going to rest upon the angry waves, she will lay out the heaviest gale that ever made you doubt living long enough to see another sunrise. —Joseph Conrad, *The Mirror of the Sea*, 1906

They do not want us in Hong Kong. They deported us from Vancouver. They do not want us in India. They wish to keep us forever in the new Andamans, viz., the *Komagata Maru*, in the Japanese waters. They have made us beggars, slaves, close prisoners in solitary confinement for an indefinite period in a steamship in the mid sea; 352 human beings confined in one small sea-house cut off from all intercourse with mankind and outside world. —*Komagata Maru* Passenger, "Tyranny over the 'Komagata Maru' Passengers in Kobe," c. August 1914

Gurdit Singh's maritime ambitions were not limited to the *Komagata Maru* alone. This was not his first attempt to secure an oceangoing vessel, though it would most certainly be his last. On 21 February 1914, Singh sent an advertisement to various Punjabi-language newspapers apprising his readers of a telegram that recently arrived from Ottawa. All "intending immigration [to Canada] should book directly from India and show $200 on landing," it advised.[1] These latest directives, which referenced the continuous journey regulation explicitly, troubled his plans even further. From Hong Kong, he began searching for a steamer that could depart from Calcutta, transport passengers across the Indian and Pacific Oceans, and arrive direct to Vancouver. All the legal requirements and dietary needs for such a long passage would be arranged in advance. "Rupees 350 shall be provided [and] charged as passage-ticket and Rs. 50 shall be provided to passengers with regard to their religious scruple. Those who provided themselves with their own food shall not be charged for their diet," Singh explained in his message to prospective travelers.[2] To maximize the number of passengers and to make the voyage economically viable, travel dates would be "notified through Punjab and other newspapers," and the "headmen of the villages" would also be informed as to the vessel's proposed departure.[3]

When Gurdit Singh began advertising in February 1914, he had not yet secured a ship. Nor did he have the capital to do so. At the time, he was in negotiations with Alfred W. King, a European agent, who was working on Singh's behalf to purchase the *Tong-Hong* from a "Chinese steamship company." The ship did not come cheap. To make the sale, Singh needed to pay a £5,000 deposit upfront, an additional £12,000, plus a mortgage "for the balance." In King's opinion, the vessel was well worth it. The *Tong-Hong* was "a beautiful boat" that could comfortably accommodate up to three thousand travelers. Given its size and capacity, it was "well suited" to Gurdit Singh's short- and long-term plans.[4] In order to raise funds so he could close the deal, Singh urged the Hong Kong Gurdwara to recruit passengers and investors on his behalf. But when local authorities learned of his intentions, they warned that he would not be permitted to go to Calcutta, nor would he be allowed to purchase a ship. Police attention delayed his negotiations, and the *Tong-Hong* deal fell through. One month later, Gurdit Singh met Mr. Odagiri, a shipping broker employed by Shinyei Kisen Goshi Kaisha, a Japanese firm that owned the *Komagata Maru*. This was the opportunity he had been waiting for. If his plans to charter the ship were successful, this would be the Guru Nanak Steamship Company's first vessel, and an initial step in realizing his maritime aspirations.

In 1914, the *Komagata Maru* was not suitable for use as a passenger ship. During the previous year, since the vessel had been purchased from its German owners, it was employed as a cargo ship, hauling coal from Moji to Manila and Java.[5] By the spring of 1914, the owners began searching for additional opportunities through which to expand their gamut of cargo. Their immediate plan was to transport Chinese indentured labor to ports of call along the South China Sea. In March 1914, Shinyei Kisen sent their vessel to Hong Kong with Odagiri so he could "obtain a passenger license for the China coast coolie trade." It was there, as he awaited the necessary documentation, that Odagiri was introduced to Gurdit Singh.[6] In their brief but fateful meeting, Singh expressed interest in chartering a ship so he could transport Punjabi travelers and migrants to Vancouver. Though "he had only some $2,000 of his own," the remainder of the charter-money, he assured, "was being advanced by a rich Indian merchant with offices in Calcutta and Singapore."[7] But as their deliberations unfolded, there was no further mention of this wealthy investor. Knowing nothing of Singh's financial position, Odagiri took the proposal to his clients. They were intrigued. Leasing the *Komagata Maru* to a prosperous Indian merchant seemed like a profitable undertaking. The arrangement renewed earlier histories of inter-Asian commerce. More importantly, it appeared to carry fewer risks than conveying indentured labor on "Chinese passenger ships" and under increasingly restrictive British laws.[8] Over the next seven months, the *Komagata Maru* would be at the epicenter of a series of jurisdictional, racial, and legal controversies that captured the attention of imperial authorities and Indian anticolonials alike. The vessel never transported Chinese indentured labor as planned. However, "the China coast coolie trade" remained a palpable presence in the vessel's 1914 voyage, recurring intermittently and in ways that evoked longer histories of Atlantic slavery.[9] Although the slave trade was formally abolished in 1807, more than a century before the *Komagata Maru* embarked on its journey from Hong Kong to Vancouver, transatlantic slavery animated maritime jurisprudence and presented a powerful anticolonial rhetoric, one which shaped passenger contests over the so-called free sea.[10]

The *Komagata Maru*'s voyage has typically been described as a legal test case that was intended to challenge Canada's restrictive immigration laws and the empire's promises that Indians were equal to other British subjects.[11] This may be. But Singh's determination to charter a ship was also a small step in a much larger and long-term business venture. As a railway contractor in Malaya who traveled regularly to Singapore, Singh was quite literally surrounded by the sea. He embraced it as a locus of economic and political opportunity.[12] Thus, his ambitions for the Guru Nanak Steamship Company and for the *Komagata Maru* more specifically, were as much financial as they were political. "It may be known to all, that in our country and specially [sic] in the Punjab there are many rich men, but none has dared to take up foreign trade up to this time."[13] Singh vowed to be the first. "If we give coal for the ship and pay salaries of the crew the ship may be taken to any place or port, where we may like to go," he pledged to those awaiting passage in Hong Kong. "If we can get any cargo, we can get a very good income."[14] Singh had high ambitions. Recall that the Guru Nanak Steamship Company was eventually to own four ships. These steamers would travel existing trade routes along the Pacific and open new ones across the Atlantic, positioning India at the heart of maritime worlds. In addition to transporting passengers, the company's ships were to convey "raw material consisting of iron and coal" from India and other Asian ports of call to the Americas. If a vessel was denied entry to Canada, Gurdit Singh promised to take "the same ship to Brazil and South America."[15] Indians "would become respected" again in maritime trade, just as they had been in the past and before British rule.[16] But to transform these aspirations from dreams to reality required more than will or imagination. It demanded capital. "Become share-holders," Singh pleaded; "improve business and become real leaders."[17] By traveling the Pacific, Atlantic, and Indian Oceans, the company's steamers would join east/west and land/sea. Mastering the seas, Singh claimed, would open new prospects for territorial control. Passengers who left India and arrived in North and South America could secure land for cultivation and settlement. The steamship, as Gurdit Singh envisioned it, would lead India to a prosperous future that was beyond British imperial control.

The scholarship on the *Komagata Maru*, I suggest in the introduction, has yet to address the materiality of the ship.[18] That Gurdit Singh and the other passengers traveled on a steamer, crossed the Pacific and Indian Oceans, and spent months at sea has drawn remarkably little attention. Given the prevailing focus on arrival, departure, and immigration prohibitions, the ship's longer maritime histories, including the passengers and cargoes it transported, the ports at which it called, and the jurisdictional struggles in which it was embedded, remain largely unexplored. What happened at sea and in the middle passage is a history that still needs to be told. Though oceans may be incidental and insignificant to contemporary analysts, they were central to the forms of violence experienced by those aboard the ship. According to one unidentified passenger who is quoted in the second epigraph to this chapter, "352 human beings [were] confined in one small-sea house cut off from all intercourse with mankind and outside world." This anonymous passenger compared the *Komagata Maru*'s journey to the terrors of convict transportation, which began in the Bay of Bengal and crossed the *kala pani* (black sea) to Britain's penal colony in the Andaman Islands.[19] Oceans produced additional forms of racial and colonial violence as this passenger made clear. But the sea also inspired alternative imaginaries of freedom, ones that linked past and future in the present.

This chapter foregrounds the ship as a racial and juridical form and traces the many passages that made up its multiple lives. Under the custom of the sea and in the British common law and admiralty law, vessels were designated as animate beings with specific rights and responsibilities at sea. Beginning with this maritime history of how ships became legal entities, I then trace the racial and legal status of this particular steamer through its partial biography. I start my account in 1890, with the birth of the *Stubbenhuk,* and follow the vessel as the *Sicilia* and then the *Komagata Maru.*[20] To be clear, this is not intended as a complete or comprehensive account of the ship's many incarnations. Instead, this chapter highlights several key moments: the steamer's construction on the Clyde River, its numerous transoceanic passages, and the legal contests and controversies that nurtured its reputation as disordered and lawless. Read together, these disparate moments highlight the vital role of ships in joining land and sea and in facilitating changing constellations of racial, colonial, and imperial power. In chapters 3 and 4, I consider more fully how the dispossession of indigenous people figured in jurisdictional struggles over the *Komagata Maru*. Below, I trace the currents and countercurrents of transatlantic slavery. Although slavery took many shapes and forms under British imperial rule, it was the triangular trade that became a powerful and recurring force in the *Komagata Maru*'s passage.[21] The African captive was not a reminder of a distant or bygone past but a persistent figure that shaped the present and the future. Transatlantic slavery reverberated in the ship's standing as a legal person, in its myriad routes and itineraries, and in the anticolonial vernaculars espoused by those aboard.

The chapter begins by situating the *Komagata Maru* within a set of historical debates that unfolded in British and American maritime jurisprudence. Moving between British and U.S. Atlantic worlds, this first section offers a necessary context to my argument that the ship was a legal form, one that produced distinctions between land and sea, a divide that animated the jurisdictional limits of the common law and admiralty law. Whereas the former focused on land and coastal waters, the latter addressed the supposedly shared space of the high seas. In maritime jurisprudence—with its emphasis on commerce, transport, and nautical control—the ship's status as a legal person challenged this foundational legal divide in important ways. "A ship is not a slave," Joseph Conrad declared in *The Mirror of the Sea*.[22] But the ship and the slave, I suggest below, were intimately linked through competing and overlapping legalities. Under the British common law and in British and U.S. admiralty law, the "positive personhood" ascribed to the ship was tightly tethered to the "negative personhood" imposed on the slave.[23]

Notwithstanding their anthropomorphized status, vessels remained commodities that were bought and sold on world markets, reborn, renamed, and relaunched. In the second section, I move to Glasgow's Clyde River, which was home to Charles Connell and Co. This midsized shipping firm was commissioned by the German Hansa Line to construct the *Stubbenhuk*, a steamer that was to eventually become the *Komagata Maru*. Connell's vessels traveled the earth's oceans and seas and were deeply implicated in wider circuits of colonial and racial dispossession. Many company-built ships transported European settlers to North America, others conveyed plantation commodities to ports of call in Europe and Asia, and still others were "coolie ships," contracted for the West Indian indenture trade. In the second section, I place the *Komagata Maru* in this *longer durée* of Connell's ships. The family of vessels vividly demonstrates that the Mediterranean Sea and the Pacific, Atlantic, and Indian Oceans were not separate or divided but were intersecting aqueous spaces, joined by moving ships and their histories of transatlantic slavery, indigenous dispossession, Indian indentured labor, and "free" migration. In the third section, I return to the *Komagata Maru*'s passage and to the jurisdictional and racial controversies it engendered. The vessel's 1914 voyage signaled multiple fault lines in the British Empire. For imperial authorities, the ship exemplified what was at stake if Indian claims to the free sea went unrestricted. For passengers and their supporters in India and the diaspora, the vessel's deportation underscored the racial force of British and Dominion law. "They have made us beggars, *slaves,* close prisoners in solitary confinement for an indefinite period in a steamship in the mid sea," the unidentified passenger lamented.[24] Atlantic slavery, as these charges suggest, generated potent vocabularies of anticolonial critique, resistance, and revolt.[25]

Before tracing the jurisdictional conflicts between the common law and admiralty law and the transoceanic voyages of the *Stubbenhuk, Sicilia,* and *Komagata Maru,* a point of clarification is in order. Throughout this chapter, I use "middle passage"—a maritime phrase most commonly associated with discussions of the triangular slave trade from Europe to Africa, the Americas, and back to Europe—in my discussion of the *Komagata Maru*'s journey. My engagement with this term is both historiographical and conceptual. In *Many Middle Passages,* Marcus Rediker, Cassandra Pybus, and Emma Christopher deploy the phrase as analytic ballast through which to consider additional forms of coerced seaborne migration. Their book, as they describe it, draws on the Atlantic slave trade as a way "to explore other social and cultural transformations that resulted from the transport of people around the globe." The term middle passage invites readers to consider how the voluminous scholarship on transatlantic slavery might speak "to the wider historiography of forced migration, sometimes on land but especially in ocean crossings."[26] In a similar way, I evoke middle passage to draw attention to the role of transatlantic slavery in shaping the legal status of vessels, even long after abolition, and to highlight how memories of this unspeakable racial violence at sea informed additional practices of maritime coercion and control while inspiring shipboard lexicons of anticolonial dissent.

Legal Personhood

In British and U.S. maritime cultures, ships have long been anthropomorphized as persons and legal persons, respectively.[27] In contrast to "many other objects," writes maritime historian Hans Konrad Van Tilburg, "ships (which so easily cross national boundaries), have an almost human-like aura, and certainly a recognized international status. They are born or launched, have working careers, and then are decommissioned." Vessels "have a birth . . . a life span, and a death or final disposition."[28] They often have multiple lives. For seafarers like Conrad, ships were never inanimate objects. They were living, agentive, and willful beings. Captains and crews described their vessels as having an intuitive quality called "ship sense." A vessel could make life at sea easy or excruciating, protecting and prolonging life, or expediting death. For some, ship sense was an instinct that worked like a compass. It was "seriously believed," quipped one source, "that an old Western Ocean traveller could find her way from the Mersey River [in Liverpool] to her own pier in New York without man's help."[29] Ships had "husbands" and "sisters" and were made akin to humans through gendered and heteronormative familial relations.[30] At the same time that ships were granted legal personhood, the people they transported—most notably slaves and indentures—were denied theirs.

The gendering of ships, as a hallmark of Western maritime worlds, has competing possible origins. Some argue that this ritual began in ancient Greece, where vessels were launched as brides of Poseidon. For others, feminine pronouns convey the deep, intimate, and emotional bonds that captains and crews formed with their vessels.[31] From the sixteenth century onward, in the age of European maritime expansion, female figureheads became important architectural signs that symbolized the vessel as a "protective mother," one that looked out for her "children" (captains and crew), and sheltered them from the fury of the sea.[32] But gender personification, others argue, is far less remarkable. The use of gendered pronouns to reference *things* is an English practice, a rule of grammar that does not exist in German or French, for instance.[33] Notwithstanding these rival explanations, gendering vessels has been a long-standing tradition in the male-dominated world of European mariners. The feminization of ships informs Western literature, poetry, and music. Perhaps most importantly, it animates British and American maritime law. The gendered personification of ships cannot be read as a straightforward expression of male power.[34] Specific types of vessels and those engaged in particular trades—including slave and indenture ships—were often named after women but were characterized in masculine terms, as the maritime identities of "man-of-war," "Guineaman," and "Indiaman" suggest.[35] Furthermore, the gendered identities of ships were shaped through the racial and class hierarchies imposed on those aboard. On merchant vessels, for instance, British sailors characterized themselves as "a 'maritime race'" that was superior to the "feminized and childlike 'tropical races'" of Indian sailors with whom they labored.[36] Maritime claims to masculinity, like impositions of femininity, were indivisible from assertions of racial superiority and inferiority on the so-called free sea.[37]

Ships acquired their identities through European customs of the sea, but it was under the British common law and in British and American admiralty law that they were given a distinct legal status. The British common law and the law of admiralty were established as separate legal orders. The first applied to land and territorial waters, the second to the common space of the high sea. For Schmitt, land and sea operated as a dividing line in British law. "The king's power was considered to be absolute on the sea and in the colonies, while in his own country it was subject to common law and to baronial or parliamentary limits of English law."[38] Whereas the common law extended only to fresh waterways, including rivers, lakes, and streams, the freedom of the sea, as a supposedly open space that was held in common for European navigation and commerce, demanded other juridical orders that were made up of international treaties and agreements, navigation acts, shipping regulations, and the power of ship captains.[39] Vessels were also symbols and expressions of European legality and authority.[40] Their movements connected distant places and transformed oceans into juridical spaces. But the passage of ships and the expansion of maritime commerce engendered jurisdictional disputes that demanded additional registers of law, order, and authority. To invest the sea with legal standing, Grotius turned to the law of nature and the law of nations.[41] To afford ships the status of legal persons, English jurists drew on both the common law and the law of the sea, reconciling these competing legalities in the interests of maritime commerce and control, as I discuss further below.

In England, admiralty law was formally inaugurated by a decree from King Edward III. However, a law of the sea existed in nascent form for hundreds of years earlier. It drew its authority from a plurality of sources, including maritime customs and medieval and Roman law.[42] To address the juridical conflicts that inevitably arose out of maritime worlds, England established a new Office of the Admiralty. The common law, jurists warned, could not deal with the growing exigencies of increased ocean travel. The law of the land was inapplicable to foreigners and could not restrain or punish acts of piracy in the English Channel.[43] As Britain's maritime power expanded, the common law was to be supplemented with a law of the sea. These new legal mechanisms would address the pressures of maritime commerce and imperial expansion, including piracy, prizes, contracts, liens, and eventually slavery. The British common law was believed to have originated in "time immemorial," representing the cultural superiority of the English people.[44] Admiralty law also reached back to a mythical past—"to a 'time out of minde.'"[45] Unlike the common law, which was considered to be continually evolving and responsive to the problems of the age, admiralty law was created by statute, as a result of political conflicts, negotiations, and compromises over ships and ocean regions.[46] Interactions between the two legal orders were often tense and hostile. From the fourteenth to the nineteenth centuries, common law lawyers repeatedly attacked the power of British admiralty law with the intention of limiting its authority and influence.[47] Though the law of the sea was enacted by statute and inspired by custom, its authority and jurisdiction expanded with the passage of ships on open water. In maritime jurisprudence, however, the moving vessel complicated divisions between land and sea as well as between the common law and admiralty law.

Britain's law of admiralty shaped other juridical and maritime orders. In the eighteenth and nineteenth centuries, the legal standing of ships became an important topic of debate in American courts, for example. Granting a legal status to vessels, many believed, would give judges a way to address the fraught and competing jurisdictions of ocean regions. But questions of legal status opened a series of debates about what constituted a ship. On both sides of the Atlantic, a ship was only a ship, in a legal sense, when its hull was fully constructed. "A ship within the meaning of admiralty is anything which is intended for navigation," one source explained.[48] According to an 1879 shipping manual on British and American courts, the provisions "which constitute a ship become one as soon as she is launched, but a vessel in process of construction is not 'engaged in navigation'" and, therefore, not yet alive.[49] In 1902, Justice Henry Billings Brown of the U.S. Supreme Court drew on maritime customs and British admiralty law to define a ship as follows: "A ship is born when she is launched, and lives so long as her identity is preserved. Prior to her launching she is a mere congeries of wood and iron—an ordinary piece of personal property—as distinctly a land structure as a house."[50] Following the tradition of seafarers and sailors, Brown anthropomorphized the ship in feminine terms. By reiterating the land/sea divide and by distinguishing real from movable property, he signaled two key moments in a vessel's metamorphosis from inanimate object to legal person. The first was the "baptism or the launching" in which a ship "receives her name." The second was "the moment her keel touches the water."[51] As soon as a vessel was launched down river, the law magically transformed her into "a subject of admiralty jurisdiction." When a ship "acquires a personality of her own," Justice Brown explained, she "becomes competent to contract, and is individually liable for her obligations, upon which she may sue in the name of her owners, and be sued in her own name."[52] Though Brown's description of the ship rested on the conventional notion of land and sea as incommensurable elements governed by distinct legal regimes, other jurists challenged this division in important ways. By personifying ships as legal persons, at least one Supreme Court justice, Oliver Wendell Holmes Jr., drew explicit continuities between the British common law and the law of admiralty.

British and American jurists afforded vessels a legal standing so they could address the quagmires of maritime trade. Yet the ship as a legal person continued to maintain its status as property. In early navigation acts, if a vessel was in breach of English law it was subject to forfeiture.[53] By the early nineteenth century, the practice of seizing ships and cargoes through *in rem* proceedings, and in the interests of maritime liens, became commonplace in Britain and the United States.[54] Their legal processes differed, however. While the British Office of Admiralty followed *in rem* procedurally, U.S. admiralty law pursued *in rem* actions through vessel personification.[55] Under the former, legal actions against a ship were used to secure the appearance of a ship's owners or representatives in court. Under U.S. admiralty law by contrast, *in rem* proceedings transformed a ship into a legal person, who then became the primary defendant in a legal action. Anthropomorphizing ships was not an idiosyncratic maritime custom. Rather, it granted judges a way to expand and protect American national and commercial interests across the Atlantic and beyond. Though British and American admiralty law shared common influences and mutual principles, each developed at particular historical moments that were informed by commercial interests, including slavery.[56] The "flourishing condition" of oceanic trade, remarked John Irving Maxwell in 1800, was an outcome of the "salutary conditions of the Navigation and Plantation Acts" in British colonies.[57] It was in the law of deodand that these connections between the common law, admiralty law, and slavery were most clearly materialized.[58]

The English law of deodand emerged after the Norman Conquest. It was influenced by Christian and feudal institutions and was the outcome of royal prerogative.[59] Deodand originated from the Latin *deo dandum,* meaning "that which must be given to God."[60] Any chattel property that caused the death of an adult human being was to be regarded as "an accursed thing" and to be forfeited to a higher power whose "earthly representative" was the sovereign.[61] Under the common law, inanimate and animate nonhuman entities such as animals, carts, locomotives, and ships were granted a legal liveliness that was to be taken only by the Crown. Nonhuman animals and objects that caused injury or death could be arrested, condemned, and forfeited to the sovereign, who would determine the ascribed value of the offending thing and apply its equivalent in the interests of the public good.[62] Under the British common law, offending ships that traveled on rivers and lakes, but not the high seas, were subject to forfeiture through the law of deodand.

By the nineteenth century, rapid changes in technology, including new developments in steam propulsion, put the social and political utility of deodand into question. By shortening time across distance, steam-powered transportation, including ships and trains, opened new and unprecedented horizons for colonial, imperial, and capitalist expansion. Britain's technological dominance, which transformed the island into an empire, came with high costs. In the nineteenth century, ships and trains were believed to be dangerous. Moving vessels created opportunities for indigenous and subaltern travel and anticolonial contest that threatened the empire from the sea. But ships and trains also produced a sharp rise in accidental deaths. As railroad corporations gained power, British jurists and politicians argued over the suitability and longevity of deodand. Many viewed it as an archaic law that no longer met the demands of a modern age.[63] In 1846, deodand was abolished by statute. In the parliamentary debate, it was deemed to be a "remnant of a barbarous and absurd law" that was "unreasonable and inconvenient" for the times.[64] But abolition did not mark its disappearance. In admiralty law and in the law of slavery, the deodand persisted as a recurrent juridical form, one that troubled distinctions between land and sea and their respective legal orders.

To be clear, the law of deodand was not formally adopted in Britain's former colonies, yet many of its fiercest critics were American commentators. In a 1906 article, titled "Queer Old Law of the Deodand," deodand was described as "an ancient English law" that "would have been completely forgotten . . . were its name not preserved in the history of the ancient common law."[65] The article cited William Blackstone's *Commentaries on the Laws of England.* Any "personal chattel [that] is the immediate occasion of the death of any reasonable creature" Blackstone wrote, is to be "forfeited to the King, to be applied to pious uses, and distributed in alms by his high almoner."[66] The law of deodand, as this account made clear, was derived from Biblical laws. In the twenty-first chapter of Exodus, Moses, speaking for God, decreed that "if an ox gore a man or a woman that they die; then the ox shall be surely stoned, and his flesh shall not be eaten; but the owner of the ox shall be quit.'"[67] For English and American critics, the religious foundations of deodand offered further evidence for its necessary expiration. But there were additional problems. Under the common law, deodand removed legal liability from the owner and placed it in an object or animal. Yet the proprietor was to be punished by forfeiture and was therefore held responsible for the actions of her/his chattel. If the crown destroyed the offending object, the owner's debt would be canceled. But if the owner laid claim to the animal or thing that caused injury or death, then s/he would be required to pay the sovereign. Under the law of deodand, the "killing of a person" was not assessed by the costs of human life lost. Rather, it was determined "by the *value* of that particular object, be it a sword, an ox, a *slave,* or even, once such things came into existence, a locomotive."[68] The deodand animated a non-human thing and then reduced it to a financial value. This mode of calculation would be vital to the world of the ship, as exemplified in maritime insurance.[69]

For Blackstone, ships, like trains, could be deodand but only under specific circumstances. Reiterating divisions between land and sea that differentiated the common law from admiralty law, Blackstone explained that vessels could only be deodand if the injury or death in question occurred in freshwater. "No deodands are due for accidental happening upon the high seas," he continued, as oceans were beyond "the jurisdiction of the common law." But "if a man falls from a boat or ship in fresh water and is drowned, it has been said that the vessel and cargo are in strictness of the law a deodand."[70] Although the specific place of injury or death was significant to the law of deodand, matters of time were far less precise. According to one source writing in London's *Chambers's Journal,* time figured as an "unjust" peculiarity of deodand. If a person perished "from the effects of an accident within a year and a day of such an accident," then "whatever had caused it, ox, horse, cart, pistol, &c., was deodand" and therefore subject to forfeiture. It was immaterial whether "the article had changed hands" during the year. The current owner was still required to relinquish the object to the Crown.[71] In the interests of "charity and salvation," these legal regulations authorized the sovereign to "unjustly" seize private property and transfer it to the public good.[72] By sanctioning the forfeiture of private property, the deodand undermined individual possession and ownership.

The law of deodand, as I suggest earlier, was never formally adopted in the British colonies, including the ones that formed the United States. Yet, curiously, one of its most ardent and outspoken opponents was the American jurist and Supreme Court justice Oliver Wendell Holmes Jr. In *The Common Law,* Holmes described deodand disparagingly as a medieval law that established "the liability of inanimate things."[73] Though British Parliament had abolished the deodand fifty years earlier, Holmes insisted that he could trace its common law residues in U.S. admiralty law. The most "striking example" of deodand was the ship, Holmes declared. "The ship is the most living of inanimate things. Servants sometimes say 'she' of a clock, but everyone gives a gender to vessels. And we need not be surprised, therefore, to find a mode of dealing which has shown such extraordinary vitality in the criminal law applied with even more striking thoroughness in the Admiralty."[74] Also citing Blackstone's *Commentaries,* Holmes noted that a ship on the high seas was beyond the reach of the common law and therefore was not deodand. But under admiralty law, a vessel as legal person was animated in ways similar to inanimate objects under the law of deodand, including knives, horses, trains, and slaves. "It is only by supposing the ship to have been treated as if endowed with personality," he observed, "that the arbitrary seeming peculiarities of the maritime law can be made intelligible, and on that supposition they at once become consistent and logical."[75] Through his critique, Holmes raised larger questions that challenged and even undermined the long-standing divisions between the British common law and admiralty law. Against prevailing views that emphasized their respective particularity, Holmes used American maritime jurisprudence as a way to highlight their overlaps and intersections.[76] The legal personification of ships, which originated in the customs of the sea, Roman law, and British admiralty law, was inspired by the common law of deodand, Holmes claimed.

American cases involving disputes at sea were first heard in federal court. If subject to appeal, they were then heard at the U.S. Supreme Court. Starting in the first decade of the nineteenth century, Supreme Court justices deliberated on several cases concerning "the personality of the ship." In each of these, the law of deodand surfaced, albeit obliquely. Given the jurisdictional exigencies produced through moving ships and maritime contests, several Supreme Court justices, including Chief Justice John Marshall, turned to British naval customs and laws for guidance on the legal standing of what happened at sea.[77] In Marshall's view, the legal personhood ascribed to vessels was an expedient and effective way to resolve jurisdictional conflicts on the high seas.[78] Under the common law, British jurists viewed the law of deodand largely in terrestrial terms. Focused on land, they condemned it as an archaic provision that undermined private property in ways that were especially detrimental to powerful railway companies. When the law of deodand was repositioned in maritime worlds, however, Supreme Court judges like Marshall suggested that legal personification protected capitalism and U.S. imperialism by extending order and certainty over the indeterminacy of the sea.[79] In other words, the law of deodand offered jurists a practical way to adjudicate legal issues in ocean arenas. In a series of admiralty cases that began in 1818, the U.S. Supreme Court transformed ships from inanimate objects to animate and living things, thereby echoing the British common law of deodand. An owner sent his "ships continuously over the seas," Chief Justice Marshall explained, and a "wrong may occur far from places where he is amenable to personal process."[80] Rather than initiating legal proceedings in foreign courts, an injured party could invoke vessel personification to bring a legal action against the ship itself. As a legal person, a ship on the high seas was subject to arrest, condemnation, and forfeiture, in much the same way that vessels in territorial waters were held responsible under the British common law.[81]

In 1818, in the well-known case of *Little Charles,* Justice Marshall established a clear distinction between the legal standing of a vessel and its proprietors. The legal action, Marshall clarified, "was against the vessel, for an offence committed by the vessel, which is not less an offence, and does not the less subject her to forfeiture, because it was committed without the authority and against the will of the owner."[82] As U.S. maritime activities flourished, courts were confronted by cases involving prizes, embargoes, and contests over slavery. Owners of offending vessels could avoid legal responsibility by flying multiple flags and using foreign registries.[83] Amid the jurisdictional complexities of the free sea, the anthropomorphized ship became a convenient and invaluable legal form. Through a "maritime metaphysics," vessel personification provided American jurists with "a ready-made concept" drawn from maritime histories, seafaring literatures, and from the British common law of deodand.[84] After joining the Supreme Court in 1902, Holmes remained a dissenting voice on the matter. The legal personification of ships, he insisted, was rooted in an old-fashioned and outdated law, one that recalled Britain's archaic past. For Marshall, however, the legal personhood of ships had given nineteenth-century American jurists a way of extending order and authority across the seas, especially in a thriving Atlantic economy sustained in part by slavery.[85]

Questions of legal personhood, including their political, economic, and racial effects, were nowhere more salient than in the transatlantic slave trade. Just as the law could bestow a lively existence to inanimate objects through the concept of legal personhood, it could transform sentient human beings into things, by *denying* their personhood. Thus, law's metaphysical power was multidirectional. Whereas British and U.S. admiralty law granted ships a legal personality, the laws of slavery and the laws of the sea denied African captives their humanity.[86] In the case of both the ship and the slave, legal personhood enabled private interests, including shipping companies and slave owners, to amass profits while maintaining the free sea as a space open to British and U.S. interests. The laws of slavery, as some have argued, were far more concerned with defending the rights of slave owners than they were with protecting the political and legal status of slaves.[87] This is clear in the legal concept of personhood. Slaves became legal persons in two interrelated moments: when African captives were transported on ships as cargo and when slaves were accused of committing a crime on land or at sea.[88] While the common law and British and U.S. admiralty law distinguished the ship from its proprietor, the laws of slavery differentiated the offending slave from her or his owner.[89] Admiralty law, and the laws of slavery recast African captives, first, from humans to objects and, then, from things to legal persons. The body of the slave, like the body of the ship, oscillated between personhood and property. But the imposition of legal personhood on the ship and the slave did not follow a parallel, symmetrical, or analogous process. Whereas a ship's owner could be punished by forfeiture for the lawless actions of his vessel, a slave owner was *compensated* for the death of his guilty slaves.[90]

For scholars of slavery, the transatlantic slave trade was much more than a historical event. It was a foundational moment, one that inaugurated an entire inventory of economic practices, juridical forms, and vicissitudes of racial violence that continue to persist today.[91] The slave became a racial, historical, and legal marker that embodied the transformation from human to thing and thing to legal person.[92] When situated in the so-called free sea, it becomes clear that the slave as legal person emerged from the deeply knotted entanglements between the common law and admiralty law, as evidenced in the law of deodand, vessel personification, and the polyvocal and shared jurisdiction of Atlantic worlds.[93] Importantly, the status of legal person did not afford the same rights to ships and to slaves. Positive and negative personhood—with their distinct racial logics—offered jurists practical ways to hold ships and slaves accountable and punishable, all in the interests of racial capital.[94] The authority of admiralty law, like the laws of slavery, assuaged the aporia between personhood and property so that ships and slaves could be both persons and property at the very same time.[95]

Seafarers and captains treated the ship affectionately and made it quasi-human by giving it feminine attributes, as Conrad remarks in *The Mirror of the Sea*. The transformation of the slave, by contrast, demanded an entire apparatus of racial and gendered violence.[96] These regimes of terror began on the shores of West Africa, escalated in the middle passage, and were extended from the ship to land via the plantation.[97] Turning humans into property, Ian Baucom argues, required "the violence of becoming a 'type': a type of person, or, terribly, not even that, a type of nonperson, a type of property, a type of commodity, a type of money."[98] But the violence that made people into "types" could never be achieved through abstraction alone. The legal transformation of humans—into slaves, things, and legal persons—demanded registers of force that were at once material, corporeal, epistemic, and always racial. The unidentified passenger aboard the *Komagata Maru* made this point vividly when he insisted that those on the ship had been transformed into slaves.

The transportation of "unfree" slaves on the "free sea" was thought to necessitate legal regimes of racial coercion and death aboard moving ships.[99] In common law jurisdictions, for example, judges routinely described ship captains as sovereigns of "a small government."[100] In order to manage his crew, passengers, and cargo, a captain had, under British and U.S. admiralty law, full and unquestioned authority to deploy physical violence as necessary. The putative exceptionality of the high sea, which was removed from national and imperial sovereignty, demanded violence to maintain order. Without the terrors of shipboard administration, slave ships might not have survived their passage across the Atlantic, some claim.[101] These intensifying registers of racial and gendered violence, enacted by captains and crews during the middle passage, facilitated the metamorphosis of African captives into "types" of cargo, "types" of property, and "types" of money.[102] Legal violence on the ship and the plantation, operated as structures of racial governance and modes of death that were justified through fears of mutiny, insurgency, and revolt, precisely the moments at which slaves became legal persons. Crucially, the power required to govern the free sea was only available to European sovereigns, shipping companies, captains, and crews. It was not accessible to Indian seafarers, and most certainly not to Gurdit Singh, who declared himself both the charterer and the *owner* of the *Komagata Maru*.[103]

Long after abolition, the slave remained a persistent and re-emerging legal figure at sea. Though efforts to humanize the ship and dehumanize the slave followed distinct racial and legal processes, the two were joined in the shared concept of legal personhood. Transatlantic slavery animated the corporeality of the ship and reappeared in its transoceanic travels and in ports of call. In the following section, I explore the currents of slavery through the multiple routes and itineraries of Connell's vessels.

Ship 168

In 1889, Charles Connell and Company, a family-owned business located in Scotstoun on the Clyde River, was commissioned to construct two passenger-cargo ships, the *Stubbenhuk* and her sister ship, the *Grimm*. Though Connell was not the largest or most prominent yard on the Clyde, its founder, Charles Connell, had solid credentials. He was the son of a shipbuilder and a trained shipwright.[104] In 1861, Connell took leave from the local yard where he was employed and set up his own shipbuilding company. In a relatively short time, his business flourished. At the time of his death in February 1884, following only two decades of production, Connell's estate was valued at £264,635.[105] It was the eldest son of his ten children—also named Charles—who would then manage the thriving firm. In 1902, Connell was incorporated as a limited liability company with all shares held by the family.[106] Between 1861, when the firm was established, and 1968, when it was amalgamated into the Scotstoun

Division of Upper Clyde Shipbuilders, the company built 519 vessels.[107] These ships crisscrossed the globe, transporting European settlers and Indian indentures to Canada, the United States, and the Caribbean, respectively and carrying sugar, coal, livestock, and opium along well-travelled routes to ports of call across Europe and Asia. The company's high-quality construction and the global itineraries of its ships earned Connell a reputation as "one of the most skillful designers of the day."[108] Many of its vessels called at the same seaports where slave ships had docked in earlier times.

Britain's global ascendency as a maritime empire was established through naval mastery, including its dominance in shipbuilding.[109] The empire's claims to racial and imperial supremacy were made possible through its maritime power.[110] As British admiralty ships defended the virtues of masculinity and whiteness at sea, merchant, passenger, and slave ships produced and extended the empire's racial asymmetries and civilizational inequalities. British-built vessels facilitated the large-scale transplanting of European settlers, the forced movements of African captives and Chinese/Indian indentured laborers, and expanded the imperial circuits of plantation commodities. Without its ships, writes Lincoln Paine, Britain "would have been unable to settle or conquer the Americas, to develop the transatlantic slave trade, or to have gained an imperial foothold in Asia."[111] By 1914, as the *Komagata Maru* embarked on its voyage from Hong Kong to Vancouver, 50 percent of international commerce and 67 percent of British imperial trade involved ships that flew the British flag.[112]

Given Connell's standing as a quality shipbuilder, the firm's customers were many, and not exclusively British. In 1889, Dampfshifffahrts-Gesellschaft Hansa, a German-owned company, also known as Hamburg's Hansa Line, commissioned Connell to build the *Stubbenhuk,* a ship that would eventually be known globally as the *Komagata Maru.*[113] Built in yard 168, the ship was a midsized steel-screw schooner. It was 329 feet long and 41 feet wide, with a capacity of 2,926 gross tons.[114] Its sister ship, the *Grimm,* also commissioned by Hansa and similar in size and design, was constructed in yard 167. Both were passenger-cargo vessels built specifically for the cattle and livestock trade.[115] The *Stubbenhuk* and the *Grimm,* as one advertisement boasted, had "all the modern improvements for the proper handling" of livestock (see fig. 2.1).[116] The ships were furnished with the latest technologies, ensuring passenger comfort and safety across long distances. The *Stubbenhuk* was equipped with a teak telegraph box and fitted with electrical lighting.[117] Its interiors were elegantly finished with mahogany, teak, and pine fixtures.[118] Moreover, Connell ensured that the *Stubbenhuk,* like its other vessels, had the necessary documentation for transoceanic travel, including a certificate to pass through the Suez Canal. As the "great highway of

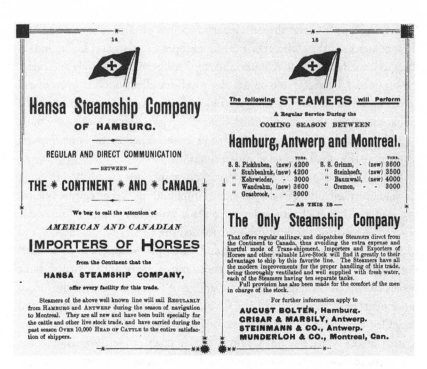

FIGURE 2.1. Advertisement from the Hansa Steamship Company (Hamburg), which commissioned construction of the *Stubbenhuk* in 1889. (Photo courtesy of *Importers' Directory: Compiled for the Use of Livestock Importers* [US Consuls Banks, 1891], 14–15)

British traffic to India, Burma, Australasia and the Far East," the canal was a clear expression of Britain's global maritime power. [119] Though the *Stubbenhuk* did not call at Mediterranean or Asian ports, these routes were well traveled by the *Sicilia* and the *Komagata Maru,* respectively.

According to the customs of the sea and admiralty law, as I discuss above, ships did not become living entities until their hulls were complete. As the *Stubbenhuk* neared the end of its construction, its identity changed from a "congeries of wood and iron" to an animate being.[120] "Ship 168," as it was known in Connell's account books, surfaced at the close of 1889. Connell assured Ferdinand Laeisz, who managed the Hansa Line, that both the *Stubbenhuk* and *Grimm* would be completed within seven months of contract. But construction was delayed for various reasons. In the case of the *Grimm,* there was an insufficient supply of steel. Production on the *Stubbenhuk* was halted for other shortages, including a "want of floors."[121] Notwithstanding these interruptions, both ships were completed by the end of summer 1890, although several months later than

FIGURE 2.2. The *Stubbenhuk,* 1890. (Photo courtesy of Ellis Island, libertyellisfoundation.org)

anticipated. As the *Stubbenhuk*'s launch date approached, Connell and Laeisz no longer called the vessel "ship 168." Instead, they began addressing her by her given name, *Stubbenhuk*. On 13 August 1890, following the ship's launch down the Clyde River, the *Stubbenhuk* officially became a legal person (see fig. 2.2). Between 1890 and 1925, the vessel would be sold, resold, relaunched, and re-named: first, as the *Sicilia* (1894); then, as the *Komagata Maru* (1913); and, finally, as the *Heian Maru* (1925). Neither Connell nor Laeisz could have foreseen how the ship's uneventful beginnings on the Clyde River would lead to a career marked by controversy, conflict, and struggle.

In his masterful photo essay *Fish Story,* Alan Sekula describes the designation of ships as a "physiognomy of vessels" that signaled national and imperial power on the high seas.[122] Traveling under the authority of specific sovereigns, falling within the jurisdiction of particular laws, and subject to regimes of personification, not all ships were considered equal. Just as vessels were feminized, they were also inscribed with racial and civilizational properties based on national and imperial affiliations. In international law, ships were permitted to fly under a single flag. This allowed owners to claim legal and political association with one nation or empire-state. Across "the mobile and fluid surface of the sea," a ship's flag signaled its identity, including the sources of law by which it was to be governed.[123] However, flags did not reflect clear or direct lines of ownership, authority, or sovereignty.[124] Though they connected vessels to national and imperial territories, a ship's legal standing was not always or easily traceable to its owners or sponsors. The flagging of ships was often decided, not as a declaration of nationalism, but in the "best interests" of maritime commerce.[125] It was not uncommon for proprietors to be citizens of one country and their vessels registered in another. These competing jurisdictional orders are, in part, what led U.S. Supreme Court judges, including Chief Justice Marshall, to champion the ship as a legal person.

As the *Stubbenhuk* neared completion, it was to be fitted with a German flag and possibly a Canadian one. "Please send us Flags," wrote Connell. This should be "a repeat of 167's [flags] with the addition of 1 Canadian Flag."[126] Given the request for two flags, Hansa was likely deciding on the most convenient and profitable place to register their ship. In October 1890, when the *Stubbenhuk* made its maiden voyage from Hamburg to Montreal, the ship flew under only one flag, a German one. Though the Hansa Line was a Hamburg-based firm, its vessels, including the *Stubbenhuk,* regularly traveled Atlantic routes, carrying passengers from Germany to eastern Canada and the United States. In 1883, Hansa began a regular service between Hamburg, Antwerp, and Montreal. In 1884, it added two more stops, Boston and Halifax. Several years later, Hansa ships sailed regularly to New Orleans, a former slave port. From 1890 to 1894, the vessel made three trips to New York City, landing at Ellis Island and bringing thousands of European travelers from Europe's "old" world to the "new." (See map 2.1.) The passengers were from Russia, Prussia, Austria, and Hungary, and included adults and young children.[127] Many were described as "protracted sojourners"; others sought permanent settlement; and some were refused entry, at least initially.

In 1891, the *Stubbenhuk* arrived in Montreal with a full complement of European passengers, including eleven Belgians and seventeen "destitute" Russian Jews. On docking, the captain failed to submit a certified passenger list. Consequently, the vessel was immediately brought to the attention of immigration authorities.[128] "The Belgians proceeded direct to Lake St. John, their destination," wrote the immigration agent to the secretary of the Department of Agriculture. However, "the Jews who are in the most destitute circumstances" were "sheltered in the Immigration Buildings."[129] These "pauper passengers" included five women and men and seven children. They "are not of a class suited for any labor offered at this agency," the agent continued, "they have no friends nor means of support and must necessarily become a burden on public charity."[130] Initially considered undesirable and thus unsuitable to enter Canada, the Belgians and Russian Jews were eventually permitted to disembark in Montreal. In 1914, 376 Punjabi passengers would arrive in Vancouver Harbour aboard the very same

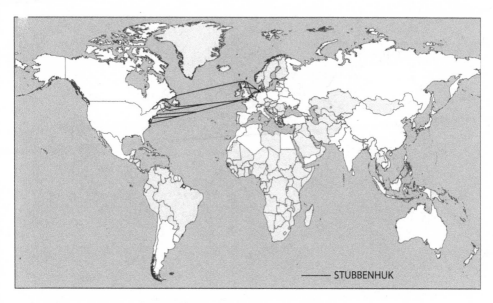

────── STUBBENHUK

MAP 2.1. Voyages of the *Stubbenhuk*, 1890–94.

ship, under new ownership, nationality, and a different name. But only twenty
would be allowed to land. The remaining passengers would be detained in Vancouver Harbour and eventually deported to Calcutta.

In 1892, the *Stubbenhuk* was sold to the Hamburg-Amerika Line. For the
next two years, it traveled under its original name. In 1894, the ship was renamed the *Sicilia*. Like Hansa, the Hamburg-Amerika Line vessels made regular transatlantic passages, departing from ports of call in continental Europe,
mostly Germany. However, its owners expanded the *Sicilia*'s route to include
several Mediterranean ports. The ship collected passengers from southern Europe and North Africa and transported them to Montreal and New York City.
Between 1894 and 1913, the *Sicilia* made sixty-two trips to Ellis Island, carrying over forty thousand people from Sweden, Germany, Italy, Greece, Algeria,
Spain, and Turkey to the eastern United States (see map 2.2).[131] Under its respective owners and changing identities, the ship was directly implicated in the
colonization and resettlement of the Eastern Seaboard. Vessels like the *Stubbenhuk* and *Sicilia* did not just bring labor and commodities; they also brought
settlers. By transporting Europeans across the Atlantic, the ship's movements
facilitated the ongoing dispossession of indigenous peoples from their ancestral
lands and waterways. This process commenced hundreds of years earlier, and
has been fiercely resisted ever since.

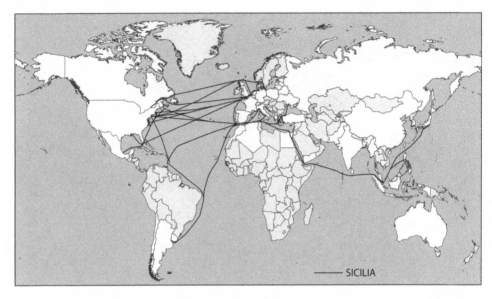

———— SICILIA

MAP 2.2. Voyages of the *Sicilia*, 1894–1901 and 1913.

Founded in 1861, Connell and Company established itself long after Britain's formal abolition of slavery. However, as the firm prospered and as its client list expanded, Connell became entrenched in global maritime circuits that were established through the transatlantic slave trade. Many Connell-built ships, including the *Stubbenhuk* and *Sicilia,* journeyed from continental Europe to former U.S. slave ports: New Orleans, Baltimore, New York, and others. Fourteen of Connell's ships also made regular passages to Ellis Island. Though widely known as an immigration entrepôt of the United States, Ellis Island had multiple histories of displacement and dispossession.[132] Long before the Dutch arrived in what is now Manhattan, the Algonquian-speaking Lenape people freely traveled between the upper and lower bays. They called this area Lenapehoking, the "place where Lenape dwell."[133] Two hundred years later, New York City would become a prominent slave port. In 1827, it was home to the largest resident slave population outside the American South.[134] Following emancipation, as Leslie Harris argues, the city became "one of the largest free slave communities in the North."[135] As this one example suggests, the resettlement of indigenous lands was inseparable from the forced transatlantic passage of African captives.

Connell's 519 vessels crisscrossed the globe. The North Atlantic was one of numerous routes traveled, and indigenous dispossession was one of many forms of racial and colonial violence in which company ships were implicated. Some Connell-built ships also journeyed across the Indian Ocean, the South Pacific, and the South Atlantic, from India to Mauritius, Fiji, and the West Indies. Unlike the *Stubbenhuk* and *Sicilia,* these vessels did not carry Europeans or livestock but "coolies" and plantation commodities, most notably sugar. Indian indentures were shipped along oceanic routes in conditions that were not much better than on slave ships, arriving at ports of call that had long been traveled to by slave ships. Both the names and the architecture of indenture ships also echoed histories of transatlantic slavery. In some cases, indenture vessels were former slave ships.[136] Indentured labor itself was a formal and direct response to Britain's abolition of slavery. From 1838 to 1917, to mitigate the effects of freedom, Britain transported more than one million Indians to its sugar plantations. Although Mauritius was the largest single recipient of indentured labor in the British Empire, almost half of these men and women were sent to the Caribbean region.[137] Indian and Chinese contract labor was transformed into racially exploitable bodies that were to replace those newly freed slaves. The overlaps and entanglements between slavery and indenture were evident in Connell's client list. Two of the firm's most valued customers—Sandbach, Tinne, and Co., and James Nourse—eventually came to dominate the Indian indenture trade.[138] In the 1870s, two decades before Connell built the *Stubbenhuk,* the firm constructed four vessels for Sandbach: the *Ailsa* (1870), *Jura* (1875), *Brenda* (1877), and *Sheila* (1877). In the last decade of the nineteenth century, as the company was building ships for Hamburg's Hansa Line, Connell built twenty-eight vessels for Nourse, including the *Volga II* (1891), *Arno* (1893), *Ems* (1893), *Forth* (1894), and *Mersey* (1894).[139] By close of the nineteenth century, Nourse owned an entire fleet of indenture ships that transported Indian contract laborers from Calcutta to Mauritius, Fiji, and the Caribbean. Though a relative newcomer to the trade, Nourse became Sandbach's fiercest rival.[140]

Demerara (subsequently British Guiana, now part of Guyana) produced and supplied more sugar than any of Britain's other West Indian colonies. It was also the first to experiment with Indian indentured labor and received the largest number of Indian contract laborers, more than any other one of Britain's Caribbean colonies.[141] Whereas Nourse capitalized on the abolition of slavery and established his fortune entirely through the indenture trade, Sandbach, Tinne, and Co. was a family empire that was founded much earlier. The firm's connections to the Caribbean date as far back as 1782, and grew directly from transatlantic slavery.[142] Formed from an amalgamation of Dutch and Liverpool merchant firms, the company owned several slave plantations in Demerara, which produced sugar, coffee, tea, and later cotton. In addition, the company manufactured rum and molasses, which it transported to Liverpool and Glasgow.[143] For many years, Sandbach enjoyed a monopoly over Demerara's slave trade and built enormous fortunes from it. The company's sailing ships brought captives from West Africa to the West Indies and transported New World commodities, including sugar, to voracious British markets. Sugar transformed British palates and dramatically shaped imperial culture. As Simon Gikandi argues, sugar was "the commodity that sweetened the pivot of coffee around which the [British] culture of taste revolved."[144] The growing consumption of sugar in Britain and in its Dominions, and colonies made the empire increasingly dependent on the horrors of slavery. The movement of slaves and the transport of sugar were equally reliant on ships, and this is where Sandbach held a clear advantage.

The enormous prosperity of slave owners in the West Indian plantations, and their influence over the development of British tastes and culture, was a direct result of dominance over land, labor, and sea. Focused on the U.S. mainland, several historians have documented the labor-land connection in important ways.[145] However, control over the seas, through the mobility of ships and the transportation of slaves was equally significant to British and later U.S. dominance and to the fortunes of plantation owners.[146] In Demerara, first the Dutch and then the British encouraged intertribal warfare among indigenous inhabitants. By devastating communities, they made land more readily available to European interests.[147] Through the importation and violent exploitation of slaves, lands were cleared and crops were grown. Thus, indigenous dispossession and transatlantic slavery overlapped and intersected through shared repertoires of racial violence.[148] But Sandbach's thriving empire exceeded this land-labor nexus in significant ways. The company's monopoly over slavery and its enormous profitability were directly linked to the sea. Sandbach owned many of the ships that transported slaves to Guiana and carried plantation commodities to Britain and to its colonies and Dominions, including Canada.[149]

The abolition of slavery, as historians and others have argued, created a set of global exigencies including an acute shortage of exploitable racial labor. The freedom of slaves, many feared, would threaten the financial, cultural, and political dominance of the British Empire, compromising its thriving appetite for sugar, tea, and cotton.[150] These conditions devastated Sandbach's empire. In 1835, the firm submitted compensation claims to the imperial government for a loss of more than three thousand slaves. As the largest slave owners in Demerara, they received the highest settlement, valued at £173,577.[151] The wealth that Sandbach accrued from transatlantic slavery was eventually invested in new ships that would be used to import indentured labor.[152] Like many plantation owners, Sandbach turned to indenture as a means of curtailing the financial losses brought about by abolition. Captain W. A. Angel, who commanded several Sandbach ships, described the dilemma accordingly: "The estates in past times have tried all expedients to obtain suitable laborers.... It goes without argument that it is impossible for white men to work in the open fields in such terrific heat." Indigenous populations were equally unsuited to field labor, he maintained, but for very different reasons. "The aboriginal races of tropical America are impossible; nothing can induce them willingly to take up any kind of labour." For Angel, it was the "African negroes kept as slaves, [who] were first class working material." Following abolition, however, this arrangement was no longer possible. "When the great scheme of manumission set in" and the slaves "were made free ... the sugar estates were practically ruined," Angel recalled.[153] After several failed attempts to import workers from Portugal, nearby Caribbean islands, and China, Sandbach eventually turned to India. "The importation of coolies from China was first tried after the Negro failure," but this scheme proved ineffective, "owing to their well-known vices."[154] In Angel's racial order, it was African slaves followed by Indian coolies who were best suited to work on the plantations. Indian labor "met with great success," he remarked. Coolies from India were not only "dependable"; they "worked well and cheerfully."[155]

Of the four sailing ships that Connell built for Sandbach's indenture fleet, it was the iron clipper *Sheila* that was most widely known.[156] Captain Angel commanded the vessel on her maiden voyage from Calcutta to Trinidad and Demerara and kept a detailed diary of the ship's journey. Connell built the *Sheila* specifically for "the special trade of carrying Indian Coolie agricultural laborers to work on the sugar plantations of the West Indies," Angel observed.[157] On her "cutwater bow," he recalled with pride, "was a beautifully carved figure-head," which was "intended to represent Mrs. J. E. Tinne," the wife of Tinne's eldest son, John. According to maritime customs, as I discuss earlier in this chapter, a feminine figurehead would protect the ship from the fury of the sea. Mrs. Tinne was present at the ship's launch on the River Clyde. She christened the vessel and sent it on its voyage from Glasgow to Calcutta.[158] After the *Sheila* reached her destination, unloaded and reloaded her cargo, she began the long journey to Demerara. The vessel carried 675 passengers, including 600 Indian indentured laborers that were soon to be employed on Sandbach's plantations.[159] The shipbuilders were instructed that "no expense was to be spared, and in the modeling everything was to give way to speed." In the world of the ship, time was money. By "conveying upward of six hundred Coolies ... even a day saved on the passage" was significant, Angel declared, especially given the high "cost of food."[160]

In *The Coolie Ships and Oil Sailors,* one of the few surviving accounts of indenture ships, Basil Lubbock chronicled the transition from slavery to indenture as follows. "There is probably no greater proof of progress in the history of mankind than that which is shown by a comparison of the slave trade with the coolie trade." This progress was not gradual but sudden, he claimed; the terrors of slavery were "replaced by *a humane, strictly regulated, indenture system.*"[161] Lubbock's account follows a linear and progressive arc that has been vigorously critiqued and discredited by many.[162] The abolition of slavery, as he conceived it, was the outcome of a budding British humanitarianism. In the nineteenth century, imperial authorities argued that systems of indenture were legally and politically distinct from slavery. This was a new form of labor that highlighted consent, free will, and contractual arrangements.[163] To mark these distinctions, colonial officials passed new maritime regulations. Unlike slave ships, which were overcrowded, poorly provisioned, and unseaworthy, indenture ships that traveled from India and China, to the Caribbean and elsewhere, were carefully governed and supposedly well furnished. They were four to five times larger than slave ships and were judiciously inspected, often multiple times, to ensure adequate supplies of food, water, and living space. In India, British officials enacted legislation that would allow them to govern the conditions aboard indenture ships, so that women and men would arrive healthy and ready to work. Despite regulations and inspections, illness, violence, and death remained endemic. But repeated appeals to consent and contract provided authorities with a legal vernacular that allowed them to differentiate the putative humanity of indenture from the inhumanity of slavery.[164]

In 1877, the *Sheila* commenced her maiden voyage to Trinidad and British Guiana. Notwithstanding assurances that slavery and indenture were legally and politically distinct, Indians would travel, work, and experience conditions of racial exploitation that were not radically different from those of transatlantic slavery. Despite repeated claims that indenture was not slavery, slippages materialized in the middle passage, as evidenced in Angel's diary. Slavery hovered in his account of the *Sheila*'s voyage as both distinct and inseparable from systems of indenture. Although Angel described indentured laborers as "living freight," he insisted that they were treated well as "passengers."[165] The conditions of coolie ships, he assured, were far better than they were aboard slavers. The "coolies had their own cooks," who worked "in strict accordance of their caste of faith." Women and men "consumed a great quantity of rice and curry" and were therefore well fed.[166] For Angel, the most important difference was that indentures were under contract and thus remunerated for their labor with silver coins. Indian women often melted these into jewelry, he explained. Furthermore, indentured laborers gave their consent by signing contracts and making decisions. Thus, they could not be equated with slaves. But it was the architecture of the ship—particularly the hold—that could not disguise the racial and historical entanglements at the root of the indenture system. The *Sheila* employed a number of freed black sailors who worked the lower decks. "It was comic to see that black mass of perspiring humanity," Angel remarked. It was "almost dark," and they were barely visible, "their great eyes rolling and blinking at you" while "carroling [*sic*] forth such ditties."[167] Aboard the indenture ship, which was modeled on the slave ship, the hold remained a place of death and destruction that was also a space of vitality, creativity, and mutiny.[168]

Following Connell's vessels across the Atlantic and Indian Oceans, as I do above, points to the connections between ocean regions and the intersecting histories of racial and colonial violence. From the decks of the *Stubbenhuk* and the *Sheila,* indigenous dispossession, transatlantic slavery, and Indian indenture emerge as deeply knotted historical and legal processes that were joined by the ships that crossed the so-called free sea. The currents and countercurrents of slavery, as they passed through Connell's vessels, were not only a reminder of the past but also a shadow cast on the present and future. In the third and final section, I turn to the Pacific and Indian Oceans and consider how transatlantic slavery materialized in the *Komagata Maru*'s 1914 journey. Its echoes resounded through Chinese indenture and maritime finances, as well as in the shipboard vernaculars of anticolonial critique.

The Middle Passage

In July 1913, after owning the *Sicilia* for just over two decades, the Hamburg-Amerika Line sold the steamer to Shinyei Kisen Goshi Kaisha. The small Japanese firm, which was represented by Odagiri, was made up of three men; all were domiciled in Japan. However, the *Genzan Maru No. 3,* the company's one and only steamer, was registered in Dalian.[169] Known in Japan by the name Dairen, the bustling port city in China's Liaoning Province had long been ruled by foreign interests: first British, then Russian, and, most recently, Japanese.[170] The company's newest vessel would join its existing one, doubling their fleet, expanding the company's trade routes, and increasing their profits. Together, the ships crisscrossed the South China Sea, transporting Japanese coal to other Asian ports of call. (See map 2.3.)

Immediately after purchasing the *Sicilia,* Shinyei Kisen renamed her the *Komakata Maru.* The ship's namesake was the Asakusa district in Tokyo, an

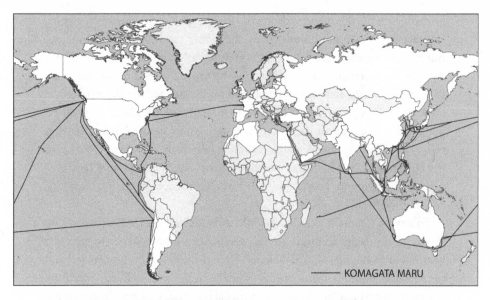

MAP 2.3. Voyages of the *Komagata Maru*, 1913–1920. In its many lives, the vessel traveled across the Atlantic, Pacific, and Indian Oceans. Only some of the voyages are pictured here. (Source: All maps are compiled from *Lloyd's Weekly Shipping Index*)

area well known for its Senso-ji Buddhist temple. Through an error in translation, the steamer was misspelled *Komagata Maru,* and listed accordingly in *Lloyd's Register of Ships*.[171] In Anglo maritime cultures, as I discuss at the outset of this chapter, ships were gendered partly through rituals of naming. In Anglo contexts including Britain and the United States, vessels were commonly named after women, as typified by Sandbach's *Sheila*. In Japan, by contrast, maritime appellations followed a different set of customs and traditions. The names of vessels—including ones that carried Punjabi migrants to Canada's west coast—often ended with the suffix *Maru*.[172] *Maru* was described as an "archaic form of masculine endearment approximating 'little boy' or 'little prince,' [and] applied to favorite possessions such as the warrior's sword or the mariner's boat."[173] Japanese vessels, including the *Komagata Maru,* were represented as youthful and impressionable boys, yet they continued to be referenced with feminine pronouns. In the spring of 1914, however, the *Komagata Maru*'s identity would undergo a radical shift. The vessel was racially marked, masculinized, and indistinguishable from the alleged radicalism and lawlessness of its Punjabi charterer.

On 23 March 1914, shortly after meeting Odagiri in Hong Kong, and following a swift and uneventful set of negotiations, Gurdit Singh signed a Charter-

Party agreement with Shinyei Kisen. Theirs was a "time charter." The *Komagata Maru* was leased to Singh for six months at a rate of $11,000 (Hong Kong) per month. The contract was to commence as soon as the ship was delivered, with the first two installments due upon receipt.[174] The Charter-Party set the conditions for law, order, and authority aboard the ship and at sea. The *Komagata Maru* "was only to be employed in strictly neutral trades." It could travel "to Asia not North of Vladivostok nor West of Suez, European Asia excluded, including Australia, but excluding Africa with the exception of the Mauritius; including West Coast of Canada, United States of North America, Mexico, Central and/or South America."[175] On the ship, Gurdit Singh was given a full range of powers that even surpassed the captain's authority. This was unprecedented. Under the law of the sea, captains enjoyed unlimited command over their vessels, crews, and cargoes.[176] In this case, the Charter-Party limited the authority of the *Komagata Maru*'s Japanese captain and forty crew members. It specified that Gurdit Singh held jurisdiction over "the whole reach and burthen of the ship," except those places reserved for the "ship's officers, crew, tackle, apparel, furniture, provisions, stores, and water." Most significantly, "the Captain (although appointed by the owners) shall be under the orders and directions of the Charterer," the agreement stated.[177]

Singh's newfound authority came with clear responsibilities. He was accountable for "all charges and expenses arising through taking steerage passengers," and was to "supply all provisions, water, galleys, cooks fittings and medicines, medical stores, also doctor and purser (if required by the Charterer) in every respect and accordance with the Hong Kong Ordinances and to the satisfaction of the Emigration Officer."[178] In return, Shinyei Kisen assured that the *Komagata Maru* would be granted a passenger license for the ship's journey to Vancouver. A "Hong Kong Passenger Certificate for a full complement of steerage passengers" and "with the necessary boats and rafts," was to "be provided by the Owners," the contract stated.[179] Thus, in Singh's view, the Charter-Party and passenger license granted the *Komagata Maru* the requisite authority to depart Hong Kong and to land without problem in Vancouver. But just to be sure, he consulted three Hong Kong lawyers who responded accordingly: "There are no restrictions upon the immigration by Indians from the Colony unless they are under contract of service (and the intending passengers were under no contract of service)."[180] By law, Gurdit Singh was transporting "free" migrants and not Indian contract passengers. Thus, the existing restrictions did not apply to him. But the system of indenture, as I discuss below, would remain a haunting presence in the *Komagata Maru*'s voyage, one that repeatedly evoked Atlantic histories of slavery.

From 1908 onward, growing concerns of Indian seafaring animated Canada's continuous journey provision and justified the Dominion's two additional orders-in-council. One required that each "Asiatic" passenger have $200 on landing. The second barred the entry of unskilled laborers to British Columbia. As officials in Hong Kong, India, and Canada shared information about the ship, and as they became more fully aware of Gurdit Singh's ambitions to establish a steamship company, charter a vessel, and carry Indian passengers across the Pacific to Vancouver, they made coordinated efforts to thwart his plans. Authorities in Hong Kong had already prevented him from purchasing the *Tong-Hong*. Shortly after Singh chartered the *Komagata Maru*, police in Shanghai and Hong Kong pursued other means of prohibiting or at least delaying the ship's planned departure. Though Gurdit Singh had unwavering support from local Indians and Gurdwaras, police averted his efforts to secure passengers and investors. As one source recalled, the "Hindus at Shanghai . . . wanted to withdraw their deposits from the Municipal Bank" so they could "render monetary assistance to the Hindu shipping venture." However, the police captain "prevented the Manager of the Bank from permitting such withdrawals."[181] According to other passengers, authorities shut down the banks in Shanghai so that prospective travelers would be unable to draw funds to pay their fares.[182] Sikhs in Hong Kong also tried sending money to the "Steamer America Fund," but they too "met with the same difficulty."[183] The Hong Kong Gurdwara "promised to send their subscriptions . . . but a telegram was received to the effect that the officers would not allow them to withdraw their deposits from the banks."[184] Even before the *Komagata Maru* lifted anchor, the Guru Nanak Steamship Company was faced with financial and legal troubles that seemed insurmountable. Over the following six months, authorities in Hong Kong, Canada, and India sought additional ways to prohibit Singh's maritime ambitions entirely and indefinitely. Based on these events, the freedom of the sea materialized as a freedom that was not available to Indian merchants or travelers, irrespective of whether they were British subjects.

Gurdit Singh's inability to secure financing delayed the ship's departure. It also alarmed prospective travelers. Though Singh "hoped to book 500 passengers," only a third of that number embarked in Hong Kong.[185] Had he sold 500 tickets, as planned, he would have collected nearly $100,000 dollars. After paying all expenses, the Guru Nanak Steamship Company would have completed its first voyage with a healthy profit of $58,000, funds that could have been invested in other ships and additional voyages.[186] But the uncertainty and delay devastated his plans and disrupted his projected revenues. Despite sending several telegrams and notifying travelers about the ship's scheduled departure, only 165 Indians boarded in Hong Kong. Another 111 embarked at Shanghai, 86 at Moji, and 14 at Yokohama. Gurdit Singh insisted that the ship could accommodate hundreds more. This remained a point of contention throughout the journey and thereafter. The vessel was fitted with only 15 passenger cabins, and one of these was intended as a Gurdwara. When Gurdit Singh assumed control over the *Komagata Maru,* he had the lower decks cleaned and fitted with wooden benches and latrines.[187] Following these improvements, he claimed that the vessel could accommodate up to 533 people on its lower decks and steerage.[188] But authorities characterized the *Komagata Maru* as "a cargo boat" that had "narrow decks and low ceilings" and "very limited accommodation for passengers."[189] In its previous lives as the *Stubbenhuk* and the *Sicilia,* the ship transported thousands of European settlers and sojourners to eastern Canada and the United States. But after purchasing the vessel, Shinyei Kisen used it primarily to carry coal. Therefore, authorities claimed that the steamer could no longer sufficiently accommodate large numbers of travelers.

Before meeting Gurdit Singh in Hong Kong, and prior to signing the Charter-Party agreement, the ship's owners, with the assistance of Odagiri, successfully secured a Chinese indenture license. This would have significant implications for the ship's unsuccessful journey and for Gurdit Singh's reputation. The Hong Kong Ordinance No. 1 of 1889, also known as the "Chinese Emigration Ordinance," consolidated all laws and regulations "relating to Chinese Passenger Ships and the Conveyance of Chinese Emigrants." The act defined a "Chinese Passenger Ship" as "every ship carrying from any port in Hongkong, and every British ship carrying from any port in China, or within one hundred miles of the coast thereof, more than twenty passengers being natives of Asia."[190] Importantly, for the purposes of the ordinance, "Asia" did not include India. Consequently, Indian indentured laborers were beyond its jurisdiction.[191] The ordinance outlined, in minute detail, the regulations that were to be followed by captains of vessels, who were transporting "contract" and "free" Chinese labor from Hong Kong and the mainland. It established the requisite minimum standards to ensure the well-being of Chinese contract laborers and the seaworthiness of the ships that transported them. "The number of passengers to be carried shall in no case exceed one passenger for every ten tons of the registered tonnage of such steamer," the ordinance specified.[192] The *Komagata Maru* measured 2,926 gross registered tons. Despite Gurdit Singh's insistence that the steamer was equipped to accommodate more than 500 travelers, by the terms of the ordinance, it could carry a maximum of 292. Given the seasonal onset of bad weather, indenture ships, unless propelled by steam, were not permitted to travel "westward of the Cape of Good Hope or to any port in Australia, New

Zealand, Oceania, or Tasmania . . . between the months of April and September inclusive."[193] They were also to be adequately provisioned and properly organized. Indentures required sufficient space on lower decks, male and female passengers were to be separated, and all ships needed a "hospital or sick bay."[194] The vessel and those aboard were to be properly cared for, or captains could be subject to severe penalties.

To be clear, the Hong Kong ordinance made no explicit reference to the transatlantic slave trade. Yet the figure of the slave and the horrors of the slave ship remained a palpable presence. The ordinance, like many other laws surrounding indenture, was a juridical and political response to slavery.[195] The law distinguished indentured labor from slavery by foregrounding consent and by calling indentures "contract passengers." Furthermore, those aboard "coolie ships" were subject to a double inspection, first by a medical officer and then by an emigration official. These examinations were to take place "on shore before embarkation as well as on board the ship after embarkation."[196] Ship decks were to be thoroughly inspected for proper ventilation; shipmasters were required to hire doctors; and all vessels were to be fully operational, with sufficient food and water. Vessels that did not have valid licenses and those with "prohibited fittings" could be searched, seized, and detained and the "owner, agent, or master of any ship" would be found "guilty of an offence against this ordinance."[197] Notwithstanding determined efforts to draw distinctions between slavery and indenture, both in the ordinance and in nonlegal contexts, "coolie ships" served as a repressed reminder of slavery. Systems of indenture were made possible by the juridical and financial forms of enslavement and by the profits accumulated from the transatlantic slave trade. Sandbach's sugar empire was a clear case in point.[198]

The eighth schedule of the Hong Kong ordinance included a "Form of Contract Passage Ticket." Since the *Komagata Maru* was authorized to transport Chinese indentures from Hong Kong, the tickets issued permitted the vessel to land in Victoria and Vancouver. On its outbound journey, Gurdit Singh gave each passenger two tickets: one blue, one white. The blue permits were "class passenger tickets" administered by the "Guru Nanak Steamer Co," and included a receipt for the payment of a £20 fare (see fig. 2.3).[199] The white passes were distributed under the eighth schedule of the Hong Kong ordinance, and were "intended for the use of [transporting] indentured Chinese Emigrants to Vancouver" (see fig. 2.4).[200] Gurdit Singh likely acquired the white tickets from Odagiri. According to Indian authorities, he used these passes to deliberately defraud passengers, convincing them that the tickets were "issued by the Government," thereby allowing each "recipient to enter Canada." The white tickets

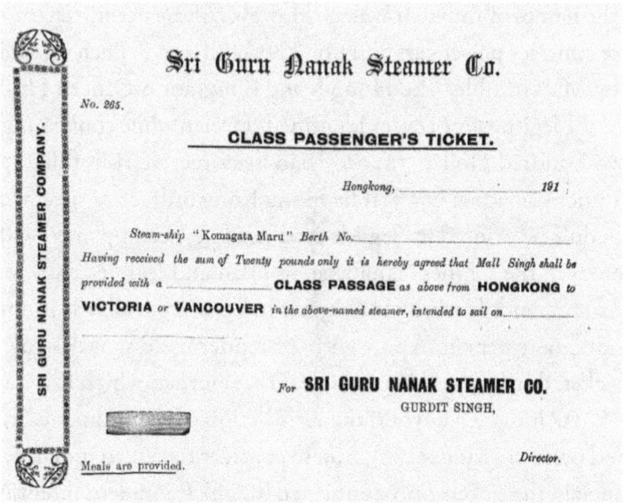

Sri Guru Nanak Steamer Co.

No. 265.

CLASS PASSENGER'S TICKET.

Hongkong, _____ 191

Steam-ship "Komagata Maru" Berth No. _____

Having received the sum of Twenty pounds only it is hereby agreed that Mall Singh shall be provided with a _____ **CLASS PASSAGE** as above from **HONGKONG** to **VICTORIA** or **VANCOUVER** in the above-named steamer, intended to sail on _____

For **SRI GURU NANAK STEAMER CO.**
GURDIT SINGH,

Meals are provided.

Director.

FIGURE 2.3. "Blue Ticket" issued by Gurdit Singh as director of the Guru Nanak Steamship Company to passengers on board the *Komagata Maru*. (Photo courtesy of British Library)

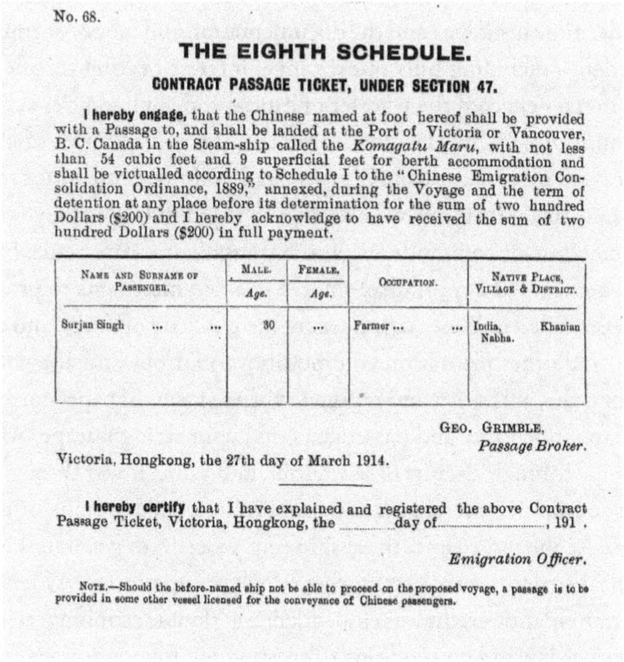

No. 68.

THE EIGHTH SCHEDULE.

CONTRACT PASSAGE TICKET, UNDER SECTION 47.

I hereby engage, that the Chinese named at foot hereof shall be provided with a Passage to, and shall be landed at the Port of Victoria or Vancouver, B. C. Canada in the Steam-ship called the *Komagatu Maru*, with not less than 54 cubic feet and 9 superficial feet for berth accommodation and shall be victualled according to Schedule I to the "Chinese Emigration Consolidation Ordinance, 1889," annexed, during the Voyage and the term of detention at any place before its determination for the sum of two hundred Dollars ($200) and I hereby acknowledge to have received the sum of two hundred Dollars ($200) in full payment.

NAME AND SURNAME OF PASSENGER.	MALE. Age.	FEMALE. Age.	OCCUPATION.	NATIVE PLACE, VILLAGE & DISTRICT.	
Surjan Singh	30	...	Farmer	India, Nabha.	Khanian

GEO. GRIMBLE,
Passage Broker.

Victoria, Hongkong, the 27th day of March 1914.

I hereby certify that I have explained and registered the above Contract Passage Ticket, Victoria, Hongkong, the _____ day of _____, 191 .

Emigration Officer.

NOTE.—Should the before-named ship not be able to proceed on the proposed voyage, a passage is to be provided in some other vessel licensed for the conveyance of Chinese passengers.

FIGURE 2.4. Contract passage ticket or "White Ticket" issued by Gurdit Singh to passengers on board the *Komagata Maru*. (Photo courtesy of British Library)

included the names of Indian travelers. However, these permitted the transport of Chinese contract passengers and not "free" Indians.[201] Each one was "signed in blank by Mr. Grimble," the Hong Kong Emigration Officer. His signature sanctioned the legitimacy of every identified traveler, while confirming that "the sum of two hundred Dollars ($200) [had been received] in full payment" as required under Canadian law.[202] The Hong Kong ordinance specified that the eighth schedule be printed in "legible type" and be "accompanied with a translation thereof in the Chinese language, in plain and legible characters."[203] No person was to "fraudulently alter or cause to be altered, after it is once issued, or shall induce any person to part with, or render useless, or destroy, any such contract ticket, during the continuance of the contract which it is intended to evidence."[204] As India fell beyond the jurisdiction of the ordinance, there were no specified penalties for issuing Chinese contract tickets to Indian passengers. But for officials, the tickets only confirmed Singh's fraudulent intentions. "The Committee found vouchers in my office," Gurdit Singh would later write. They "tried in vain to prove that the pass tickets were counterfeit ones, by alleging that they were white."[205]

Transatlantic slavery inaugurated new financial arrangements, legal structures, and economic institutions that featured prominently in Atlantic economies.[206] Maritime insurance and the documentation and modes of enumeration it demanded—including bills of exchange, interest-bearing certificates, and ship manifests—enabled the transfer of capital and commodities across time/distance and land/sea.[207] Maritime commerce demanded forms of credit and debt that were extended through protracted and uncertain seaborne movements. These financial forms were as vital to shipbuilding as they were to the purchase and sale of commodities. In the transatlantic slave trade, bills of exchange, which served as promissory notes, enabled merchants to procure provisions to be traded in West Africa, secure the purchase of slaves, and transport sugar, tea, and other plantation commodities to Europe and elsewhere.[208] As symbols of order, authority, and rationality, these forms of paper currency traveled on slave, indenture, and passenger ships, connecting Europe, Africa, and the Americas through circuits of law, profit, and value. It was through transatlantic economies that merchants and captains were able to transform humans into cargo. At the same time, these shipping procedures generated economic and political structures that strengthened white superiority. As Ian Baucom explains, transatlantic credit was embedded in a "double economy: an economy of monetary value and an economy of trust whose foundation was the credibility, the character, the trustworthiness of the person signing the bill over *and* the value of the trust that person had placed in the previous owner."[209] Bills of exchange enabled white European men to lend money, accumulated via slavery, to other white European men, with the intention of procuring and transporting unfree black bodies across the free sea. Credit was based on an "economy of trust" and those granted credit were assumed to be of good (racial) character.[210]

These racial instruments of finance that were foundational to maritime commerce and to admiralty law also operated as systems of colonial and imperial governance. Bills of exchange and promissory notes offered yet another way for imperial powers to ensure that the free sea remained firmly under British control. Gurdit Singh was not a Liverpool or London merchant. According to authorities in Hong Kong, Canada, and India, he was an audacious and duplicitous colonial subject. The financial worlds that engendered thriving maritime economies, along the Atlantic and in other ocean regimes, were inaccessible and even foreclosed to him. Credit was about much more than financial accounting. It demanded "a phenomenology of transactions, promises, character, [and] credibility" that did not extend beyond northern Europe and certainly not to an Indian populace thought to be corrupt, scheming, and mendacious.[211] Gurdit Singh was already barred from the world of shipping and global capital. Local police disallowed the Gurdwaras and potential passengers in Hong Kong and Shanghai from withdrawing their money in support of the Guru Nanak Steamship Company. But these obstacles neither dissuaded nor discouraged him. Well-versed in the art of commerce, Singh assembled his own maritime economy of credit and debt that aimed to replicate the Atlantic versions from which he was excluded. To ensure that the *Komagata Maru*'s voyage unfolded as planned, Singh distributed passenger tickets and introduced interest-bearing certificates to instantiate his own systems of accounting (see fig. 2.5).[212] Of the 376 passengers on the ship, only 350 paid full fares. The twenty-six who did not, including nineteen Muslims, were required to sign a promissory note agreeing to pay £40, "double what was due from them."[213] In the end, and notwithstanding Singh's elaborate system of documentation, the Guru Nanak Steamship Company had no way of collecting unpaid fares and no way to complete its 1914 journey.

Given the financial difficulties that Gurdit Singh encountered from the very outset, and with no other options at hand, he borrowed money from approximately 100 passengers aboard the ship. According to Kirpa Singh, these funds were used to purchase coal in Moji. "Gurdit Singh said the ship was rolling very much," he recalled, "and it was necessary to buy some coal to keep her steady."[214] Singh delivered a lecture, Pohlo Ram recounted, "saying that passengers could advance money which would be refunded afterwards."[215] Following Singh's appeals, 94 passengers agreed to lend him any monies they had, so he

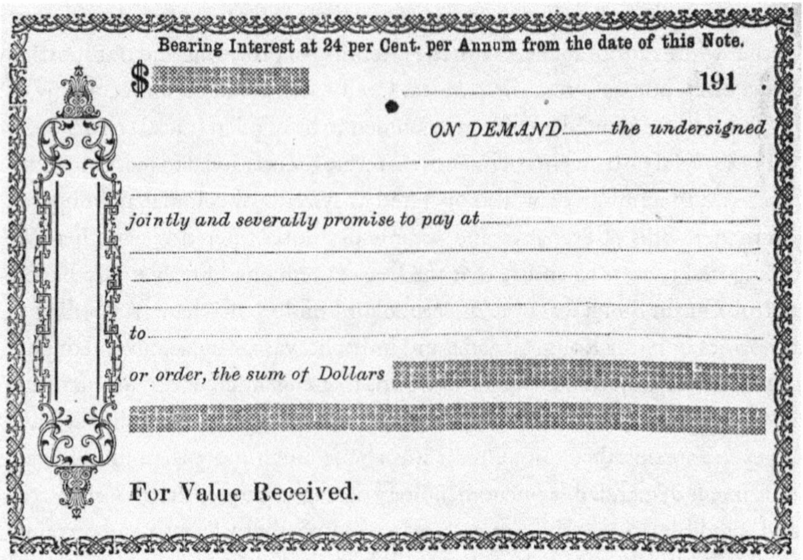

Bearing Interest at 24 per Cent. per Annum from the date of this Note.

$ ▓▓▓▓▓▓▓▓▓▓▓▓   191 .

ON DEMAND............the undersigned

jointly and severally promise to pay at..

to..

or order, the sum of Dollars ▓▓▓▓▓▓▓▓▓▓▓▓▓▓▓▓▓▓

▓▓▓▓▓▓▓▓▓▓▓▓▓▓▓▓▓▓▓▓▓▓▓▓▓▓▓▓▓

For Value Received.

FIGURE 2.5. Interest-bearing certificate found among Gurdit Singh's papers aboard the *Komagata Maru*. (Photo courtesy of British Library)

could purchase coal, and complete the journey. To document these transactions and to establish the terms of their arrangement, Singh crafted "An Agreement Signed by Certain Passengers": "The sum of money which we deposited on the 29th of April 1914 for the purpose of defraying occasional expense incurred for necessary requirements and up-keep of the vessel, and the interest of which sum was to be paid to us, *will be recovered by us from the Khalsa Diwan Committee of Vancouver,* who are trying their best for our welfare."[216]

To authenticate their contract, Gurdit Singh added a guarantor. After the ship landed in Vancouver, he explained, the Khalsa Diwan Society, which had already been campaigning to raise funds for their safe passage, would repay the passengers whatever he owed them. In the event that the Khalsa Diwan Society would not pay his debts, the passengers could "recover [their money] ... from Bhai Gurdit Singh." His creditors could not seek their "deposits from the Bhai Sahib (Gurdit Singh) as long as he is on the vessel," the agreement specified.[217] Their money would be repaid once the vessel made landfall and could not be honored at sea. To authorities in India, the financial orders that Gurdit Singh initiated aboard the ship were not evidence of his business acumen or his maritime ambitions, but of his duplicity and criminality. One official with the Indian Criminal Intelligence Department accused Singh of extorting money.

The passengers were to "raise a subscription among themselves if they wanted the ship to proceed to Vancouver," he charged.[218]

Ship manifests, including passenger and freight lists, were vital to trans-oceanic commerce and to maritime governance. These inventories were especially vital to the slave and indenture trades, recording credit, debt, profit, and value. By the early 1800s, with the deregulation of transatlantic slavery, new rules demanded that ship captains enumerate the African captives aboard their vessels.[219] All ships traveling the Atlantic were required to carry individual registries that itemized their cargoes and calculated their individual and collective worth. Captains were not required to identify the names, places of origin, or even gender of those captured.[220] Through single entries arranged in tabular columns, human beings were made into inanimate things. Slave manifests and freight lists, combined with shipboard violence worked together to supplement law's "maritime metaphysics." Through forms of enumeration and modes of abstraction, humans as cargo were valued as much in life as they were in death.[221]

The format and layout of Singh's contract with travelers is as suggestive as its content. Singh penned his "Agreement Signed by Certain Passengers" on the "Summary of Freight List," which was written in English and likely accompanied the *Komagata Maru*. In long tabular columns, he and his associates had listed the names, villages, and districts of passengers, including signatures and "thumb impression[s]."[222] By registering each traveler, Singh and his counterparts retained detailed accounts of who was aboard and of money lent and owed with interest. Writing the names of passengers on the "freight list," he evoked memories of slave manifests and in so doing emphasized the destitution and despair of the *Komagata Maru* passengers. Above one page of the list was a note, scribbled quickly and urgently in disjointed prose (see figs. 2.6 and 2.7). Written in a religious, deferential, and desperate tone, the message was an appeal to the Khalsa Diwan Society that was addressed to the highest priest of the Gurdwara. The memo was a plea to those in Vancouver—including Husain Rahim, Bhag Singh, and other members of the shore committee—to assist Singh by raising $11,000. These funds would be used to pay the next charter installment, which was already long overdue. If Gurdit Singh did not fulfill the provisions of his agreement with Shinyei Kisen, the ship and the passengers would be deported to Hong Kong. "Please help us get off the ship. We are ready to do service for you. Please don't let us be sent back. Until we are able to pay you back, we will be at your mercy."[223] The note was signed "gulam," meaning defenseless.

Writing on the freight list and conveying a sense of desperation under the imminent threat of deportation, Gurdit Singh gestured to the entangled histories of transatlantic slavery, Chinese indentured labor, and so-called free migration.

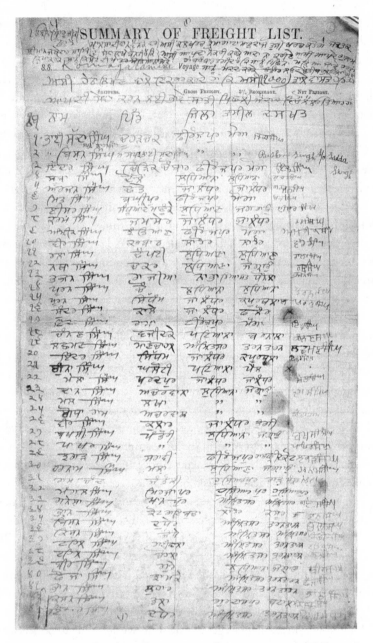

FIGURES 2.6 and 2.7. List of passengers and urgent message to Khalsa Diwan Society written on a summary of freight list. Note the signatures and thumbprints on the right. (Photo courtesy of National Archives of India, Private Collections)

SUMMARY OF FREIGHT LIST.

S.S. _____ Voyage _____ ⊙ _____

SHIPPERS.	Gross Freight.	5%. Brokerage.	Net Freight.

Several passengers drew similar connections, as they condemned the deplorable conditions to which they were subject aboard the ship. "The captain has refused to give us any lights," wrote Amir Muhammed Khan, one of Gurdit Singh's closest associates. "Three hundred and seventy passengers are confined in a dark prison house at night . . . We are treated very badly," Khan continued. "We are treated as mere chattel."[224] Another passenger described conditions aboard the vessel as unlivable. "Lights have been stopped; decks not washed; water stopped; steam for cooking food stopped; sea water put into our provisions; sickness prevails; no doctor."[225] Daljit Singh, Gurdit Singh's secretary, offered the most damning critique of all: "The *feranghis* treated us as inanimate objects, which did not want food or water."[226] To Gurdit Singh, Amir Muhammed Khan, and Daljit Singh, those on the ship were not *like* slaves. Rather, they were subject to forms of racial violence that emerged and expanded from transatlantic slavery. By referencing the terrors of the middle passage and replicating the financial and juridical forms of maritime worlds, Singh and his associates conveyed their desperation as linked to the fate of African captives who were forcibly imprisoned aboard slave ships in another ocean and at another time.[227] The rhetoric of slavery allowed Singh and the other passengers to challenge the freedom of the sea and to dispute the status of Indians in the British Empire.

Authorities in Hong Kong and Vancouver collectively and deliberately produced the appalling conditions that Gurdit Singh and the other passengers evoked in communicating with those on shore. Colonial officials blocked the movements of money, delayed the ship's departure, and detained the vessel for two long months in Vancouver Harbour. The passengers not only had insufficient supplies of food and water; they also lacked electricity to power lights. The police in Shanghai and Hong Kong made sure that Singh was unable to sell tickets. Thus, he could not raise the necessary funds to make his payments under the Charter-Party. Furthermore, Singh was unable to provide provisions to the passengers, as he promised. By borrowing money from passengers and purchasing coal in Moji, Singh planned to offload the coal and resell it in Vancouver. But once again, Singh's entrepreneurialism was thwarted and his access to the sea prohibited. "The quality of the Moji coal is not up to the standard of the local coal fro [*sic*] steaming purposes," wrote Herbert Clogston, a retired officer from Bengal and a resident of Vancouver who was appointed to oversee a local inquiry into the ship's journey.[228] Gurdit Singh was forbidden to sell the coal and was unable to repay the passengers.

The Khalsa Diwan Society did receive Singh's appeal. Shortly after the *Komagata Maru* laid anchor, Bhag Singh and Husain Rahim began circulating their call to secure funds.[229] That call was sufficiently persuasive to enable the

Khalsa Diwan Society to raise more than $70,000 for the purpose of resuming the Charter-Party and providing the passengers adequate food and water.[230] But in the end, this was not enough, and the vessel was deported. The financial worlds of maritime commerce that were engendered through the racial violence of transatlantic slavery were reserved for European men alone. Notwithstanding claims that the sea was free, oceans remained inaccessible to Indian travelers, traders, and migrants. Ultimately, the challenges that Gurdit Singh initiated against the Canadian, British, and Indian government carried high political, legal, and financial costs. After reaching Calcutta, Singh spent seven years as a fugitive and five years in prison. His reputation was shattered, and his life savings were lost. The shore committee, including Husain Rahim and Bhag Singh, never recovered the $14,000 they put forth in efforts to secure the ship's landing.[231]

THE VESSEL THAT would come to be known as the *Komagata Maru,* which drew global attention and engendered new and repressive legal regimes in Canada and India, spent thirty-six years at sea. Apart from its 1914 passage, the vessel's movements were routine and largely unexceptional. Voyaging first as the *Stubbenhuk,* then as the *Sicilia,* and eventually as the *Komagata Maru,* the steamer crisscrossed ocean arenas, transporting settlers and assorted commodities, most notably livestock and coal, to distant ports of call. By being attentive to its hundreds of voyages, and situating the steamer within a larger fleet and longer history of Connell's ships, we can trace a set of transoceanic itineraries that connected discrepant histories and geographies. By traveling the "free sea," Connell's ships joined transatlantic slavery, indigenous dispossession, and Chinese/Indian indenture to "free" Indian migration. In its many lives, the steamer linked the Atlantic, Pacific, and Indian Oceans to the Mediterranean Sea and the South China Sea, uniting ocean regions, connecting continents, and producing the earth as an uneven and indivisible whole.

Slavery in Atlantic worlds was formally abolished more than a century before the *Komagata Maru*'s 1914 journey. Yet, the figure of the slave, as I argue in this chapter, remained foundational to the ship and the sea as racial and juridical forms. Specifically, slavery reverberated in a number of related registers: in the juridical status of ships as legal persons; in the routes traveled by Connell's vessels and the ports at which many called; and in Chinese/Indian indentured labor as legal and political responses to abolition. In the *Komagata Maru*'s middle passage, slavery recurred in other ways. It afforded a shape and structure to shipboard arrangements of credit and debt and animated the anticolonial lexicons of Gurdit Singh and his contemporaries. During the ship's passage along the Pacific, Atlantic slavery was powerfully refracted through systems of Chinese indenture. Read through the moving ship, histories of slavery, indenture, and so-called free migration defy the successive and linear arc of historical time and the teleology ascribed to British law. In the intersecting authority of the common law and admiralty law, transatlantic slavery remained a tangible current in maritime worlds, one that was inextricably tied to the legal status of ships and to oceanic governance.

In the following chapter, I consider the jurisdictional struggles over land, sea, and subjecthood that were spawned by the *Komagata Maru*'s arrival to Vancouver Harbour. To do so, I shift my focus from the high seas to coastal waters and from slavery to indigeneity. Chapter 3 examines *Re Munshi Singh,* a "test-case" that was heard at the Immigration Board and the British Columbia Court of Appeal and which ultimately determined the *Komagata Maru*'s fate and future.

Land, Sea, and Subjecthood

For it is here shown that by nature neither land nor sea is the property of anyone, but that land through nature can become property, while the sea cannot.—HUGO GROTIUS, "Defense of Chapter V of the *Mare Liberum*," c. 1615

We admit being "intruders upon the native possessors of the country" and, on the whole, the Canadian government's treatment of them has been fair and just. But you would have us extend to the British East Indian privileges which we deny to our own native Indians, who have prior claim upon us.—MAXWELL SMITH, *Vancouver Sun*, June 1914

The *Komagata Maru*'s arrival in Vancouver unleashed a series of jurisdictional struggles that were global and local, terrestrial and oceanic, spatial and temporal. A ship registered in Dairen under a Japanese flag, chartered by a British subject originally from Punjab and domiciled in the Straits Settlements, carrying Punjabi passengers from ports of call in Hong Kong, China, Japan, and elsewhere, and arriving along the west coast of Canada, a Dominion with its own racial and political divides, posed pressing questions regarding the legal authority of the empire and the rights of British subjects to travel within it. Though these concerns were not new, they became newly politicized with the vessel's landing. Critics and onlookers viewed the *Komagata Maru*'s detention and deportation through exigencies that had long been fermenting within imperial debates over Indian mobility. Did British subjects from India, like their white counterparts elsewhere, enjoy the same rights to travel and settle across the British Empire? Could the Dominions, which were concerned with large-scale indigenous dispossession and European resettlement, legally prohibit the entry of Indians who were also British subjects? If so, on what legal grounds? How did the Coast Salish and other indigenous nations figure in Canada's claims to political and legal autonomy? The ship's journey, as it was widely reported in newspapers and periodicals in the United States, Australia, South Africa, Singapore, and India, repositioned these questions on a global stage. Legal deliberations over the *Komagata Maru's* fate galvanized an attentive though impatient audience. While some, including Maxwell Smith defended the role of settlers as "intruders upon the native possessors of the country," as the opening epigraph above suggests, the ship's supporters repudiated the presumed authority and legitimacy of the Dominion. Together, these disparate views and the debates they engendered exposed the empire's racial, territorial, and temporal asymmetries and placed them into sharp dispute.

In a brief article titled "*When* Is a British Subject?," the *New York Times* addressed the *Komagata Maru's* legal and political implications accordingly.[1] "These Hindus, who proclaim themselves to be British subjects, wish to change their abode from one part of the British Empire to another."[2] However, they are "prevented from so doing by the Government of the Dominion of Canada, which according to the [British] North American [*sic*] act of 1867, can make and enforce its own immigration laws." Despite the Dominion's resolve to govern its territorial boundaries, the *New York Times* questioned Canada's claims to sovereignty and autonomy, insisting that immigration laws could not "be made legally operative against British subjects, whether these subjects were born in India, Africa or Australia."[3] Yet, Indian laborers in South Africa, the paper continued, were repeatedly denied the rights they "enjoyed in India." Given these geographical disparities and racial inequalities, many demanded to know "just what is meant by the term 'British subject.'" When domiciled in India, the *New York Times* continued, Indians were taught that to be a British subject "carried with it a certain status of citizenship which placed them under the laws of the empire in what ever part of the empire they might be."[4] Though Indian rights to mobility were observed and upheld in England, they were "not in South Africa." Claims to British subjecthood, as the *Komagata Maru's* arrival so vividly demonstrated, did "not work at all in the Dominion of Canada."[5]

As the vessel sat anchored in Vancouver Harbour, legal and political conflicts developed among the governments of Canada, Hong Kong, and India, and between Dominion and provincial authorities. These disputes centered on which government held authority over the ship and its passengers and where their respective jurisdictions began, coincided, overlapped, and ended. By demanding the status and rights of British subjects, Gurdit Singh, the passengers, and their supporters from near and far demanded to know the legal and political origins of Dominion sovereignty. Their transpacific voyage challenged the racial and territorial constraints imposed on British subjecthood, and in so doing, posed difficulties for the present and future of colonial and imperial governance. For many, the heightened mobility of Asiatics that threatened the ostensibly free sea was most vividly demonstrated in the white Dominions. Officials were especially concerned with how Indian migrants and travelers were to be distinguished—legally, politically, and civilizationally—from Britons and indigenous peoples and how their entry might trouble the racial balance these governments sought to achieve in their respective jurisdictions.[6] Though Gurdit Singh, Husain Rahim, and many others imagined the British Empire to be a limitless and contiguous horizon, and declared their right to move freely across its vast landmass and flowing seas, restrictive and prohibitory immigration laws enacted in South Africa, Australia, New Zealand, and Canada maintained oceans as European spaces and the Dominions as white settler colonies.[7] "British authority in India," wrote the *New York Times,* "has been built up on the idea of equality among British subjects. How can a Hindu, how can any one, be made to understand that, although his citizenship means the same thing in London as it does in Calcutta, it means something else in Cape Town, and still something else in Vancouver?"[8] Imperial territories were interconnected and interdependent, but contrary to the beliefs of Singh and Rahim, they were organized vertically in a hierarchy of racial worth and value. This chapter examines the Board of Inquiry hearing and the case at the British Columbia Court of Appeal that authorized the *Komagata Maru*'s deportation from Vancouver. Specifically, it considers the vertical relations of imperial rule that were established through jurisdictional contests over land, sea, and subjecthood and that reaffirmed the flagrant inequalities between Dominions and colonies and citizens and subjects.

Britain asserted its claims to imperial sovereignty with confidence. However, as imperial and world historians have argued, the British Empire was never founded on a centralized, unified, or contiguous authority emerging in the metropole and extending outward.[9] Like other empires, it was a spatial and temporal composite of oceans, colonies, protectorates, and territories that were ruled, unevenly and often tenuously, through multiple juridical and political arrangements.[10] Imperial polities were fragmented, divided, and bounded by fluid and permeable borders.[11] As a maritime empire, Britain staked its legal and political control over a vast and heterogeneous global topography. Imperial authorities produced an assortment of jurisdictional spaces that held unequal claims to sovereignty, legality, and political autonomy.[12] This unevenness, as I have already suggested, was particularly evident in the contrast between the "youthful" Dominions and Britain's supposedly older and archaic colonies, including India.[13] As imperial territories were increasingly unified through global conceptions of space and time, and as the Dominions asserted their own autonomy and authority, the empire's racial and temporal, asymmetries were maintained through a number of overlapping legal processes, including immigration restrictions and maritime regulations. Passengers aboard the *Komagata Maru* and their supporters around the world expressed frustration and disaffection on "the uncertainty and lack of uniformity" in immigration law, as enacted "by the different states of the empire."[14] Racial inequality and inconsistency, many would soon realize, was not accidental or exceptional but formed a legal and political structure through which the British Empire was ruled.

To foreground the porous, plural, and overlapping dimensions of political and legal authority over land, sea, and subjecthood, this chapter focuses on the jurisdictional contests initiated by the *Komagata Maru*'s arrival in Vancouver Harbour. In its widest sense, and as I note briefly in the introduction, jurisdiction is a form of legal authority that recognizes the power and influence of law to speak on its own behalf.[15] Recent scholarship distinguishes jurisdiction from sovereignty in several key ways. First, sovereignty implies a uniformity, coherence, and infallibility thought to coalesce in a state or polity. Assertions of centralized control, critics argue, obscure the "degrees" and "layers" of sovereignty and belie the polycentricity of juridical power.[16] Jurisdiction, by contrast, emphasizes the multiple and competing foundations of law as well as the limits of legal control. It directs attention away from sovereign *states* to jurisdictional *processes* that encompass many constituencies and often a myriad of legal systems.[17] Second, and relatedly, studies of sovereignty do not often attend to the coexistence, opposition, and overlap between different legal orders. Yet, from the very outset, the British common law was made up of competing legalities that coexisted with religious, personal, and indigenous law, even if it did not often appear that way.[18] The tensions and overlaps between the common law and admiralty law, as I discuss in chapter 2 and elaborate further below, present one example among many of legal plurality in colonial and imperial contexts. By emphasizing the multiple sources of law, jurisdiction opens fruitful possibilities for examining the projected, partial, and disputed legalities that established the grounds for British imperial power. Law and order were extended unpredictably across the putatively free sea via ships and were enforced inconsistently and unequally on land. Though immigration regulations figured prominently in the *Komagata Maru*'s arrival, detention, and deportation as many have argued, admiralty law was also important in changing the vessel's course and determining its future. The ship manifest, I suggest below, incited an ongoing dispute between admiralty and immigration law, becoming a catalyst for wider struggles over imperial, Dominion, and provincial control.

Jurisdiction is commonly viewed as a territorial and spatial concept. Although the relations between sovereignty, territory, and state are now firmly embedded in contemporary legal and political thought, their associations are relatively recent.[19] Until the early nineteenth century, jurisdiction was expressed through subjecthood and status. It was only with the rising dominance of modern cartography that jurisdiction and territory became deeply intertwined.[20] But if the "logic of government *is* the logic of jurisdiction," as Richard Ford argues, territory constitutes only one of its many elements. Jurisdiction, I suggest in this chapter, operated as a form of colonial and imperial governance that worked through a number of registers including race, time, and territory.[21] Cartographic practices may have encouraged a new geographical perspective, however, maps were also visual representations of race, space, *and* time, as evidenced in the legal and political asymmetries and inequalities of the British Empire. By plotting the itineraries and journeys of travelers and marking the distances between places, early modern mapmakers characterized time in terms of movement and mobility.[22] These temporal grids did not taper or diminish with the rise of a global legal order. Rather, the quest for a measurable and universal time persisted and even intensified through maritime expansion, as the imperial quest for longitude suggests.

The racial, territorial, and temporal characteristics of jurisdiction are especially clear in the inauguration and extension of colonial and imperial law across land and sea.[23] In Schmitt's account, the *nomos* of the earth was a spatial project that emerged from Europe's so-called discovery of the New World. The founding violence of law—its imposition by European powers—he argued, began exclusively with land. "The constitutive process of a land-appropriation is found at the beginning of the history of every settled people every commonwealth, every empire," Schmitt claimed.[24] Yet, land appropriations, including the deterritorialization of indigenous peoples, could not have been possible without ocean travel. Perhaps more importantly, the territorial claims of European empires did not stop at land or littoral but regularly extended across the sea, as the Dutch and Portuguese contests over the *Santa Catarina* suggest. Three centuries later, Canada and Australia would defend their territorial sovereignty both terrestrially and oceanically, through the continuous journey regulation and the white Australia policy, respectively.[25] Efforts to dispossess indigenous peoples and resettle the Dominions had other implications that were inspired and shaped by maritime worlds. "Discovery" and conquest joined the "arrival" of white colonists with the beginning of universal history, placing indigenous peoples and colonial populations beyond European time.[26] The mythical origins of colonial law thus established new legal regimes that produced temporalized conceptions of territory and subjecthood through shifting chronologies of past, present, and future.[27] It was precisely this sequential linearity—of youthful Dominions, old colonies, "vanishing Indians" and stagnant British subjects—that Gurdit Singh and the *Komagata Maru* passengers challenged in their aspirations to cross the sea and in their resounding demands to be recognized as British subjects.

Focused on legal deliberations surrounding the ship and its passengers, this chapter takes its cue from the *New York Times* article with which I begin. By posing the question "when is a British Subject?" rather than "where or who is a British subject?" the article invites novel ways to explore jurisdiction as a racial and temporal force and not just a territorial one. In the first section, I introduce the Board of Immigration's inquiry through the *Komagata Maru*'s ship manifest. The manifest, I argue, worked as an administrative tool that joined land to sea and admiralty law to immigration law. To establish the legitimacy and legality of ships, their passengers and cargoes, manifests served as early forms of border control that governed the movements of vessels, goods, and peoples. Read oceanically, the history of these registries connects transatlantic slavery to other forms of racial administration, including "Asiatic" exclusion. In the second section, I turn to the Court of Appeal's deliberations in *Re Munshi Singh*.[28] Specifically, I use this case to analyze the debates on race, territory, and time that the *Komagata Maru*'s arrival initiated. Political asymmetry and racial inequality, the court agreed, were not irregular, anomalous, or unjust. Rather, they were foundational to the vertical divides between Britain's Dominions, colonies, and their respective inhabitants. The third section also centers on *Re Munshi Singh* but takes a different tack. Moving to questions of status, I examine the racial struggles over British subjecthood that emerged in the case. Here, the Court of Appeal marshaled a number of arguments to maintain the presumed autonomy of a white Canada. The past and future of indigenous peoples became one strategy to justify the Dominion's legal, political, and territorial control. When read alongside the court's discussions of racial fit and admissibility, indigenous protection, it appears, lent additional traction to the *Komagata Maru*'s deportation, thereby establishing a long era of Indian exclusion.

Admiralty Law and/as Immigration Law

One month after the *Komagata Maru* anchored in Vancouver Harbour, and as passengers remained detained on board the ship, tensions between provincial and Dominion authorities and Vancouver's Indian residents continued to escalate. Facing pressure from the imperial government and from the ship's supporters in London, India, and South Africa, and with no clear resolution at hand, the Dominion of Canada conceded, albeit reluctantly, that one passenger could come ashore to act as a legal "test-case" to assess the lawfulness of Canada's immigration regulations. These proceedings were to determine, once and for all, the fate and future of the ship and its 376 passengers: could they stay, or were they to be returned to Hong Kong, India, or some other British jurisdiction? At issue were the three orders-in-council: the first disallowed the entry of unskilled laborers and/or artisans to British Columbia, the second required each "Asian" entrant to be in possession of $200 upon arrival, and the third stipulated that passengers had to have made a "continuous journey" from their place of origin to Canada.[29] The immigration hearing and legal proceedings that followed were to address the following questions: Was Canada legally authorized to deny entry to British/Indian subjects, or was the Dominion bound by other legal and political obligations determined by the British Crown? Were the orders-in-council, which demanded passengers make a continuous journey, be in possession of $200 upon arrival, and which singled out the "Asiatic race," discriminatory? And finally, were those aboard the *Komagata Maru* "Asians" or "Caucasians," and what kind of undesirable influences might their entry to Canada have on whites and indigenous peoples?[30]

On 25 June 1914 one month after the *Komagata Maru* berthed in Dominion waters, the Board of Inquiry—made up of three Canadian officials, including Malcolm Reid, Canada's immigration agent—was finally set into motion. By this time, only twenty passengers—those who could prove previous domicile in Canada—had been allowed to disembark.[31] The remaining passengers were forcibly confined to the ship, where many would be held until late September, before the *Komagata Maru* made landfall outside Calcutta. Given the successful legal challenges initiated by Husain Rahim and others, Dominion authorities remained apprehensive and uncertain as to how the courts would assess the ship's arrival. Well aware of the high political stakes that followed, they deliberately stalled legal proceedings, a tactic that only exacerbated the deplorable conditions aboard the ship. Supplies were running low, the vessel was infested with rats and flies, and toilets were overflowing.[32] Immigration authorities hoped that these dire circumstances would lead to exhaustion, exasperation, and ultimately desperation, forcing Gurdit Singh and the passengers to leave of their own accord, and before their case was heard by the Immigration Board. Singh remained resolute, however. He and many of his supporters believed that a court would decide in their favor. Appearing before the law, Gurdit Singh avowed, would reveal the profound injustices committed by the British Empire against Indians at home and abroad.[33]

As the ship sat anchored in the harbor, Husain Rahim, Bhag Singh, and other members of the shore committee recruited J. Edward Bird to represent the vessel and its passengers. With only a few days to prepare their case, Bird hastily reviewed the ship manifest. Of the hundreds of passengers listed, he identified Munshi Singh, a twenty-six-year-old from the village of Gulupore in the Hoshiarpur District of Punjab, as the most suitable person to appear before the board. Like many others on the manifest, Munshi Singh was listed as a "farmer." He had very little money and did not come to Canada via continuous journey. After leaving Calcutta, he stopped first in Hong Kong and then in Yokohama. By openly and explicitly contravening all three orders-in-council, Munshi Singh, in Bird's opinion, presented the strongest challenge to Canada's immigration regime. But he was not Bird's first choice, nor was he the choice of the other passengers. As the charterer of the *Komagata Maru,* Gurdit Singh insisted that he should be the one to appear before the board, to represent both the vessel and the passengers detained aboard. Bird agreed. On 14 June, eleven days before the hearing, Gurdit Singh wrote to Malcolm Reid charging that "the men called for the Board of Enquiry, are not according to the Manifest List." As the charterer, it was his "right to come first before the Board of Enquiry."[34] But his letter received no reply. Three days later, Gurdit Singh's secretary, Daljit Singh, wrote to Reid, arguing once more that immigration authorities were obligated to call on Gurdit Singh. "If the Board of Inquiry is working according to the Manifest, it should call the first man on the manifest," Daljit Singh explained. "As the Board of Enquiry is not working according to the manifest then it was my right to be called upon first so that I might be able to procure food and to arrange for my merchandise," he wrote on behalf of Gurdit Singh.[35] Under admiralty law, the ship manifest was a legal document that authorized the sovereignty of the ship's captain and crew. Though Gurdit Singh was listed as the charterer, and was granted legal command over the vessel, Reid refused to recognize his position of authority. Your "status is that of a passenger on board the 'Komagata Maru,'" he eventually wrote back, "and an applicant for admission into Canada."[36] Reid assured Gurdit Singh that he would be the last one to be called ashore.

Ship manifests, as I discuss in the previous chapter, were central to racial, colonial, and imperial administration across oceans and in ports of call. For Grotius, the physical properties of the sea — its continual movements and ceaseless change — rendered it a space that could not be owned or occupied, though it could be controlled. On the vast, fluid, and dynamic surfaces of the sea, it was the ship's flag, colors, and manifest that served as sources of legal authority. Like the flags under which ships traveled, manifests also conveyed the sovereignty of ships, owners, and sponsors. Perhaps more importantly, the ship manifest functioned as a jurisdictional hinge between "firm land" and "free sea." Under admiralty law, a shipmaster was to submit a detailed manifest within a specified time of arrival in port, anywhere from forty-eight hours to ten days, depending on the location. Vessels were not allowed to anchor or offload goods until a signed and sworn record of crew and cargo was submitted to immigration and port authorities. The document was to provide a wide array of information, including the shipmaster's surname, the ship's name, its tonnage, and its ports of embarkation. But manifests had other objectives. As modes of enumeration, they were also intended to prevent fraud in the securing of bounties and to forestall the clandestine re-landing of goods.[37] If a manifest did not contain a detailed specification of all goods, including the dates, times, and places of their procurement, the shipmaster could be fined. Port authorities were authorized to seize any items found on board a ship that were not included on the manifest. If goods were listed in the document but could not be located on the vessel, the shipmaster was subject to additional penalties. In some places, separate manifests were required for high-value commodities, including wine and tobacco.[38] Failure to provide a signed manifest could result in the forfeiture of goods or fines, or both, causing economic losses for shipping companies and sponsors, while also tarnishing their reputations.[39] Ultimately, ship manifests determined the legality and legitimacy of people and goods that were transported across the high seas.

In the case of Munshi Singh, the Board of Inquiry's task was to determine whether his arrival on the *Komagata Maru* contravened the three orders-in-council and whether he and the other passengers were to be deported. Throughout their deliberations, the questions posed by immigration authorities centered on borders and immigration regulations but also maritime law. Indeed, the ship manifest emerged as a point of vigorous debate on the competing authority of admiralty law and immigration law and on the Dominion's jurisdiction over land and sea. When Munshi Singh was asked how much money he had in his possession, he told the board via an interpreter, that he had only six sovereign coins but that the remaining $200 was readily available from his bank in India. Officials rejected this argument. Passengers had to produce the money "on *the ship's deck*," they claimed, before the vessel made landfall.[40] Next, Reid asked Munshi Singh why he did not travel from India via continuous journey, and why he stopped in Hong Kong and Yokohama. He departed India three months earlier, in search of a transpacific passage to Vancouver, he recalled. In 1908, after the first continuous journey provision was enacted, the Canadian and imperial governments notified steamship companies that all Calcutta-Vancouver routes were to be halted immediately. Not all companies complied, however. Fearing financial losses, Canadian Pacific ignored government directives and continued their service as usual. It was only after British and Canadian authorities reissued their warnings, and the continuous journey provision was amended and reenacted, that Canadian Pacific reluctantly agreed to terminate the route.[41] There was still at least one "steamship company plying from India," Bird would later claim, "but the Immigration Officials have control of that because they won't take any Hindus on board."[42] The Dominion's border was not fixed to land but was extended via moving ships outward and across the sea.

Like thousands of Indians aspiring to reach Canada and the United States, Munshi Singh began his journey in Calcutta. He crossed the Bay of Bengal, the Indian Ocean, and the South China Sea, and finally arrived in Hong Kong weeks later. From the late nineteenth century onward, many Indian travelers and migrants followed similar routes, departing Punjab for Calcutta, Hong Kong, China, Japan, Malaya, and Singapore. Some, including Gurdit Singh and Husain Rahim, traveled as merchants seeking new commercial opportunities, others left as Sepoys and security personnel who were employed by the British Crown.[43] By the early twentieth century, with the rise of immigration regulations in Canada and the United States, Hong Kong became a crucial transition point for Indian travelers and migrants seeking passage across the Pacific. Many waited at the local Gurdwara where news of steamship arrivals, departures, and itineraries was discussed, shared, and circulated. It was here, while in transit, that Indians were allegedly radicalized and turned against British imperial rule.[44] But Munshi Singh's layover in Hong Kong was brief. After arriving at the island, he "came to know the Komagata Maru has gone to Yokohama." He followed the ship, Bird told the court, but "did not find the Komagata Maru there." Munshi Singh then "wired to Moji where the Komagata Maru was" anchored.[45] After receiving the telegram, and anticipating new passengers and additional revenues, a struggling Gurdit Singh ordered the vessel's return to Yokohama. Given Munshi Singh's many failed attempts to secure passage to Vancouver, he boarded the *Komagata Maru* and willingly paid $20 for a one-way ticket.[46] Like others on the ship, he would be unprepared for the legal and political spectacle that awaited them after they arrived in Canadian waters.

H. W. D. Ladner, the lawyer for the Immigration Department, was not convinced by Munshi Singh's explanation of events. Passengers aboard the ship, Ladner urged, were part of a much larger plot initiated by Gurdit Singh, whose intention was to knowingly defy Canada's immigration laws. Although Ladner was aware that steamship companies were no longer running a direct service between Calcutta and Vancouver, he questioned Munshi Singh repeatedly as to why he traveled to Hong Kong and Japan, and why he did not take direct passage from India. It "is impossible to get a ticket from Calcutta to Vancouver direct," Bird replied on his behalf.[47] Even at Hong Kong, no shipping companies would issue him passage. One by one, Ladner disputed these rejoinders. The Blue Funnel Line, he maintained, was still operating a direct service between Calcutta and Vancouver. In addition, there were "regular steamers coming from Hong Kong," and Munshi Singh could have boarded any of these.[48] He visited the Blue Line office and also sought passage via other companies, Bird retorted, but none would take him. "Was it not on account of the immigration law of Canada," Ladner questioned, that the shipping companies "refused you a ticket"? Munshi Singh denied any knowledge of Canada's immigration prohibitions. The repeated refusals of steamship companies to grant him passage across the Pacific, Bird maintained, were discretionary and discriminatory, entirely dependent upon "the will of the Companies," which were directed by the Canadian, Indian, and British governments not to carry Indians to Canada.[49]

Although the continuous journey regulation was intended to prohibit the transpacific movements of Indians, it enabled the Dominion government to expand its immigration regulations to the Pacific and Indian Oceans, preventing Indians from boarding steamers in Calcutta or Hong Kong. Canada's immigration regulations directly overlapped with admiralty law, as evidenced in contests over the ship manifest. At the Board of Inquiry hearing, as Ladner reviewed the items placed in exhibit, he asked William Hopkinson, the immigration agent who was also acting as interpreter for the Dominion, to identify Munshi Singh's ticket. "The blue paper is the steamship ticket as handed to me by the applicant," Hopkinson replied. Indian officials alleged that each passenger aboard the *Komagata Maru* was given two vouchers, one white and one blue.[50] By issuing tickets twice, they claimed that Gurdit Singh deliberately deceived travelers, giving them Chinese indenture tickets and thus leading them to believe that the Dominion had sanctioned and approved the ship's journey. Munshi Singh's ticket was "No. 350," Hopkinson told the board, "which corresponds to the number as given on the Manifest."[51] Ladner used Hopkinson's reply as an opportunity to question the authority, veracity, and credibility of the manifest. "You referred just now to the Manifest, Mr. Hopkinson, is that the Manifest that was furnished [to] you as an Immigration Officer by the ship's officers or their agents, in accordance with law?" he asked.[52] While inspecting the ship, Hopkinson explained, he witnessed a representative of the steamship company sitting with Daljit Singh and preparing a document. But he could not confirm with any certitude which one of these men actually composed the manifest.

By the nineteenth century, as the British Empire expanded its reach through the movements of imperial and merchant vessels, ship manifests performed a number of other important legal functions, beyond the enumeration of crews, passengers, and slaves. To begin with, a manifest documented a ship's status by providing a detailed inventory of its cargo and the ports where goods and people were collected and offloaded. Such a list was meant to provide "a particular account and description of all the packages on board" as attested to by the signatures of the shipmaster and other authorized personnel, including the ship's surgeon.[53] By itemizing goods, manifests were used to keep accounts, including those related to credit, duties, customs, revenues, and losses. In so doing, they created legal and financial records of the movements of ships, commodities, and people across the seas. Manifests governed the mobility of persons and nonpersons long before imperial immigration controls were established and enforced. These modes of enumeration were especially vital to the transatlantic slave trade, as I discuss in the previous chapter. By ascribing a monetary value to goods and a moral worth to persons, manifests determined the legal status of slaves as commodities as well as their desirability and admissibility.[54] The modes of documentation operated as violent processes of abstraction.[55] "African men, women, and children ... were stripped of all specificity, including their names," writes M. NourbeSe Philip. Their financial worth as chattel property was "recorded for insurance purposes," so that shipowners and proprietors could be compensated for any losses that took place at sea.[56]

Also organized in tabular columns, the *Komagata Maru*'s manifest was considerably more detailed than those used on slave ships. It listed passengers by name, age, gender, marital status, place of birth, race, religious affiliation, occupation (both in their place of origin and as intended in Canada), and ticket number, as well the amount of money in their possession (see fig. 3.1). Interestingly, the manifest did not specify gender, though it did list the numbers of adults and children. The register was also supposed to include health reports and all stops listed by ports of call. Captain Yamamoto, along with Raghunath Singh, the ship's doctor, and Malcolm Reid, the immigration inspector, signed the first page. As the secretary for Gurdit Singh, Daljit Singh signed the top of the following page. With their signatures, the document granted legal authority to the shipmaster, charterer, doctor, and immigration officers. Together, their names functioned as expressions of order and authority on land and sea without the need for additional forms of legal certification. Thus, the manifest operated as a legal decree that specified the ship's transoceanic movements and enumerated and estimated the value of its passengers and cargo. As a result, it established the boundaries between legality and illegality and between legitimacy and illegitimacy. The Board of Inquiry's reading of the *Komagata Maru*'s manifest led it to conclude that all but twenty passengers

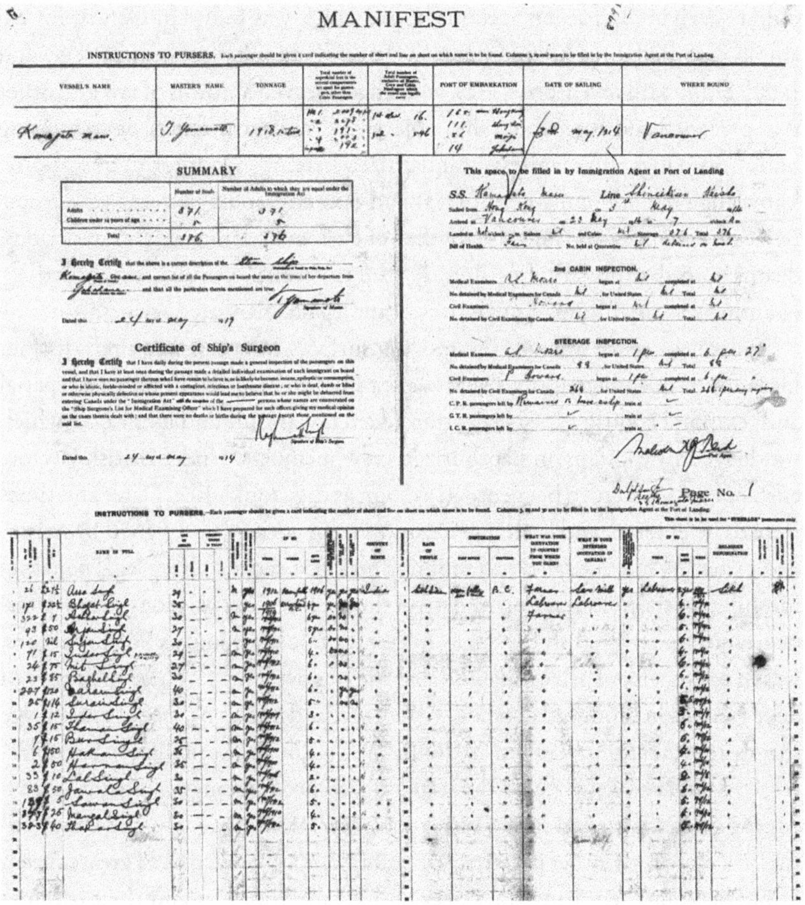
MANIFEST

INSTRUCTIONS TO PURSERS.

SUMMARY

Certificate of Ship's Surgeon

This space to be filled in by Immigration Agent at Port of Landing

2nd CABIN INSPECTION.

STEERAGE INSPECTION.

Page No. 1

INSTRUCTIONS TO PURSERS.

FIGURE 3.1. The *Komagata Maru*'s manifest, pages 1–2. (Image courtesy of Library and Archives Canada, Canada Department of Immigration, 24 May 1914. Accessed from http://komagatamarujourney.ca/node/3262)

were "illegals" and "undesirables" and would not be permitted to enter the Dominion.[57]

In her influential study, *The History of the Modern Fact,* Mary Poovey argues that early modern bookkeeping provided the origins for what we now call objective and indisputable truths.[58] Interestingly, many of the mercantilist sources that Poovey draws on are texts that address long-distance travel and trade via sea. Yet nowhere does she consider how the emergence of the modern fact evolved from maritime worlds. Oceans and ships as juridical forms were central to practices of enumeration, classification, and documentation. The oldest surviving European account book, which was found in Genoa, for example, recorded three Mediterranean voyages that took place between 1156 and 1158.[59] Shipboard inventories, logs, and ledgers served as forms of law and order that preceded and augmented the "objectivity" and "neutrality" of accounting books. Ship logs and manifests standardized heterogeneous forms of seaborne knowledge including meteorological and oceanographic patterns (the recurrence of storms, swells, and the rhythm of currents), commercial transactions, deaths, and disciplinary measures. By the thirteenth century, shipboard accounting was significant enough to warrant legally mandated scribes.[60]

Unlike the fixity of land, the moving surfaces of oceans required distinct methods of documentation. Events at sea were to be listed in terms of spatial and temporal coordinates. Navigation relied on latitude and longitude, which was logged by captains and authorized crew members. Under British law, occurrences at sea were to be recorded as soon as they took place. Dates and times were to be entered, and each line item was to be verified and signed by master and mate.[61] While the failure to submit a manifest carried severe legal penalties for shipmasters, the alteration or destruction of logbooks was considered a misdemeanor under English law.[62] Double-entry bookkeeping, as Poovey argues, was in effect a form of writing *and* a mode of governing.[63] These processes of documentation produced detailed, systematic, and uniform types of knowledge that carried an unprecedented credibility and authority, seen then to be "objective."[64] Manifests were vital to the standardized production of maritime knowledges that could be used to track the movement of ships, people, and commodities. By plotting weather patterns, for example, mariners acquired greater levels of predictability, ensuring the safety and security of ships and their cargo at sea. As a technology of jurisdiction, ship manifests afforded legal authority to shipmasters and crews. By drawing on maritime expertise, manifests rendered oceans to be intelligible and thus potentially governable.

In its dual authority at sea and in port, the ship manifest reconciled the competing jurisdictions of the common law and admiralty law. It offered one way of linking land, sea, and littoral in legal regimes. As ships traveled from the high seas to the three-mile territorial border and into ports of call, their legal status changed in ways that generated jurisdictional disputes. According to Sir Francis Taylor Piggott, an English lawyer and colonial administrator, ships were "part of the territory of the country to which they belong: *i.e.* in which they are registered." As such, they came under the authority "of the country whose flag they are entitled to fly." Piggott called this "the 'floating island' theory," whereby ships became an extension of the empires and polities they represented.[65] Appointed first as the procurer-general of Mauritius and later as chief justice of

Hong Kong, Piggott resided on islands and was therefore surrounded by water. As a result, he was well aware of the legal tensions between land, sea, and territorial waters in ports of call. In *Nationality: Including Naturalization and English Law on the High Seas and Beyond the Realm* (1907), he characterized admiralty law and the common law as overlapping and interconnected legal orders, rather than distinct or separate ones. If ships were "floating islands" while at sea, what happened when they reached land, he asked. Though Piggott saw merchant ships as "private property protected by the flag," their legal identity became far more ambiguous and uncertain when vessels anchored in coastal areas. For Grotius, the distinction between land and sea was elemental, juridical, and beyond question. In Piggot's view, which was closer to Welwod's, these divisions were plural and open to debate. "When ships leave the high seas and enter foreign harbors or other dominion waters, questions of considerable difficulty arise," Piggott claimed. "Does the jurisdiction of the Legislature of the flag absolutely prevail? or does it absolutely cease? or does it continue to some limited degree by general consent?"[66] The landfall of ships, Piggott continued, put "the 'floating island' theory to the touch: What in fact is the law governing ships in foreign ports," he queried.[67] The *Komagata Maru*'s landing in Vancouver Harbour repositioned the legal status of the ship and its passengers from a quotidian jurisdictional question to an urgent Dominion and imperial concern.

By the early twentieth century, manifests were no longer significant to the sea alone. They were absorbed into wider structures of terrestrial and territorial control. Under admiralty law, shipmasters had to swear to the accuracy of their manifests under oath. As a result, these modes of documentation were often called as legal evidence in commercial disputes and criminal proceedings, including those involving "alien immigrant passengers."[68] At the Board of Inquiry in Vancouver, as Hopkinson read Munshi Singh's age, marital status, and occupation from the manifest, Bird immediately protested. "I object to the Manifest being put in in that way as it is not evidence," he argued. It "should not be read as to any statements therein contained without the evidence of the man who made up the manifest, to show that these statements were made by this man."[69] However, Bird's objections were promptly dismissed. In Malcolm Reid's assessment, ship manifests were not only an expression of admiralty law but also an extension of immigration regulations. By characterizing the manifest as a form of authority that controlled who could enter the country, Reid responded to Bird as follows: "Before any passengers are permitted to leave the Vessel, in Canada, the Immigration Officer in charge, or any Officer directed by me, may go on Board such vessel and examine and take extracts from the Manifest of passengers and their bill of health."[70] The ship manifest, he insisted, was necessary to ensure the effective administration of immigration policy. "These manifests are prepared according to the requirements of the company and under the supervision of the Superintendent," Reid asserted, "and if Mr. Bird's objection was sustained in this case it would simply mean that before any ship is allowed to disembark with passengers, we would have to doubt the manifest entirely."[71] Any suspicions regarding the authority and legitimacy of the manifest, he continued, "would simply tie up the whole work of the Immigration Department."[72] Though Hopkinson could not verify who authored the manifest, only that it was "prepared on Board the Komagata Maru after her arrival," Reid insisted on its authority and legality. The manifest was "prepared according to the [Immigration] Act" and was therefore to "be accepted as credible evidence."[73]

As systems of enumeration, ship manifests furnished local authorities with information that was vital to the regulation of territorial borders. In August 1914, as the *Komagata Maru* was en route from Vancouver to Calcutta, and as the Indian government was finalizing the Ingress into India Ordinance, the manifest became key to monitoring the entry and exit of all Indian nationals suspected of being radicalized while abroad. It allowed colonial officials to identify and apprehend Indian passengers suspected of sedition and criminality, before they landed and disembarked. "All steamers on arrival put in a list of passengers," wrote R. E. Enthoven on behalf of the Indian colonial government. "We can, therefore, arrange to let the police know at once of these men's arrival."[74] Ship manifests granted Canadian and Indian authorities the power to identify, arrest, and detain seaborne Indians who would prove elusive once they reached land.

At the end of a long day of testimony that centered on the competing and overlapping jurisdictions of admiralty law and immigration law and the accuracy and authority of the ship manifest, the board reached a unanimous decision. Munshi Singh violated all three orders-in-council. He did not have $200 on his person; he did not arrive in Canada via continuous journey; and he was far more likely to become a laborer in British Columbia than a farmer. But Hopkinson questioned the veracity of the manifest by highlighting its conflicting and fraudulent details. Munshi Singh, he insisted, was "likely to be a public charge owing to the fact that he has a very small amount of money, namely the sum of $20.00." Though he has "declared on the Manifest as a person who intends to be a farmer in this country, and he has reiterated that statement to me in my preliminary examination," Hopkinson continued, "I believe that the man has no more intention of being a farmer than I have." The "reasons for this are, that the man, for a start, has not sufficient money to make a living for a month, much less to buy a farm in this country." Ninety percent of the "2500 East Indians resident in this country," Hopkinson charged, "are engaged as Labourers and the remaining 10% are divided between farmers and real estate operators."[75] Disputing the "facts" of the manifest and turning the document against its own prescribed legal authority, Hopkinson claimed that Munshi Singh would most certainly become a laborer in British Columbia. Under the Dominion's immigration laws, including its three orders-in-council, and notwithstanding what was recorded on the manifest, he and the remaining passengers were to be deported.

The Board of Inquiry hearing marked the beginning of a set of legal deliberations regarding the competing authority of admiralty law, immigration law, and much more. The board's decision raised a set of urgent questions as to where Dominion, imperial, and provincial jurisdiction began and ended. After receiving news of the unfavorable decision, Bird immediately filed a writ of habeas corpus with the British Columbia Supreme Court. But the writ was denied. He then appealed to the British Columbia Court of Appeal, which happened to be sitting in Victoria the following day. Robert Cassidy, a local lawyer who had considerable experience with Japanese immigration accompanied Bird as senior counsel.[76] On 29 and 30 June 1914, they argued their case before five appellate court judges, Chief Justice J. A. MacDonald and Justices W. A. Galliher, P. A. E. Irving, A. Martin, and A. E. McPhillips. One week later, following a vigorous set of deliberations over the jurisdictional divides between land, sea, and subjecthood, the court reinforced Canada's authority and autonomy. In so doing, it fortified the racial, territorial, and temporal asymmetries of the British Empire, the vertical relations between Dominions and colonies, and the appropriate place and time of Indian subjects.

Munshi Singh and "the Law of the Land"

Efforts to exclude British subjects from the Dominions, as the *New York Times* article of 20 July 1914 suggests, prompted a spirited debate on the racial and legal divisions and the spatial and temporal arrangements that formed the basis of imperial authority. The *Komagata Maru*'s detention in Vancouver Harbour grounded these discussions in local contests over jurisdiction, particularly the shared and overlapping Dominion and provincial orders, including the extent to which their respective domains of authority extended over land, sea, and coastal waters. While the ship was on the Pacific and en route to Vancouver, immigration officials and politicians insisted on Canada's legal authority and legitimacy to control its territorial borders. As the Court of Appeal viewed it, jurisdictional lines were firm and fixed: "The Canada Parliament is a sovereign parliament," Justice McPhillips argued, and it held the right to decide on the inclusion and exclusion of immigrants, irrespective of whether they were British subjects.[77] However, jurisdictional uncertainty and ambiguity featured prominently in Bird and Cassidy's legal strategy. By emphasizing the juridical and political divides between Britain, Canada, and British Columbia, they questioned the origins and foundation of Dominion sovereignty. Which laws were applicable to itinerant British subjects who crisscrossed the so-called free sea via ship? Did the *Komagata Maru*, while anchored in Vancouver Harbour, fall under federal jurisdiction or had the vessel already landed in British Columbia? Did the ship's arrival come under the domain of immigration controls, or were passengers as British subjects, to be granted civil rights? Whose authority prevailed, that of Britain, of Canada, or of British Columbia?

By posing these questions to the court, Bird and Cassidy sought to undermine the Dominion's legal and political authority in several ways. Canada, they argued—echoing the *New York Times*—could not lawfully prevent the entry of British subjects. Though the Dominion had recently dealt with whether "aliens," including Chinese and Japanese migrants, were permitted to enter the country, there was "no case yet tried or decided" in any court, "where the question of a British subject's right to come into Canada has been dealt with."[78] If the three orders-in-council that sought to prohibit the admission of Indian migrants were applicable to British subjects, Bird added, they would surely impinge on British imperial sovereignty and would therefore be "contrary to justice."[79] The ship had already been anchored in Vancouver Harbour for over a month (see fig. 3.2). As a result, it fell under the authority and jurisdiction of British Columbia. Since all the passengers were British subjects, the legal issues at hand were not matters of immigration, Bird and Cassidy maintained, but of civil rights. "A law for the detention and deportation of a person rejected as an immigrant," they explained, "is certainly an interference with 'civil rights within the Province' which all immigrants possess from the moment they enter the province, i.e. Provincial waters."[80] Despite his legal and political status as a British subject, Munshi Singh was "rejected as an immigrant" by the Board of Inquiry. He was "ordered to be deprived of his liberty" by being "imprisoned on a ship [in provincial waters] and carried over seas against his will."[81] Civil rights, Bird and Cassidy reminded the court, were not a federal matter; they were under "the exclusive control of the Provincial legislature." Finally, the continuous journey legislation, they insisted, was explicitly and incorrectly aimed at curtailing the flow of Indian migration across the Pacific only. Like the order-in-council that prohibited unskilled laborers from entering British Columbia, this regulation was also aimed at restricting admission to Canada's

FIGURE 3.2. The *Komagata Maru* anchored in Vancouver Harbour within the three-mile territorial line. (Photo courtesy of City of Vancouver Archives)

west coast. The continuous journey provision did not apply to Indians who crossed the Atlantic or those "coming in from Montreal, or Quebec or other places," Bird and Cassidy argued.[82] Its unequal application and enforcement are precisely what prompted Husain Rahim to propose the Atlantic as a viable route of travel. By denying entry only to those at Pacific ports, Bird and Cassidy urged, the Dominion openly violated the federal/provincial division of powers. In other words, Canada exceeded its legal, political, and territorial authority by extending its rule westward and across the sea.

While the ship manifest featured prominently in the Board of Inquiry hearing, the juridical status of oceans and ships became critical to the Court of Appeal's deliberations over the extent and limits of provincial and Dominion control. As the *Komagata Maru* sat detained in Vancouver Harbour and within the three-mile limit prescribed by British and international law, Bird and Cassidy argued that the passengers had already reached British Columbia. Though confined on an anchored ship, they were visibly proximate to the shoreline and had technically made landfall. As British subjects, the passengers were not to be treated as immigrants or "aliens," they claimed, but were to be granted the same rights as residents of the province. The "moment a British subject comes to Canada," Cassidy explained, and "comes within the three-mile limit," he should be allowed to disembark. Even though "the Dominion upon the subject of immigration may have just passed a law" that states that "he is not to be allowed to enter Canada," the Dominion cannot then declare, "Not only shall you not enter Canada, but we will arrest you—we authorize your arrest, we authorize your detention and we authorize your deportation."[83] To do so would be to violate that person's civil rights.

Under the British North America Act, the Dominion government held responsibility over coastal waters, maritime navigation, aboriginal peoples, and reserve lands. The provinces, by contrast, were responsible for labor, education, natural resources, and civil rights. The two governmental entities shared jurisdiction, often uneasily, over matters of immigration. That the passengers were detained aboard a ship that was still anchored in port only exacerbated these tensions further. But the court used this to its advantage and disagreed with Bird and Cassidy's arguments, regardless of how well they were crafted. It "is rather interesting," Chief Justice MacDonald opined, that "when this man [Munshi Singh] was on board ship" and "within the 3-mile limit," you described him as being "within British Columbia."[84] Yet, the Dominion "has authority over the waters of Canada, even the harbours of Canada, which would include Vancouver." Was Munshi Singh "really in British Columbia, or under the jurisdiction of British Columbia" or was he in Canada if he was not yet "on a British shore," Justice MacDonald queried.[85] In his rejoinder, Cassidy challenged these jurisdictional divides even further by distinguishing the anchored ship from the passengers on board. "I quite agree that the Dominion has exclusive jurisdiction over harbours and may make any regulation with regard to ships," he explained, "*but not persons found upon ships in British Columbia.*"[86] The Dominion may have legitimate control over "Harbours, Waters, Ships, Navigation," but "with regard to the civil rights of the people on the ships I think these are within the jurisdiction of the Province."[87] Echoing Sir Francis Piggott, Cassidy also disputed the "floating island theory." When in port, the ship became a legal entity that was situated somewhere between land and sea and between federal and provincial control.

Bird and Cassidy probed even further. If Indians as British subjects were peripatetic, continually crossing imperial jurisdictions via ship, how was their legal and political standing to be decided? In other words, how was British subjecthood to be defined and determined within the itinerancy of maritime worlds? "There are cases in the books with which lawyers are familiar," Justice McPhillips replied, "where British subjects have lived in India and Canada who originally came from the British Isles." The question of which law applied was often prominent "in cases of intestacy as to the personal estate, under which law should it be distributed."[88] British subjects, McPhillips reasoned, could not make a choice as to which law was most relevant or applicable: "Just because you are a British subject . . . can you come from India to Canada" and claim you now "have all the rights of a Canadian, and return to India and have all English rights"?[89] One must "have domicile to get a civil status, and [to] have the local law applied." Therefore, a British subject "may not leave India and come to British Columbia," and the minute he is "within the 3 mile limit" say that he is "clothed within the attributes of a citizen of Canada."[90] An immigrant, Justice Martin added, "is not immediately . . . freed from the operation of laws relating to the subject-matter of immigration merely because he happens to come within the three-mile-limit."[91] Dominion jurisdiction, he clarified, remains attached "to him at least till after he is permitted to land in conformity with the [Immigration] Act."[92] The "exercise of Federal jurisdiction," Justice Martin added, "necessarily affects civil rights, including . . . personal liberty." The most vivid illustration "occurs in connection with quarantine . . . wherein whole shiploads of people, traders, merchants, tourists, immigrants and others, have been frequently detained for weeks at a time in quarantine stations on shore."[93] The *Komagata Maru* passengers were well within the three-mile limit, all agreed. However, the court concluded that their arrival directly contravened Canada's Immigration Act. Irrespective of whether they were British subjects, they were not domiciled in British Columbia or Canada, and thus were not entitled to the civil rights that Canadians could claim.

Ultimately, the jurisdictional tensions between land and sea, port and ship, and province and Dominion that Bird and Cassidy deployed as part of their legal arguments before the Court of Appeal were superseded by deliberations over the court's own authority. After hearing the case, the Court of Appeal concluded that under the British North America Act, it held no jurisdiction to evaluate or assess the laws of Parliament. The court, Chief Justice MacDonald clarified, "cannot review a decision upon a question which the board was authorized to decide."[94] The court was not hearing an appeal "from the decision of the Board of Inquiry," Justice Irving added. The issue at hand was whether Munshi Singh had been illegally restrained, not whether he should be allowed off the ship and into Canada.[95] In public debate, the court's authority emerged as the most significant jurisdictional question at hand. On 8 July 1914, two days after the Court of Appeal issued its judgment, the following cartoon appeared in the *Vancouver Sun* (see fig. 3.3). The caricature depicts an Indian migrant, who as a proxy for the *Komagata Maru* passengers, is lawfully prevented from entering Canada. Despite the decision, he sits patiently though hopelessly at the Dominion's door. Only the minister of the interior—a federal official—held the authority to hear his appeal. The minister had sole prerogative to reverse

FIGURE 3.3. "The Hindu Question as It Stands." *Vancouver Sun,* 8 July 1914, 1. (Image courtesy of *Vancouver Sun*)

the Board's decision, unlock the door, and grant the Indian entry. "There is a complete chain of authority from the Sovereign, with the assent of Imperial Parliament, down to the Board of Inquiry," Justice Irving insisted, "and the proceedings are, on their face, regular in every respect."[96] The Court of Appeal, Justice McPhillips clarified, "cannot attract themselves to jurisdiction. Jurisdiction must be conferred" only by parliament.[97] Inscribed on the Dominion's door was "THE LAW" of "CANADA," which authorized and sanctioned its immigration regulations. By evoking parliamentary statute as the ultimate and incontestable source of Dominion authority, the *Vancouver Sun* reinforced the court's decision and the jurisdictional chain of command that it established. The "law of the land," as the law of Canada originated with the arrival of the British.[98] The British North America Act granted the Dominion undisputed authority to enact and enforce legislation and to safeguard its territorial borders from the encroachment of "aliens" and from the influx of undesirables, including British subjects. These legal determinations, the *Vancouver Sun* implied, were secured as much by territory as they were by race and temporality. After all, the Sikh was *waiting* at the Dominion's door.

For scholars writing on late nineteenth- and early twentieth-century Chinese, Japanese, and Indian migration to the Dominions, race has figured prominently as a historiographical explanation for immigration exclusions and prohibitions.[99] In much of this scholarship, however, race is defined narrowly through the prevailing ideologies of colonial and imperial authorities. "As a consequence of white settler attitudes," Robert Huttenback argues, "a main goal of colonial legislation became the curtailment of non-white immigration."[100] The cultivation of whiteness, others have suggested, was a national and transnational project to which restrictive immigration laws were central.[101] But racial inclusion/exclusion was not the result of attitudes or ideologies alone.[102] Race worked as a regime of power, as a structuring and persistent force, that operated through land/sea, space/time, and people/populations.[103] As my reading of *Re Munshi Singh* suggests, racial power gained its force jurisdictionally, by dividing people into nations and civilizations and by inscribing them into vertical geographies and developmentalist histories. Racial superiority/inferiority circulated in multiple directions as a politically and legally charged mode of government, one that conferred meanings on place, status, and subjecthood, while ascribing a force and legitimacy to British, Dominion, and Indian authority. Imposing symbolic and material import to the territorial and temporal divides between Dominions, colonies, and protectorates, and producing variegated conceptions of British subjecthood, racial power was fused to the very foundation and architecture of imperial rule.[104] The shaded regions of the British Empire, as I suggest earlier in this chapter, only fortified territorial divisions in racial and temporal terms.[105] Whereas India was viewed as a land and people without history, the Dominions—including Canada—were characterized as "the strong and fruitful daughters of Britannia."[106] Moving ships, like the *Komagata Maru,* brought these racial, territorial, and temporal asymmetries directly to the fore and into conflict and dispute.

Shortly after the vessel arrived in Vancouver, the *Leader,* an Allahabad newspaper, reported that "another steamer" was scheduled to depart "Hong Kong for Canada with a number of Indian passengers on board."[107] By the 1910s, this was a familiar and recurring narrative. But what was unusual in this particular account was the author's description of the empire as unequally divided between Dominions and colonies. "India is cheerfully content to be part of the empire but not as the footstool of Canada and Australia and South Africa and New Zealand." Rather, "a nobler destiny was promised her by the Sovereign and the Parliament of the United Kingdom, and she is preparing herself assiduously for the ideal of equality and internal self-government with the generous aid and under the wise tutelage of England herself."[108] Some Indian observers readily accepted these assessments of the racial and temporal lag between India and Britain. But it was a condition of the present that would eventually diminish in the future. Others had little patience for the exalted Dominions. "The convention has grown up that the self-governing colonies should not be interfered with," wrote *Indian Opinion,* Gandhi's Natal newspaper. Yet "Imperial obligations have been incurred in India and other Eastern dependencies which cannot possibly be ignored." The trouble "is that the people who direct imperial affairs cannot decide how to bring the two jarring elements into harmony, nor do they see how severely they are straining the bonds that unite the dependencies to the Empire."[109] India's "self-respect and honour will only be satisfied if Indians in the colonies get the identical treatment that colonists get in India."[110] For Indian migrants, traders, and travelers, the empire could only be symmetrical if racial inequality—expressed in terms of time, space, and status—was finally eradicated.

The racial and temporal logics of jurisdiction were equally evident in discussions of British subjecthood. In "The Dominions and India," an essay penned by Hy S. L. Polak, a prominent lawyer and honorary secretary of the Indians Overseas Association in South Africa, the inhabitants of the empire were sharply divided into two classes, "British citizens" and "British subjects." The latter, "including the people of India," were believed to be "subordinate to the former."[111] "'British citizens,' merely by their being self-governing, in the political sense," Polak continued, "are fitted to control the destinies of the subordinate class of 'British subjects.'" Indeed, "it is their 'supreme duty' to do [so], until the latter have achieved the sublime heights of self-government already gained by the more fortunate and superior—in fact, the Imperial—class." These differentiations, Polak charged, were "merely Teutonism in another form, though its authors do not appear to be aware of it."[112] The distinction between "citizens" and "subjects," Mahmood Mamdani argues in another context, created a foundational dividing line in British colonial and imperial governance. It categorized populations as either "natives" or "settlers," and in so doing introduced an entire bureaucracy of direct and indirect rule.[113] Importantly, these methods of colonial classification and administration were configured as much by race and time as they were by geography and territoriality. The "British rulers of India," remarked Henry Sumner Maine, "are like men bound to make their watches keep true time in two longitudes at once."[114] Citizenship would remain "a privilege of the civilized; the uncivilized would be subject to an all-round tutelage."[115] In *Re Munshi Singh,* the Court of Appeal endorsed this separation between "citizen" and "subject." The presumed racial and temporal aperture that distinguished India from the Dominions ensured that British subjecthood would remain unequal, and the empire would endure as racially, territorially, and temporally divided and irreconcilable.

Like supporters and sympathizers across the Pacific and Indian Oceans, Bird and Cassidy were well aware that imperial divisions were racially charged. At the Court of Appeal, their other strategy was to dispute the temporal and territorial claims to Dominion jurisdiction by revealing its underlying racial foundations. To begin with, Bird questioned the relevance and meaning of the order-in-council, which stated that "no immigrant of any Asiatic race shall be permitted to land in Canada unless such immigrant possessed $200."[116] The term "Asiatic," he argued, was "ethnologically incorrect and too indefinite to be capable of application" to Indians.[117] There is "no such thing as an Asiatic Race" he charged, and its use in the statute "is incapable of any understanding and is liable to lead to confusion and uncertainty."[118] According to the *Hindu International Encyclopedia,* which Bird consulted, and from which he read aloud in court, the "entire population of Asia is composed of three great races," including the "white race." The "white inhabitants indigenous to Asia constitute about a tenth of the total population" and represent "a wonderful diversity of type, both mental and physical." Asia's white races embraced "peoples in various stages of civilization, ranging from the cultured Hindu with their great cities, down to the tribes of the Desert."[119] Both "Caucasians and the Semites," he elaborated, "have been the original occupants of Asia Minor." The Caucasians of Asia "are of the same branch as the peoples of England," he continued, "and 99 per cent of applicants for admission to Canada are broadly speaking" from this part of "the Asiatic race."[120] According to these sources, and against prevailing views, Bird insisted that whites and Asians were racially indistinguishable. "Our forefathers," he declared proudly, "are of the same race as the Hindus — the Caucasian race."[121] "Asiatics," including Indians, he concluded, should be allowed to travel along the free sea and to enter the white Dominions.

Given the high legal and political stakes of racial categorization, it is hardly surprising that the appellate court rejected Bird's arguments so vehemently. "It was asserted by counsel for the appellant," replied Justice McPhillips, "that the Hindus are of the Caucasian race, akin to the English."[122] Membership in the "Asiatic" race was "in no way crucial" to the Dominion's case, McPhillips continued. Canada has "the right to deport under the provisions of the Immigration Act and the orders in council irrespective of race" and "irrespective of nationality." In crafting his argument, Justice McPhillips invoked an alternative and more conventional genealogy of race that he narrated through British colonial history.[123] When "the words 'Asiatic race' are used in the order in council, PC 24, the words are, in their meaning, comprehensive and precise enough to cover the Hindu race, of which the appellant is one," he explained. As "early as 1784, an association was formed and named the Asiatic Society in Calcutta to extend knowledge of the Sanskrit language and literature." According to "the History of India," edited by "A. W. Williams, Professor of Indo-Iranian languages in Columbia University," we "read of the 'Asiatic races' including therein the people of India."[124] To support his claim that Indians were "Asiatics" and not Caucasians, McPhillips turned to the *Encyclopedia Britannica* (1910):

> The Aryans of India are probably the most settled and civilized of all Asiatic Races. . . . Asiatics stand on a higher level than the natives of Africa or America, but do not possess the special material civilization of Western Europe. . . . Asiatics have not the same sentiment of independence and freedom as Europeans. Individuals are thought as members of a family, state or religion, rather than as entities with a destiny and rights of their own. This leads to autocracy in politics, fatalism in religion, and conservativism in both.[125]

The order-in-council, Justice McPhillips urged, was purposefully and legitimately directed at the "Asiatic race," which, based on the sources of "expert knowledge" he consulted, included British subjects from India. Not commenting directly on the purported superiority of "Asiatics" over "the natives of Africa or America," McPhillips explained that the Dominion's refusal to allow entry to Indian migrants and travelers was premised on questions of racial desirability, suitability, and assimilability. The British North America Act, or the law of the land, authorized Canada to pass legislation in the interests of peace, order, and good government.[126] The orders-in-council, including the continuous journey regulation and the one that required "immigrants of any Asiatic race" to have $200 on arrival were enacted in this spirit.

In defending the term "Asiatic" and in assessing its relevance to the case at hand, Justice McPhillips reinscribed the racial, territorial, and temporal divides that separated Dominion and colony and citizen and subject. The "Hindu race, as well as the Asiatic race in general," he maintained, were "in their conception of life and ideas of society, fundamentally different to the Anglo-Saxon and Celtic races, and European races in general."[127] Indians who left the subcontinent and migrated elsewhere, he opined, might be superior to other races in the empire including "natives of Africa or America," but given their customs, habits, and political-legal orientations, they remained unsuited to reside as equals among whites. "Further acquaintance with the subject shews that the better classes of the Asiatic races are not given to leave their own countries—they are non-immigrant classes, greatly attached to their homes." The ones "who become immigrants," McPhillips continued, are "without disparagement to them, *un-desirables in Canada,* where a very different civilization exists. The laws of this country are unsuited to them, and their ways and ideas may well be a menace to the well-being of the Canadian people."[128] The conceptions of racial inferiority evoked by McPhillips encouraged Indians not to pursue transoceanic travel and to remain on the subcontinent. His position directly opposed the advice given by Husain Rahim and Gurdit Singh, who encouraged their countrymen to leave India and travel to North America. In his reasoning, Justice McPhillips reinforced the position that the sea was free only to Europeans and, in so doing, fortified the British Empire as an unequal and asymmetrical whole.

Unlike earlier objections to Indian migration that centered on climate, Justice McPhillips emphasized the racial unsuitability of Indian migrants and travelers on account of their ostensibly strange beliefs and customs, especially the "very different character of their family life, rules of society and law."[129] The historical, cultural, and religious philosophies practiced by Indians, irrespective of region, religion, or caste, rendered them racially and temporally incompatible to Canadian ways of life. For McPhillips, it was in the best interests of Indians as British subjects and of the empire as a whole, if they stayed "within the confines of their respective countries in the continent of Asia." Indian "customs are not in vogue" in Canada, he continued, and "adhesion to them" only results in "disturbances destructive to the well-being of society and against the maintenance of peace, order and good government."[130] It was the personal law system in India, Justice McPhillips added, that was most objectionable and even antithetical to Canadian ways of life. To emphasize this point, he turned to Lord Watson's decision in *Abd-ul-Messih v. Chukri Farra* (1888), a case heard by the Privy Council, the empire's highest court. According to the laws of India, Watson opined, "certain castes and creeds are ... governed by their own peculiar rules and customs." As such, "an Indian domicile of succession may involve the application of Hindu or Mohommedan [*sic*] law; but these rules and customs are an integral part of the municipal law administered by the territorial tribunals."[131] These personal laws, McPhillips cautioned, would only undermine what the *Vancouver Sun* characterized as "THE LAW" of "CANADA." Personal laws "will not conform with national ideals in Canada," and "to introduce any such laws ... or give them the effect of law as applied to people domiciled in Canada" would produce much discontent. For Justice McPhillips, "peoples of non-assimilative—and by nature properly non-assimilative—race should not come to Canada" and should "remain of residence in their country of origin and there do their share, as they have in the past, in the preservation and development of the Empire."[132] Thus, Indians were locked once more in the "waiting room of history" until they were ready to travel the seas and live in the Dominions among whites.[133] The court's findings were portrayed vividly in the *Vancouver Sun*'s depiction of *Re Munshi Singh*.

The five appellate judges agreed, albeit for different reasons, that Canada's Immigration Act was not discriminatory or ultra vires. Justice Irving stated that the orders-in-council were applicable to everyone, including British subjects, irrespective of their race or nationality. These latest exclusions only added to a long and expanding list that included "persons mentally and physically defective; diseased persons, criminals, beggars and vagrants; [and] charity immigrants."[134] For Justice Martin, charges of racial inequality, such as the ones brought forth by Bird and Cassidy, glossed the marked realities of racial difference and the necessary force of imperial governance. British subjects did not enjoy equality in political or legal status, he claimed. Nor were they entitled to fair and equitable treatment in the Dominions and beyond. Three of the five judges made this point explicitly. Justice McPhillips cited the *Encyclopedia Britannica*, which characterized Indians as more civilized than indigenous peoples in North America and Africa but racially inferior to Europeans. Justice MacDonald recognized that specific sections of the orders-in-council "could not be" and were "not intended to have been made operative without discrimination in favor of some races whose legal *status* to be admitted to Canada was already fixed by statute or treaty."[135] Looking inward, Justice Martin emphasized the inequalities inherent in British subjecthood. These asymmetries were especially evident in the conditions facing indigenous peoples. "Much was said about discrimination between the citizens and races of the Empire," he remarked. It "was suggested [by Bird and Cassidy] that Canada had not the right to exclude British subjects coming from other parts of the Empire."[136] But for Justice Martin charges of discrimination were "not a ground of attack upon an Act of Parliament within its jurisdiction." The enactment and enforcement of immigration legislation, he elaborated, "constantly and necessarily involves the different treatment of various classes, *even of the Crown's own subjects*."[137] To make this point as clear as possible, Martin invoked the case of indigenous peoples in Canada. To fortify Dominion claims to territorial autonomy, as I discuss further below, the court mobilized indigeneity as yet another reason why the *Komagata Maru* and its passengers needed to be deported.

"Our Own Native Indians"

The Court of Appeal argued that Canada's authority to prohibit the *Komagata Maru*'s landing was drawn from the laws of Parliament, which originated in the British Imperial government. The British North America Act united the provinces of Canada, Nova Scotia, and New Brunswick into one Dominion for "the welfare of the provinces" and to "promote the interests of the British Empire."[138] In legal proceedings surrounding the ship, the act was invoked repeatedly as both the origin and the legal and political foundation of Dominion authority. In terms of Schmitt's sociopolitical philosophy, the British North America Act was a founding law, one that afforded an order and orientation to land appropriations.[139] The act permitted Canada to enact legislation in matters of immigration and territorial sovereignty. Its undisputed authority as "the law of the land" was used to dispossess indigenous peoples, while maintaining Canada's place within the British imperial whole. As the *Vancouver Sun* characterized it, the Dominion's jurisdiction over its borders was derived from "THE LAW" of parliamentary statute and not from "the law" of judicial authority. Recurring references to the British North America Act implied that Canada was established on a monolithic and unitary legal order, one that drew a clear and direct line of sovereignty and authority from London to Ottawa and Vancouver.

The inauguration and imposition of British law in colonial contexts, no matter how negotiated or translated, was always already an act of racial and colonial violence.[140] For Schmitt, the seizure of land is "the primeval act in founding law."[141] Though *The Nomos of the Earth* makes little mention of indigenous peoples, Schmitt acknowledges that the commencement and expansion of European resettlement in the "New World" and elsewhere necessitated processes of large-scale and violent displacement. The deterritorialization of indigenous peoples was instantiated in a myriad of ways, including regimes of private property that distinguished "firm land" from "free sea." Recall that in Grotius's view land could be owned and occupied in ways that oceans could not. Private property, many insisted, was deeply entangled with racial conceptions of citizenship. Maxwell Smith put it accordingly: "This country [Canada] has been pioneered, opened up and developed to the status of a nation by white people and we contend that the full privileges of Canadian citizenship and the right to own property within the Dominion should be withheld from all save qualified and desirable members of the white race whether British subjects or not."[142]

In *Re Munshi Singh*, "THE LAW" of the land rendered Indians, irrespective of their legal and political status, racially unsuited for entry to the Dominion. Recurring references to "THE LAW" reaffirmed Dominion authority in other ways as well, suggesting that there was only one law, thereby effacing the presence of indigenous legal and political orders. To be sure, the Squamish, Musqueam, and Tsleil-Waututh had their respective conceptions of sovereignty and authority. They never ceded their ownership over land, sea, waterways, or natural resources. Yet, in *Re Munshi Singh*, indigenous peoples were recognized momentarily, only to be erased repeatedly, through the court's affirmation of Dominion authority. Significantly, the court's evocation of indigeneity would coalesce unexpectedly with anticolonial contests over the *Komagata Maru* in Vancouver and beyond.

If the origins of law and history were dated from the arrival of Europeans, as myths of colonial resettlement suggest, then the relationship between indigenous peoples and the colonial state has always existed in temporalized form.[143] Legal redress for territorial dispossession and other forms of colonial violence has demanded that indigenous communities be prepared to trace their existence "as peoples" to a time before European arrival.[144] The law's desire for proof of "priorness" has always been refracted through a linear chronology, one that has placed indigenous peoples in an impossible position of trying to establish their existence in multiple temporalities at once.[145] Heterotemporality may be a rich lived experience, but it is not easily recognizable or reconcilable in law.[146] These temporalities of settler colonialism, as Chickasaw scholar Jodi Byrd argues, are not specific to legal contexts alone. In the literature on U.S. imperialism, she argues, indigenous peoples are characteristically evoked "as past tense presences" as "*spectral,* implied and felt."[147] In colonial mythologies inspired and informed by national legalities, she claims, indigenous peoples have been identified as prior and thus vanishing. The court's invocation of indigeneity in *Re Munshi Singh* called forth another temporal order. Theirs was not an appeal to an imaginary past but to the present and future. Justice Martin and Justice McPhillips cited indigeneity as a temporal figure, one that emphasized the present legal status of indigenous communities, while also anticipating their political futures.[148]

In their arguments to the British Columbia Court of Appeal, Bird and Cassidy insisted that Canada held no jurisdiction to prohibit the entry of Indians. In response, W. B. A. Ritchie, a lawyer for the immigration department, drew the court's attention to a lengthy history in which British subjects were regularly excluded and disenfranchised. The Dominion legislature "or the local legislature of any province has an authority as plenary and as ample as the Imperial Parliament in the plentitude of its powers," he explained.[149] Legislatures were known to prohibit entry to British subjects on the basis of race and nationality and could also reject those naturalized. The racial restrictions and exclusions imposed on British subjects, Justice McPhillips added, were especially salient in the case of indigenous people. "The original sons of the soil of Canada," he explained, "are aborigines, and to-day they are deprived of a good many civil rights. They are not enfranchised, they cannot vote." Their subordinate status, which was never questioned or challenged by the judges or lawyers in the case, was determined by their putative racial, temporal, and civilizational differences from Europeans. Indigenous people in Canada, Justice Martin insisted, were "an absolutely distinct race." On the "American continent," he continued, there were "three main races and two sub races."[150] It was because of these infallible racial divides that indigenous peoples were granted a subservient legal status. Aboriginal peoples "are wards of the Crown, though adult," McPhillips claimed. They "were born here and were the earliest sons of the soil," yet, in the eyes of the court, they remained racially and civilizationally inferior to whites.[151] For Justices McPhillips and Martin, Canada's indigenous populace offered a clear and relevant example of how racial superiority and inferiority, combined with the arrow of time, informed the variegated inequalities of British subjecthood. The diminished status of aboriginal peoples as "wards of the Crown" provided further evidence as to why the racial asymmetries of imperial jurisdictions and the inequalities of racial governance remained a legal and political necessity. Whereas Indian migrants came within the jurisdiction of British imperial rule, indigenous peoples fell firmly under Canadian authority, until they were ready to govern themselves.[152] Neither Indians nor indigenous peoples, the court concluded, were suited to live as equals among whites.

If competing jurisdictions were apparent in the tensions over land/sea and immigration law/admiralty law, they were further evidenced in the juxtaposition of Dominion and indigenous legalities. In what is now Canada, indigenous law preceded European contact and settlement for millennia. It forged the foundations on which Dominion authorities established their unstable, tenuous, and fragile claims to sovereignty. Although many colonists and jurists of the time regarded aboriginal peoples as "lawless"—a lack that supposedly verified their inferiority, legitimized land appropriations, and reinforced the sovereignty of imperial polities—indigenous legalities were the oldest sources of law in what is now Canada.[153] In the view of John Borrows, an Anishinabe/Ojibway legal scholar, indigenous peoples were the first legal practitioners in North America. Indigenous conceptions of law were symbolized, narrated, and conveyed to subsequent generations in a variety of different formats, including stories, totems, and wampum belts.[154] These juridical forms forged the historical and contemporary basis for indigenous sovereignty and legality, even if colonial and imperial authorities did not formally recognize them as such.

According to Borrows, the wampum was one of the founding constitutional documents of the land. Following the Royal Proclamation of 1763, indigenous leaders were invited to attend a summer peace conference that was to take place the following year in Niagara. In the winter preceding the conference, people of the Algonquin and Nippissing nations met with Sir William Johnson, superintendent of Indian affairs, at Oswegatchie, where he persuaded them to invite members of other indigenous communities to attend the gathering. Subsequently, representatives from these nations traveled across the region with a written copy of the Royal Proclamation and several wampum strings. The result was extraordinary. Approximately twenty-four nations and two thousand chiefs were present to witness the event.[155] A two-row wampum belt, originally used as a diplomatic agreement between the Iroquois and Europeans, was exchanged at Niagara to convey indigenous respect and understanding of the proclamation and to affirm the treaty.[156] This was an arrangement based on peace, friendship, and mutual respect, Borrows maintains, an understanding that "discredits the claims of the crown to exercise sovereignty over First Nations."[157] For indigenous peoples, the events at Niagara recognized the plurality of indigenous law and its coexistence with the British common law, while also marking indigenous rights to land, place, and territory. By invoking "THE LAW" of "CANADA" and by designating indigenous peoples "wards of the crown," the Court of Appeal disregarded these rich histories of multiple sovereignties and plural legalities.[158] Characterizations of colonial and racial dependency further eroded the self-determination of indigenous peoples in British Columbia and Canada.

The subject-citizen distinction that figured so prominently in *Re Munshi Singh,* and that legitimized the exclusion of the *Komagata Maru* passengers, was addressed, albeit briefly, in the court's references to indigenous peoples. As British subjects, how were migrants and sojourners from India to be legally categorized in imperial jurisdictions that were home to a large indigenous populace? Did Indians have the same legal and political rights as aboriginal peoples? Were they equal or unequal? Justice Martin addressed these questions directly. The order-in-council that excluded "labourers, skilled or unskilled" from British Columbia, he opined, was enforceable against "British subjects residing in other parts of the Empire," but could just as easily be applied to individuals and populations living "in Canada itself."[159] No one "has ventured to suggest any reason why a native East Indian British subject and labourer from Punjab should be allowed the special privilege of entering the Province of British Columbia," he declared, when "*even a native Canadian Indian, a British subject and labourer from, say, the adjoining sister Province of Alberta, who attempted to cross the boundary into this Province and work in a salmon cannery or a logging camp would be turned back.*"[160] The order-in-council, which was directed at unskilled laborers and artisans, he maintained, was not for use against Indian migrants alone. Nor was it aimed at the Pacific region, as Bird and Cassidy alleged. Instead, Canada's order-in-council could just as easily be used to administer continental movements from east to west and to govern the internal migrations of indigenous peoples as they traveled within the Dominion and across provincial borders.

Justice Martin's comparison between "native Canadian Indians" and Indian migrants referenced another set of racial, territorial, and temporal asymmetries that were foundational to British subjecthood. His logic drew on conceptions of civilizational superiority/inferiority that were expressed through the duties and obligations of the white Dominions. All colonial localities, he intimated, were responsible first and foremost to those residing within its borders. Thus, Canada was directly accountable to British subjects domiciled in the country, including "native Canadian Indians." To permit the entry of unskilled laborers from India, Martin J. opined, would only result in a grave injustice to the country's indigenous peoples who were the "original sons of the soil" and now "wards of the Crown." This would produce "a strange conception and perversion of British citizenship," Justice Martin continued, one that "would give to others [not resident] greater rights and privileges in Canada than are therein possessed and enjoyed by Canadians themselves."[161] Justice Martin's reasoning in *Re Munshi Singh* shared troubling similarities with the arguments advanced by Maxwell Smith, as indicated by his statement with which this chapter begins.

In 1914, indigenous peoples were not "Canadians." Their lands and lives remained firmly under Dominion and provincial control. In what is now British Columbia, aboriginal peoples never ceded their lands through treaty, conquest, or any other means. Only fourteen treaties were signed in the province, and all of these on Vancouver Island.[162] Yet the British Columbia Court of Appeal did not acknowledge the ongoing sovereign claims made by the Coast Salish to land and sea. Under the Indian Act, indigenous peoples across Canada were forcibly placed on reserves, disenfranchised, and pushed beyond any collective national imaginary.[163] Through the violent force of law, they were transformed, in the eyes of the colonial government, from formidable sovereign nations into "wards of the Crown."[164] In his brief reference to "native Canadian Indians," Justice Martin, like Justice McPhillips, reinforced the need for an unequal topography of British subjecthood. Indigenous peoples residing in Canada, he claimed, were to be afforded legal and political rights that could not be extended to Indians from India, even if "Asiatics" stood "on a higher level than the natives of Africa or America."[165] In *Re Munshi Singh,* indigeneity shaped determinations of British subjecthood. Extracted from the lived realities of indigenous peoples, including their ongoing struggles against the Dominion and the province, indigeneity was mobilized by the Court of Appeal as a racial, territorial, and temporal figure that called the presumed equality of "British subject" into question. The judges' deployment of indigeneity brought "native Canadian Indians" from the past—as the "original sons of the soil"—into the present as "wards of the Crown." As dependents of Canada, Justice Martin and

McPhillips insisted, they required legal and political protection that was to be extended from the present indefinitely into the future. Ultimately, indigenous protection necessitated the exclusion of undesirables, including migrants and sojourners from India.

Dominion claims over indigenous peoples were by no means unique to Canada. From the nineteenth century onward, "the colonial mission" in Africa, Mamdani argues, "shifted from civilization to preservation and from assimilation to protection."[166] In 1911, Sir Montagu de Pomeroy Webb, a prominent businessman in India and a founder of the Sind Light Railway and the Karachi Electrical Supply Company, remarked at length on the overlaps and entanglements between indigenous protection and immigration prohibitions in another British Dominion:

> South Africa has a perfect right to say in her own interest whom she will admit and whom she will not admit. (I myself—with all other passengers—was compelled to conform to the requirements of the Immigration Act before the shipping companies would contract to land me in Cape Town). In preparing the New Immigration Act provision has no doubt been made for the exclusion of all undesirables—white and coloured. Such people will be prohibited to land in British Africa, not because they are Indians, or Asiatics, or Syrians, or Russian Jews, *but because as individuals, they do not possess the education or the ability, or the means or the moral and physical attributes of the standard deemed necessary by Government to assist in building up, and carrying forward Great Britain's work amidst South Africa's aboriginal millions.*[167]

There were "roughly, eleven aboriginal inhabitants to every white man, and six or seven white men to every Indian" in South Africa, Webb claimed. But the influx of Indians into the Transvaal, the Orange Free State, and the Cape Colony was upsetting this delicate racial balance.[168] In Webb's view, Indians were not prohibited from South Africa because of their purported racial unsuitability. Rather, like Syrians and Russian Jews, Indians were restricted entry because their arrival and resettlement disrupted the racial-colonial project of aboriginal uplift. In South Africa, as in Canada, the protection of indigenous peoples worked as a jurisdictional claim for the colonial state, one that was as racial and temporal as it was territorial. In the end, it legitimized the exclusion of Indians from the white Dominions.

In contests over the *Komagata Maru*, the courtroom was not the only place where indigenous peoples were simultaneously evoked and erased. Passengers aboard the ship also referenced indigeneity, often as an absent presence in their claims to inclusion. As the vessel awaited deportation, and as Canadian officials began deliberations with the imperial government and with authorities in Hong Kong, Japan, and India as to where the ship should be sent, the passengers grew increasingly beleaguered and desperate. Dismayed and discouraged by the Board of Inquiry's ruling and the Court of Appeal's decision, several passengers sent an urgent plea to the governor-general in Ottawa: "We passengers of 'Komagata Maru' indicate our sorrow to judgment Board of Enquiry regarding our deportation, and humbly have the honour to appeal before Your Royal Highness for our landing on following reasons."[169] They began by reiterating their status as British subjects. Then they claimed that if their "coming was unsuitable" to the Dominion, the government should have prohibited the ship's departure from Hong Kong and not it's landing in Vancouver. The passengers went on to describe the sea as a juridical space and invoked the authority of admiralty law to challenge the jurisdiction of the Board of Inquiry and the Court of Appeal. The "ship was duly gazetted in Hong Kong," they wrote, and "our necessary and legal papers were not produced in appeal court because Mr. Gurdit Singh was not allowed to see his counsel." Though the manifest authorized Singh as the charterer, whose authority outweighed that of the ship's captain, he was confined to the vessel. Finally, the legal and political right to travel freely across the land and sea, they urged, was not only their right but also an obligation of British subjecthood. It was "the duty of the Indian government to form and carry out a great scheme of Indian colonization within the British Empire," they claimed.[170] The shipload of passengers brought to Vancouver by Gurdit Singh was trying to do just that. The manifest listed most of those on board as farmers. One of their objectives in coming to Canada, they claimed, was to advance resettlement. "Our brothers ashore can collect sums to arrange for land and everything," they wrote. "Some blocks of land should be awarded in any part of Canada to cultivate." Settler colonialism, as twinned projects of indigenous dispossession and racial labor exploitation, was not solely the responsibility of white colonists alone. It was also the duty of Indian migrants. "Kindly take pity and award blocks of land to improve Canada progress and to make land fertile," they pleaded. "Shall die if return," they stated in one final appeal. "In prison for four months. No bodily strength to cross Pacific."[171]

THE *KOMAGATA MARU*'S passage has typically been narrated in terms of Canada's exclusionary immigration laws, particularly its three orders-in-council, of which the continuous journey provision was most egregious. At the Board of Inquiry and the British Columbia Court of Appeal, as my discussion in this chapter makes clear, immigration officials and appellate court judges most certainly deliberated on whether Munshi Singh, as a representative of the other passengers, violated Canada's immigration regulations. But in making their determinations on the legitimacy of Dominion claims to sovereignty, they referred to multiple, competing, and overlapping legal orders in which admiralty law featured prominently. The persistent historiographical emphasis on the law of the land has obfuscated the law of the sea.

In regard to the Board of Inquiry hearing, both Reid and Hopkinson focused their attention on the *Komagata Maru*'s manifest, albeit for different reasons. This document, in their respective readings, was not merely an instrument of admiralty law. As an itemized list of passengers and cargo, and as a document authorized by the ship's captain, doctor, and by immigration officials, it operated as an additional modality of border control that was used to verify the legality of persons entering the Dominion. At the Court of Appeal, the five judges underscored the British North America Act as "THE LAW" of "CANADA" and as the foundation of Dominion authority. The act sanctioned the appropriation of land, the imposition of law, and the legal and political arrangements between the provincial governments and Ottawa, to which indigenous dispossession remained crucial. As the court's deliberations unfolded, however, it became evident that Canadian sovereignty was not manifest in "THE LAW" as a unified or monolithic expression of power. Rather, Dominion authority was composed of intersecting and opposing legalities, forcibly written over indigenous laws and bringing the British, Dominion, and provincial governments into conflict. Reconceptualizing jurisdiction as a racial, territorial, and temporal logic of colonial government, as I have endeavored to do here, emphasizes land/sea, subject/citizen, and indigenous/Indian as legal and political divides that were animated by the racial asymmetries and inequalities of the British Empire, brought to the fore by the *Komagata Maru*'s voyage, and vigorously disputed by Bird, Cassidy, Gurdit Singh, and the other passengers.

As struggles over the steamer unfolded in Vancouver Harbour and in other parts of the imperial world, indigeneity materialized as a powerful transoceanic vernacular that produced opposition and contestation from both far and near. While transatlantic slavery generated a potent anticolonial lexicon that was evoked intermittently by passengers aboard the ship, indigeneity engendered an equally forceful critique of immigration prohibitions, but one that worked ambiguously, and in ways that both challenged and fortified Canadian claims to territorial control. The Court of Appeal drew on the past, present, and future of indigenous peoples as "sons of the soil" and as "wards of the Crown." They marshaled aboriginal dependency to fortify Dominion sovereignty. Justices

McPhillips and Martin claimed that, given Canada's duties and responsibilities to its original inhabitants, parliament had the right to protect itself against the influx of foreigners, including Indian migrants and travelers, irrespective of whether they were British subjects. Importantly, the court's decision in *Re Munshi Singh* was not the last time indigeneity was evoked in contests over the *Komagata Maru*. The ship's deportation, its passage across the Pacific and Indian Oceans, and its landing outside Calcutta incited a transoceanic response to which indigeneity, in its multiple, historical, and geographical registers, featured prominently. The ascendency of a global and itinerant politics of indigeneity in struggles over the ship is the subject of the following chapter. It shifts the discussion from jurisdiction as territory to jurisdiction as status, and expands the book's geographical frame from Canada and the Pacific to South Africa, India, and the Indian Ocean arena.

Anticolonial Vernaculars of Indigeneity

England has to fulfill a double mission in India: one destructive, the other regenerating the annihilation of old Asiatic society, and the laying the material foundations of Western Society in Asia.—KARL MARX, "The Future Results of British Rule in India," July 1853

Examined on its merits, the doctrine that this is a white man's country cannot be defended. It was originally a red man's country, until we were told that the only good Indian was a dead Indian.— "Canadian Gentleman," *Hindustanee,* June 1914

On 30 May 1866, Gyanendra Mohun Tagore delivered an evening address on the "Future of India" at the St. Thomas School in Howrah. A member of the prominent Tagore family, the first Indian to be called to the bar from Lincoln's Inn, and a professor at University College London, he drew a diverse audience, including "natives" and "a good number of European gentlemen and several ladies."[1] This was Tagore's first public appearance since returning from England, and those in attendance were "curious to see how the new Barrister would acquit himself." After openly admitting his lack of preparation, Tagore spoke briefly yet passionately about India's future. In looking forward, he immediately turned back:

> How can you know the future unless you know something of the past? Is it right for a Hindoo to ignore his past history? Is it *Ethnical?* . . . A man is nothing without his pedigree, and no nation should forget its past history. Then, where did we Brahmins come from? We came from Medes, across the Himalaya mountains and settled in the Punjab. We came on a

mission of civilization, conquered the aboriginal tribes, and established the Brahminical Institutions. These institutions became effete in process of time, and then the Mussulmans came to rob and plunder us. They did India no good... After the Mussulmans came the English, but not as conquerors. They came as peaceful traders... *They came merely as guardians to the natives of India.*[2]

Narrating the history of India as a history of conquest, Tagore's account shares striking resonances with India's history as Marx described it. In "The Future Results of British Rule in India," published thirteen years earlier, Marx claimed that India "could not escape the fate of being conquered." The Turks, Russians, Persians, Britons, and others "founded their empires on the passive basis of that unresisting and unchanging [Indian] society."[3] The history of India was "the history of the successive intruders," he wrote.[4] From Tagore's point of view, the origins of India also began with conquest. However, the colonists in his chronology were not the Turks, Russians, or Britons, but the Brahmins and Muslims. Indeed, the British were not "conquerors," Tagore claimed, but "co-operators" who would grant India a future but only by destroying its past.[5]

The successive conquests of India, as Tagore described them, were clearly territorial, but they were also racial and temporal. If India's "aboriginal tribes" were firmly rooted in the past, the country's "natives," as non-indigenous peoples, were its future. "You are the heirs of this glorious inheritance," Tagore said encouragingly to his audience, "the English are only your guardians till you come of age and are able to manage your own property."[6] When the time is right, "India will one day be yours." If Tagore viewed India as lacking history beyond conquest, in the present and under British rule, it still had the potential to make a history of its own. The English "will of themselves leave the country whenever you are fit to govern yourselves," he urged. Then "your future relations will be purely international!"[7] Tagore's observations were myopic in some respects and prescient in others. In 1914, as the *Komagata Maru*'s voyage captured the attention of Indians across the subcontinent and diaspora, history, futurity, and indigeneity would emerge as a firmly sutured entanglement, one that engendered a series of anticolonial vernaculars that circulated across the Pacific and Indian Oceans, most vividly in Canada and South Africa.

At first glance, the portrayals of India offered by Marx and Tagore echo each other, particularly in the civilizational telos they ascribed to conquest. When situated in longer colonial and racial histories, however, their accounts appear markedly distinct. First, Tagore drew on temporal registers to distinguish India's "aboriginal tribes" from its "natives," populations that were undifferentiated in

Marx's writings on India.[8] Second, Tagore's chronology was familiar in some ways and questionable in others. He described aboriginal peoples as the "original inhabitants" of India, only to erase them from his visions of the country's future. They were not India's "supreme destiny," he claimed.[9] They were to be eradicated through "England's annihilation of old Asiatic society," a process similar to what Marx described in the epigraph at the outset of this chapter.[10] As indigenous scholars have argued, this is a violent and persistent temporalization of indigenous peoples, most clearly represented in the trope of the "vanishing Indian."[11] But when Tagore's remarks are situated within the transoceanic movements of peoples and news via ships and telegraph cables, they seem somewhat surprising. From the 1860s onward, Indian English newspapers and periodicals published in major Indian cities including Allahabad, Amritsar, Bombay, Calcutta, and Lahore and in the diaspora, most notably Natal, routinely reported on the conditions facing indigenous peoples as the original inhabitants of India, South Africa, and Canada.[12] In some imperial jurisdictions, "aboriginal" and "native" were distinct personages (India); in others they were undifferentiated and interchangeable (South Africa and Canada). From the late nineteenth to the early twentieth century, as Indian anticolonial struggles intensified on the subcontinent and across the diaspora, reaching an apogee with the *Komagata Maru*'s passage, indigeneity emerged as a dynamic figure of anticolonial critique that crisscrossed the Indian and Pacific Oceans, gaining traction in its rebuke of Dominion legalities and imperial policies. Viewed from the sea, indigeneity appears as a mobile and itinerant force that was not confined to specific territories, to the past, or to history. Rather, it materialized as a powerful current that compressed the past and future into the present. An anticolonial vernacular of indigeneity connected the Indian and Pacific Oceans and their corresponding histories of colonial and racial violence. However, its circulations did not disrupt racial regimes of power and often worked against the legal and political interests of indigenous communities.

In this chapter, I trace the multiple figures of indigeneity who emerged from the anticolonial struggles leading up to and surrounding the *Komagata Maru*'s journey. Whereas the previous chapter centered on jurisdiction as territory and temporality, exploring how the British Columbia Court of Appeal mobilized the past, present, and future of indigenous peoples to authorize the ship's deportation from Vancouver, this chapter considers jurisdiction in terms of racial status and subjecthood. Specifically, I explore the ways in which the vessel's supporters in South Africa and India drew on indigeneity to advance their legal and political rights as British subjects, both to cross the putatively free sea and to enter the so-called white Dominions. Operating in different tones and registers, indigeneity featured prominently in anticolonial contests in South Africa, India, and Canada, gaining momentum as the *Komagata Maru* crossed the Pacific and Indian Oceans. Whereas some passengers presented themselves as colonists who would help to advance Canada's mission of territorial appropriation and resettlement, as I discuss in chapter 3, many of the ship's supporters directly challenged Dominion claims to sovereignty and authority, by insisting that Britons and Europeans were foreign intruders and settlers who occupied lands that did not belong to them. According to the "Canadian gentleman" writing for the *Hindustanee* in 1914, as quoted in the second epigraph to this chapter, Canada had no legal or political grounds to exclude Indians or anyone else. The Dominion was not a white man's country, he argued, but a "red man's country," a truth that was repressed through racial and colonial force but equally resisted.[13]

It is vital to note that in contests over colonization and Indian migration in the vernacular press, which is the subject of this chapter, indigenous peoples did not speak in their own interests or on their own behalf. Instead, colonial administrators and Indian migrants and travelers strategically appropriated and deployed indigeneity as an abstract, racial, and temporal figure that might further their respective agendas. The appellate court judges acknowledged that aboriginal peoples were the "original inhabitants" of the land but transformed them from sovereign nations into "wards of the Crown." These evocations effaced indigenous claims to autonomy and territoriality, affirmed Canada's right to control its borders, and denied the *Komagata Maru* passengers entry. An equally contentious politics of indigeneity also surfaced in South Africa and India. In each of these locales, indigeneity worked as a critique of immigration regulations, a challenge to imperial sovereignty, and a racial, temporal, and civilizational claim to inclusion in the imperial polity.[14] Like discussions of indigeneity in *Re Munshi Singh,* the anticolonial versions deployed by Indian migrants, travelers, and onlookers were produced in the interstices of racial coercion administered by imperial authorities across the Dominions, colonies, and territories. These vernaculars revealed the colonial asymmetries of British subjecthood and fortified the unevenness of imperial power that informed it. To be clear, indigeneity operated in several competing registers at once. It was a potent effect of racial power that was evoked oppositionally but inconsistently, lending traction to anticoloniality and featuring with regularity in the politics of Indian migration and settlement along the Indian and Pacific Oceans.[15] Its emergence in India preceded the *Komagata Maru*'s journey by many decades, as Tagore's remarks suggest. Its recurrence augmented global struggles over the ship, as I elaborate below.

From the 1860s onward, the Indian reading public was well aware of the dire conditions of violent dispossession that confronted indigenous communities in South Africa, Canada, and the other Dominions. Indian English newspapers and periodicals routinely published articles regarding the fate of aboriginal peoples on the subcontinent and elsewhere. Many of these articles were ethnological: they described the civilizational characteristics, linguistic features, and disposition of hill peoples and tribal communities in the eastern, western, and central provinces. If some European and Indian commentators, including Tagore, viewed "aboriginal tribes" as preceding colonization and as firmly rooted in the past, others insisted on their vibrancy, tenacity, and strength amid the devastating conditions produced by British colonial and imperial rule.[16] Importantly, these accounts were not specific only to the subcontinent. Indian English newspapers frequently reported the conditions of violence confronting indigenous peoples in other parts of the British Empire, including the white settler Dominions. In one brief article, issued the same year as Tagore's address, the *Pioneer,* one of Allahabad's most influential papers, recalled the intensification of anti-Maori violence in New Zealand. The article described the fierce and protracted battles in Tauranga, a region that had long been a site of New Zealand's land wars.[17] "The Government has called a meeting, or as we should say in India, held a Durbar of all the rebel and friendly chiefs, and arranged amicably, the terms of a treaty." The *Pioneer* was sympathetic but not optimistic: "European civilization either kills off the aboriginal native, or drives him year by year further off. We are not confident that this treaty will be kept, but for present the war is over."[18]

As newspaper reports and their global circulations expanded, thereby connecting distant regions of the empire, idioms of indigeneity as a reproach to imperial and colonial policies and as a claim to equality and inclusion also flourished. These lexicons followed the circuitous maritime routes well traveled by Indian indentured laborers, sojourners, and so-called free migrants. However, debates surrounding indigeneity in one imperial context were not simply transplanted elsewhere.[19] They were shaped by longer histories of racial classification that animated the oscillating divides between "aboriginal" and "native." Transoceanic contests over Indian migration, when informed by a politics of indigenous dispossession, influenced anticolonial struggles in unpredictable, unexpected, and sometimes disconcerting ways. In South Africa, which had the lengthiest and most troubled history of Indian migration, the deterritorialization of indigenous Africans was woven into legislation aimed at prohibiting the entry of "free" Indians.[20] Here, colonial authorities and missionaries took care to differentiate indigenous peoples and Indian indentured labourers and migrants, racially and temporally. Yet in the practical interests of colonial governance, these distinctions were sometimes effaced and collapsed. In India and

Canada, by contrast, onlookers invoked indigeneity to critique the violence of colonial rule and to insist on their own "coming of age," as Tagore described it.[21] While some recalled the territorial dispossession of indigenous peoples, as a clear example of British colonial violence and as a challenge to restrictions on immigration, others mobilized indigeneity to assert their own self-serving claims to civilizational and racial superiority. In these opposing positions, one thing remained constant. Indigenous peoples were not vanishing or in the past. Rather, indigeneity materialized as both the present and future. Whereas some Indian migrants and travelers recalled the dispossession of indigenous peoples as a way to express their solidarity and to condemn Dominion claims to sovereignty, others sought to disrupt the linear chronology of a global and universal history by placing European time "out of joint."[22] Irrespective of their intentions, these invocations often worked against the political and juridical ambitions of Indian sojourners and migrants, and opposed the collective demands of indigenous peoples.

The politics of indigeneity, as troubling as it may appear in my discussion below, cannot be reduced to the opinions, attitudes, or ideologies of Indian migrants alone. As a vernacular of anticolonial critique, indigeneity was an effect of racial and colonial power, produced through protracted struggles and violent histories of British imperial rule. The anticolonial politics that called forth different figures and forms of indigeneity may have been itinerant and global, as I suggest, but those figures and forms emerged from very specific conditions of dispossession, deterritorialization, and resettlement. To emphasize this point and to draw attention to its interconnections and overlaps with racial administration in the white Dominions, in the first section of this chapter, I offer a brief account of immigration prohibitions directed at Indians in South Africa. Though the *Komagata Maru* never crossed the western Indian Ocean or called at African ports, news of the vessel did. In fact, some of the most forceful critiques of the Dominion's treatment of the ship's passengers and of indigenous peoples came from Natal. In the second section, I follow the circuitous movements of indigeneity between India and Canada, and through the transoceanic responses to the *Komagata Maru*'s passage. In their repudiation of immigration restrictions, Indians on the subcontinent and in the diaspora claimed that aboriginal peoples were the original inhabitants of Britain's most northerly Dominion and were the targets of a deliberate, sustained, and ongoing program of racial and colonial force. In section three, I chart the movements of indigeneity across the western Indian Ocean arena between India and South Africa. Responding to the *Komagata Maru*'s unsuccessful journey, Indians on the subcontinent drew on the presence of "native South Africans" as a way to emphasize their purported racial and civilizational superiority and their readiness to join the imperial polity. When repositioned from land to sea, indigeneity emerges as a circulating and oppositional force, produced out of specific histories of territorial dispossession and also emerging from a politics of anticolonial struggle. Viewed from the ship, indigeneity is no longer a white settler formation. Rather, it materializes as a global and itinerant force that connected South Africa, India, and Canada in a variegated and uneven topography of British imperial control. Importantly, what these multiple deployments of indigeneity, as I trace them below reveal, is that anticolonialism did not often translate into antiracism, and certainly not in any direct or straightforward way. As moving targets, Indian migrants and travelers marshaled indigeneity in different registers and for distinct purposes. In so doing, they disputed some racial, temporal, and territorial divisions while reproducing and reinforcing others.[23] Contra Marx, it was through a *racial politics* and not solely an economic and political one that England laid "the material foundations for Western society in Asia."[24]

To fully appreciate the extent to which indigeneity as a racial, temporal, and transoceanic force animated anticolonial critiques of the *Komagata Maru,* a discussion of colonial and racial politics is necessary. In the first section, I begin with South Africa's restrictive and exclusionary responses to Indian migration and settlement. Here, I sketch the overlaps and interconnections between Indian exclusion and indigenous administration, configurations that would shape racial and colonial contests in other Dominions, including Canada.

"What Is a Native?"

Of all the Dominions, South Africa experienced the most protracted and arduous history of Indian migration, one that has now been well documented.[25] What remains unclear, however, is how exclusionary laws directed at Indian migrants and travelers intersected, juridically and politically, with histories of indigenous dispossession. In South Africa, as in other colonial contexts, British rule created an entire bureaucracy aimed at classifying indigenous peoples and others. Under the auspices of protection, aboriginal peoples were distinguished from colonial subjects and "foreigners," including "Asiatics" and "coloureds."[26] From the late nineteenth century onward, partly in response to rising rates of immigration from India and China, processes of colonial distinction and division intensified. In efforts to protect a putatively endangered indigenous population from the projected influx of "Asiatics," Natal, the Transvaal, the Orange Free State, and the Cape Colony each established legal and political regimes aimed at defining, circumscribing, and regulating those defined as "natives."[27] Colonial authorities did not count and classify indigenous peoples as the original inhabitants only to distinguish them from European and migrant populations. Aboriginal protection and administration, as I argue in the previous chapter, offered a political rationale for the introduction of immigration prohibitions directed at migrants from India.

In South Africa, native administration provided a crucial and enduring template for the legal exclusion of so-called free Indians. The prohibitions placed on Indian migrants and sojourners seeking admission to South Africa, combined with efforts to disenfranchise those already there, were initiated by Dutch settlers and subsequently absorbed into British colonial policy.[28] The "great majority of Afrikaners," Sir Montague de Pomeroy Webb claimed, have no knowledge or experience with "any other kind of coloured man than the aboriginal savage whom they have subdued by violence, and now employ on their farms, etc." This "lack of experience," with the colored races, he continued, "has been revealed in their disinclination to show any more consideration for Indians than they customarily exhibit towards Africans."[29] The "conduct of the Transvaal and of Natal towards their settled Asiatic population," remarked another English observer, "is all of a piece with the native policy. . . . It is almost certain that the Anti-Asiatic attitude is, to a great extent, a corollary of that policy." The Dominions, including South Africa, he opined, have aimed to "either rid themselves of their Asiatics or to reduce them to the dead level of the native."[30] These overlaps between indigenous administration and racial exclusion directed at Indians and other "Asiatics" did not produce racial symmetry in colonial administration. Rather, by creating different types of subjects, it reinforced the empire's racial, temporal, and territorial unevenness. Migrants from India were indeed the targets of racial and legal violence in South Africa. But for Webb, "the Indian is almost as far ahead of the Kaffir as the Anglo-African himself is ahead of the South African Indian!"[31] A prevailing view of the time was that native Africans and Indians were distinct races that exhibited fixed characteristics and were situated in distinct and immutable stages of civilization. But in the pragmatic interests of colonial governance, the racial and temporal divides between these communities were occasionally collapsed and conflated. As British subjects, indigenous peoples and Indian migrants were *subject* populations. Though they were presumed to be racially distinct, they were both assumed to be subordinate to Europeans. The legal expansion and contraction of the term "native" as it developed in South Africa partly influenced the contours of indigeneity as an anticolonial force in India and Canada.[32]

Indian Ocean migrations from the subcontinent to South Africa are often regarded to be a nineteenth-century phenomenon. Although large-scale migration did not begin until the mid-nineteenth century, Indians first arrived in the Cape Colony two hundred years earlier when Dutch merchants returned with slaves that they captured from the subcontinent. Between 1657 and 1808, approximately 25 percent of all slaves in the Cape Colony were from India.[33] From 1856 to 1859—forty years after British sovereignty was formally recognized by Europeans in the Cape and more than twenty years after Britain's Colonial Office formally abolished its transatlantic slave trade—the forced migration of Indians via indenture accelerated.[34] In particular, as British administrators initiated plans to begin sugar production in Natal, they looked to India as a primary source of cheap and exploitable racial labor. The largest numbers of Indians, recruited via systems of indenture, arrived in Natal from Madras and Calcutta, located on India's eastern coast.[35] From 1860 to 1911, estimates suggest that over 150,000 Indian workers were successfully conscripted under coercive regimes of labor exploitation, which some have termed "a new system of slavery."[36] After completing their requisite terms, Indian indentured laborers in Natal were encouraged by colonial officials to renew their contracts or return home. Despite pressures to leave, many stayed. Between 1902 and 1913, only 32,506 Indians who arrived in South Africa as indentures eventually returned to India.[37]

Driven by the uneven demands for cheap and exploitable labor and inspired by the possibility of new opportunities for economic trade and settlement, patterns of Indian migration to South Africa followed discrepant trajectories. Given its experiments with sugar production and its reliance on indenture, Natal had the longest history of Indian migration and was home to the largest resident Indian community. By the late nineteenth century, for example, the number of Indians in Natal almost matched the population of European settlers. The 1893 census enumerated 500,000 Africans, 43,742 whites, and 41,208 Indians.[38] By the turn of the century, there were smaller but growing Indian communities in the Transvaal, the Cape Colony, and the Orange Free State.[39] Though Indians were regarded as vital to the economic engine of South Africa, colonial officials complained that people from the subcontinent posed a direct challenge to the viability and longevity of British imperial rule. Specifically, Indian migration and settlement, some charged, held deleterious effects for indigenous Africans. Give the Cape Colony's "mixed population of British and Dutch, Zulu and Hottentot," wrote John Cowen, South Africa "can never be a white man's land."[40] Yet "it aspires to be the strictest of all colonies," he remarked, with "its exclusion of the Asiatic." Whereas the Transvaal "imposes registration and severe restrictions" on Indians, Natal has "sought to reduce the number of 'free Indians' and admit natives of India only as indentured laborers."[41] Cowen's view of Indian migration was in no way typical, however.

Many argued that the arrival of Indians disrupted visions of white settlement by endangering South Africa's indigenous peoples.[42]

In 1920, Charles F. Andrews, a former Anglican missionary and a close friend and associate of Mohandas K. Gandhi, quoted a recent Economic Commission Report, which made these arguments explicitly. "The moral depravity of the Indian is equally damaging to the African, who in his natural state is at least innocent of the worse vice of the East."[43] Would the future of South Africa be determined by "the vital interest of the African" or by the ambitions of the Indian, the authors asked? According to the report, Indian migration created serious problems for British rule.[44] "On purely economic grounds, we submit that the admission of the Indian [to Africa] was a cardinal error of policy," the commission charged. "It involved the economic stagnation of the African throughout a large tract of [South and East] Africa." The importation of Indians, the report continued, "produced a consequent retardation of progress," and merely for "a temporary convenience."[45] It was the uplift of the aboriginal and not the cultivation of sugar that was to be Britain's primary and long-term objective in South Africa, the authors insisted. "It is our firm conviction that the justification of our occupation of this country lies in our ability to adapt the native to our own civilization."[46] The "racial problems" between the white settler, the Indian, and the native South African, as Winston Churchill argued the following year, were "delicate and baffling... The native population must be regarded as the greatest trust," he urged, and it was Britain that was "charged with that responsibility."[47]

To be sure, the migration of Indians to South Africa and the responses it engendered were shaped and influenced by the political status of its four colonies.[48] Whereas Britain occupied Natal and the Cape at various points in the early to mid-nineteenth century, the Transvaal and the Orange Free State remained Afrikaner republics until 1902, when they too came under British control.[49] In 1910, the four colonies were consolidated as a union under British rule. Despite their historical, political, and jurisdictional differences, each government shared the view that Indian migration was an urgency that demanded concerted attention. Restrictive, coercive, and prohibitive legislation, especially in Natal and the Transvaal, as Cowen pointed out, was deemed necessary not to prevent Indian migration altogether, but to discourage the permanent settlement of "free" Indians. For some, this was especially significant in a Dominion where white settlers were vastly outnumbered. "In Canada and Australasia," wrote one English commentator, "we witness the spectacle of a handful of 'whites' monopolizing continents.... In South Africa the situation is complicated by the fact of a large and growing indigenous population, plus a considerable number of settled immigrants from Asia." In such a racially mixed milieu, "the 'white man's country' doctrine" appears "particularly incongruous," this commentator observed.[50] It was the presence of Indians in the colony, and their increased interactions and associations with Africans, many British observers believed, that threatened the future of colonial rule. "Long association with European settlers has had the effect of quickening indigenous evolvement." But the introduction of Indian labor in Natal and the Transvaal had "a dangerous influence upon the quickening self-consciousness of the native."[51] By politicizing concerns of aboriginal protection, and providing legal precedents for Indian exclusion, British authorities in what was to become South Africa established a set of prohibitions that would inspire those instituted elsewhere, including the orders-in-council directed at passengers aboard the *Komagata Maru.*[52]

There is little doubt that the restrictive and coercive legislation passed in Natal and the Transvaal was intended to dissuade permanent Indian settlement. In 1880, twenty years following the arrival of the first indentures, after thousands completed their requisite five-year terms, refused to renew their contracts, and claimed residence under the banner of freedom, anti-Indian sentiments intensified. Growing concerns of Indian settlement were institutionalized through a series of punitive and exclusionary laws. Although Natal was committed to maintaining its steady supply of indentured labor, authorities strongly discouraged Indian settlement. To do so, they passed legislation aimed at limiting Indian mobility and restricting access to housing, marriage, and education.[53] Through the legal and political disenfranchisement of ex-indentures, "colonial-borns," and those newly arrived, and by curtailing the freedoms of so-called free Indians by limiting their prospects for long-term resettlement, these laws were intended to make Natal unlivable for Indians, and thereby making them temporary residents. It was amid these racially charged conditions that a politics of indigeneity became critical to immigration controls and to anticolonialism.

In 1895, to take one well-known example, all non-indentured adult Indians in Natal were required to pay a three-pound annual tax, an imposition that would later become one target of Gandhi's satyagraha campaign.[54] The following year, Natal disenfranchised all Indians, except those already registered on lists of voters. Notably, this law never cited Indians explicitly or directly. Rather, it stipulated that "those 'who (not being of European Origin) are Natives or descendants in the male line of Natives of countries which have not hitherto possessed elective institutions,' unless exempted by the Governor in Council," were not permitted to vote in parliamentary elections.[55] Recall that in Tagore's address, the "aboriginal" and the "native" were distinct personages. In late nineteenth-century Natal, under the auspices of this particular legislation, these communities were conflated and thus legally indistinguishable. As India was ruled by Britain and did not yet enjoy "elective institutions" of government, the term "native" in the Natal Act was interpreted broadly. For the purposes of the law, anyone who could not be racially classified as European would be counted as a "native." This conflation of racial-legal categories would continue intermittently in colonial laws and policies, drawing rebuke and repudiation from Indians in South Africa and from those in India.

In British-controlled jurisdictions, racial categories carried high legal and political stakes. Yet in Natal, these taxonomies were introduced and often circulated without clear or explicit definition.[56] Even after colonial-racial classifications were legally defined and institutionalized, racial designations remained ambiguous, inconsistent, and highly mutable. Whereas colonial officials in South Africa, London, and elsewhere debated their meanings and effects, educated Indians also fiercely disputed racial categories. In *Indian Opinion,* Gandhi's weekly newspaper, contributors openly questioned the legal and political meanings of racial classifications. Articles titled, "What Is a Native?" and "What Is an Asiatic?" appeared recurrently in the first decades of the twentieth century, as Indians contemplated the legal and political consequences of racial classification in Natal and elsewhere in South Africa. For many, this ambiguity and confusion was especially acute in deliberations over "nativeness." Although the term "native" was intended to describe the original inhabitants of the region, it was highly elastic, as the Natal law revealed. "One of the first difficulties presented in connection with the consideration of laws by the recent South African Native Affairs Commission," claimed one observer in 1905, "was the varying definitions therein of the term 'Native.' So great indeed is the variation that in the same colony it has several meanings."[57] At specific historical moments, colonial authorities expanded and contracted definitions of "native," always with the intent of excluding "Asiatics" and "coloureds," including Indians.

The opacity of "native," "coloured," and "Asiatic" materialized in a range of legislation, from restrictive by-laws to immigration regulations. Unlike the Natal Act, which did not identify Indians explicitly, subsequent laws openly expanded definitions of "native" to incorporate Chinese and Indian communities. The most coercive of these was introduced in the Transvaal, where Indians had been settling since the 1880s.[58] Here, as one source explained, the Kruger government "proposed to interpret the term 'Natives,' occurring in the London convention to include Asiatics."[59] In 1885, the Transvaal passed Law 3, which was openly and directly aimed at Indians, requiring their compulsory registration in the colony, restricting their access to property, and segregating them in specific neighborhoods. Due to concerns over Indian resistance, the law was passed but not enforced. Following Britain's victory in the Second Boer War, many anticipated greater equality for Indians in South Africa, but this turned out not to be the case. In 1907, the Transvaal Asiatic Registration Act was the first law to be passed by the newly self-governing colony. It expanded and fortified Law 3 by classifying Indians as "natives." This time, Britain did not intervene. The legislation mobilized vigorous Indian resistance across the colony and served as a catalyst for Gandhi's satyagraha campaign.[60] In mass protests, Indians objected to their forced registration and repudiated the law for its devastating effects on their communities. More importantly, many vehemently rejected the comparisons that authorities drew between indigenous peoples and migrants from India.

The Asiatic Restriction Act, many Indian critics claimed, failed to adequately distinguish the Transvaal's racially diverse populace. The law "makes no distinction between British and alien Asiatics," one source charged, "it reduces British Indians to a lower status than that of the aboriginal or coloured people of South Africa, and it places greater disabilities on the Indian than they even suffered under the Boers."[61] An "aboriginal native is not required to carry a pass under penalties laid down in the Ordinance . . . nor, again, is a native liable to have his children registered and to furnish means of identifying them from birth upwards," this particular observer noted.[62] Mr. L. W. Ritchie, a longtime resident, lawyer, and secretary of the South Africa British Indian Committee, condemned the act as "humiliating legislation." The law classified Indians "with the native savage as Kleurling," he claimed, "because forsooth his skin is brown."[63] The Transvaal British Indian Association, founded by Gandhi, also condemned the law. The "term 'natives,' whatever else it may mean, can never include British Indians," it urged. "The statute-book of the Colony is replete with laws which deal with the 'natives,' but which admittedly do not apply to Asiatics or British Indians." Most significantly, the Transvaal's Law 3 dealt "specifically with Asiatics" and yet did "not apply to the 'natives.'" Since the "Transvaal laws have almost invariably distinguished between 'Natives' and 'Asiatics,'" the Transvaal British Indian Association concluded, the two must remain racially and legally distinct.[64]

"Who is a Native" remained a point of contention among Indians and colonial administrators alike. It was a conversation from which indigenous peoples were excluded, and one that was never fully resolved. Lord Milner, the high commissioner to South Africa and the governor of the Transvaal and the Orange River Colony noted that in the Treaty of Vereeniging, which followed the Second Boer War, the term "native" did "not include all coloured people." As "the question was never discussed," Milner continued, "each member of the Peace Conference appears to be at liberty to place upon the word 'native' the construction which to him seemed right."[65] For many years, South Africa imposed "a distinction between coloured people and aboriginal inhabitants of the country," Milner recalled. Yet there was "no uniform definition of either."[66] His own view was as follows: "I have always held that the word 'native' in the Terms of the Surrender meant natives, and not coloured people." The "universal use of language in South Africa makes a clear distinction between the two," he maintained, "and I have never myself heard Cape boys—much less Asiatics— spoken of as 'natives.'"[67] For the Native Affairs Commission, he clarified, the word "native" was "strictly confined to aboriginals, and persons both of whose parents were aboriginals." If the Boers wanted to include all persons of color "in the term 'native,' why did they not use the term 'coloured person'" instead, he asked.[68]

By the first decades of the twentieth century, the juridical and political boundaries between Indians and native Africans, in all of their oscillations and ambiguities, remained fiercely disputed. In 1906, *Indian Opinion* reprinted a commentary that raised the question of racial classification directly and took it up head on. Originally published in the *East London Daily News,* a paper that circulated in the Cape Colony, the article questioned the legal meaning of the term "native." Of particular import were its political implications for Indians and other non-British Asiatics: "There has been a good deal of controversy as to the proper definition of the word native, and the question has, we see, been raised in the House of Commons [London], where Mr. Winston Churchill recently, in reply to an enquiry, said he believed the meaning attached to the word in South Africa was a native of any country other than a European country."[69] Indian readers were outraged by Churchill's remarks. "Considering that Mr. Churchill has been out in this country [South Africa], and knows something about it, it is extraordinary that he should make such a blunder," one critic argued. Most colonists, the *East London Daily News* explained impatiently, "attach no meaning to the word." For them, the native "is one of the aboriginal inhabitants of South Africa. Whoever speaks of Indians, Chinese, or Japanese as natives?" they demanded.[70]

In their efforts to secure a future in South Africa, Indian travelers and migrants might have made claims to the soil. This was a population that crisscrossed the western Indian Ocean, cultivated the land as indentured laborers, and enjoyed a long history of settlement in the region. But, instead, to assert their civilizational differences from native South Africans and to emphasize their proximity to Europeans, many drew on the racial, territorial, and temporal vernaculars put into motion by British imperial rule. Unlike indigenous peoples, who allegedly required the guidance and tutelage of their British rulers,

Indians insisted on their own readiness to join the imperial polity. *Indian Opinion* offered a vibrant forum for public debate on the matter.[71] Contributors used the periodical to problematize, challenge, and undo the racial and temporal taxonomies imposed on Indian traders, sojourners, and migrants. Some voiced concerns regarding the putative uniformity and equality between aboriginal, native, and Indian. "This struggle of the Transvaal Indians to resist further encroachment upon their status and to avoid degradation in the eye of the law to the level of the savage aboriginal has now lasted three years," wrote Ritchie in 1910; "no grievance has stirred deeper and more widespread indignation in India than this."[72] As the *Komagata Maru* was detained in Vancouver Harbour and awaited deportation, the ship's supporters in South Africa and India would insist on the imposition of racial and temporal divides to separate Indians from native Africans. To fortify Dominion control and to legitimize the ship's deportation, the British Columbia Court of Appeal evoked similar oppositions.

Importantly, Indians were not the only ones to dispute the racial categorizations that were applied to them by the colonial governments of South Africa. In the interests of native protection and administration, missionaries and Indian sympathizers also insisted on maintaining the racial and temporal divides that separated these communities. As John Cowen put it, "Asiatic" migration to the Dominions was essential to imperial progress. Asiatics, including Indians, he insisted, were inheritors of an ancient history and civilization that only enhanced the advancement of British imperialism. "Supposing that Canada, Australia, South Africa, and the rest of the colonies, contrived to exclude, not only the Asiatic but all that the Asiatic has stood for in the highest sphere of human life," he argued, "they would have to shut out Christianity, Mahomedism [*sic*], Buddhism, [and] Confucianism." Prohibiting the "Asiatic" from entry would obscure "all the marvelous creeds and heavenly visions of Palestine, Arabia, India, China, and Japan," Cowen continued. Human civilization "would sink back to the totems of the aboriginal Maoris, the medicine-man magic of the bushmen, and the demonology of the American Indian."[73] Cowen, like many of his contemporaries, held an expansive geographical perspective of the earth, but one that was arranged through a teleological view of history. In his chronology of imperial progress and civilization, indigenous peoples were not a vanishing race. Rather, the ongoing presence of native South Africans helped to underscore the merits and virtues of Indian migration, in the present and future.

The Aborigines Protection Society of the Orange River Colony also expressed its opposition to legislation that did not clearly differentiate indigenous peoples from Indians. In the village of Odendaalsrust, a new law was recently enacted which made native administration exceedingly difficult, the society explained. "Besides imposing exceptionally severe restrictions on the native," this legislation expanded the definition of the term.[74] The regulations "direct that the word 'native' shall be so interpreted as to include, not only all members of South African native tribes, but also 'all coloured persons, and all who, in accordance with law and custom, are called colored persons or are treated as such, of whatever nationality or race they may be.'" In its condemnation of the law, particularly the expanding definition of "native," the Aborigines Protection Society directed attention to Lord Milner's final speech in Johannesburg: "We got off the right lines in this matter (the colour question) when we threw over the principle of Mr. Rhodes—equal rights for all civilized men." In Milner's view, racial and temporal distinctions of status and subjecthood were crucial to the efficiency and success of British colonial and imperial policy. The British Empire could not "throw all people of colour, the highest as well as the lowest, into one indistinguishable heap," he maintained. Instead, "it needed to follow closely the difference of race, of circumstances, and of degrees of civilization."[75] The Aborigines Protection Society urged the Orange River Colony to legally and politically differentiate natives from colored peoples, including Indians, and therefore to uphold Milner's advice. Ultimately, aboriginal protection and administration demanded the unequal division of race, territory, and temporality, distinctions that underpinned the British Empire and animated the asymmetries of British subjecthood.

If some critics looked to South Africa as a site and source of racial exclusions that were directed at "free" Indians, others shifted their gaze in the opposite direction, across the Indian Ocean, and toward the subcontinent. It was India's history of caste, some claimed, that informed and directly shaped racial regimes of power in the white Dominions. South Africa, C. F. Andrews cautioned, "is now in great danger of becoming a caste-ridden country." When India "is at last trying to throw off he [sic] caste habit. . . . South Africa, with all the feverish haste of youth and inexperience, is seeking to impose the caste system, not on others, but on herself."[76] For Andrews, caste was "nothing extraordinary, nothing mysterious, nothing peculiarly 'Oriental.'" Rather, it was "simply the same word as 'color' or 'race.'" Although racial segregation was "being spoken about in South African politics to-day, as though it were a new discovery," he charged, it had ancient roots that were traceable to "India somewhere between 1700 B.C. and 1000 B.C.," and "has been the curse of India ever since."[77] The origin of caste, as Andrews saw it, was part of India's long history of conquest. Caste was mobilized by the Aryan conquerors, in efforts to differentiate themselves from "the dark aboriginal races with which the white invaders came into contact."[78] Thus, it was foreigners who brought caste to India and ultimately transformed it into an enduring form of racial power. Prohibitions directed at Indians in South Africa, Andrews insisted, were borrowed directly from Indian history. It "is the very caste system which many are feverishly attempting to build up within the South Africa Union," he lamented.[79] But the translation of caste from India to South Africa was possible only because Dominion and colony were located in different spaces and times of civilization. Andrews, like many of his contemporaries, viewed South Africa as a young Dominion. The "Indian continent, nearly four hundred thousand years ago, must have been in striking respects similar to that of South Africa today," he remarked.[80] Caste in India had only one objective, he contended—to distinguish the aboriginal from the European. "Everything was directed to that end," and "in the final segregation of the aboriginal or pariah races of India from the so-called higher races, it has fatally succeeded."[81] As an expression of racial power, caste traveled to new jurisdictions via imperial expansion and colonial migration. It morphed and mutated across the seas, often with devastating effects. Indians in South Africa, who were "Indians of the higher caste" in India, Andrews observed, "have been made the 'untouchables of Africa.'"[82]

By 1914, these legal, political, and racial struggles over indigeneity, history, and futurity in South Africa would crisscross the Indian and Pacific Oceans, becoming powerful currents and crosscurrents that animated anticolonial struggles in India and Canada. Laws enacted in Natal and in the Transvaal that collapsed racial distinctions between aboriginal, native, and Indian would produce novel expressions of anticolonialism. Racial, territorial, and temporal invocations of indigeneity, as I discuss in the following section, informed contests over the *Komagata Maru,* lending traction to critiques of white superiority and undermining Dominion claims to legal authority and political autonomy.

"No Open Door for the Indian!"

In the first decades of the twentieth-century, multiple figures of indigeneity circulated along the Indian and Pacific Oceans, connecting South Africa, Canada, and India. In struggles over the *Komagata Maru,* indigeneity took distinct juridical and political formats and carried a myriad of intended and unintended effects. Indigeneity was deployed as a territorial challenge to Canada's claims to land, sea, and sovereignty and was aimed at undermining the legal and political foundations of Dominion rule. The vessel never crossed the western Indian Ocean, however, the long histories of Indian migration and exclusion in South Africa, especially its entanglements with indigenous dispossession that I discuss above, became a formidable presence in disputes over the ship. In 1914, as Indians across the empire rebuked Canada's prohibition against the entry of Gurdit Singh and the *Komagata Maru* passengers, indigeneity emerged with a patterned regularity in both Indian and Canadian periodicals. Diasporic Indians, along with those on the subcontinent, drew on the beleaguered experiences and fierce resistance of indigenous peoples to challenge Dominion authority and to condemn the colonial and racial violence on which it was founded and expanded. In so doing, many rejected linear chronologies of universal history that placed indigenous peoples in the past. Despite sustained efforts aimed at deterritorialization, critics considered indigenous communities to be the present and future of the Dominion. The *Komagata Maru*'s supporters in both India and Canada mobilized potent figures of indigeneity, which allowed them to question the legality and legitimacy of Canada. If the land belonged to aboriginal peoples, some asked, then how could "THE LAW" of "CANADA" reign supreme as the Court of Appeal claimed in *Re Munshi Singh* and as the *Vancouver Sun* reiterated in its caricature of an Indian waiting at the Dominion's door? How could Indians as British subjects be prohibited from entering and residing in imperial jurisdictions that had always been inhabited by indigenous peoples? One observer put it thus: "Who gave the whites the title deeds of Alberta and British Columbia, or any other settled or unsettled portion of the earth?"[83] For supporters and onlookers in India, Canada, and South Africa, the *Komagata Maru*'s journey exemplified much more than the Dominion's immigration restrictions. The ship's voyage struck at the very heart of the British Empire, revealing the racial and legal unevenness of imperial rule over land, sea, and subjecthood.

On 3 May 1914, as the steamer journeyed along the Pacific Ocean, nearly three weeks before it arrived in Vancouver, the *Hindi Punch,* a well-known Bombay periodical, published a cartoon that provocatively questioned the boundaries between indigeneity and Indianness (see fig. 4.1). At first glance, the image appears to be markedly different from the racially charged politics of indigenous dispossession and Indian migration as evidenced in South Africa. Here, the native, aboriginal, and Indian were not juridically conflated as they were in Natal or in the Transvaal. In a staged standoff between a youthful male figure—bearing the imperial name "Miss Columbia"—and an older, unidentified turbaned Sikh, indigeneity and Indianness were visibly differentiated and hierarchically organized through the use of exaggerated cultural signifiers and in a clever play on gender. By arranging these two British subjects unequally within the same frame, the *Hindi Punch* boldly captured the racial and temporal unevenness of the empire as evidenced in debates on status and subjecthood, and which Indian

FIGURE 4.1. "No
Open Door for the
Indian!" *Hindi Punch,*
3 May 1914, 16.
(Image courtesy of
British Library)

NO OPEN DOOR FOR THE INDIAN!

migrants and travelers were disputing in the various Dominions. As such, the
image might be read as a problematization of several colonial motifs at once.
First, by foregrounding indigeneity in terms of Dominion control, the cartoon
parodied European claims to autochthony. Second, it diminished the legitimacy
of indigeneity as a jurisdictional claim of Dominion command, a rationale that
authorized Indian exclusion in Canada and South Africa. Finally, the cartoon
undermined the gendered trope of the "vanishing Indian."[84] Represented as an
arbiter, defender, and symbol of Canada, "Miss Columbia" did not symbolize
the past. Rather, *she* represented a spectacular collision of past and future in a
way that placed colonial resettlement and its time "out of joint."[85]

Published weekly in Gujarati and English for an elite Indian readership, the
Hindi Punch was modeled on the famous English *Punch.* In the 1840s and 1850s,
as the magazine *Punch* was gaining prominence in London, many believed that

its measured style of satire and humor would find a flourishing market and wide readership in India. And it did. The English *Punch* made a deep impression on Indian audiences. It introduced the cartoon as a distinct genre of parody as social critique and, in so doing, produced a plethora of similar and related periodicals.[86] But as Urdu, Hindi, Gujarati, and other "vernacular doubles" appeared on the literary scene and gained popularity across the subcontinent, Indians lost interest in the British metropolitan version.[87] Founded by N. D. Apyakhtiar, an affluent Bombay Parsi, the *Hindi Punch* was originally named the *Parsee Punch*. Apyakhtiar's nephew Barjorjee Nowroji, an influential figure in his own right, later acquired it.[88] He changed the magazine's name, broadened its readership, and increased its circulation. With a weekly distribution of eight hundred copies and a hardcover edition featuring annual highlights, the *Hindi Punch* was featured in Bombay literary circles as one of the more widely read *Punch* magazines in India.[89]

Over the span of its long career (1878–1930), the *Hindi Punch* came to be known as a temperate version of the vernacular *Punches*.[90] Through its satirical imagery, subtle and lively humor, and liberal commentary on local, national, and imperial politics, including events unfolding in the Indian diaspora, the magazine established a solid reputation. It was lauded within and beyond the subcontinent as staging a powerful yet moderate forum for political satire and critical commentary. By the first decades of the twentieth century, as the Indian colonial government expressed increasing concerns regarding anticolonial activities at home and abroad, and as they declared magazines and periodicals such as the *Hindustanee* to be seditious, vernacular *Punches* (including the *Hindi Punch*) became subject to increased scrutiny. The Indian colonial government routinely hired English-educated Indians to work as translators and informants, drawing vernacular magazines and local readers into wider transoceanic regimes of surveillance. "For the colonial state," writes Ritu Khanduri, "comic papers were particularly contentious because political cartoons and caricature blurred the distinction between factual reporting and clever play of meanings, posing a challenge to the interpretation of local news and editorial content."[91]

Anticipating the *Komagata Maru*'s arrival in Vancouver, the *Hindi Punch*, with its excerpts from Canadian newspapers and its ironic play on indigeneity, offered a compelling though elusive condemnation of Dominion authority, one that blurred the lines between fact and fantasy. Whereas the Sikh was depicted somewhat predictably as male and visibly foreign and standing at the Dominion's door, a depiction that has clear resonances with the illustration in the *Vancouver Sun,* the indigenous figure was far more ambiguous. Was Miss Columbia male or female? Was she a comment on the ongoing and gendered violence of colonial occupation facing indigenous peoples in Canada? Was she a critique of Dominion authority, indigeneity, or both? Did Miss Columbia represent autonomy and self-governance or was she a "ward of the Crown" who remained under Dominion control? By caricaturing a European "playing Indian" was the *Hindi Punch* approving or denouncing the legal and political origins of Dominion sovereignty, including Canada's efforts to administer its territorial borders across land, sea, and coastal waters?[92]

The stylistic tone, features, and subtle humor that became trademarks of the *Hindi Punch* were clearly evident. In an unconventional way, the image foregrounded Canada's restrictive immigration policies, the purported undesirability of Indian migration, and the exclusion of Indians from the Dominion. The double standard of mobility that became a point of vigorous debate, as so-called free migration from India increased and as Indians asserted their rights to travel freely across aqueous and terrestrial spaces as British subjects, was also apparent. The *Hindi Punch* suggested that Indians, unlike their white counterparts, were restricted and even barred from entering white settler colonies while holding no comparable jurisdiction over India. Despite its spirited and provocative illustration, the magazine did not offer an explicit critique of the Dominion or imperial governments, or of their respective laws and policies. In the caricatured encounter between an indigenized, youthful, and visibly male "Miss Columbia" and a Sikh arriving at the Dominion's door, the image intimated that the political and legal status of British subjecthood was premised on a variegated hierarchy, racial inequality, and a disputed temporality, configured by European supremacy and shaped also by indigeneity. Here, the *Punch* echoed contestations over racial temporalities in South Africa and those in *Re Munshi Singh*. The aboriginal, the Indian, and the European were each located in different times of origin, arrival, and civilization, a linear and racial chronology that formed the foundation of British colonial and imperial rule. As the original inhabitants, indigenous peoples were absorbed and consolidated into the figure of Miss Columbia, who excluded Indians from India on Canada's behalf.

As news was increasingly shared across ocean regions, the *Komagata Maru*'s failed journey became a global event.[93] Indeed, it was the transoceanic circulation of information that catalyzed such a widespread response to the ship and its passengers. Indian English papers routinely republished reports of the voyage, which they drew from the British and Canadian press. Below the *Hindi Punch* image, for example, was an excerpt drawn from Victoria and Ottawa dailies:

> It is reported that the *Komagata Maru* has sailed from Shanghai for Victoria with 400 Hindus on board. . . . The vessel is said to be under charter

to a wealthy East Indian named Gurdit Singh. . . . In the House of Commons yesterday Mr. Stevens, Member for Vancouver interrogated the Government on the subject of the press dispatch stating that 400 Hindus had left Shanghai for Vancouver. Mr. [Roche], Minister of the Interior, replied that instructions had been sent to the immigration officers to prevent the landing of the Hindus.[94]

Many of the details printed here were incorrect. The ship disembarked from Hong Kong and stopped only briefly in Shanghai. It carried 376 passengers, and not 400. Gurdit Singh was not a "wealthy East Indian"; as the ship's charterer, he was in a desperate financial state. Notwithstanding the factual inaccuracies, what this excerpt suggests is that Canadian newspapers did not question the Dominion's self-proclaimed authority. Nor did provincial or federal politicians, for that matter. The Dominion of Canada ostensibly enjoyed an incontrovertible right to legal and political autonomy, to regulate its borders, and defend its racial identity as a white settler colony.[95]

As processes of resettlement unfolded in the Dominions, British and European claims to indigeneity became common. British settlers often asserted themselves as the original inhabitants of the territories they colonized. One tactic was to use the trope of the "vanishing Indian"; another was to invoke the doctrine of *terra nullius*.[96] The two operated simultaneously and inseparably as land was appropriated and as indigenous peoples were displaced materially, symbolically, and violently. In 1907, Richard Jebb, a journalist and conservative commentator of imperial politics, presented a paper titled "Notes on Imperial Organization" to the Royal Colonial Institute in London.[97] Between 1898 and 1901, Jebb had toured Australia, Canada, and other parts of the British Empire. In 1906, five years after his first imperial expedition, he visited South Africa.[98] In his remarks to the Institute, which were meant to offer a "modern view of imperial evolution," Jebb drew on the comparative knowledges he acquired during his oversea travels.[99] "His Majesty's subjects," Jebb claimed, were divided into two distinct classes: "citizens" and "subjects." Citizens were those who ruled in the "autonomous partner nations," and subjects were "the people of the Dependencies."[100] The former comprised the white residents of Canada, Australia, and South Africa; the latter included the inhabitants of India. For Jebb, "citizens," unlike subjects, held prior claims to the land, which granted them an undisputed right to control immigration:

> In South Africa, the Rulers, *being a nation indigenous to the land,* have
> to consider the safety not only of their democratic political institutions,
> but also of their racial position, which is threatened economically by the

unequal competition of the Indian trader. Surely, therefore, if the Rulers in India are justified in restricting the political rights of Indians in India itself, the Rulers in South Africa are justified in restricting both the political and the commercial rights of the Indians in a country where the latter are, in actual fact, alien immigrants.[101]

Excerpts of Jebb's paper were reprinted in *Indian Opinion*. Readers strongly objected to his remarks. One source described his address disparagingly, as "a mass verbiage redolent of triviality and surface thought."[102] What critics found most troubling was not Jebb's racial commentary on Indian traders and laborers, but his unabashed appropriation of indigeneity. "For Mr. Jebb," one critic charged, "the 'Rulers' of South Africa (with a capital R) are indigenous to the land! We always thought that the natives were, and that the Rulers (still capitalized) were interlopers."[103] To the audiences of *Indian Opinion*, the logic of Jebb's argument was outrageous and nonsensical. It led to "the absurd conclusion that the European immigrant and the aboriginal are identical," an equivalence that undermined the racial asymmetries and hierarchies by which the empire ruled.[104]

In South Africa, Canada, and the other Dominions, European assertions of indigeneity were made as autochthonous claims to land and belonging. This served as one foundation for indigenous dispossession and deterritorialization from both land and sea. Autochthony, which was symbolically and materially central to European myths of belonging, held devastating consequences. As Grant Farred explains it, the "settler wants to ensure that there is no difference between the settler and the land, so that expropriation becomes—through time—narrativized as historic affiliation with the land."[105] These racial affinities between Europeanness and territoriality provided one rationale to exclude Indian migrants and travelers from South Africa and Canada. But time, as Farred explains, made the settler vulnerable to history.[106] No matter how much the European colonist performed indigeneity in efforts to be one with the land and to belong to the land, the ongoing presence of indigenous peoples and their fierce resistance to colonial rule disrupted the pretense of these claims. Indigenous people could never be fully assimilated, integrated, or annihilated.[107] Indigenous resistance to European colonization had long persisted in multiple ways that were troubling the very foundation of the Dominion's legal and political authority. In the *Hindi Punch,* Canada was represented not as an imperiled white colonist, as one might expect, but as a young, male, and European-looking indigenous figure. Miss Columbia was adorned with mismatched cultural signifiers, a Plains/Prairie war bonnet, a Prairie/Subarctic hide robe with fur cuffs, and a parodied wampum belt, thus embodying indigenous and Canadian sovereignty at the very same time. In combining these competing sovereignties, the *Hindi Punch* displayed the multiple, overlapping, and incommensurable jurisdictional claims that informed Dominion control: indigenous peoples made claims to sovereignty and autonomy as self-determining nations; Indian migrants and travelers asserted their rights to move freely across the seas and settle in various parts of the empire as British subjects; and Canada claimed the authority and legitimacy to protect its borders from the influx of "Asiatics." By evoking indigeneity and Indian migration simultaneously, the *Hindi Punch* temporarily disrupted the foundational racial and juridical order that engendered and authorized white resettlement in Canada.

The *Hindi Punch* appropriated indigeneity as a way to question the legitimacy of Dominion command. Miss Columbia stood before a door displaying what appears to be the Dominion's crest and pointing to a sign that read "NOTICE: NO INDIANS ADMITTED." Her youthful European features represented a temporal assertion made routinely by the white Dominions, who viewed themselves as young colonies and as new "Rulers" who eventually became "indigenous to the land."[108] The belt, imprinted with "CANADA," was especially telling in its political and legal appropriations of indigeneity. The wampum, as John Borrows explains, signaled a legal agreement between two sovereign powers.[109] But its reterritorialization in the *Hindi Punch* only affirmed the strength and jurisdiction of Dominion authority. Through its luminous satire, the *Hindi Punch* inserted an ambiguously gendered indigeneity into discussions surrounding the *Komagata Maru*'s arrival in Canadian waters. Echoing racial, territorial, and temporal distinctions, however unclear, between native, aboriginal, and Indian in South Africa and Canada, indigeneity was made momentarily present, thereby highlighting the racial logics that provided a fragile basis to Dominion jurisdiction.[110]

Despite its nuances and its indeterminacy, the *Hindi Punch* offered one clear message: indigenous dispossession and immigration prohibitions were tightly intertwined. The dialogue between the two Indians pointed very suggestively to the racial unevenness of colonial subjecthood as it was advocated by Lord Milner in South Africa and reaffirmed by the Court of Appeal in *Re Munshi Singh*. Miss Columbia, as a newfound symbol of Canada was positioned *against* the Hindustani. "NO OPEN DOOR FOR THE INDIAN!" the text proclaims. "MISS COLUMBIA—Begone, sir! Don't you see this notice? There's no place for such as you here! INDIAN—Ha! Suppose I put up a similar notice on the doorsteps of my Indian home against you? MISS COLUMBIA—I know you can't, you daren't!" Racial distinctions between indigenous peoples and Indian migrants, the *Hindi Punch* suggested, were informed by shifting conceptions of civilizational superiority and inferiority, and by the corresponding rights and responsibilities they put into place.[111] For Justice Martin in *Re Munshi Singh*, Canada already held authority over an indigenous populace, one that required the Dominion's attention through colonial administration and protection. By projecting indigeneity as "the priority of the prior" and thus as the legitimate temporal foundation of the Dominion, Canada's legal and political authority in the *now* was represented through the past *and* future of indigeneity.[112] Reclaimed by the Dominion, Miss Columbia was depicted not as a sovereign or autonomous character, but as a dependent that was to defend Canada's immigration policy, and as such, became the ultimate embodiment of Dominion sovereignty.

Importantly, the figure of indigeneity in the *Hindi Punch* cartoon did not represent indigenous peoples in Canada or British Columbia. Rather, the image served as an abstraction on several registers.[113] First, Miss Columbia was a pastiche of cultural and legal signifiers appropriated from indigenous communities in the Canadian Prairies and Arctic regions and displaced to the west coast. As a clear exaggeration, the visibly male figure did not reflect the experiences of indigenous peoples. On the contrary, she was extracted from violent histories and lived realities. Second, through her feminized name, Miss Columbia signaled the gendered violence of colonial rule. Efforts to assimilate aboriginal peoples into the Dominion were initiated primarily through the Indian Act. Indigenous women, men, and children were subjected to multiple and escalating forms of coercion and violence that promoted racial segregation and deterritorialization through restrictions on marriage and forced education, all in the interests of assimilation. The loss of Indian status for women who married outside of their communities was especially vital to the colonial project of assimilation as elimination and figured prominently in the erasure of the "Indian" as a juridical concept.[114] Through the figure of indigeneity, the *Hindi Punch* represented aboriginal administration as deeply embedded in the exigencies of Indian migration, albeit in different ways than in South Africa. Specifically, the *Hindi Punch* offered a potent reminder of the racial force that underpinned British colonial expansion through laws aimed at land-appropriation, of which Canada's Immigration Act was only the most recent. The figurative encounter between the two Indians suggestively conveyed the productive aspects of colonial power. It highlighted the mobilities and collisions of race engendered by British colonial and imperial rule and resettlement.

Though the *Hindi Punch* was unique in its representations of indigeneity, it was not atypical in its critique. Indeed, the magazine was not the only periodical to evoke indigeneity as an anticolonial vernacular. Other newspapers and magazines in India and Canada also drew on the violence of white resettlement and its effects on indigenous peoples to denounce the Dominion government's treatment of the *Komagata Maru* passengers. The *Modern Review,* a weekly periodical published in Calcutta under the editorship of Ramananda Chatterjee, offered one such intervention.[115] In July 1914, as the *Komagata Maru* was preparing to leave Vancouver, with no firm destination in view, one commentator invoked the territorial dispossession of indigenous people to condemn Dominion claims to sovereignty and to challenge the racial disparities of British subjecthood:

> The attitude of the Canadians and all white men who support them, is quite iniquitous. While white men claim, at the point of the bayonet when necessary, to go and settle or sojourn anywhere on the surface of the earth, "coloured" men, particularly Indians, are supposed not to possess the right to labour for wages in a "white" colony. *There is a humorous side to this claim of the colonists to exclude "coloured" labourers. For these "white" colonies rightfully belong to "coloured" aborigines, who have been deprived of their patrimony by force and in many places totally annihilated.* By their attitude the white colonists seem to say, "We have the might, and we will do what we please." But this naturally excites a bellicose mood among non-whites, and so ultimately makes for breach of peace. *For he does not know history or has read it in vain who thinks that races of men are destined to occupy their respective positions of superiority and inferiority forever. The whirligig of time brings on strange revenges.*[116]

The *Review* article explicitly rejected the claim that Canada held the authority to control its territorial borders, especially when the land it was defending was not its own. Similarly, the *London Statist* maintained that "the Canadians are all settlers from foreign lands or descendants of such. They are intruders upon the native possessors of the country and hold their position only because of the protection of the British empire."[117] If the white Dominions "rightfully" belonged to Indigenous peoples, many reasoned, then white colonists could not lawfully or legitimately exclude "coloured" laborers, sojourners, or migrants.

In June 1914, the *Hindustanee* published a lengthy article in its final issue. Titled "The Exclusion of Hindoos," it was penned by an unknown author, described obliquely as a "Canadian gentleman," and who boldly condemned the devastating conditions that confronted indigenous peoples in Canada. The article had been forwarded to Bird, Munshi Singh's lawyer, by a law firm in eastern Canada. "We have never seen such a comprehensive and sound analysis of the Hindu Question," Husain Rahim wrote in his opening editorial. As "it comes from the pen of a Canadian gentleman, we take great pleasure in giving it room in these columns."[118] The commentary, which quite fittingly followed the final installment of Rahim's chronicle, "Canada as a Hindu Saw It," began somewhat predictably. It disputed prevailing claims that Indian migration posed racial threats to white labor. But the "gentleman's" commentary then took an unexpected turn. It questioned the legitimacy of Canada's identity as a white settler colony. "Examined on its merits, the doctrine that this is a white man's country cannot be defended," the author charged. "We have succeeded in almost exterminating the original occupants of our soil, but it is fair to contend that there is nothing really and inherently objectionable in people of one or two more distinct races living side by side."[119] If race-mixing was as perilous as colonial authorities insisted, then the empire was in serious trouble: "why should white men go into Africa, inhabited by blacks, and into China and Japan inhabited by Mongolians, as well as into India peopled with an immense population of a race essentially our own (that is Aryan)."[120] The basis of these arguments, which informed Indian exclusion in Canada and South Africa, revealed the inequalities of British colonial and imperial rule, thereby exposing the inherently delicate legal, political, and racial foundations of Dominion power.

In the *Hindi Punch,* the *Modern Review,* and the *Hindustanee,* indigeneity emerged as a powerful and itinerant force of anticolonial critique, one that circulated in multiple directions across the Pacific and Indian Oceans, connecting Canada, India, and South Africa. Through a combination of subtle satire and explicit disapproval, the articles cited above questioned the legal and political basis of Dominion authority and its violent effects on indigenous communities. Importantly, the forms and figures of indigeneity that were mobilized by Indians and their supporters were disruptive but not always emancipatory. As figures of indigeneity moved across the seas and settled in British jurisdictions, their deployment undermined some racial histories and geographies and reinforced others. If the presence of indigenous peoples in South Africa and Canada led the *Komagata Maru*'s supporters to ask whether a "white man's country" was ever possible, in India indigeneity gave added traction to demands for British subjecthood. In response to the *Komagata Maru*'s failed journey, Indians on the subcontinent, like their counterparts in Natal and the Transvaal, also drew on conceptions of indigeneity to assert their readiness to become part of the imperial polity. To do so, many distinguished themselves from the "natives" of South Africa. It is to India and the politics of indigeneity that I now turn.

"Coloured Subjects of the Crown"

As the *Komagata Maru* awaited its deportation from Vancouver Harbour, and as Canadian officials began deliberations with the Imperial government and with authorities in Hong Kong, Japan, and India as to where the ship should be sent, English-language newspapers located in major cities on the subcontinent published regular—in some cases daily—updates about the vessel's fate. In India, news of the *Komagata Maru*'s journey—its arrival, detention, and anticipated departure from Vancouver—was frequently reported and vigorously debated by the Indian middle classes. For English-language papers published in Amritsar, Allahabad, Lahore, and Calcutta, the *Komagata Maru* became a politically charged site of struggle in which a number of imperial urgencies coalesced: the legality of restrictive legislation in Natal, Canada, and Australia; the imperial government's responsibilities to its Indian constituencies as British subjects; the authority and reach of Dominion jurisdiction; and the legal and political possibilities of "imperial citizenship."[121] Figures of indigeneity featured prominently, though differently, throughout these deliberations. The Indian reading public, for instance, routinely invoked the "native South African" in ways that shaped wider discussions on migration, mobility, and settlement. By positioning themselves *against* indigenous peoples, with whom they had been politically and legally equated in late nineteenth- and early twentieth-century South Africa, some drew on indigeneity as further evidence of their own racial and civilizational superiority and their readiness to join the imperial polity. Anticolonialism, therefore, was not always opposed to or disruptive of racial and colonial histories, even though it emerged in and through them.

Race, as I suggest throughout this book, cannot be conceptualized solely as differences in skin color, phenotype, history, language, and/or geography. Instead, to understand its jurisdictional and structural force, race must be conceived of as a modern strategy of power, one that shaped foundational divides of land/sea, time/space, citizen/subject while also affording meanings to somatic, psychic, and cultural distinctions, often to violent effect.[122] What counted as racial difference in the early twentieth century, as my discussion of *Re Munshi Singh* suggests, was highly politicized, fiercely contested, and intensely generative. Racial distinctions were imported and translated, in collision (and collusion) with people and populations that existed in other histories and geographies. Whereas Bird insisted that the *Komagata Maru* passengers were "Caucasians" and shared racial origins with Europeans, Justice Martin characterized Indians as "Asiatics" who were situated in a different civilizational time, one that was anathema to Canadian ways of life. As the deliberations in *Re Munshi Singh* illustrate, discussions of race and imperial belonging, no matter how luminous or obscure, held political and legal consequences that were fraught and not always straightforward in their effect. Racial differentiations, as my discussion of South Africa suggests, were not solely aimed at marking out and excluding bodies and populations; they were also embedded in and productive of regimes of inclusion *and* exclusion and of superiority *and* inferiority that drew on different genealogies, including caste, and that assigned legal rights and political privileges unequally.[123] Approaches that view race as an expression and effect of modern power have drawn varying degrees of inspiration from the work of Michel Foucault.[124] Among his most prescient and compelling insights was that power is not just a centralized, repressive, or external force imposed upon individuals and populations by sovereign command. To be politically effective, power also circulates through the polity, permeating its subjects so they might eventually govern themselves.[125] If power is a mobile and dynamic force, as Foucault claimed, its effects are not easily foreseeable or predictable. As an effect of racial power, the itinerant politics of indigeneity that I am tracing below, through a transoceanic anticolonialism, fortified and undermined Dominion authority and British imperial command.

Indian claims to racial superiority over native Africans, as they surfaced in South Africa, journeyed across the Indian Ocean region. By 1914, as Indians in the empire followed the *Komagata Maru*'s arrival, detention, and deportation, these assertions materialized with growing frequency in English-language newspapers both in India and the diaspora. That Indians would be embedded in and would knowingly and strategically exploit colonial-racial taxonomies is more fully explicable, beyond the familiar and insufficient explanations of racist attitudes, when race is analyzed as an organizing power and power is analyzed as a motile force that penetrates, animates, and constitutes its subjects. To be clear, my arguments about the motility of race are not intended to draw attention away from the racial and colonial violence of British imperialism and resettlement, the forces of white superiority that enabled colonial rule to flourish, or from the intersections between indigenous dispossession, antiblack racism, and immigration prohibitions that were manifestations of racial power. On the contrary, as I argue in chapter 3, race worked as a jurisdictional logic and a structuring force that underpinned strategies of rule across land and sea, informed conceptions of subjecthood, and organized the empire as an uneven whole. As British subjects and subjected peoples—indigenous, Indian, and African—were produced and differentiated through shifting intensities of colonial power. Attending to the unequal contours of status and subjecthood provides one way of redirecting analytic concerns from the *intent* of colonial actors to the multiple, contradictory, and indeterminate *effects* of imperial command.[126] To be sure, race as a modern regime of power operated not solely through exclusion and repression but also through productive forces, rhythms that were similar to those materialized in the changing force of ocean currents. The ceaseless mobility of race subsumed colonial subjects within wider regimes of power/knowledge and coercion/defiance. In South Africa, Indians rejected the comparisons that colonial administrators drew between them and native Africans. In India, the reading public deliberately and strategically invoked their putative differences from indigenous South Africans to achieve particular legal and political ends. In so doing, they drew from longer histories of racial antagonism and antinomy that transcended the ship and its unsuccessful journey. These histories were not always explicitly articulated in public discussions of the *Komagata Maru*. Rather, they operated as a muted though palpable presence, one that surfaced intermittently and in ways that shaped contests over transoceanic mobility, British subjecthood, and imperial politics.

Indian English newspapers in India published accounts of racial and colonial force directed at indigenous peoples in the Dominions. Unlike the *Hindi Punch* and the *Modern Review,* however, they did not often connect these to Indian migration. In reports of the *Komagata Maru*'s journey, the Indian press often downplayed and erased the violence aimed at indigenous peoples by reminding the Indian reading public of the severe racial conditions that confronted their "country-men in South Africa."[127] Many Indians, including Nanak Chand, a lawyer who spoke at a meeting on Indian migration and the *Komagata Maru* in Lahore, argued that these trials and tribulations needed to be overcome if Indians abroad were "to maintain the good name of this country."[128] Amid extreme adversity, Chand argued, Indians in South Africa were supposed to "establish that they were as good British subjects as those in various parts of the world."[129] Tellingly, his point of reference was not the "colored races" of the empire but white Britons. The "Indian community of Africa," the *Khalsa Advocate* explained, has "for years past, been the victims of grave wrongs and injustices."[130] The wrongs to which the paper referred were ones that whites inflicted on Indians and not ones that Europeans or Indians directed at Africans. Thus, for many, Indian migrants and travelers to South Africa and Canada were the targets (and not the perpetrators) of violence under British colonial and imperial rule.

Discussions of racism in Indian migrant and diasporic histories, such as the ones referenced by Chand and others, have been firmly cast "along a brown-white axis."[131] Until recently, historians have been hesitant to trace the contacts between Indians and Africans and particularly reluctant to analyze the racial contests that organized their everyday encounters.[132] As is true of colonial legal historiographies in Canada and other settler colonies, Indian migration to South Africa has typically been disconnected from histories of indigenous dispossession. Even as colonial historiographies of the Indian Ocean and of East and South Africa point to the transoceanic mobility of Indian travelers and migrants, these accounts are often narrated as though Indians journeyed to and settled in places inhabited by native Africans, yet never came into contact with them. The "history of Indians in South Africa," Antoinette Burton argues, "turns on several racialized axes at once."[133] Burton's interest is in literary and fictional narratives that capture what cannot easily be deciphered from colonial archives. Cross-racial intimacies were often family secrets that escaped the documentation practices of the colonial state, she claims. The "consolidation of a common 'settler' identity," Burton explains, "derived from racially discriminatory treatment under both the colonial and the apartheid state was always already shaped by anxieties about, proximity to, and dependence on, 'native' Africans."[134] As Indians imagined themselves through the disavowal of caste, blackness, and indigeneity, they revealed a set of deeply conjoined histories of colonial and racial violence that continue to be suppressed, even today.[135] The tensions between Indians and Africans, and the role of the African in the constitution of an Indian subjectivity, point to the far reaches of the British Empire, including the shifting constellations of racial power that it inaugurated and through which it unevenly ruled its Dominions, colonies, and distant territories.

In South Africa, as in Canada, authorities instituted a racial regime of government that depended on and augmented the empire's unequal topography. State initiatives aimed at affirming and maintaining white superiority assembled a legally sanctioned racial hierarchy that placed Indians and native Africans on profoundly uneven terms. In his speech to Natal's parliament, Sir Liege Hulett insisted on the centrality of Indian labor to Natal's economic and political progress. Natal "never had been, and never would be a white man's country," Hulett claimed.[136] However, he did not want Natal to become "a desolate wilderness; he did not want to see Victoria County—which was now almost one unbroken field of cultivation from the Umgeni to the Tugela—go back to its *aboriginal darkness*."[137] In 1920, six years after the *Komagata Maru* arrived in Calcutta, the *Natal Advertiser* characterized Indian-African relations as follows. The Indian "is not to be confounded with the native of South Africa. In colour he is dark, and in social status far below the European. But in intelligence and habits of industry he more nearly approximates to the white man than to the black." In his intellectual capacity, the Indian is "no more subject to arrestation than John Smith or Patrick Murphy. Politically and numerically he can never in this country constitute a menace, such as the black man potentially always does. He is an alien in this country in the same sense that a great many people here are aliens; and, with them, he is immeasurably above the aboriginal, whose country this is."[138]

The tense and hostile relations, produced from the vicissitudes of being subject to colonial rule, were further exacerbated by the implementation of colonial laws, policies, and state practices that were aimed at distinguishing *and* consolidating Indians and native Africans. As targets of colonial racism, Indians were not outside or immune to racial power but were produced by and embedded in it. During his time in South Africa, Gandhi repeatedly gestured to the putative racial superiority of Indians over Africans. An Indian's elevated moral status, he argued, was especially manifest in his investments in labor and in his virtuous qualities of hard work, self-discipline, and cleanliness.[139] "Gandhi's touting of Indian industriousness," Sukanya Banerjee contends, was established through and "capitalized on colonial perceptions of 'native laziness,'" which overlooked "the visible exploitation of native labor."[140]

On 17 June 1914, as the *Komagata Maru*'s passengers and supporters awaited the decision about its fate and future, the *Civil and Military Gazette,* an English daily in Lahore, published a provocative article on the racial asymmetries of empire. Outraged by the events in Canada, especially the Dominion's refusal to allow Gurdit Singh and the ship's passengers to enter, the *Civil and Military Gazette* raised a series of difficult questions that incited a protracted and lively discussion foreshadowing many of the issues that would emerge in *Re Munshi Singh.* Specifically, the article emphasized the racial inequities by which imperial subjecthood was organized. "Indians have claimed that the rights which they enjoy in India and England should also be extended to them in the colonies," wrote the *Gazette.* The "colonial governments, they say are making naught of the promise Queen Victoria gave to India, and as the King of England is King also of each colony, his promise ought to hold good in every unit of the Empire." Pointing briefly to the events in Vancouver, the *Gazette* asked its readers, "How can the King both affirm and deny. How can he as Emperor of India grant rights which he confirms as King of England, while as King of South Africa or King of Canada he denies those rights."[141] The answers to these questions, the *Gazette* advised, were dependent on prevailing racial distinctions that were used to differentiate Europeans from Indians. Any resolution of these matters necessitated a much wider discussion of whether Indians were comparable or equal to whites. In short, the *Gazette* encouraged its readers to consider where Indians were positioned in imperial hierarchies of race. Were Indians, like other "coloured races," in need of further moral instruction and guidance from their British custodians, or had they now reached a higher stage of civilization and development after hundreds of years of foreign rule? More importantly, could Indians move out of "the waiting room of history," travel across the supposedly free sea, and make claims to the rights that followed from British subjecthood?[142]

Reprinting an article that originally appeared in the *Pioneer,* another English daily with which the *Civil and Military Gazette* was affiliated, the paper reaffirmed the racial unevenness of the British Empire in the following ways. To begin, the *Gazette* highlighted the civilizational divides by which British rule operated and organized its Dominions, colonies, and protectorates, a constellation of race in which Indians were deeply invested. Second, it outlined the foundational paradoxes and instabilities of imperial promises. Although "the King is the same everywhere, the crown is in each case but part of a constitution and a Government," the paper explained. Contrary to the beliefs of many Indians, the "Governments of the United Kingdom, of India, of South Africa and of Canada *are not identical.*"[143] The *Gazette* elaborated as follows:

> Many imperialists are deeply distressed that the feelings of Indians should be thus wounded and are themselves hurt by the charge that the Empire demands loyalty without giving a proper equivalent. But it should be remembered that there are dangers in the theory that all British subjects have equal rights wherever the Union Jack flies, and that in the future, Indians themselves might [suffer] from the universal acceptance of such a principle. Indians are not the only coloured subjects of the British crown. The Empire contains Chinese, Malays, Polynesians, Red Indians, and Negroes *in various stages of civilization or barbarism. Indians themselves would not maintain that a "Hubshi" ought to have the same rights as an Englishman. Indians are fully aware of the inferiority of the African natives both to themselves and to the Europeans.* And once an exception (an exception which applies to millions of souls) is granted, the whole theory of the equal rights of all British citizens falls to the ground.[144]

The *Gazette* clearly recognized that British imperialism rationalized its geographical reach in racial, territorial, and temporal terms. In an empire that was divided historically and civilizationally, British subjecthood did not carry the same meaning everywhere. Indians, the *Gazette* pointed out, were firmly embedded in existing imperial hierarchies. Their claims to racial and civilizational superiority were asserted against native Africans. But for Indians to demand equality with *all* British subjects, the *Gazette* cautioned, might invite unsavory comparisons of various kinds. Indians could just as easily be contrasted with "hubshis" as they could with white Europeans, with whom they sought affinity.[145] These racial affiliations, which were already initiated in South Africa, might potentially undercut the place of Indians on the British imperial map, thereby unraveling their claims to racial supremacy over *anyone.*

Questions of racial inequality, hierarchy, and taxonomy that emerged in South Africa and resurfaced in struggles over the *Komagata Maru,* which were initiated by the *Pioneer* and reprinted in the *Civil and Military Gazette,* generated contests in other English language newspapers as well. "A curious question has been asked by the *Pioneer* whether the people of India would have no objections if the black races of South-Africa were allowed to settle in India," wrote the *Tribune*. In "the first place we deny the attempted analogy that we are to the people of Canada what the Negroes are to Indians." And second, the *Tribune* continued, "*if we had as extensive and unoccupied tracts of land as Canada and Australia, we would certainly welcome any people on earth to fill them up on equal terms with other British subjects and we would never raise such absurd objections.*"[146] Here, the *Tribune* made two contradictory assertions that closely paralleled British liberal thought: a universal claim to liberty and equality and a deep and continued investment in racial superiority and inferiority.[147] Viewing Canada and Australia as "unoccupied tracts of land," the *Tribune* echoed claims made by several of the *Komagata Maru* passengers. In so doing, the paper deliberately effaced indigenous peoples. The *Tribune* also claimed that there were clear distinctions between native Africans and Indians. Like Justice McPhillips's reasoning in *Re Munshi Singh,* however, the authors did not elaborate on exactly what these differences were. It was implied that Indian subjects, unlike their native African counterparts, had sufficiently benefited from British colonial rule. Thus, Indians held a newfound appreciation for British legality and equality and were ready to migrate to settler colonies, to cultivate and resettle indigenous lands, and to live as equals among whites. In *Re Munshi Singh,* Bird and Cassidy advanced the argument, albeit unsuccessfully, that Indians were Caucasians and thus enjoyed an intimate and even filial relationship with Britons and other Europeans. In Indian English papers, the *Komagata Maru*'s supporters crafted a different racial claim. Also contingent on prevailing colonial-racial orders, but ones that emerged out of longer histories of Indian migration to South Africa, their argument held that the presumed superiority of Indians over native Africans was further evidence of their preparedness to join the imperial polity. These constellations of race offered some of "the material foundations of Western Society" that England sought to establish in India, through what Marx described as the empire's "double mission" of destruction and regeneration.[148]

INDIAN STRUGGLES AGAINST British imperial rule that drew on the territorial dispossession of indigenous peoples, as powerful as they are, cannot be read in terms of solidarity and collaboration among colonized peoples alone. Nor can they be interpreted as an alibi for the colonizing role of Indian migrants. To be sure, political alliances and intimacies between Indians, indigenous peoples, and Africans were inevitable in colonial contexts as were contentions and conflicts.

However, the dynamic relations of colonial rule that I draw out in this chapter highlight a productive force of racial power that defies any straightforward or easy conclusions.[149] Indians in South Africa and Canada regularly described themselves as "pioneers" and "settlers." For some sojourners and migrants from the subcontinent, "free migration" was vital to the British Empire and especially to the territorial resettlement of the Dominions. "There is a crying need for labour on the unsettled lands," wrote the *Hindustanee,* as the *Komagata Maru* was anchored in Vancouver Harbour.[150] We "are confronted with the rapid awakening and expansion of coloured peoples who have never acquiesced in the theory that certain lands should be set aside for white colonization only," remarked *Indian Opinion.*[151] Many Indians viewed themselves as civilizationally advanced, further along in the forward march of history, and thus ready to be equals in the imperial family. Their claims to racial superiority were based on a "coming of age," as Tagore put it and on the esteemed virtues of labor and industriousness that were so vital to Gandhi's anticolonial visions. Bound up in contests against British rule, the figures of indigeneity invoked by Indian migrants, travelers, and the *Komagata Maru*'s supporters, which circulated across the Indian Ocean between India and South Africa and across the Pacific to Canada, had multiple, unpredictable, and coercive effects. These anticolonial vernaculars did not assist Indians in reaching their objectives and they certainly did not work in the interests of indigenous communities.

Through their seaborne movements, Indian sojourners and migrants developed an expansive view of the British Empire. Looking out to the ship as it traveled along the Pacific and then the Indian Ocean, the *Komagata Maru*'s advocates in India and the diaspora marshaled a number of rhetorical strategies to assert the passengers' rights to enter Canada. They cited imperial citizenship, emphasized the deterritorialization of indigenous peoples in the white Dominions, and asserted claims as British subjects who were equal to white Britons, and therefore should be permitted to travel and trade on the free sea. Some onlookers, as I suggest above, offered highly sophisticated and compelling anticolonial critiques, which connected indigenous dispossession and immigration prohibitions through race, territory, and temporality. In the following chapter, I examine these connections further. Specifically, I argue that unprecedented access to steamship travel from the late nineteenth century onward, nurtured critical anticolonial imaginaries among Indian subjects, most notably Gurdit Singh. From his voyages to Malaya, Singapore, India, Hong Kong, and to Canada's west coast, and through his fugitivity on land, Singh drew powerful links between transatlantic slavery, systems of Indian indenture, and immigration regulations as the violent command of British imperial rule. But like many of his counterparts aboard the *Komagata Maru* and on shore, Gurdit Singh said nothing of the racial and colonial violence that was directed at indigenous peoples in Canada, India, and the Straits Settlements. Despite these omissions, however, Singh's discerning critique of the empire highlighted the ways in which racial power moved with changing intensities, connecting land, sea, and littoral and puncturing the divides between past, present, and future. In his anticolonial writings, Singh foregrounded the overlapping, shared, and competing legalities that extended the empire's reach. These jurisdictional tensions, as he conceived them, opened opportunities for new contests and different futures.

The Fugitive Sojourns of Gurdit Singh

Gurdit Singh

O Gurdit Singh! O Gurdit Singh! / Why did you to this country bringh
A crowd of Hindus 'neath your wing / Against our laws, O Gurdit Singh?

O Gurdit Singh! O Gurdit Singh! / You knew you could not have your flingh,
Nor round your finger like a ringh, / Twist our enactments, Gurdit Singh

O Gurdit Singh! O Gurdit Singh! / Your ship at anchor there will swingh
And turn to junk or anythingh / Before you land, O Gurdit Singh!

O Gurdit Singh! O Gurdit Singh! / You and your legal friends may wringh
Your hands and curse your stars and singh / Another tune, O Gurdit Singh!

O Gurdit Singh! O Gurdit Singh! / I guess you've found us tough as *lingh;
Now "git" by way you came, nor bringh / Another shipload, Gurdit Singh
—FRANK L. VOSPER, *Vancouver Sun,* June 1914

This sacrifice of flesh and blood [slavery] to Mammon in no way less reprehensible than
the cannibalism of the savage races, is a legacy of Spain and Portugal to Europe. The big
powers gradually felt the inequity of the custom and are said to have met in a conference in
1833 to stop the practice.... The negro slave trade being closed to them, they turned their
attention upon Hindusthan [*sic*]—GURDIT SINGH, *Voyage of the Komagatamaru,* 1928

Prior to the *Komagata Maru*'s 1914 voyage, Gurdit Singh was only vaguely
familiar to colonial judges and administrators. He appeared before criminal
and civil courts in Punjab, Malaya, and Singapore, often for minor offenses and

FIGURE 5.1. Gurdit Singh in his best clothes, c. 1914. (Photo courtesy of Library and Archives Canada. Photographer: W. Kaye Lamb, C026547)

disputes, and was characterized as a local agitator who marshaled British and colonial laws for his own pecuniary gain.[1] Singh's ambitions to begin a steamship company and his efforts to transport Punjabi travelers and migrants from Hong Kong to Vancouver, in violation of Dominion legislation and in direct defiance of a British imperial and racial order, gained him a newfound prominence (see fig. 5.1). He and the ship were the focus of hundreds of letters and telegrams and the subject of two government enquiries. The *Komagata Maru* was the most recent target of Canada's orders-in-council and a direct catalyst for India's new border control regulations. Singh's transpacific expedition, albeit unsuccessful, inspired respect, admiration, and encouragement from Indian observers in the subcontinent and the diaspora, and drew condemnation from white colonists, as the poem by Frank Vosper quoted above suggests. Ultimately, the six-month voyage transformed Singh from a "wealthy businessman" and railway contractor into a seafaring "mutineer."[2] Though he was born in the village of Sirali, in the

Amritsar district of a landlocked Punjab, his seafaring aspirations earned him the title "Bengal ka Kaptan."[3]

From the seventeenth century onward, as I have argued throughout this book, Dutch, British, and, later, American jurists debated the racial and legal status of oceans. Amid ongoing disagreements as to whether the sea was open or closed, one point was clear: the freedom of sea was a freedom for European men and not for indigenous peoples or colonized subjects.[4] Like many before him, including lascars, sailors, fugitive and freed slaves, Singh embraced the sea as a space of freedom and a site of resistance against colonial, imperial, and racial rule.[5] In 1845, Frederick Douglass wrote longingly of oceangoing vessels as places of refuge from the horrors of slavery. "You are loosed from your moorings, and are free; I am fast in my chains, and am a slave! You move merrily before the gentle gale, and I sadly before the bloody whip! You are freedom's swift-winged angels that fly round the world; I am confined in bands of iron! O that I were free!"[6] The world of the ship, as Douglass imagined it, would open new routes of escape, and it did.[7] Almost seventy years later, Gurdit Singh looked out to the sea as an endless horizon filled with opportunities for commerce, political autonomy, and escape from the tyrannies of British command. Given his travels between Punjab and the Straits Settlements, Singh was well aware that Britannia's efforts to rule the waves were ambitions and objectives that were not often successful in practice. Maritime vulnerabilities, as he viewed them, opened lucrative prospects for mobility, trade, and anticolonial contest.[8]

Competing visions of the sea—as *mare liberum* and *mare clausum*—collided in the *Komagata Maru*'s arrival at Vancouver. On 13 June 1914, three weeks after the vessel laid anchor, as Gurdit Singh and the other passengers were confined on the ship awaiting news on whether they would be granted a legal hearing on shore, the *Vancouver Sun* published the poem with which this chapter begins.[9] Titled "Gurdit Singh" and written by Frank L. Vosper, a prolific essayist, civic "pioneer," and esteemed member of Vancouver's Methodist Church, the poem was placed inconspicuously near the bottom of the page. Readers would have needed to look hard to find it. But Vosper's satire was timely. The poem, though focused on Singh and the *Komagata Maru*, gestured to existing anxieties of Asiatic travel and to the racial and political consequences of unregulated maritime worlds. In stanza after stanza, Vosper assured his readers, with unremitting confidence, that the free sea remained a European domain, one that was well protected by the rule of law and by racial rule. The *Komagata Maru*'s landing, Vosper insisted, would not yield the liberatory outcomes that Singh envisioned. Rather, his seagoing aspirations would only unleash additional forms of maritime control and new restrictions on mobility, culminating in greater unfreedoms for Indians on land and at sea. Vosper's poetic voice was prescient. Six weeks later, Canada's immigration laws, including its newly revised continuous journey regulation, ensured the *Komagata Maru*'s deportation. Moreover, the ship's landing outside Calcutta, which is the subject of this chapter, inaugurated a new security regime in colonial India that held devastating consequences for Gurdit Singh, the passengers, and thousands of Indian nationals well into the 1920s.

Even before the steamer lifted anchor and embarked from Hong Kong, Gurdit Singh became a person of mounting interest. He appeared with regularity in government correspondence and in newspaper coverage in Canada, India, and beyond. In many of these accounts, Singh's business acumen and maritime entrepreneurialism were questioned and undermined by recurring allegations of his militancy and criminality. During the vessel's protracted journey, authorities characterized him in disparaging terms, as scheming, fraudulent, and not particularly clever. Gurdit Singh is "a man of little intelligence" and "suffers from an inflated idea of his own importance and that of his 'Komagata Maru' venture," one source charged.[10] Singh's "lurid past," another claimed, placed him "among Sikh extremists." He was described as "an irreconcilable opponent of Government and more or less involved in every form of extremist agitation in the Punjab."[11] He and his "immediate adherents," C. A. Barron, the chief secretary of Punjab concluded, were "violent and dangerous persons."[12] Indian officials insisted repeatedly and tirelessly that Singh was an affiliate of the Ghadrs. "During both the [vessel's] outward and return voyages," the *Ghadr Directory* stated, "Gurdit Singh posed openly as a revolutionary leader." Literature from "the Ghadr Party in America was circulated on board and the passengers were incited to raise the standard of revolt against the British Government on their return to India."[13] Yet Singh's visions of anticolonialism, as I argue below, offered a distinct approach and a dramatic departure from existing repertoires of Indian radicalism. While the Ghadrs unequivocally rejected British law and called for armed revolution, Singh encouraged an anticolonialism that embraced oceans, maritime commerce, and British legality.[14]

Gurdit Singh's standing as an outlaw and his alleged affiliations with the Ghadrs were not benign characterizations. Rather, they motivated a series of violent legal responses from the Hong Kong and Canadian governments, and from the Indian colonial state. In September 1914, in anticipation of the *Komagata Maru*'s arrival, Indian authorities hastily enacted new emergency legislation. Many worried that the steamer's landing would incite further unrest and agitation, exacerbating revolutionary activities already underway in the former capital.[15] On 28 July 1914, shortly after the vessel departed Vancouver Harbour,

World War I commenced. The "Great War" only amplified and exacerbated these fears.[16] To prepare for the return of a shipload of passengers suspected of disaffection and disloyalty, the Indian colonial government passed the Foreigners Ordinance and the Ingress into India Ordinance.[17] Together, they granted police, magistrates, and other authorities unprecedented and sweeping powers to arrest and detain "aliens" and nationals arriving in India by land or sea and who were thought to be involved in anticolonial activities abroad.[18] As a direct response to the *Komagata Maru*, the Ingress transformed Gurdit Singh and hundreds of others from law-abiding subjects into "criminals" who posed imminent threats to British imperial rule. The ordinances were to be terminated six months following the end of war but remained in effect much longer. The Ingress did not expire until February 1922, three months after Singh's arrest, conviction, and imprisonment.

This chapter tracks the fugitive sojourns of Gurdit Singh, beginning with his absconding from Budge Budge in September 1914 and ending with his dramatic surrender in Sheikhupura, Punjab, in November 1921. The vessel's outbound voyage from Vancouver and its landing on the Hooghly River, thirty kilometers south of Calcutta, have received surprisingly little consideration, as have Singh's escape and submission to police.[19] In the first section, I follow the ship's passage from Vancouver to Budge Budge. My interest is not solely in filling a historical gap, as necessary as this is, but in exploring the *conditions* of political, legal, and racial violence that the *Komagata Maru*'s voyage initiated and established following its arrival to Calcutta. India's security regime, which targeted foreigners and nationals alike, was partly motivated by Singh's seaborne ambitions and was tightly bound up with maritime regulations. The politically charged circumstances under which these ordinances were signed, combined with their extensive and coercive powers, made fugitivity Singh's only viable possibility. In the second section, I track Singh's clandestine itinerancy, his surrender, and his sedition trial in Amritsar. Though he was never formally charged with events related to the *Komagata Maru*, Singh's efforts to commence a shipping line and to assert his rights to the sea, firmly established him as a criminal, an outlaw, and an enemy of the colonial state. In the final section, I turn to Singh's anticolonial writings. Published first in Gurmukhi as *Zulmi Katha,* and then in English as *Voyage of the Komagatamaru, or India's Slavery Abroad,* Singh's "life history," as he called the English version, echoed several genres at once, including autobiography, travel narrative, and legal testimony, though never fully embodying any one of them.[20] The *Voyage,* which is the focus of my attention here, was intended as a legal rejoinder to the charges of corruption, despotism, and sedition that were laid against him by the Dominion of Canada and the governments of

Hong Kong, Bengal, and Punjab. Fugitivity is palpable in the text's form and content. The manuscript was written while Singh was at large and completed retrospectively, during his time in prison. An undulating rhythm and disjointed temporality are discernable throughout the text, evidenced in its rhetorical strategies, its inconsistencies, and ultimately, its lack of closure.

Maritime worlds, as I have argued throughout, point to overlapping histories and geographies that are often hidden from view. As an alternative to analytic frameworks that focus on terra firma, I draw on fugitivity as a concept that foregrounds mobility across land and sea. My discussion of fugitivity draws from two disparate sources and places them into conversation: the first comes from Singh's brief but persuasive remarks on the transatlantic slave trade, and the second from scholars of slavery. In the *Voyage,* as indicated in the epigraph above, Singh viewed abolition not as freedom but as the inauguration of additional forms of bondage, most notably indentured labor. Yet Singh's critique of British rule did not center on the subcontinent or on Indians alone. Rather, his anticolonial imaginary reached much further back, to earlier eras, additional ocean regions, and other manifestations of racial violence. His condemnation of the empire was animated by discrepant histories that commenced with the Atlantic slave trade, joined the Indian and Pacific Oceans, and were echoed in the oppressive conditions that he and his countrymen confronted in India, the Straits Settlements, and the white Dominions, as well as at sea. The clandestine mobility of fugitivity, as the writings of Douglass and others suggest, was often inspired by maritime worlds. Lines of escape that joined land and sea engendered freedom and unfreedom, not as distinct states, but as deeply conjoined processes.[21] By "stealing away," Saidiya Hartman argues, slaves embodied a transgression of law that placed them in a continual state of flight, one that was marked by the ongoing threat of reenslavement.[22] It was in this interval between liberty and capture that fugitivity produced newness, creativity, and possibility.[23] Singh's fugitive wanderings, as I discuss in the third section, generated dynamic repertoires of anticolonialism, which were inspired by the sea and which embraced it as a domain of freedom from British rule.

My turn to transatlantic slavery, I should say at the outset, is in no way intended to equate the figure of the forced migrant with that of the slave. Nor is it to draw their intensities of racial violence into analogous or parallel terms. Rather, fugitivity, as I see it, offers a productive schema through which to consider racial restrictions on maritime mobility, the memories of slavery that informed them, and the radical imaginaries they made possible. In the eighteenth century, for example, the legal architecture of fugitive slave laws in the southern United States borrowed directly from maritime legislation aimed at ship-jumping sailors.[24] In the nineteenth century, as I suggest in chapter 2, the ship and the slave were racial and juridical forms joined through idioms of legal personhood. If the sea was a source of racial, colonial, and legal violence, as evinced in the middle passage and in coerced migrations across the *kala pani,* it was also a space of refuge that inspired escape and new ways of being.[25] For Singh, the sea was filled with possibilities not yet realized, and which dramatically shaped his radical imaginary.

Situating Singh's fugitivity within histories of transatlantic slavery breathes a much-needed plurality into studies of Indian radicalism. Just as Singh's absconding from Budge Budge and his seven years of flight unleashed new forms of colonial and legal force and generated unprecedented constellations of racial power in British-controlled India, it inspired alternative vernaculars of freedom and justice that opposed and even challenged Ghadr radicalism. But tracing Singh's itinerary and his anticoloniality, let me first turn to the legal and political circumstances surrounding the *Komagata Maru*'s landing, as these were the conditions that necessitated his fugitivity in the first place.

The Budge Budge Massacre

The British Columbia Court of Appeal's decision to deport the *Komagata Maru* may have been unanimous and uncontroversial, but the vessel's actual deportation was not. Deliberations over the ship's outbound journey and its final destination became points of fierce contention, affirming the British Empire as an uneven composite of Dominions, colonies, and territories that did not always work efficiently as a coordinated imperial whole. The court's deliberations in *Re Munshi Singh* opened a series of jurisdictional questions: who was responsible for the ship and its passengers? Where was the vessel to be sent—to Hong Kong, Japan, India, or elsewhere? The Charter-Party presented some direction in this regard. As the law of the ship, it specified that if the schedule of installments or any other conditions of the contract were violated, the vessel was to be "redelivered in Hong Kong."[26] For the ship's owners, the island colony was the *Komagata Maru*'s rightful port of return. After learning of the court's decision, many passengers anticipated that they would be sent to Hong Kong, as nearly half had boarded there. Others hoped this to be their final destination, so they could be closer to other Asian port cities, including Shanghai, Singapore, and Manila, where many passengers had been employed as security guards and night watchmen. Opportunities for steady employment were more crucial now than ever, so passengers could recover the devastating financial losses they incurred while at sea. But Gurdit Singh's reputation as a criminal and outlaw, combined with allegations that he had radicalized passengers aboard the ship, drastically altered the vessel's prospects for landing. Authorities in Hong Kong, Japan, and Singapore accused Singh and others of being seditionists, criminals, and revolutionaries who would not be permitted entry under any circumstances.

As the vessel prepared to leave Vancouver Harbour, with no clear destination at hand, the governor general of Hong Kong telegrammed the governor general of Canada, assuring him that the passengers would not be allowed to land. "Not only is it probable that the greater number of these men will not find employment here," he wrote tersely, "but they are all now apparently disaffected and it would be highly undesirable to have them in this Colony where they may contaminate the Indian troops and the heterogeneous agglomeration of Indians who find employment as private watchmen."[27] That the passengers had been subjected to radical influences under Gurdit Singh's command became a common refrain that was invoked to justify the ship's exclusion from Hong Kong and Singapore. As deliberations on the fate of the ship continued, the *Komagata Maru* anchored in Yokohama. While in port, Singh received a letter from the Hong Kong colonial secretary "informing him that the Government of that Dependency considered it undesirable that any of the passengers should land . . . and threatening to enforce a local Vagrancy Ordinance against any who might attempt to" do so.[28] In many parts of the British Empire, authorities used vagrancy laws against colonial subjects, especially those suspected of engaging in "disorderly" behavior, including prostitution, trespassing, and homelessness.[29] In Hong Kong, the Vagrancy Ordinance explicitly targeted foreigners who arrived by ship. Here, a "vagrant" was defined as "any person other than a Chinese found asking for alms or without any employment or visible means of subsistence."[30] If non-Chinese persons were not suitably employed within seven days of arriving in the colony, they faced detention and/or deportation. The ordinance specified that shipmasters were to be held financially responsible for any passengers deemed indigent or undesirable.[31] If the *Komagata Maru* attempted to lay anchor, the governor general assured the secretary of state for the colonies, the "Master owner or agent of steamers by which they are brought back will be held liable for all charges incurred by Government of Hong Kong in connection with . . . repatriation of destitutes."[32] By regulating the passage of ships and those aboard, the Vagrancy Ordinance, granted authorities in Hong Kong additional ways to extend their jurisdiction from land to sea.

Given the hostile reaction from Hong Kong, the Dominion and Indian governments began negotiating alternative final destinations for the *Komagata Maru*. After stopping in Yokohama, where a dozen passengers disembarked and several others boarded, the ship docked in Kobe. Authorities alleged that Indian radicals embarked and delivered seditious speeches. Others claimed that revolvers were smuggled aboard the ship and were part of a mutinous plan.[33] As deliberations continued, the governments of Canada and India agreed to share the costs of the voyage. Since all the passengers were originally from Punjab, Indian officials reluctantly agreed to permit the vessel to land in a designated Indian port. But Gurdit Singh had other plans. On 16 September, while the *Komagata Maru* was en route to the subcontinent, it passed through the Straits of Singapore. This was the very place where Dutch vessels, under the command of Jakob van Heemskerk, attacked the *Santa Catarina* more than three hundred years earlier. These waters spawned the European debates on the free sea, in which Gurdit Singh and the *Komagata Maru* were now firmly embedded. Like many of the other passengers, Singh had no desire to return to India. Instead, he hoped to disembark in Singapore, where he still had commercial interests and personal contacts. Indeed, the Guru Nanak Steamship Company was registered in Singapore, and Singh's address was listed as the Singapore Gurdwara. But when he "attempted to get special permission to go on shore to purchase stores" the Captain recalled, his request was flatly denied.[34] As the Great War was already under way, Singapore was subject to martial law, and authorities "refused to allow any one to land."[35] The *Komagata Maru* "remained at a distance of five miles" from shore, beyond the three-mile jurisdictional line "where the steamers usually lie at anchor."[36]

Dominion and Indian authorities readily acknowledged that the passengers "did in fact not want to return to India."[37] But those on the ship were considered dangerous and mutinous and there were few remaining options. Initially, officials made arrangements for the vessel to drop anchor in Madras, where the "atmosphere was less excitable than [it was in] Calcutta."[38] But Gurdit Singh and the others demanded to go to Calcutta. Given heightened fears of radicalism in the former capital city, authorities grudgingly granted their permission. As soon as the ship berthed, Bengal and Punjab police would be on site to escort the returnees to the Budge Budge railway station where they would be placed on a special train and sent to their respective villages in Punjab. Anticipating unrest and seeking assurances that their plans would be followed, the Indian colonial government hastily enacted new legislation. On 12 September 1914, Lord Hardinge signed the Ingress into India Ordinance, which was linked directly to the Foreigners Ordinance that had been passed one week earlier. The Foreigners Ordinance was intended to manage the entry and exit of all "aliens" into India. The Ingress, by contrast, was aimed at Indian nationals but motivated by similar concerns. It targeted any nationals "entering British India, whether by sea or land, in order to protect the State from danger of anything prejudicial to its safety, interest or tranquility."[39] Gurdit Singh, seen as an outlaw, and those under his persuasion were believed to pose serious threats to the order and authority of the Indian colonial government.

The Ingress into India Ordinance was signed seventeen days before the *Komagata Maru* arrived in Calcutta. Since conditions at sea made it difficult to predict when a ship might enter port, the ordinance was to be enforced retroactively, against any Indian national arriving on the subcontinent after 5 September. Though the Ingress applied only to Indian nationals entering India or Burma by land or by ship, foreignness was its governing logic.[40] The Ingress "is another instance of 'Emergency Legislation,'" one memo explained. "It gives power in the interests of the state *to treat persons in British India in the same manner as foreigners—even though they are not foreigners in fact—*in regard to restriction of their liberty and the other matters dealt with in the Foreigners Ordinance [of] 1914."[41] Although the Ingress could not deny Indian nationals reentry, fears of sedition and criminality granted the colonial government new powers to govern recent arrivals as though they were foreigners in their own land. As Gurdit Singh and many other passengers had been domiciled elsewhere, in Hong Kong, Shanghai, Kobe, and Singapore, District Magistrate Mr. Donald, proceeded to describe them as "emigrants from outside India."[42]

At what was thought to be a high-water mark of radicalism and anticolonialism, the Ingress granted authorities expansive powers to govern those arriving from aboard.[43] It authorized local police to search, register, arrest, and detain persons suspected of endangering national security, and to curtail the movements of nationals in various parts of the subcontinent. Magistrates and police were authorized to prevent anyone from interacting "with any class of persons with whom such communication or intercourse may be prohibited." They could lawfully confine suspects to their respective villages, requiring them to make daily appearances before a supervising officer.[44] Imprisonment was indefinite and release was "pending inquiry."[45] Thus, the *Komagata Maru*'s arrival radically altered India's security regime. Gurdit Singh had planned the voyage partly as a challenge to the racial and legal restrictions imposed on Indian migrants and travelers seeking entry to Canada. When the ship anchored in Calcutta, however, this new law awaited them, one that was equally repressive in its efforts to control Indian mobility. The onset of the First World War granted Indian officials additional ways to justify and legitimize their new repressive powers. The Ingress was necessary, one source asserted, "on general grounds appertaining to a state of war" and not on account of internal or local threats of sedition.[46]

Positioned along the eastern and western Indian Ocean regions and with growing numbers of nationals abroad, some officials argued that India was especially susceptible to external seaborne threats. Maritime governance featured prominently in India's emergency legislation, just as it did in Canada's continuous journey provision and in Hong Kong's Vagrancy Ordinance. In all three jurisdictions, control over migration and mobility began at sea and was subsequently extended to land. The success of legal enforcement depended to a large extent on the coordination and cooperation of shipping companies. Like their Canadian counterparts, who enlisted ship owners and operators into the domain of immigration law, Indian officials also advised steamship owners and managers to uphold and abide by the newly enacted ordinances. Shipping companies were instructed not to book "aliens to ports other than Calcutta, Madras, or Rangoon."[47] The Foreigners Ordinance differentiated "aliens" into "enemies" and "friends." The former included residents of Germany, Austria, and Hungary, which were at war with Britain; the latter were residents of countries at peace with the Crown. But even "'alien friends' (Belgians or Dutch) [who] are booked to Bombay, Karachi or other ports [other] than those named above," Indian authorities cautioned, "will meet with difficulty on arrival." To enter ports of call "without special permission" from the relevant governments was "punishable with imprisonment or fines."[48]

Indian authorities vowed that they would enforce this new security apparatus to the fullest extent possible. However, the Foreigners Ordinance was applied selectively, unevenly, and racially. Whereas Canada's continuous journey regulation targeted and thus excluded Indian sojourners and migrants, the Foreigners Ordinance ensured the unrestrained mobility of white British subjects. Several days after the *Komagata Maru* anchored on the Hooghly River, eight Canadian missionaries commenced their sea bound passage from Liverpool to Bombay.[49] As white subjects of the empire, they could not be denied entry to India. Under the newly enacted Foreigners Ordinance, however, they were restricted to specified ports of call, and Bombay was not one of them. Given India's recent border regulations, all Canadian travelers were advised to "provide themselves with passports or other satisfactory evidence" proving that they were British subjects.[50] In the case of the Canadian missionaries, British officials advised India's Home Department accordingly: "It may be worth while to caution your officers not to treat Canadians as foreigners," especially "when travelling in company with Americans."[51] As was the case with Canada's continuous journey regulation, India's Foreigners Ordinance maintained a selective freedom of mobility, but one that expanded the racial and legal status of the free sea well beyond the contours of British subjecthood. Oceans were no longer domains of European control. There were spaces where whiteness could flourish.[52]

As the specific targets of the Ingress, Gurdit Singh and the other passengers suffered devastating consequences. If the ordinance was inspired, in part, by Singh's alleged criminality, it certainly produced the conditions of his fugitivity. Authorities were quite literally armed with the law as they awaited the ship's landing. District Magistrate Mr. Donald, who was accompanied by several British and Bengali officers, met the *Komagata Maru* in Kalpi. By official accounts, authorities "interviewed the passengers and explained the intentions of [the Indian colonial] Government" to send the passengers to Punjab.[53] The police then examined their luggage "for arms and seditious literature" which was thought to be smuggled aboard at Yokohama and Kobe. Several "of the returning Indians were also searched," authorities reported.[54] But Amir Muhammed Khan, one of Gurdit Singh's closest associates, remembered the ship's arrival differently. The passengers were all lined up, arranged by their village districts, and examined "very roughly," he recalled.[55] They were not "told that they were to travel to the Punjab from Budge Budge or that any of them were to be subject to restraint either in Bengal or on arrival in the Punjab."[56] Two days later, when the ship anchored at the jetty in Budge Budge, the passengers "were directed to disembark and to proceed to the special train."[57] On another visit to the ship, Mr. Donald "clearly read out" the Ingress and, in so doing, startled those on board. "The Ingress into India Ordinance was the last thing in the world those passengers who had been refused ingress into the colony [of Canada], were in a fit condition to understand and properly appreciate," the *Leader* reported.[58] The vessel had only just anchored after a long, dramatic, and arduous six-month journey, during which the passengers were detained at sea, deprived of food and water, attacked by police, and denied entry to Canada, Hong Kong, and Singapore. Though "Gurdit Singh and other Sikhs understood English," the *Tribune* claimed, "they absolutely refused to go."[59] Some feared imprisonment in their villages. Others stayed with Gurdit Singh so that they could collect the money he owed them and had promised to repay at landfall.

According to passenger Bhan Singh, Gurdit Singh did not intend to defy the police. "At first, when the Ordinance was shown to him his intention was to go by the train" to Punjab. But "when he went near the *Granth Sahib* . . . he changed his mind."[60] Before proceeding back to his village in Amritsar, Gurdit Singh decided to visit the Gurdwara at Howrah. There, he would deposit the Sikh holy book that accompanied the passengers on their protracted journey. At Howrah, he could also settle the accounts he kept at sea. Perhaps most importantly, Singh planned to file a complaint with the Indian government, listing the privations that he and the passengers suffered over the course of their six-month voyage.[61] Though Singh's preference was to land in Singapore, he was optimistic that the *Komagata Maru*'s arrival in Calcutta would avail him opportunities to seek justice. "There existed in our breasts a ray of hope that once in India and the real facts are layed [*sic*] before the Indian Government," he and the others "would be redressed." But "fate was holding a different cup for us at Budge Budge," Singh lamented. "Little did we knew [*sic*] that like wild beasts we would be hunted and shot on the very soil of our mother land with no one to raise a voice for us and on our behalf."[62] The full weight of legal force was unleashed against the passengers. It was justified by Singh's presumed lawlessness, his alleged radicalism during the middle passage, and ultimately, by the outbreak of war.

Given the flurry of telegrams that were exchanged between authorities in Canada, Hong Kong, and Japan, Indian officials fully expected that the passengers would arrive in an indignant and desperate state. "The vast majority of the passengers," wrote the Home Department's R. H. Craddock, were "misled and deluded by Gurdit Singh." They "had suffered so much hardship, and had been for so many weary months shut up on board the ship" that they were angry and disgruntled on their return.[63] Contrary to these accounts, most of the passengers laid fault with the Dominion, Indian, and British imperial governments and not with Gurdit Singh. Passenger Surain Singh described their grievances accordingly: "First, we used to go to Australia and the Government stopped that, then we used to go to America and the Government stopped that also." Now, "the Government has taken possession of the ship; the Government is doing great *zoolum* to us . . . the Government considers us *badmashes*. The Government mistrusts us and the Government will surely punish us on our return."[64] On their outbound voyage, the passengers met with opposition and hostility at Hong Kong and Singapore. Many anticipated that their landing at Budge Budge would provoke a similar response. Given rumors of seditious plottings at sea and of mutinous plans involving revolvers, authorities expected that many of the returnees would "resort to undesirable agitation."[65]

Despite the growing speculations on the disaffected state of the passengers, David Petrie, the assistant commissioner of the Criminal Intelligence Directory (CID), openly admitted that he "did not know" what Gurdit Singh and the others "were going to do" on their arrival. His "impression was that they might hold meetings" in Calcutta or give "inflammatory speeches" against the government.[66] They might instigate "inflammatory newspaper articles, or an assassination or some outbreak or something like that," he explained.[67] The special trains to Punjab were intended to circumvent these opportunities by preventing Singh and his supporters from staying in Calcutta and thus forestalling any plans they might have to incite trouble. In the first decades of the twentieth century, Calcutta remained a politically charged space that was marked by a long history of revolutionary activity.[68] In September 1914, three years after the capital was moved to New Delhi, Petrie still described the city as a hotbed that was "full of combustible material."[69] Long after the passengers disembarked, fears of what the ship represented and of radicalism at sea continued to reverberate in Calcutta. There is "evidence to prove that, after the arrival of the 'Komagata Maru,'" wrote the *Komagata Maru* Commission of Inquiry, "there has been a large influx of Indians to Calcutta from America. It is believed that many of these returning emigrants are infected with seditious views and have returned to this country with the avowed intention of promoting a rising against Government."[70] These allegations only encouraged further calls for maritime regulation, all the while sanctioning India's repressive security controls.

By official accounts, the *Komagata Maru* passengers "steadily refused to disembark," despite "the efforts of the various officers to induce them to do so."[71] District Magistrate Mr. Donald warned that if those aboard did "not go ashore within an hour's time, the steamer will be sent . . . to the Andaman Islands," Britain's most notorious and reviled penal colony.[72] After multiple threats of being returned to sea and forced to cross the *kala pani*, the passengers were "induced to take their luggage off the vessel." But of the 321 who landed, only 59 willingly boarded the special train to Punjab. This included 17 Muslims from the Shahpur District. The "Muhammadans managed to elude the efforts of their fellow passengers to detain them and entered the special train not only willingly but gladly," one source claimed. The Muslim passengers were allegedly "subjected to great ill-treatment by Gurdit Singh on the voyage," allegations that directly opposed the reports of religious unity and solidarity advanced by Bhag Singh, Husain Rahim, and Gurdit Singh.[73] Recall that at different moments during the voyage, each of these men maintained that the ship's passage had united Sikhs and Muslims against British imperial rule. "The Muhammadans were on Gurdit Singh's side," passenger Hazarah Singh asserted, but most had not paid their fares.[74] Together, the men owed at least £130 and were thus "ready to go" to Punjab as they did not have the funds to repay Singh.[75] Only one Muslim passenger by the name of Baru stayed behind.[76]

Notwithstanding the concerted efforts made by local authorities to send the passengers to Punjab, those who remained did not go to the train station as directed. Instead, they began marching toward Howrah. Despite the violent greeting they received on their arrival, the passengers formed a procession, sang hymns, and displayed good spirits. Their march to Howrah was "headed by the Granth Sahib, the holy scripture of the Sikhs, which was carried by some of the passengers," authorities reported.[77] Many of the returnees, including Baru, "were creditors of Gurdit Singh." They followed him with the intention of recovering the money that he owed them. As per the shipboard agreement that Singh signed with the passengers, he was obligated to repay his debts once the vessel reached land. Many of those who lent him money had lost their entire life savings. They expected Singh to honor his debts and to return half their fares, as promised.[78] The passengers "did not like to leave him," several officers concluded, "for they were afraid of losing their money." Singh had his own reasons for going to Howrah. According to passenger Pohlo Ram, Singh's intention was to "ask for the appointment of a Commission . . . [so] that Government should hear" the passengers' devastating stories of deprivation and loss while they were imprisoned aboard the vessel.[79] Notwithstanding the many injustices wrought by the vessel's ill-fated journey, Gurdit Singh maintained the belief that if he appeared in court, he would receive a fair and impartial hearing. Indian authorities, he claimed, would surely agree that both the Hong Kong and Dominion governments mistreated them, and in reaching this decision, would compensate their losses. But Singh and the others never made it to Howrah as planned. A struggle ensued in which forty passengers, bystanders, and police were killed and many others injured.

What happened at Budge Budge remained a point of dispute for years to come. According to the *Leader,* the "Sikhs were excited by disembarkation arrangements and started to march to Calcutta. They were taken back by a force of police and military and [that] suddenly opened fire."[80] However, the passengers claimed that the local police escorted their convoy to Howrah (see fig. 5.2). En route, their procession was confronted by a motorcade of British officers who were armed with "bamboo sticks." The officers surrounded them and demanded to speak to Gurdit Singh, passenger Bishen Singh recounted.[81] When Singh came forward, they exchanged hostile words and the crowd was suddenly "fired upon."[82] In what came to be known as the "Budge Budge Massacre," nineteen of the forty people killed were passengers.[83] More than two hundred passengers were arrested and imprisoned without charge. Thirty-nine others, including Gurdit Singh, remained at large. For anticolonials in India and the Indian diaspora, the *Komagata Maru*'s deportation from Vancouver and the Budge Budge Massacre became formative moments in struggles for Indian independence. To Indian officials, the "riot" only solidified Singh's status as a criminal and outlaw.[84] "Many of his countrymen are ready to sympathize with Gurdit Singh as the brave, heroic leader of the forlorn hope against the

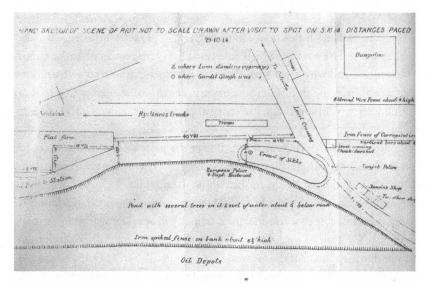

FIGURE 5.2. Hand-drawn map of Budge Budge during the "riot," which marks the position of Gurdit Singh and the returnees. (Photo from *Report of Komagata Maru Committee of Inquiry* [Calcutta, 1914])

inhumanity and wickedness of the Immigration laws of Canada, and against the tyranny of Government," Francis Slocock of the CID charged. But "they should realize that he never intended to be and never was the self-sacrificing, high minded patriot."[85] Rather, Singh was an "unscrupulous adventurer."[86] He was "a man of some cunning" who had "no experience of shipping business or accounts" and was "attempting to carry out a difficult undertaking without any capital . . . without any expert assistance" and solely for his own financial gain.[87] These portrayals of Singh were ubiquitous and unrelenting, solidifying the alleged dangers he posed to Canada, India, and the British Empire.

The Indian colonial government immediately appointed a commission to investigate the events at Budge Budge, but not on Gurdit Singh's advice. The "Komagata Maru Committee of Inquiry" was convened shortly after the massacre. It was composed of British officials from Bengal and Punjab, as well as two Indian princes who had close ties to the colonial administration.[88] Following six weeks of hearings, twenty-seven meetings in Calcutta, Budge Budge, and Jullundur, interviews with 201 witnesses—including the captain and crew, passengers, police, government authorities, and shop owners—and after generating thousands of pages of testimony, the commissioners reached conclusions that did not bode well for Gurdit Singh.[89] The *Komagata Maru*'s voyage and the Budge

Budge "riot," they decided, were entirely the fault of Singh alone. Given their findings, he had very little hope of initiating a legal case as he intended. To make matters worse, an iron safe, which contained his correspondence with various governments and with legal authorities, as well as a diary he kept at sea, was confiscated from the ship. These documents, Singh maintained, were proof of his innocence. Without them, fugitivity became Gurdit Singh's only prospect for survival.

Following the shootings at Budge Budge, 211 passengers were arrested and interned under the Ingress into India Ordinance. The men were detained indefinitely and without charge in the Alipore Central Jail.[90] On 30 November, two months after the ship docked, all of the passengers remained in prison. "It is highly improbable that criminal proceedings will be taken against more than a very few for want of specific proof," Bengal authorities admitted, "and then only with the approval of the Government of India."[91] Sardar Daljit Singh and the Maharaja of Burdwan, both members of the Committee of Inquiry, wrote a joint letter to Sir James DuBoulay, Lord Hardinge's private secretary. Gurdit Singh and several others "were responsible for the deplorable occurrence at Budge Budge," they insisted. Most of the men in prison had little involvement and should be released immediately. The detainees had already "suffered considerable punishment," they noted, including the voyage at sea, "the loss of money in consequence . . . the loss of life and property in the riot at Budge Budge and the fairly long internment in jail." Most "were not in themselves dangerous."[92] Bengal authorities conceded that the men no longer posed an immediate risk. However, their release would be contingent on the Committee's final report. The men were to remain in the Alipore Jail until "the Lieutenant-Governor of the Punjab has had an opportunity of considering the report of the Committee and advising on the lines of action which should, in his opinion, be taken in any individual case."[93]

After exchanging memos and telegrams on the fate of those who were still confined, Bengal and Punjab authorities agreed that most of the prisoners should be discharged. "I have been giving deep consideration to the matter in communication with Bengal," wrote the lieutenant governor of Punjab, "and have already suggested the immediate release of 92 [inmates] and their return to the Punjab." As for those remaining, "enquiries are being made from their homes, and I propose, subject to Committee's report and Government's orders thereon, to recommend the release of all but the ringleaders and dangerous characters."[94] The "ringleaders" ostensibly included twenty to thirty men in prison and several others at large. The most dangerous and conspicuous of these was Gurdit Singh. The lieutenant governor claimed to have "evidence that at least two of the passengers, who escaped from Calcutta" were "members of a revolutionary body" that had been "stirring up sedition since their return." Along with "other returned Sikhs," they were "also participating in violent crimes to raise funds for a campaign against [the] Government."[95] In light of these reports, Lord Hardinge ordered the men to "be removed from jail and sent to the Punjab with as little delay as possible." Whereas "the invasion of returning Sikhs from British Columbia, all of them in the worst possible frame of mind, and with the evident intention of making trouble, is quite a serious matter," he conceded, "it will be easier to deal with them in the Punjab in their own villages than if they are herded together in jail in Calcutta or elsewhere."[96] The physical proximity of confinement—aboard the ship and in prison—produced perilous conditions in which radicalism would only flourish.

From his cell in the Alipore Central Jail, Amir Muhammed Khan penned an urgent plea to his countrymen requesting their immediate attention and assistance. "I respectfully and with my folded hands submit before all the Hindu Sikhs and Muhammadans," so that "the leader of the Hindustan will come down to Calcutta and help us," he wrote. There are 120 "confined in the jail, 12 are wounded, and it is said that 120 are shot." We are "all entirely innocent," he maintained.[97] The Ingress, Khan warned, unleashed a violent force of law that was unprecedented in India. "This new oppression has been done to us in Calcutta, which we cannot express," he lamented.[98] Along with their property, which had been violently searched, the personhood and freedom of the passengers was taken without any just grounds. Khan's cautions were entirely justified. For seven years, the Indian colonial government enforced the Ingress with unmitigated harshness. The law was administered in various parts of India and Burma and used to detain anyone suspected of anti-British activities, irrespective of whether these had any legitimate basis. Indefinite detention was justified and rationalized in the broadest possible terms. Indian men thought to be associating with the Ghadrs were detained without charge, sometimes for years.[99] Between 1915 and 1916 in Punjab alone, over three thousand men were imprisoned and/or restricted to their respective villages.[100]

In February 1915, five months following the ship's arrival, British authorities in London sent a memo to their Indian counterparts asking "what punishment, if any, has been inflicted on the organizer" of the *Komagata Maru* expedition.[101] The Indian colonial government could not issue a firm reply, as there was still no sign of Gurdit Singh. Some claimed he drowned in the Hooghly River during the Budge Budge "riot." Others suspected he fled and remained in hiding. It was not until 15 November 1921 that Gurdit Singh resurfaced and finally surrendered. The Ingress could not reach its expiration without being used against the target of its creation. The law was not repealed until Singh was successfully arrested and imprisoned.

"Fugitive Wanderings"

Following the massacre at Budge Budge, Gurdit Singh and thirty-eight passengers narrowly escaped. His associates from the ship protected him from the police, Singh would later write, so he could remain beyond the law, free to chronicle their devastating journey, including the injustices he and the passengers suffered at the hands of the Hong Kong, Canadian, and Indian governments.[102] But the Bengal police were determined to find the absconders. They called on local residents and bystanders to assist in their search for the dangerous "mutineers."[103] According to several unsubstantiated reports, the returnees were "acting under guidance from Germany."[104] They were a threat not only to the safety of India but also to Britain and the empire. Although these allegations were eventually discredited, they recast the *Komagata Maru* from an exceptional and unprecedented voyage to an urgent matter that demanded national and imperial attention. Most of the escapees were arrested the following day. However, Gurdit Singh successfully fled the police. After hiding at the home of a Budge Budge resident, Singh took a ferry across the river. At the Howrah railway station, he met a passerby who advised him to travel south to Jaganath Puri (Orissa) "and [to] wait there till peaceful times returned."[105] The man offered Singh refuge but only if he "assumed the dress and figure of a Bengali." Gurdit Singh adamantly refused. Bengali men "wear short hair and their chins are clean shaven," he replied. "I was a Sikh and prefer death to any sacrilege of my Keshas. I told him it was impossible."[106]

As a fugitive, Gurdit Singh traveled by day and night, on foot, by train, and bullock cart, covering considerable distances across the subcontinent. Over the course of his seven years at large, his journey followed a circuitous path that moved initially from east to west, then north, and farther south (see map 5.1). Occasionally Singh journeyed with companions, but most of the time he traveled alone. Though he was not formally trained as a seafarer, Singh's maritime knowledge proved vital to his inland sojourns. "Guided in my course by the stars," he wrote, "I traveled along fields, jungles, dry land and swamps, villages and wilds."[107] Singh's "fugitive wanderings" along these diverse landscapes were fit for an adventure story in which he was the main hero.[108] In villages and towns, he claimed to have met women and men whom he suspected might eventually betray him.[109] In forests, so Singh claimed, he encountered "wild beasts," including "tigers, bears, and leopards."[110] To avoid the dangers posed by humans

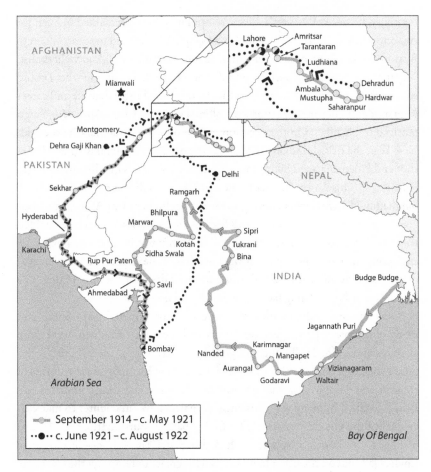

MAP 5.1. This map of Gurdit Singh's fugitive sojourns is re-created from the itinerary that he describes in *Voyage of the Komagatamaru or India's Slavery Abroad* (1928). It is not easy to determine where exactly Singh stopped or for how long as he sometimes refers generically to "village," "town," and "city."

and animals alike, he occasionally went days without food. Early in his escape, as Singh was en route to Godarvi, he recalled eating a fruit called "kothi." This was "a tasteless thing eaten by the poor," he explained. But "who could be poorer than myself in such circumstances," he retorted. "Even a poor man is free, but I was a fugitive who was being ruthlessly pursued."[111] In Singh's account, freedom was a moving horizon that was always slightly beyond reach.

In September 1916, after nearly two years on the run, Gurdit Singh arrived in Savli near the city of Baroda in Gujarat. Exhausted and beleaguered by his fugitivity, he decided to settle, albeit temporarily. Singh remained in Savli for two and a half years. By reading local newspapers, he learned to speak Gujarati. By studying books on natural remedies, he soon became a well-known herbalist. "My medicines began to become popular, and I decided to live on what I could earn by their sale," he recalled.[112] But his efforts to establish a new life and career were suddenly cut short by reports of colonial violence. On 19 April 1919, Singh received tragic news. On the occasion of Baisakhi, a festival marking the Sikh New Year, the British Indian army, under the orders of General Reginald Dyer, shot and killed unarmed Sikh protestors and worshippers in Jallianwalla Bagh, Amritsar.[113] This was in Singh's home state. He was distraught and outraged. Singh immediately began planning a visit to Gandhi in nearby Ahmedabad. But given the tense political climate, and fearing for his personal safety, he decided to delay.[114] In early 1920, after learning that Gandhi was in Bombay, Singh traveled along the coast and settled at the outskirts of the city. Once again, he was drawn to maritime worlds. Singh was employed first as a doctor and then as a manager in a shipbuilding factory owned by a fellow Sikh.[115]

Canadian and Indian authorities repeatedly described Gurdit Singh and many of the other passengers as radicals and revolutionaries who were close affiliates of the Ghadrs. Though Singh condemned British rule in India, he did not advocate violent overthrow. Instead, he actively encouraged other forms of resistance and opposition that prominently featured maritime commerce and British legality. In many ways, his anticolonial visions ran counter to many elements of the Ghadr message. "The *Ghadr* party is outside (the application) of English law," one article stated. "It is above such law. It does not recognize English law and on the other hand looks with great contempt on the law made by the English dacoits because these dacoits frame laws according to their own will."[116] British legality was dynamic, the unknown author of this article argued, but only so it could be more repressive. "The English book is not a religious book which cannot change. This law has been framed by the English on new methods and they will twist and turn it as they like or will make a new law." It was only "foolish and timid people" who did not "properly understand the principles of mutiny and independence" and who went "to the English courts," the article continued.[117] With an anticolonial vision invested in British legality, Gurdit Singh, by this account, was among the "foolish and timid."

Singh was more closely aligned to Gandhi's teachings than he was to Ghadr ideology. In the *Voyage,* for example, he openly and repeatedly identified as an admirer and follower of satyagraha. By his own account, he visited Bombay several times, with the intention of meeting Gandhi. But it was not until his third attempt that Singh was finally successful. In their initial encounter, Singh offered Gandhi his few possessions, including a coat. This was to be auctioned, and its proceeds were to be used toward the Jallianwalla Bagh relief fund. In his writings, Singh claimed to have visited Gandhi "every now and then." The two men discussed various political urgencies and also deliberated on the timing and staging of Singh's surrender.[118] On 13 March 1921, during their third meeting, this time in Ahmedabad, Gandhi advised Singh to turn himself in. Though Singh held Gandhi in the highest regard, he had his own plans on how to proceed. Before surrendering, Singh explained, he needed to have "necessary interview[s] with other important persons," including nationalist leaders.[119] Shortly thereafter, he left Ahmedabad and spent the next several months traveling north to Sind, Karachi, Lahore, Ludhiana, and Dehradun.[120]

In this final leg of his fugitivity, Singh met with members of the Khilafat Movement and the Indian National Congress and consulted them on his plans for surrender. It had been nearly seven years since the Budge Budge Massacre, and his fugitive wanderings had taken a physical and emotional toll. Singh "was tired of disguising himself" and was now ready to submit to police.[121] But those he consulted asked that he wait, at least until the Sikh League met in Lyallpur.[122] Singh acquiesced. In November 1921, he traveled to Delhi to attend an assembly of the Indian National Congress. There, he again raised the issue of his surrender. But, once more, he was advised to delay. The committee "unanimously restrained me from surrendering to the Government," he claimed. "They said that the atmosphere was poisonous and the attitude of the Government was not at all good." The Ghadrs' call to revolt, both during and after the war, had put the Indian colonial government on high alert.[123] If Singh submitted to police, his advisees warned, he would surely be hanged; India would "lose an innocent worker and our work for [the] country's cause will suffer greatly."[124] But Gandhi remained steadfast on the question of Singh's surrender. Nothing could be gained from the fugitive's efforts "to roam hither and tither disguising himself," he believed. Gurdit Singh had "once shook the Government [and] made a voyage to Canada, [he] awoke the sleeping India and exposed the bureaucratic policy before the general public."[125] Now it was time to claim his place as a national hero. Gandhi insisted that Singh's opposition to the Canadian and British governments not only advanced freedom for India. Rather, the *Komagata Maru*'s journey also "helped the Indians in Africa." In the years that Gandhi spent in South Africa, he became intimately familiar with the "distressed condition[s]" facing the Indians there. His own experiences with racial violence profoundly shaped his anticolonial views and strategies.[126] Singh's surrender, Gandhi counseled, would bring "forth some good for the country" while at the same time improving the lives of those abroad.[127]

After months of consultation with the Indian National Congress, Gandhi, and other nationalist leaders, Gurdit Singh began preparing his surrender. He wrote several letters to the Punjab police, alerting them to his intentions and inviting them to attend the Nankana Festival on 15 November 1921, where he would submit himself before his admirers. This was an auspicious occasion that marked Guru Nanak's birthday. Therefore, "almost all the Sikhs would assemble" to celebrate.[128] His surrender would be a majestic event, witnessed by tens of thousands of his countrymen. Gurdit Singh had long anticipated the day that would end his fugitivity. Though his surrender would certainly lead to imprisonment and possibly death, it would also open new opportunities to seek justice. Despite the many failures of law that he and the passengers experienced over the course of the ship's passage, he remained hopeful. A court hearing would allow him to tell the *real* story of the *Komagata Maru,* he claimed, especially "Canada's hideous crime under the cover of law."[129] Confronting the law with the law was not a foolish or timid act, as the Ghadr circular suggested it to be. Rather, it afforded Singh a long-awaited opportunity to challenge the legitimacy of Dominion sovereignty and to condemn the colonial government's violent use of force at Budge Budge. This would be Singh's chance to argue his innocence, to affirm his standing as a law-abiding British subject, and to insist on India's readiness for self-determination. But the weight of the charges against him in Hong Kong, Canada, and India were too substantial. Singh's legal struggles did not produce the outcomes he anticipated or desired. Instead, they generated the very conditions of unfreedom that Vosper had forecast in his ode to Gurdit Singh.

On 15 November 1921, in a well-orchestrated event, Gurdit Singh arranged his surrender via a letter to the district magistrate of Sheikhupura:

Dear Mr. Barry,

With all the police and the ever vigilant C.I.D. at its back [the] Government has failed to arrest me during the last seven years while I have [been] freely going about through India. My object in evading arrest has been to bring to light the true facts about Sri Guru Nanak, the steamer Komagata Maru and the Budge Budge Massacre. Now that my Panth and my country have decided that we must undergo all conceivable sufferings at the hands of the bureaucracy in order to gain religious freedom and Swaraj I have come here to be arrested. Will you please let me know per bearer the time and place where I should make myself over to the brave police.

Yours truly,
Gurdit Singh[130]

Despite Singh's mocking tone, the magistrate's reply was delicate but immediate. "I am glad to learn from your letter that you are prepared to give yourself up," Mr. Barry responded. "I trust you will use all the influence you have with your supporters" to prevent "attempts at violence as we are naturally anxious to avoid all risk of bloodshed."[131] That very afternoon and without incident, Gurdit Singh was arrested before thousands of Sikh supporters and was imprisoned under the Ingress into India Ordinance.

Characterizations of Singh as a mutineer and an outlaw circulated along the Pacific and Indian Oceans and set the conditions for his fugitivity and his eventual arrest. Hong Kong authorities maintained that even before the *Komagata Maru* embarked on its passage, as Singh was still finalizing the ship's itinerary, he had already broken the law. On the eve of his planned departure, the Hong Kong police arrested Singh for failing to provide a signed passenger license even though Shinyei Kisen had provided him with one. "No charge was framed against me nor was I told what I had done to incur Governmental wrath," he declared. "Obviously, this was done to scare away my followers. Woe to those who dare to make such a bold venture!"[132] The "bold venture" for which he was guilty was to assert the rights of Indians to travel and trade on the so-called free sea. In India, government reports and correspondence regarding the voyage and the violence at Budge Budge only confirmed these charges of criminality. In *The Report of the Komagata Maru Committee of Inquiry* published in December 1914, the members of the investigative commission described Singh as "a person of strong character" who "succeeded in a short time in acquiring great influence over his fellow countrymen in Hong Kong."[133] Though "he was well aware of the restrictions imposed by the Canadian law on the immigration of Asiatics into that country," he allegedly deceived those aboard the ship into believing that the "law had been declared . . . invalid."[134] As several passengers would later testify, Singh assured them "that he had obtained authority from the Government of Hong Kong to take passengers by the *Komagata Maru* into Canada, and that there would be no difficulty in securing admission there."[135] By Singh's account, however, the *Komagata Maru*'s landing was guaranteed by the vessel's owners and then corroborated by three Hong Kong lawyers. But Indian authorities argued otherwise. "It has been freely suggested," wrote one official, that Gurdit Singh and his followers "were well aware that the emigrants would not be allowed to enter Vancouver." Yet, he still "took money from the passengers with the deliberate intention of defrauding them." He "dishonestly misappropriated the money paid for fares," another source charged, "and in this way made a large profit out of the present venture."[136] These allegations were directly contradicted by the dire financial circumstances that confronted

Gurdit Singh, which necessitated his shipboard financial arrangements. After weighing the evidence, the commissioners reached the unanimous decision that "Gurdit Singh took money from the passengers with the deliberate intention of defrauding them" and so that he could make a profit from the venture.[137]

Charges of duplicity and greed were among the many leveled against Singh. The *Komagata Maru* Committee of Inquiry reminded the Indian colonial government that Singh had a lengthy history of criminal misconduct. In 1907, when he returned to Punjab from Malaya and Singapore, he was charged with sedition. Between 1909 and 1912, when he traveled to Punjab from the Straits Settlements once again, the police arrested him on similar grounds.[138] His radicalism, several sources charged, only intensified at sea. As the *Komagata Maru* was en route to Vancouver, some claimed that Singh delivered lectures "in which disloyal and seditious language was used."[139] Each morning, passenger Pal Singh reported, Gurdit Singh and his associates would gather everyone on deck with a bugle call, and "anyone who did not go was threatened."[140] But the content of these meetings remained in dispute. According to one passenger, Singh implored them "not [to] *Salaam* the English." Others spoke of his lectures as religious sermons that centered on the teachings of Guru Nanak and Guru Gobind and did not promote insurgency of any kind.[141] But authorities approached the middle passage as a space-time of insurrection. Singh preached sedition, many claimed, and circulated copies of the Ghadr newspaper to those aboard the ship. All "the methods advocated by the Ghadr to effect revolution," others explained, were already "in the minds of the revolutionists when leaving America." Although the passengers were forcibly returned to the subcontinent, after being barred entry to Canada, Hong Kong, and Singapore, anticolonial rebellion, one source claimed, "was the express object of the emigrants in sailing to India."[142]

As the ship made its way to Calcutta, Singh was believed to have complete control over those on board. Many of the returnees "had been excited to a state of serious disaffection towards the Government," the *Komagata Maru* Committee of Inquiry concluded, and "a considerable number of them were armed and prepared to go to almost any length in their opposition to the authorities."[143] Inspired by admiration and fear, Singh was thought to have a dangerous influence over his countrymen "that was paramount." While some passengers exalted him as "their 'guru' and the champion of their rights," others portrayed him as despotic.[144] When the ship was at sea, one Indian official explained, Singh assumed "the powers of a magistrate," usurping the shipmaster's authority and breaking the conventions of admiralty law. He "punished men by telling them off to act as cooks, and carry coal," saving "his own pockets," and thereby securing profits from the venture.[145] Under "various pretexts," Singh allegedly convinced "the passengers to deposit all their money and valuables with him." Though he charged exorbitant fares and borrowed money from nearly one hundred travelers, Singh failed to provide sufficient provisions, authorities maintained. "The food was of the worst description," sanitation was deplorable, and "flies and rats" were rampant.[146]

In the end, the *Komagata Maru* Committee of Inquiry concluded that Gurdit Singh's efforts to plan and execute the voyage were "characterized by a reckless disregard both of his promises to the passengers and of his obligations to the ship's owners." This "so-called Sri Guru Nanak Steamship Company, which he freely advertised, styling himself manager or director," the committee charged, "was a bogus concern, in which the solitary shareholder was Gurdit Singh himself, and which possessed only one vessel, the *Komagata Maru,* and that a hired one."[147] After reviewing the evidence, David Petrie, who was injured in the shootings at Budge Budge, characterized Singh as "a thorough megalomaniac." Another official described him to be bordering "on insanity."[148] Charges of sedition, criminality, and madness, lodged by authorities in Hong Kong, Canada, and India, had less to do with the laws that Singh breached in planning and executing the *Komagata Maru*'s voyage and more to do with the maritime dangers he represented to the so-called free sea. Though Singh was never charged with any activities or events related to the *Komagata Maru,* in November 1921, following his surrender at Sheikhupura, claims about his radicalism and despotism served as further evidence of his guilt.

During his seven years on the run, Singh was characterized as a significant threat to Indian national security. Yet his surrender to Mr. Barry generated a series of disagreements between the Bengal and Punjab governments. Their disputes centered on matters of jurisdiction: who held the authority to charge Singh, for what offense, and under which law? Following the massacre at Budge Budge, Singh was "'wanted, for rioting and murder.'" The Indian government immediately offered a Rs. 1,000 reward to anyone who would help secure his arrest.[149] But in November 1921, more than seven years had passed. The *Komagata Maru* and the Budge Budge Massacre were faded memories, superseded by a series of other momentous events. The Great War had started and ended; anticolonial insurgency was thought to be rampant; and Gandhi's noncooperation movement was gaining momentum, disrupting the order and authority of the Indian colonial government. As a result, Singh's arrest was no longer as urgent as it had once been. After learning of his surrender, the Bengal government notified the Intelligence Bureau that they did "not wish to proceed with the case against Gurdit Singh."[150] As Budge Budge came under the jurisdiction of Bengal, officials in Punjab were well aware that they could not charge Singh for his involvement there. Given his reputation in India and abroad, authorities agreed that a legal response was no longer urgent but remained necessary: "some action" must be taken against Gurdit Singh, one government memo advised, so he does not become "a national hero."[151]

In February 1922, three months after Singh's dramatic surrender, he had still not been charged with any specific offense. The Ingress expired, and Singh was released from prison. But his freedom was short-lived. One week later, he was arrested again, this time on two counts of sedition. The most recent charges centered on a speech that Singh gave in Amritsar to "a crowd of ten to twelve thousand men." In anticipation of his arrival, supporters decorated the bazaars, assembled "triumphal arches," and "were on the tiptoe of expectation."[152] When Singh appeared before the crowd, he was "given a tremendous ovation," which was magnified by a "long procession of about half a mile," featuring tens of thousands of followers and supporters. He "received welcome addresses from [the] Khilafat and Congress Committees and made a speech in reply."[153] To excite and unite the crowd, Singh remarked on the recent acts of gendered, racial, and religious violence committed by the British in India:

> In this country, the faces of your mothers and sisters were unveiled and spit on. Can you be called Hindus? In your country, the Government slaughters thousands of cows. You can be called Hindus when all such evils are removed from the country. The country rendered great assistance during the Great War. In reward, the Government gave us the Jallianwalla Bagh, in which our children and brothers became targets for the bullets and a tyrant like General Dyer was given a robe of honour on behalf of the Durbar Sahib.[154]

When Singh arrived in Amritsar, the Jallianwalla Bhag Massacre was very much in the air. Authorities alleged that "anti-Government propaganda of a violent nature" was circulating throughout the district. "Unlawful organizations variously known as Khilafat, Congress and National volunteers" were moving "about in processions with the avowed object of breaking the law."[155] The Seditious Meetings Act was in effect and was willfully violated by Singh's remarks.[156]

Gurdit Singh's speeches, therefore, built on and intensified the city's fraught political atmosphere. After weighing the seriousness of his address along with his reputation as a fugitive and outlaw, Punjab authorities charged Singh under the sedition provisions of the Indian Penal Code. He was immediately imprisoned in the Dera Gazi Khan Jail.[157] Four months later, when Singh appeared before the court, the past charges against him accumulated, and he was already thought to be guilty. Lala Amarnath, the district magistrate in Amritsar, regarded Singh's speeches as inciting animosity and enmity against British rule. "The language of the accused is so plain, clear, and unambiguous," he opined, "that it does not need the slightest remark on my part to show that it contains imputations against the Government and that these imputations are calculated to cause 'disaffection' within the meaning of Section 124A."[158] Notwithstanding the force of Singh's address and his deliberate attempts to agitate the crowd, Amarnath called his lectures "nonsensical." Gurdit Singh simply presented "an enumeration of the evils of the present Government." His list of atrocities committed by British authorities against Hindus and Sikhs moved "before the eye like the films in a cinema show." Whereas clear associations joined the pictures in films, Singh's address had "absolutely no inherent connection between the various subjects embraced by the speech," Amarnath continued.[159] A "slaughtering of cows, however bad it may be," he argued, "has nothing whatever to do with the Komagata Maru the Jallian-wala Bagh and the prisoner's own detention in jail." Singh's sole objective in addressing his large and excitable audience at Amritsar was not to air a specific grievance, the Magistrate concluded, but "to discredit the British administration in India."[160]

Shortly before Singh's trial commenced, authorities notified him that Gandhi's noncooperation movement was under way and that he would not be given a lawyer. Singh would be required to act in his own defense.[161] Standing before the law as a fugitive and an outlaw, he would temporarily become a man of law.[162] To fulfill the obligations of his newly inherited vocation, Singh presented an initial draft of the *Voyage*. The document was made up of "350 foolscap pages" written in Gurumukhi, to be translated into Urdu and read aloud to the court.[163] His text offered a vigorous rebuttal to the various charges of criminality directed at him in Hong Kong, Canada, and India. It also presented a counter-history of the *Komagata Maru* and the events at Budge Budge. Finally, the manuscript included a legal archive containing copies of correspondence that Singh exchanged with various government officials during the ship's journey, detention, and deportation.[164] Ultimately, the text was to serve as a testament, as testimony, and as a defense refuting all the charges laid against him.[165] But Amarnath refused to accept it. "The statements are totally devoted to the accused's own story of the Komagata Maru expedition and the Budge Budge Riot," he claimed. "It is intended presumably to be a reply to the report of the Komagata Maru Committee of Inquiry and is not relevant to the case" at hand.[166] In addition, Singh submitted a list of twenty-two witnesses to be called before the court. These included the colonial secretary of Hong Kong; Malcolm Reid, the Canadian immigration officer; members of the *Komagata Maru* Committee of Inquiry; and Muhammed Ali Jinnah, a barrister of the

Bombay High Court and member of the All-India Muslim League, who was to become Pakistan's first governor general.[167] The magistrate also disallowed Singh's witnesses, dismissing all but two as irrelevant. This was devastating. When Singh surrendered at Sheikhupura the previous year, he believed that a court appearance would grant him a long overdue opportunity to demand justice. But his efforts to confront the British, Canadian, and Indian governments were repeatedly dismissed. British and colonial law could not hear the voices of its racial and colonial subjects.

Singh's sedition case was widely reported in Indian English newspapers and drew spirited comment from local readers. At least one observer noted the ironies that informed the magistrate's reasoning. The sedition case against Singh, Amarnath insisted, had nothing to do with the *Komagata Maru*. Yet, in his own deliberations and judgment, the ship's voyage featured prominently and in ways that only reinforced the accused's presumed lawlessness. "Before detailing the facts of this case," Amarnath explained, "it is necessary to cast our eyes back upon the year 1914 and to know what were this Komagata Maru expedition and the Budge Budge Riot." Looking back *"is necessary for the purpose of acquainting ourselves with the accused's personality* and for explaining certain passages in the speech which are the subject of present charge," he claimed.[168] "But it must be clearly understood that it is not my objective . . . to discuss the merits of the Komagata Maru expedition or to sit in judgment upon the Budge Budge incident." Each of these events is "irrelevant to the present case, except insofar as they are introductory to or throw light upon the facts with which I am here concerned."[169] Amarnath's deliberate disregard for Singh's written statement and his list of witnesses, one observer noted, "greatly prejudiced" his defense.[170]

At trial, Amarnath drew repeated attention to Singh's status as an outlaw. Singh's written account contains "a long list of the tyrannies committed by the Government against him." Singh "declares that this Government bore, towards him an old standing enmity," but "the statement is also full of invective and vituperation," Amarnath added. "It is idle, under the circumstances to imagine that at the time of making his speech the prisoner was animated by a spirit other than that of animosity."[171] Ultimately, Singh's reputed lawlessness became an aggravating factor in his sentencing. "As regards the punishment to be awarded," the magistrate maintained that "it must be commensurate with the offense." Gurdit Singh "is undoubtedly an influential man in the province" of Punjab, he continued.[172] After being released from jail, "wherever he went thousands of people uninvited came out to greet him." These "unsolicited greetings" on such a grand scale "indicate what sway the prisoner exercised over the minds of his countrymen." The "mischief intended [by Singh] was incalculable,"

Amarnath continued, "and I think nothing short of an exemplary sentence would meet the ends of justice."[173] In the end, Singh was not sentenced to hang as his compatriots had predicted. Instead, Amarnath sentenced him to five years transportation. In India, transportation was a punishment worse than death. For many, the treacherous journey across the *kala pani* and into the unknown was a penalty with devastating corporeal, emotional, and existential effects. Shipboard conditions—where bodies were confined to lower decks, and where food was prepared with little regard for religious or caste observances—was a transgression of religious rites that resulted in a loss of self. The conditions of the journey made the return to India difficult to contemplate, if not impossible to achieve.[174] For reasons of caste purity, Hindus were prohibited from crossing the sea.[175] But Singh was a Sikh and an aspiring seafarer. A punishment at sea was therefore no punishment at all. His "monstrous sentence" was commuted. Gurdit Singh was condemned to five years in the Mianwali Jail, a prison known to some as the "Andamans of Punjab."[176]

How do we make sense of Singh's fugitive sojourns, especially when they generated ever-greater conditions of unfreedom, not only for him, but also for thousands of others on the subcontinent and elsewhere in the empire? Writing of the fugitive slave, Samira Kawash cautions that fugitivity cannot be considered an oppositional act of resistance. "Reading the *corporeal topography* of the space of fugitivity," she explains, makes one "increasingly skeptical of the blithe, celebratory invocations of the subversive powers of boundary crossing, nomadism, or excess—all figures that *might* be mobilized to describe the space of fugitivity."[177] When read corporeally and spatially, the fugitive's body, "exposes, in fact, embodies, the violence necessary to preserve order, hierarchy, boundedness, propriety, and property."[178] As my discussion above suggests, Singh's fugitivity unleashed shifting intensities of violence that were deemed necessary to preserve Britain's colonial and racial order in India and at sea. Following his surrender, Singh was faced with unrelenting juridical force: the Ingress into India Ordinance, sedition charges under the Indian Penal Code, Amarnath's judgment, and Singh's five years in the Mianwali jail. But while his clandestine itinerancy drew the full strength of the Indian colonial government, his fugitivity engendered and nurtured creative imaginaries, as was true for Frederick Douglass and other fugitive and freed slaves. The interval between freedom and capture proved to be dangerous but also generative. Informed by the limitless horizon of the sea, Singh's "fugitive wanderings" spawned disjointed temporalities of anticolonial critique and alternative visions of freedom from British rule.[179] It is to his critical imaginaries that I now turn.

Singh penned the *Voyage* in fits and starts, in conditions between itinerancy and confinement. He began writing during the *Komagata Maru*'s voyage from Yokohama to Calcutta, continued to commit his thoughts to paper in his seven years on the run, and completed the text during his five years in prison. In the time that Singh was at large, he wrote several versions of the manuscript, burning at least one of them when he believed police capture was imminent. Each account was written retrospectively, composed of close and distant memories and organized through different periods of his life: his years as a railway contractor in Malaya, the time he spent organizing and commanding the *Komagata Maru*'s voyage, and, more immediately, as a fugitive seeking justice. In the preface to *Zulmi Katha,* Singh claimed that he commenced writing in Yokohama. As the vessel sat anchored in port, awaiting word of its final destination, a group of young Indian students came to pay him homage. Inspired by Singh's defiance against Canada, India, and the British Empire, they encouraged him to chronicle the ship's passage. The voyage, they insisted, would one day be recognized as a vital moment in India's history against British rule. The Punjabi and English versions of Singh's text were distinct; though informed by competing motivations, addressed to specific audiences, and written in different affective registers, they nevertheless shared several resonances. The English *Voyage* began by echoing the Indian students, even if Singh never referenced them directly. "The unfortunate voyage of the steamship 'Komagatamaru' to Canada and the incidents arising therefrom make a very important chapter in this present day," Singh wrote. The "event may be rightly described, with others of varying degrees of importance, as one of the chief eye-openers to India's real situation as also a material contributor to the latter day national efforts for the change of her political condition."[180] The *Komagata Maru* may have failed its immediate objectives as the first ship to travel under the Guru Nanak Steamship Company. However, it would be a formative moment in the longer struggle for Indian independence.[181]

The *Voyage,* as I have indicated, was not a direct translation of the Punjabi version; it presented a much subtler critique of British rule.[182] Singh's primary objective in writing the manuscript was to offer his own account of the *Komagata Maru*'s passage. However, the English text had several additional purposes. To begin, it was to serve as a testament to the many illegalities committed by the Canadian and Indian governments under the sanction of British and colonial law. "The siren of Komagatamaru was a surprise for Canada," Singh declared. The government "had no lawful means to stop our admission except unlawfully and unlawfully they refused Admission in which our Indian Government seconded the motion."[183] The text was to act as a defense of his reputation as a law-abiding British subject and to serve as a rejoinder to the governments of Hong Kong, Canada, and India. However, "the journey on the high seas" would not be included, Singh explained, "owing to the fear that the size of the book will increase."[184] Gurdit Singh had kept a detailed journal of the ship's transoceanic passage.[185] But when the vessel anchored on the Hooghly River, authorities raided the ship and confiscated his diary, papers, and other belongings. Inverting the language of piracy—which Britain deployed strategically to maintain its legitimacy as a maritime empire and to expand its territorial control across the sea—Singh accused the Indian police of "looting . . . the ship treasure."[186] His safe held key legal documents that verified his innocence and were crucial to his quest for justice. The *Voyage* would serve as an alternative account. The iron safe also contained bank notes in several currencies, including Japanese yen. Singh desperately needed this money to repay his debts to passengers. Following his release from prison, he spent years writing to the police. However, his epistolary efforts were to no avail. The safe and his diary were never recovered.

The *Voyage* was not an autobiography or memoir in the conventional sense. Rather, Singh's text was a composite of recollections and a patchwork of writing styles that traversed genres. His purpose in writing the *Voyage*, as he explained it, was to narrate his life, but only as it related to the "voyage of the ill-fated Komagata Maru."[187] Thus, the text said nothing of his childhood, family, or village, save for a few references to his father, sister, and to his six-year-old son, Balwant, who accompanied him on the journey to Vancouver, and from whom he was separated at Budge Budge (see fig. 5.3). Origins are crucial to autobiographical writings. However, Singh's *Voyage* had no identifiable beginning or end. His narrative did not start with an event, nor did it follow a smooth or linear chronology. Rather, fugitivity and itinerancy were structuring elements, organizing the inconsistencies of form and content. The *Voyage* had an errant and unfinished quality. It drifted on a circuitous path and followed a disjointed temporality, much like Singh's own journeys. The text was arranged into two sections, each with multiple chapters. The first was unnamed and unidentified. It became "Part I" only when the reader reached "Part II." Moreover, there was no discernible conclusion. The manuscript ended quickly and abruptly with an unfinished section titled "British Justice." This was accompanied with a promise to complete the text in the future. The pagination between the two parts was discontinuous, defying a progressive chronology while retaining some continuity. As a personal account of law's colonial and racial force, the text was written in three concurrent temporalities: in the past of the tea and rubber

FIGURE 5.3. This photo of Gurdit Singh and his son Balwant, standing on one of the decks of the *Komagata Maru* as it was anchored in Vancouver Harbour in 1914, has now become an iconic representation of the ship's journey. (Photo courtesy of Vancouver Public Library)

plantations, in the present of so-called free Indian migration, and in the future of Indian independence. For Singh, these fragmented temporalities were not discrete periodizations but shared historical moments in Britain's larger project of colonial and imperial expansion. It was his own clandestine mobility across land and sea, over the Indian and Pacific Oceans and through the subcontinent, that positioned him in the interstices between freedom and unfreedom. It was from within this interval that Singh reflected on the overlapping histories and geographies of racial violence unleashed by the Dominion of Canada and the governments of Hong Kong, India, and Malaya, and ultimately sanctioned by British law.

Unlike *Zulmi Katha,* which was an anticolonial and nationalist view of India's past and future, the *Voyage* was intended to defend Singh's name and restore his reputation.[188] Presented initially as testimony in his sedition trial, the text closely resembled a legal brief and offered a statement on his innocence. Throughout, Singh continually reasserted himself as a law-abiding subject. "I did not violate the regulations laid down by the Canadian government to make a direct voyage to Canada," he declared.[189] "I have got copies of documents in my possession to prove that we engaged a lawyer as soon as our ship arrived in Vancouver. Had it been our intention to go against law we would well have spared ourselves the fees that we paid for legal advice."[190] In his efforts "to get justice done by law courts," Singh maintained that he "was careful to stay on the right side of the law." He was "suffering so much" when he "was strictly subservient to legal limitation," he explained. "Had I transgressed [the law] . . . I do not know what would have happened to my people."[191] But the Dominion of Canada, Singh alleged, "wanted to make the whole thing appear like a farce to the outside world . . . they restrained me from landing by resorting to force and fraud."[192] As the ship's charterer and commander, it was his responsibility "to load and unload cargo" and to purchase supplies for the passengers. Under "the charter contract [Singh] had to pay customs and other duties, and pur-chas [sic] provisions and victuals." Therefore, he "had every right to land" in Vancouver.[193] As the "merchant and charterer of a ship," Singh clarified, he was "immune from the disabilities attaching to an 'immigrant' and could not un-der any circumstances be debarred from landing according to the clearly stated terms of the law."[194] Thus, both the Dominion and Indian governments acted unlawfully and illegally, he charged. The Indian government "joined with the Canadian government in an unholy alliance to deprive us of our legal rights." The two "Governments violated and ignored the laws of their own creation."[195]

As an effort to restore his reputation, the *Voyage* was deeply personal. As a counter-history, however, it offered an acerbic critique of British colonial and imperial rule. Singh narrated the *Komagata Maru*'s unsuccessful journey, not as a single or exceptional incident, but as a tragic moment in a much longer tra-jectory of crimes committed by Britain against its colonial and racial subjects. In Singh's view, Britain extended its imperial reach across land and sea by way of distinct but entangled forms of racial, colonial, and legal violence. Transatlantic slavery, Indian indenture, and immigration prohibitions, he claimed, overlapped and intersected in ways that were not easily divisible. Positioned within this longer history, the *Komagata Maru*'s detention in Vancouver, its deportation to Calcutta, and the subsequent massacre at Budge Budge were part of a much broader constellation of racial power, one that structured imperial relations and colonial populations civilizationally, temporally, and unequally. To develop this argument, Singh drew fleeting but compelling links between transatlantic slavery and systems of Indian indenture, and subsequently between indentured labor and immigration prohibitions. In his assessment, indenture was yet another system of bondage that grew directly from the abolition of slavery.[196] Given the years he spent as a railway contractor in Malaya, Singh was especially critical of Britain's reliance on Indian indentured labor in the tea and rubber plantations. The indenture system, as Britain established it in the Straits Settlements, and which he witnessed firsthand, was an exploitative arrangement of racial labor that echoed the inhumanity of Atlantic slavery. Slavery continued in the Straits Settlements even after it was abolished in Britain's colonies. British authorities portrayed it in benign terms, as a system of domestic servitude that was radically different from its transatlantic counterpart.[197] Plantations relied on systems of indenture, debt, and bondage that were officially outlawed in 1843, but which persisted long thereafter.[198] To register the wanton violence directed at Indian indentured laborers in Malaya and to condemn British administration over the region, Singh recalled the memory of transatlantic slavery, transposing it to another time and place, and with specific anticolonial objectives.

Though Britain's ties to Malaya date as far back as the eighteenth century, it was not until 1824, after the signing of the Anglo-Dutch Treaty, that Britain formally took legal and political control. Initially, the East India Company governed the islands of Penang, Malacca, and Singapore. But after the company was dissolved, the region came under the jurisdiction of the Bengal presidency. In 1867, when the Straits Settlements was granted status as a Crown colony, the locus of power shifted again, this time from Calcutta to the Colonial Office in London.[199] Amid these jurisdictional shuffles, Malaya became extremely profitable. As with many other colonies, the region became a laboratory for a range of plantation commodities, in this case tin, tea, pepper, and, perhaps most significantly, rubber.[200] Between 1876 and 1877, the Colonial Office began experimenting with the transfer of rubber trees. By 1900, it was clear that these trees, which were imported from Brazil and took six years to fully mature, could flourish in local environments.[201] The thriving success of rubber produced additional demands for land and labor. In 1897, one year before Britain established the Federated Malay States, colonial administrators initiated a series of land reforms through the introduction of the Torrens system of registration.[202] Named after Sir Robert Richard Torrens, a politician in South Australia who was eventually to become the colony's third premier, this system of land registry was borrowed directly from the world of imperial shipping.[203] As a customs officer, first in London and then in Adelaide, Torrens viewed the tabular columns of shipping indexes to be a concise, convenient, and effective way to record the sale and transfer of land.[204] Title by registration was introduced first in South Australia in 1858, and later exported to various places in the British Empire, including British Columbia, Hawai'i, and Malaya.[205] For Torrens, landed and movable property shared marked similarities. Both could be extracted from prior histories of ownership and assigned a financial value.[206] Through processes of documentation that erased social relations and kin networks, registries, with their indexes and line items, transformed land into sellable commodities.[207] By way of violent abstraction, shipping registries and later land registries, operated along similar lines as slave manifests.

Title by registration held devastating consequences for the territorial, legal, and political self-determination of indigenous peoples.[208] In South Australia and British Columbia, for example, processes of registration produced a "logic of abstraction that shaped a new grammar of property ownership" and instantiated private property as a new juridical form.[209] Land became commodified as a product that could be bought, sold, and transferred. Written registries made this process easier and more efficient than the cumbersome models of land tenure that had existed for centuries in England.[210] By creating new legal regimes of private property and an entire bureaucracy to manage it, title by registration expanded, authorized, and legitimized indigenous dispossession.[211] In Malaya, the introduction of the Torrens system granted British administrators the legal mechanisms they needed to set aside fertile lands for rubber production.[212] By introducing new forms of individualism, the Torrens system dramatically altered social and economic relations among ethnic Malays.[213] Many took ownership of their land and began selling it to foreigners. In 1913, amid escalating fears that Malays were competing with planters both by growing rubber and by transferring land, British administrators introduced the Malay Reservation Enactment.[214] Under the auspices of indigenous protection, the Reservation Enactment set aside small tracts of land where indigenous Malays were required to work and live. By targeting ethnic Malays, the law created a new "indigenous" identity while safeguarding their "continued existence as a peasantry."[215] To avert potential rivalries with planters, ethnic Malays who lived on reservations were encouraged to cultivate rice and were prohibited from growing rubber. By the 1920s, British-produced rubber dominated global markets, and Malaya was its chief source.[216]

During his time in Malaya, Gurdit Singh lived in the Selangor State, an area well known for tin and rubber production.[217] As a railway contractor and supposed rubber planter, Singh had remarkably little to say about these land reforms, though he likely witnessed their implementation firsthand. Plantations were connected to inland regions and to port cities through transport systems, including trains, boats, and ships, which also facilitated the movement of indentured laborers and crops.[218] Singh benefited from the construction of roadways and railways, but he said nothing as to how plantations, which transformed "the lands of no one into the lands of someone," encroached on and overwrote the territorial ownership of indigenous Malays.[219] As much as the Coast Salish were obscured and ignored in Husain Rahim's column, "Canada as a Hindu Saw It," indigenous Malays were equally absent from the *Voyage*. Singh mentioned indigeneity only obliquely, generically, and disparagingly in his reference to the "cannibalism of the savage races."[220]

Given Singh's maritime ambitions and aspirations, he was far more attentive to coercive regimes of labor than he was to the violent appropriation of land, even though the cultivation of rubber demanded both. The years that Singh spent in Malaya and Singapore, he claimed, gave him "first-hand knowledge" of the worth that Europeans ascribed to "the labor of an Indian," and how it compared to that of "a lower animal." Indeed, it was during his many years in the Straits Settlements that he gained an understanding as to how structures of racial exploitation could be maintained and sanctioned through the expansion, circulation, and mutability of British law.[221] In 1834, Britain's abolition of slavery generated acute labor shortages in its West Indian plantations. Freedom for slaves, many opponents of abolition argued, endangered the commodities, profits, and tastes that were firmly embedded within British imperial culture.[222] "When the slave trade was abolished by an agreement of the European powers," Singh explained, "about fifty companies had been engaged in capturing Negroes in Africa and selling them to different countries of the world. Of these, fourteen were English Companies."[223] As soon as the "Negro slave trade" was "closed to them, they turned their attention upon Hindustan" and "the helpless laborers of India henceforth became their victims in the place of the Negroes."[224] Though the abolition of Atlantic slavery was not directly relevant to the Straits Settlements, Singh marshaled this history as a powerful point of reference to underscore the deplorable conditions that Indian indentured laborers were forced to live and work in.[225] In the Caribbean, systems of indenture mitigated the exigencies wrought by the formal end of slavery. In the Straits Settlements, systems of indenture provided a steady supply of exploitable South Indian labor.[226] Although Britain insisted on freedom of contract, as it did elsewhere, Singh viewed indenture as a system of bondage that emerged directly from abolition. The subtitle of the *Voyage*, "India's Slavery Abroad," underscored these connections. It gestured to the shared histories of racial subjection in West Africa, the Caribbean, India, the Straits Settlements, the United States, and elsewhere. Singh's expansive geographic imaginary and the discrepant histories he evoked were produced in and nurtured by his own itinerancy across land and sea and by his struggles against British command.

The abolition of slavery and the introduction of indentured labor, critics have argued, was part of an expanding regime of racial and colonial control that Britain used to differentiate freedom (indenture) from unfreedom (slavery).[227] In the *Voyage,* Singh drew on transatlantic slavery to condemn Britain's reliance on Indian indentured labor, which he described as a legal expansion of racial *unfreedom:*

> While a contractor in the Malaya States I had the first opportunity to see for myself what an Indian coolie, bound for a British colony to help it in its industrial progress, was like. There I first learnt from a British employer of labour himself that an Indian coolie is not worth even a small fraction of what a horse fetches him. And this, inspite [*sic*] of the fact that the early coolie immigrants were the pitiable victims of the recruiter's machinations and the main props of European industry in the Colonies.... In the Malaya States the Europeans happen to be the owners of many tea and rubber gardens.... They badly needed Indian coolies to work these gardens and to place them in riches. But once when I visited these coolies' quarters, I was struck-dumb to find that human beings, helpful in the production of wealth, could thus be denied even a contemptible beast's accommodation.[228]

Abolition did not eradicate or arrest slavery. Rather, "under the euphemism of [an] 'Agreement of Coolies,'" Singh charged, the violence of slavery continued unabated.[229] In the Straits Settlements, Europeans treated animals as though they had more value than Indian laborers. Whereas "a horse would bring... Rs. 1500-" to its proprietor," Singh observed, a coolie would garner no more "than Rs. 40/- or Rs. 50/-."[230] The differential value ascribed to human and animal labor and life was also evidenced in the quality of their care. If the horse cost "Rs. 4/- per day for its fodder and upkeep," a coolie "was made to live and keep fit on one anna and six pies a day"[231] In Singh's calculation, "one horse cost as much as 42 human beings."[232]

Gurdit Singh's movements along the Indian and Pacific Oceans availed him new opportunities to witness the racial violence of British and colonial law first-hand. The view from the sea afforded him a wider perspective from which to chart the deep entanglements between different manifestations of imperial coercion, and to create a forceful critique. Indian indenture was joined to transatlantic slavery through shared objectives and juridical forms. But in Singh's account, slavery and indenture spawned additional racial injustices as evidenced in restrictive immigration regulations. Indentures were not only distinguished from slaves but also from "free" Indians. When placed in relation to indentures and slaves, it was clear that they too were not truly free. In the case of Indian sojourners and migrants, the "different colonies" legislated "immigration law as a standing monument to their selfishness and colour-prejudice," Singh claimed. These laws were used to restrict Indian mobility across the so-called free sea and to exclude migrants and travelers from entering the white Dominions. The repressive force of law was as evident in Australia as it was in Canada, he maintained. In his efforts to draw connections between slavery, indenture, and immigration prohibitions, Singh argued that British colonies exploiting indentured laborers and rejecting "free" Indians had not invented a new form of subordination. Rather, the status of Indians abroad—in the Dominions, protectorates, and colonies—was an extension of their inferior racial standing in India under British rule. "Those who have no status at home are *ipso facto* deprived of any abroad."[233]

For Singh, the overlaps between distinct forms of racial violence and among Britain's Dominions, colonies, and territories were especially apparent in the events of 1913. This was a particularly tragic year for India, he recalled. First, the Canadian government prevented "respectable Indians" who were British subjects, from entering Canada "to take to manual labor for a living."[234] Second, Gandhi and his wife Kasturba, along with "thousands of Indians[,] courted imprisonment fighting for the rights of Indians in South Africa."[235] In addition, this marked the year that the Indian colonial government demolished the Gurdwara Rakab Ganj in Delhi, thus desecrating a Sikh holy place. Finally, in 1913 the government of the Malay states, "without the least show of an excuse" sent sixty Sikhs to jail and then forcefully "expatriated them to Madras where they were left stranded and penniless."[236] Most indentured laborers in the Straits Settlements were recruited from Madras. But Madrasi was a language "quite foreign" to Sikhs, Singh explained. Therefore, those Sikhs that were forcibly sent to South India were displaced and deracinated, and they "could not maintain themselves [even] by begging."[237] These memories of violence might have been one of the many reasons why Singh and his associates refused Madras as the *Komagata Maru*'s final destination.

Once complete, Singh's *Voyage* was eventually to include three parts. Parts one and two were to focus on the past, enumerating the violence of British and colonial law, joining transatlantic slavery, Indian indenture, and immigration prohibitions. Part three, which remained incomplete, was to look backward and forward simultaneously, to racial histories of British legality and to the promises of freedom and justice to come. But the *Voyage* ended suddenly, noting that a third part would "be published in the near future."[238] These unwritten pages were also meant to apprise readers of Singh's own personal quest for justice, including the civil case he would eventually file in the High Court of Bengal. This case, which he initiated against the Indian colonial government, centered on a sum of "Rs. 250,000 that the police allegedly confiscated from his safe aboard the ship.[239] This final part of the *Voyage* was also supposed to instruct Singh's readers as to what really happened when the *Komagata Maru* anchored on the Hooghly River, and to memorialize those "brave comrades who fell at Budge Budge."[240] In short, the third part of the text was to recall the past while also reflecting on the present and future. It was to foreground the great advancements of Indian migrants and travelers by chronicling their financial achievements, their role in "the new world," as well as their ongoing struggles against the British administration in India and abroad. Finally, Singh promised to provide some direction for the long route to freedom. In so doing, he would remark on "how and when . . . India, will be India for Indians."[241] Attentive to racial histories under British colonial and imperial control, the final pages were to expand into an unknown and uncertain future, ruminating on the possibilities of British law in Singh's personal quest for redemption and in his peoples' struggles for self-determination.

Fugitivity, as several scholars of slavery have argued, staged a collision between past and future, of what *was* and what *might be.* For Stephen Best and Saidiya Hartman, "the political interval in which all captives find themselves—the interval between the no longer and the not yet, between the destruction of the old world and the awaited hour of deliverance"—was bursting with newness and possibility. It was in this gap that "fugitive justice" emerged.[242] Singh's conceptualizations of "British justice," which emerged out of his fugitivity, followed a similar temporal rhythm that oscillated between past and future and coalesced in the present. His condemnation of British rule demanded a rearrangement of discrepant oceanic histories and geographies, a reordering that clearly disjointed time. By sketching a wider constellation of racial and colonial violence, and by connecting transatlantic slavery to Indian indenture and so-called free migration, Singh disrupted the temporal linearity that was so central to universal history and to British legality. The visions of freedom and justice at play in Singh's text emerged directly from his own circuitous mobilities.[243]

For Gurdit Singh, the promise for the future, despite the past, could be found in the rule of law. The last section of the *Voyage,* titled "British Justice," began somewhat expectedly with a critique of British law, including its claims to equality, impartiality, and universality. "Once an English gentleman prided on the British Justice" observed that "English law permits a hundred criminals to escape in doubtful cases in order to escape the sin of punishing an innocent person," he recounted.[244] But this was not how law worked in colonial India. Ordinary people, like himself, Singh maintained, were routinely accused of breaking the law. "Our English masters raise sky high the praises of the English Law," he charged. Yet the law "is only available for the wealthy and not the poor." Such flagrant inequalities were "some of the causes of Indian slavery," he claimed.[245] Notwithstanding Singh's trenchant critique of British rule, however, he remained steadfast in believing that British law might eventually lead him to justice. The "innumerable iniquities" to which he and his "comrades were subjected" during the *Komagata Maru*'s voyage, he remarked, were the result of a *mishandling* and *misapplication* of law, especially by lower officers. "I do feel and fell [*sic*] keenly," he wrote, "that it is the intention of the Government to administer 'JUSTICE' in its true sense."[246] Singh's writings were translated from Gurmukhi into English, he explained, so that he could "draw the attention of the superior authorities of the various departments of the Government," and alert them to the injustices administered against him and the other passengers. "If my life story paves the way of repetition of any such single inequity being impossible, on any one in future, I shall die in happiness to know that I had done my duty."[247]

Foregrounding the shared and underlying structural force of racial violence under British rule, Singh's *Voyage* might be read as a critical reflection on the mutability of law. Much like the Ghadr circular that I discuss earlier, Singh also viewed "English law" as ever changing. Transatlantic slavery, systems of indenture, and immigration prohibitions revealed an expansion of racial un-freedom. At the same time, however, these racial and legal regimes served as clear evidence that British law held the possibility of becoming something else, something otherwise. Singh commenced the *Voyage* by reflecting on the potential of British legality and justice. He ended abruptly but on a similar note: "To suppress the country is the easiest thing for a mighty government to do but if the government wants the country's love then let her give justice."[248] To be clear, Gurdit Singh never offered a definition of justice, nor did he elucidate its relationship to law. Rather, he characterized justice in reference to properties that were similar to those of the sea—ineffable, indefinite, and open to the future. The fractured temporalities that Singh ascribed to British and colonial law allowed him to invoke it strategically and opportunistically, and as a firm rejoinder to the charges levied against him by the colonial governments of Canada, Hong Kong, and India.

Throughout the *Voyage,* oceans emerged faintly and intermittently, as both a metaphor and a materiality that hovered in Singh's imaginary. The elemental properties of oceans, including their vertiginous currents and ceaseless change, invited pathways toward Indian independence. Singh remained as steadfast on this point as he did on the potentiality of British law. "After countless sufferings and prosecutions, after losing all my worldly possessions and at such an advanced age of 70 years," he wrote, "I am still at the *helm* and would not prefer any other death but in harness of my country."[249] Here, "helm" conveyed multiple meanings. It gestured to Singh's maritime ambitions, his seaborne command, and his efforts to lead the *Komagata Maru*'s passengers across the Pacific and to a new life abroad. In addition, "helm" signaled a plan for the future. The steamer's maiden voyage was clearly unsuccessful. However, Singh did not give up on his dreams to begin a transoceanic shipping firm. Near the end of the *Voyage*, he encouraged the "youths and wealthy" of his "beloved land" to fulfill his aspirations for "a Steamship Company." Financial and political developments in shipping, he urged, would bring India's illustrious past into the future, enabling his "poor countrymen to go to foreign shores and learn and earn and come back better men."[250] Recall that Singh had already planned out two possible itineraries. The Calcutta-to-Canada route was no longer an option, given the *Komagata Maru*'s failed voyage. However, the Bombay-to-Brazil route remained a viable prospect. In the final section of the text, Singh included documents and correspondence that supported such a venture. In a letter addressed to immigration officials in Rio de Janeiro, Singh asked about Brazil's "rules and regulations for immigrants": whether "Europeans, Asiatics, and particularly Indians will be given the same privileges" of entry and whether they would "have the same rights" as nationals. If there was "any difference in rights, privileges and treatment with any particular nationality mentioned above," then Singh demanded to know "what and why."[251] Indians would willingly cross the Indian and Atlantic Oceans from Bombay to Brazil, especially if they were given "a definite assurance that the Indians' rights in the National territory" would "be retained as shown in . . . the coming future."[252] Ocean crossings, Singh intimated, were as vital to subjective awakenings as they were to nationalist and anticolonial ones.

Years after the *Komagata Maru*'s arrival to Budge Budge, Singh's maritime imaginaries continued to draw interest from abroad. In 1926, two years before the *Voyage* was published and as Singh was completing his sentence at Mianwali, Indian authorities intercepted a letter from Gyani Hanam Singh, a "highly educated Sikh" who was "very seditious in his utterances," and who served as the secretary of the Khalsa Diwan Society in Vancouver. The letter referred "to a donation of 100 dollars" that Gyani Hanam Singh "says he dispatched some time ago to the man who is looking after the education of the addressee's son," Balwant. The seized letter also made reference to "Gurdit Singh's scheme of starting a 'Sri Guru Navigation Co.'" If the project was "undertaken in a thoroughly businesslike manner, he (the writer) will have no difficulty in raising a sum of Rs. 50,000 among the Canadian Sikhs," the letter stated.[253] Although the Guru Nanak Steamship Company was an aspiration that was never achieved by Gurdit Singh, it was one that continued to inspire others.

GURDIT SINGH NEVER completed the *Voyage* as promised. In 1954, at the end of his life, the text remained just as it was in 1928, incomplete. There was no further discussion of the heroes that fell at Budge Budge and no reflections on India's maritime potential. After his release from prison, Singh moved on to other things. He worked for the Indian National Congress, was arrested on another three occasions, and eventually settled in Calcutta. In August 1947, he witnessed India's independence firsthand, including the effects of partition, which were most devastating for Punjab.[254]

Singh's maritime ambitions, his itinerancy, and fugitivity engendered conceptions of freedom and self-determination that followed interesting trajectories. His seaborne travels, as I argue above, gave him a perspective from the sea, one that enabled him to connect constellations of race across histories and geographies of British imperial control. By enumerating Britain's expanding regime of juridical violence, and by tracing the overlaps and interconnections between slavery, indenture, and so-called free migration, Singh's *Voyage* refuted prevailing temporalities of progress. Fugitivity, as Singh's own itinerancy made clear, was never a simple, linear, or straightforward pathway to freedom. Lines of flight produced additional registers of racial and legal violence and produced multiple temporalities. In so doing, fugitivity generated spaces for creative imaginaries and new possibilities, and for a future that was yet to be realized. For lascars, sailors, and fugitive/freed slaves, oceans were concomitant sites of violence and refuge that inspired inconsistent, disjointed, and errant conceptions of freedom.[255] These themes were also evident in Singh's *Voyage*.

In the view of Frank Vosper, who authored the poem to Gurdit Singh with which this chapter opens, Indian seafaring was not only dangerous, but also unthinkable. The *Komagata Maru*'s landing in Vancouver overtly challenged the racial and legal status of the sea as it had been envisioned and dictated for over three centuries, first by European empires and then by the white Dominions. Singh's maritime ambitions, which included trade, mobility, and anticolonialism, defied Britannia's efforts to rule the waves. His commercial and political aspirations could only be rendered legible through charges of lawlessness, madness, and criminality. Characterizations of the free sea as a racial and juridical space, and the purported criminality of non-Europeans who risked their lives to claim it by crossing it, are not limited to history alone. Rather, struggles over the sea remain urgent problems that continue to persist in the troubled global present. Maritime disputes that are unfolding today in different ocean regions, including the Mediterranean and the South China Sea, echo the *Komagata Maru*'s 1914 journey and the accusations directed at Gurdit Singh. In the epilogue, I turn to contemporary struggles over the free sea and to other ships and captains.

Race, Jurisdiction, and the Free Sea Reconsidered

Where are your monuments, your battles, martyrs?
Where is your tribal memory? Sirs,
in that grey vault. The sea. The sea
has locked them up. The sea is History.
—DEREK WALCOTT, "The Sea Is History," 1978

It is now clearly believed that Sri Guru Nanak Steamship Company's Steamers
will be around the whole world in the future.—GURDIT SINGH, c. 1914

In his 2006 Caird Lecture, David Armitage remarked that the opposition between empires of land and sea were "at once among the most basic yet also
least investigated themes in western historiography and political thought."[1]
His observations, as I understand them, signal a much wider problem, one that
necessitates a critical rereading of the land/sea divide in colonial, imperial, and
legal history. The distinction that animates terrestrial and maritime empires
is assumed to come from an elemental order. This may be one reason why it
has received so little scholarly attention. Upon closer scrutiny, it becomes clear
that the distinction between land and sea is not primeval or natural. As I have
argued in this book, through the passage of the *Komagata Maru,* their juridico-
political separation was inaugurated, enacted, and fortified through European
and later British expansion, an imperial reach that imposed spatial, temporal,
and racial inscriptions across the earth, and which has been contested ever
since.

The separation of land and sea was produced in part through moving ships. At the same time that developments in shipbuilding and navigational technologies transformed Britain into a maritime world power, vessels that traversed the high seas generated legal and political distinctions between oceans, continents, space, and time.[2] As European, British, and later American ships move farther along the high seas, aqueous regions were further differentiated into territorial waters (first, three miles, then twelve), contiguous zones, and exclusive economic zones.[3] A set of juridico-political lines that were formalized by the Dutch seizure of the *Santa Catarina* in 1603, laid the groundwork for a European legal order that has not only animated international law, but has dramatically shaped how we write history and approach (geo)politics.

In 1609, Hugo Grotius invoked the land and sea divide as an elemental edifice from which to develop his arguments on the freedom of Dutch trade. The publication of *Mare Liberum*, as I discuss in chapter 1, fortified the juridical standing of oceans at a key moment of European expansion, one that authorized "free trade" in the East Indies as a natural right of the Dutch East India Company. The physico-material properties that Grotius attributed to the sea, and which established its incommensurability with land, led him to clarify a range of legal concepts, including common space and private property. If the ever-changing sea placed it beyond occupation and ownership, Grotius argued, the fixity and immovability of land situated it firmly within the realm of possession. This opposition inspired regimes of landed property as well as other legal instruments through which indigenous peoples could be dispossessed and colonial populations deracinated.[4] Ultimately, Grotius's writings carried far-reaching consequences, affording a material and symbolic force to the racial and legal status of oceans and a legal architecture to Europe's resettlement of the "New World." Its colonial and racial effects continue to animate the divisions between East/West, North/South, and Orient/Occident and are evident in contemporary forms of maritime violence aimed at protecting Europe and its ostensibly free sea from yet another so-called migrant crisis, a point I return to below.[5]

Following Grotius, other European thinkers also arranged the earth in elemental terms. Hegel, for example, drew on conceptions of land and sea to position Europe, Asia, and Africa in a descending order of civilizational superiority and inferiority.[6] But it was in the mid-twentieth century, with the writings of Carl Schmitt, that the "cleft between land and sea" was further elaborated as "an expression of different worlds" and opposing legalities.[7] In the period preceding and then following the Second World War, Schmitt argued that the *nomos* of the earth was on the precipice of a profound historical shift: "The new *nomos* of our planet grows, unceasingly and irresistibly. It is summoned by the new relations of humans to the old and to the new elements, and the altered measurements and relations that compel it."[8] For Schmitt, technology dramatically advanced the project of human mastery over nature. "The sea is today no longer an element as it was in the time of the whale hunters and corsairs," he claimed. "Today's transportation and communications technology has made the sea into a space in the contemporary sense of the word. Today, in times of peace, every shipowner can know daily and hourly at which point in the ocean his ship on the high sea is to be found." In a clear departure from the age of sail, "the world of the sea" under the dominance of steam was "elementarily altered for humans," Schmitt argued.[9] With new developments in navigation, the uncertainty and unknowability of oceans, which at one time terrified captains and crews, became a distant memory of a bygone era. "Some believe themselves to be experiencing the end of the world," he remarked, but what "we are only experiencing [is] the end of the relation between land and sea."[10] Notwithstanding Schmitt's speculations on a changing imperial order, and his prediction that the rise of German airpower would eventually triumph over British maritime dominance, the world's oceans and seas remain crucial to struggles over migration, trade, and planetary control.[11]

Against Grotius and Schmitt's accounts of the purportedly free sea, *Across Oceans of Law* argues that the sea has always been a vibrant site of maritime crossings and of legal, political, and racial contests. The *Komagata Maru*'s journey, as I narrate it in this book, presents one moment in a much longer history of circulation, exchange, solidarity, and struggle. When the ship is unmoored from land, extricated from prevailing narratives of immigration and arrival, and situated in the Pacific, Indian, and Atlantic Oceans, its voyage offers a productive aperture and a wider vista through which to explore the vessel's maritime and global significance. From the decks of the ship, oceans appear not as empty or divided spaces successfully conquered by human prowess, but as densely woven sites of encounter. Oceans were scenes of conviviality, contest, and collision, where legal disputes over race, mobility, and jurisdiction unfolded with potency, urgency, and often in multiple temporalities. Tracking the movements of the *Komagata Maru* through time and space, while trailing the aspirations of its itinerant Sikh commander, underscores the significance of the sea, both as a domain of violence and a site of imagination. Following a single ship across seemingly disparate ocean arenas, and placing it within European debates on the freedom of the sea, offers one way to problematize the elemental divide between land and sea not solely as an undercurrent of terrestrial and maritime empires, but as an enduring juridical, political, and racial effect of imperial power.

As with all oppositions, land and sea have never been equal, symmetrical or proportional. According to Nicholas Mirzoeff, "There is a remarkable investment (in all senses, whether economic, psychoanalytic, or emotional) in the imagining of the marine as elemental, primordial, and unchanging, a dialectical corollary to the biopolitical struggles over land."[12] If terra firma supposedly grounded modern law, setting the conditions for land appropriations and property regimes, oceans, by contrast, were seen to be infinite, thereby lacking legality, politics, and sociability.[13] By diminishing the significance of the sea, Schmitt found additional ways to emphasize the legal and political import of land. The ocean, in his formulation, featured as a negative space and a vacant backdrop, one that afforded substance and meaning to law and empire as terrestrial and spatial arrangements. Recall that Schmitt dated the rise of a European global order to 1492, to Columbus's so-called discovery of the Americas. Curiously, he paid little attention to Columbus's ships or to the arduous Atlantic crossings that brought his fleet to the "New World." The sea, as Schmitt viewed it, was not a domain of imperial or legal struggle. Nor was it a space of anticolonialism.[14] Beginning and ending with land and with Europe, Schmitt ignored the vital role of the sea in non-European worlds.[15] His Eurocentric and terracentric order erased the symbolic and material significance that the Pacific, Indian, and Atlantic Oceans held for indigenous peoples, Muslim travelers, African seafarers, "Asiatic" traders, and many others who drew their individual and collective identities and livelihoods from the sea. Moreover, his *nomos*—as a European spatial order—obscured the challenges that racial and colonial subjects waged against the juridification and securitization of ocean arenas through their continued crossings. The epigraphs from Derek Walcott and Gurdit Singh that open this epilogue, when read alongside Grotius's free sea and Schmitt's empty one, serve as a critical riposte and as further evidence of the presence and persistence of other oceanic histories. For colonial and racial subjects—compelled to cross the sea, as slaves, indentured laborers, and forced/ "free" migrants yet prohibited at different times from engaging in maritime trade and mobility—oceans were neither open nor empty. They were space-times of racial terror, dispossession, and death but also lively arenas of commerce, trade, pilgrimage, and revolt. For Gurdit Singh and Husain Rahim, oceans formed a capacious site of creativity, struggle, and ultimately a route toward freedom from British imperial rule.

Across Oceans of Law conceives of the Pacific, Indian, and Atlantic Oceans not as discrete regions but as overlapping and intersecting histories and geographies. What I have termed "oceans as method" draws deliberately on the dynamic materiality and rich metaphoricity of the sea as both a technique of writing colonial legal history and as a conceptual frame that foregrounds movement and change. In his influential writings on ocean currents, the Scottish scientist,

James Croll, who we encountered in the introduction, described the earth's watery spaces as follows: "Leaving out of account a few small inland seas, the globe may be said to have but one sea, as well as but one atmosphere."[16] Attuned to the interconnections among ocean arenas, joined by their intersecting and interdependent currents, I direct attention away from the coordinates of arrival and departure that have figured so prominently in histories of the *Komagata Maru* and in literatures on Indian migration and radicalism. Instead, I turn to the free sea, the ship, its commander, and the middle passage. This reorientation, as I see it, invites a wider set of historiographical discussions on the sea as a racial *and* legal history; on currents and countercurrents of law and anticolonialism; and of time and jurisdiction as potent registers of imperial control. In my discussion of the overlaps and intersections between immigration and admiralty law, I argue that the transoceanic itineraries of moving ships facilitated an uneven expansion of racial and imperial power that was advanced through multiple, competing, and conflicting legal orders. These juridical inscriptions—as they recast the earth into a seemingly unified spatial and temporal whole—worked to overwrite indigenous and subaltern cosmologies, albeit never entirely.[17]

From the 1880s onward, as steam opened maritime travel and made it more widely accessible to "Asiatics," ships offered additional prospects for solidarities, anticolonial networks, and radical imaginaries. In my retelling of the *Komagata Maru*'s 1914 journey, I suggest that colonial authorities and Indian radicals questioned the division between land and sea, albeit in different ways and with competing objectives. Whereas Canadian and Indian officials perceived oceans, littorals, and inland regions to be inextricably linked through a knotted regime of maritime controls and immigration regulations, seaborne Indians, including Gurdit Singh and Husain Rahim, unraveled these elemental divides through their expansive visions, anticolonial writings, and their transoceanic itineraries. The counter-*nomos* of the earth envisaged by Rahim openly disputed the freedom of the sea and proposed alternative routes of transoceanic travel. In his anticolonial writings, Singh viewed oceans, islands, and distant continents as interconnected through circuits of racial violence. His critique of the British Empire disrupted the lines of the cartographer's map and the linearity of historical time. For Singh, the sea invited a looking back to India's illustrious era of shipping, and a projection forward to Indian independence. History and futurity were condensed in the present, a moment marked by struggles against British control over India, the seas, and the Dominions, colonies, and territories.

By recentering maritime space, oceans as method invites a rethinking of historical time. When the Pacific, Atlantic, and Indian Oceans are placed together within the same conceptual frame, the struggles waged by Gurdit Singh, Husain

Rahim, the *Komagata Maru* passengers, and their supporters in India and the diaspora echo other times and places, and in ways that trouble a progressive view of history. The racial, territorial, and temporal disputes over jurisdiction and British subjecthood, which came into sharp focus with the ship's arrival in Vancouver Harbour, were produced from and animated by protracted and sedimented histories. Indigenous dispossession, transatlantic slavery, systems of Chinese/Indian indenture, and so-called free migration are too often studied as distinct processes, confined to specific terrestrial and oceanic regions and within discrete historical periods.[18] When viewed from the ship, they appear simultaneous rather than successive: through shared juridical forms, most notably the concept of legal personhood; in changing registers of racial and legal power that produced the conditions for enslaved and forced labor, and informed restrictions on mobility; and in anticolonial vernaculars inspired by histories of transatlantic slavery and shifting figures of indigeneity. Moving from Schmitt's *nomos* to the oceanic worlds of Indian migrants, sojourners, and travelers, however restricted and prohibited these worlds were, offers an alternative set of coordinates and chronologies through which to analyze circuits of law, race, and empire as regimes of power that worked horizontally, vertically, and in several dimensions. Rather than drawing a fixed line in the soil as the basis of a modern European legal order, oceans as method emphasizes the sea as a polycentric, polyphonous, and variegated space marked by continual movements, circulating legalities, and by competing jurisdictional claims.[19] Though the freedom of the sea was established at a specific moment in the concomitant expansion of European imperialism and colonial capitalism, it endures into the present day. As an ongoing scene of racial violence, the "free sea" and its opposition to land continues to demand critical attention, perhaps with even greater urgency.

This book centers on the *Komagata Maru*'s journey. But is also a reflection on a more distant past and how it shapes our troubled global present. Today, oceans remain vibrant spaces of law, politics, and poetics, as they were when Grotius, Rahim, and Singh were writing their competing visions of the earth. The debates over *mare liberum* and *mare clausum* that were formalized in the early seventeenth century, which shaped racial and jurisdictional struggles from the age of "discovery" to "free trade," through transatlantic slavery, to indenture and "Asiatic" migration, continue to persist in different forms and intensities. The voyage of the *Komagata Maru*, as Gurdit Singh's commercial, political, and legal challenge to the purported free sea, to the British Empire's restrictions on mobility, and to Canada's immigration prohibitions, reverberates in distinct registers and tones, in the thousands of migrants aspiring to cross the Mediterranean under unspeakable conditions of life-and-death. The *Sicilia,* as the *Komagata Maru*'s previous incarnation, made regular stops along the Mediterranean, thus it seems fitting to end here.[20]

Perceived as a maritime border that separates North and South, East and West, the Mediterranean is thought to be in need of protection from the small, precarious, and overcrowded vessels that have long been viewed as the antithesis of Europe. Growing militarization has resulted in tens of thousands of deaths. From 1998 to 2012, official estimates suggest that more than 14,000 people have perished while trying to make the passage from North Africa and the Middle East to Southern Europe.[21] Drawing on more recent data, the International Organization for Migration's Missing Migrants Project reports that between 2013 and 2017, more than 3,000 people have died each year while attempting to cross Europe's primordial sea.[22] To be sure, these official numbers do not sufficiently capture the actual scale of death. Many people remain missing and unaccounted for. But as the Mediterranean (re)materializes into a deadly space, evocations of land continue. Recent deaths at sea are described, not as maritime violence, but in terms of landfall, nation, and sovereignty, as Europe's latest "migrant crisis."

The Mediterranean Sea is not the Pacific, Atlantic, or Indian Ocean. The open boats, unseaworthy and overcrowded, are not British-built steamships. It would be a completely different experience to cross the Pacific on a steamer, a voyage that took the *Komagata Maru* six-weeks, than it would to cross the Central or Eastern Mediterranean aboard a dinghy. While there are stark differences between the Mediterranean and other ocean regions, and between crossings past and present, these contemporary sea passages might be read as the most recent struggles in a much longer genealogy of the "free sea." Currents connect the Mediterranean and Atlantic at the Strait of Gibraltar, Croll observed. The force of currents and countercurrents continue to move people and goods, join disparate regions of the earth, and produce entangled histories. The perilous migrant journeys across the Mediterranean and the tens of thousands of deaths at sea echo the forced passages of slaves, indentured laborers, and of other involuntary and "free" migrants.[23] Together, these passages make up the battles, martyrs, monuments, and memories contained in Walcott's "grey vault," a reminder that "the sea is history," a history that can be otherwise.

In many ways, Gurdit Singh's efforts to charter and command a ship across the Pacific are no longer as exceptional today as they were in 1914. The contemporary Mediterranean is filled with vessels, under the supposed command of black and brown captains. Like Singh, many of these men have been characterized as corrupt and despotic criminals, and in more recent idioms, as "human traffickers." In April 2015, the Mediterranean became international news yet again when eight hundred people drowned after a fishing trawler sank off the coast of Libya.[24] The twenty-meter fishing boat collided with a Portuguese merchant ship that was allegedly coming to its rescue. Of the eight hundred passengers aboard, only twenty-eight survived, and only twenty-four bodies were recovered.[25] According to the United Nations High Commission for Refugees, 350 of the passengers were Eritrean. Others were from Syria, Somalia, Mali, Senegal, Gambia, Ivory Coast, and Ethiopia. All were seeking a new life, free from the conditions of occupation, civil war, and environmental degradation that have made life unlivable for people in these regions and horrific voyages across the Mediterranean a necessary means of escape. The captain of the trawler, Ali Malek, a Tunisian national, along with one of his crewmen, Mahmud Bikhit, a Syrian national, were charged with "reckless multiple manslaughter, causing a shipwreck, and aiding illegal immigration."[26] Rather than locating this tragedy where it belongs, in Western intervention and occupation, it was cast as preventable, a loss of life caused by Malek's negligence. There are eerie resonances. Recall that the *Komagata Maru*'s unsuccessful journey—its detention and deportation, as well as the massacre at Budge Budge—were believed to be the sole responsibility of Gurdit Singh. My intention in drawing these connections is not to make equivalences between today's migrant deaths and the *Komagata Maru*'s 1914 voyage. Though nineteen passengers were killed at Budge Budge and another two in the Alipore Jail, there were no reported deaths at sea. What deserves attention, however, is how the freedom of the sea engenders a mutability of maritime jurisdictions. To protect Europe against these most recent racial threats, and "to avoid engaging in rescue missions, states have strategically exploited the partial and overlapping sovereignty at sea and the elastic nature of international law."[27] Forces of global power have shifted, empires have crumbled, others are in decline, and new concentrations of power are emerging. Yet the contemporary Mediterranean is a potent reminder that the so-called free sea remains a domain of European and Western control.

Gurdit Singh's aspirations to initiate the Guru Nanak Steamship Company, though never fully realized, were established on other ocean histories and traditions of Indian seafaring and trade that defied the elemental orders of Grotius and Schmitt and challenged the European myth of the free sea. In his recollection of the *Komagata Maru*'s passage, Singh presented a vast and compelling anticolonial imaginary, one that emerged from his travels at sea and his seven years of fugitivity on land. In the *Voyage of the Komagatamaru*, Singh skillfully sutured seemingly distinct histories and geographies—transatlantic slavery, Indian indentured labor in the Straits Settlements, and Indian migration to Canada and Australia—positioning them in ways that disputed the opposition of land and sea and the forward march of history. Though oceans were at the heart of a global and universal European time and vital to changing registers of imperial control, Singh appreciated how their rhythmic movements and undulations linked distant parts of the earth, producing disjointed and circuitous temporalities. It was in these interstices of land/sea and time/space that he identified the potential for freedom. Today, as we witness the horrors of maritime violence as it plays out along the Mediterranean, Singh's writings provide a critical rejoinder, an alternative map, and a source of inspiration. Oceans, as he viewed them, were deadly spaces of racial and colonial violence but also moving horizons that opened commercial, political, and anticolonial possibilities. This is a urgent lesson for our time.

INTRODUCTION

1. *Report of the Komagata Maru Committee of Inquiry*, 1:2 (hereafter *Report of the Komagata Maru*).

2. British Library, India Office Records (hereafter BL/IOR), L/PJ/6/1338, file 5028, *'Komagata Maru' Committee of Enquiry: Volume III* (23 October–4 December 1914), exhibit 134: Proclamation to Indians by Sardar Singh, no date [c. spring 1914], 315. "Sardar Sing" signed the document. Gurdit Singh was the director of the Guru Nanak Steamship Company and was regularly referred to as "Sardar Gurdit Singh."

3. BL/IOR, L/PJ/6/1338, file 5028, *'Komagata Maru' Committee of Enquiry: Volume III* (23 October–4 December 1914), exhibit 85: Translation of a letter in Gurmukhi from Sardar Singh, Honorary Agent of "Bridh Sewak" [lit., old servant] Bhai Gurdit Singh, Contractor, to the Editor, Panth Sewak, 1914, 184.

4. BL/IOR, L/PJ/6/1338, file 5028, *'Komagata Maru' Committee of Enquiry: Volume III* (23 October–4 December 1914), exhibit 85: Translation of a letter in Gurmukhi from Sardar Singh, Honorary Agent of "Bridh Sewak" [lit., old servant] Bhai Gurdit Singh, Contractor, to the Editor, Panth Sewak, 1914, 184.

5. For an account of the history of shipping published two years before Singh issued his proclamation, see Mookerji, *Indian Shipping*.

6. BL/IOR, L/PJ/6/1338, file 5028, *'Komagata Maru' Committee of Enquiry: Volume III* (23 October–4 December 1914), exhibit 134: Proclamation to Indians by Sardar Singh [c. spring 1914], 315. Though the letter has no date, the *Report of the Komagata Maru* said that Gurdit Singh published an advertisement in February 1914. See *Report of the Komagata Maru*, 2.

7. BL/IOR, L/PJ/6/1338, file 5028, *'Komagata Maru' Committee of Enquiry: Volume III* (23 October–4 December 1914), Exhibit 134: Proclamation to Indians by Sardar Singh [c. spring 1914], 315.

8. There were two women on the ship, Dr. Raghunath's wife and Kishen Kaur. See Johnston, *The Voyage of the Komagata Maru*, 66, 136.

9. The year 1947 marked a year of greater independence for both Canada and India. It is the origin of Canada's Citizenship Act, which replaced "British subject" with "Canadian citizen." See Macklin, "Historicizing Narratives of Arrival," 41.

10. The passengers allowed to disembark were ones who could prove they had previously resided in Vancouver. In the historiography of the ship, the number varies between twenty and twenty-two. On the latter, see Macklin, "Historicizing Narratives of Arrival," 59.

11. For an overview of the legal framework of Indian exclusion as it relates to the *Komagata Maru*, see Macklin, "Historicizing Narratives of Arrival." In chapter 3, I offer a more detailed analysis of the laws passed by the Dominion and a close reading of the case heard by the Board of Immigration and the British Columbia Court of Appeal. For a compelling discussion of how the movements of "free" Indians, including those aboard the *Komagata Maru*, were governed through the legal framework of indenture, see Mongia, "The *Komagata Maru* as Event."

12. BL/IOR, L/PJ/6/1338, file 5028, '*Komagata Maru*' Committee of Enquiry: Volume III (23 October–4 December 1914), exhibit 45: Translation of an appeal for money printed in Gurmukhi, issued from Vancouver [c. June 1914], 93.

13. BL/IOR, L/PJ/6/1338, file 5028, '*Komagata Maru*' Committee of Enquiry: Volume III (23 October–4 December 1914), Exhibit 45: Translation of an appeal for money printed in Gurmukhi, issued from Vancouver [c. June 1914], 93.

14. Hugo Grotius's *Mare Liberum* is the subject of the following chapter. See Armitage, introduction to *The Free Sea*.

15. For an interesting discussion of the sea as European that focuses on Hegel's *Lectures on the Philosophy of World History*, see Wick, *The Red Sea*, esp. chap. 2.

16. On the policing of the free sea, see Steinberg, "Free Sea," 271.

17. There is a small but growing body of feminist scholarship that challenges the prevailing view of the sea as an exclusively male domain. See Creighton and Norling, *Iron Men, Wooden Women*; Smith, "Costume Changes."

18. BL/IOR, L/PJ/6/1338, file 5028, '*Komagata Maru*' Committee of Enquiry: Volume III (23 October–4 December 1914), exhibit 45: Translation of an appeal for money printed in Gurmukhi, issued from Vancouver [c. June 1914], 93.

19. BL/IOR, L/PJ/6/1338, file 5028, '*Komagata Maru*' Committee of Enquiry: Volume III (23 October–4 December 1914), exhibit 45: Translation of an appeal for money printed in Gurmukhi, issued from Vancouver [c. June 1914], 93.

20. BL/IOR, L/PJ/6/1338, file 5028, '*Komagata Maru*' Committee of Enquiry: Volume III (23 October–4 December 1914), exhibit 45: Translation of an appeal for money printed in Gurmukhi, issued from Vancouver [c. June 1914], 93.

21. BL/IOR, L/PJ/6/1338, file 5028, '*Komagata Maru*' Committee of Enquiry: Volume III (23 October–4 December 1914), exhibit 45: Translation of an appeal for money printed in Gurmukhi, issued from Vancouver [c. June 1914], 93.

22. On ocean and maritime studies, see Amrith, *Crossing the Bay of Bengal*; Bose, *A Hundred Horizons*; Gilroy, *The Black Atlantic*; Ho, *The Graves of Tarim*; Linebaugh and Rediker, *The Many-Headed Hydra*. For notable exceptions that explore multiple ocean arenas, see Christopher, Pybus, and Rediker, *Many Middle Passages*, Hofmeyr, "The Black Atlantic Meets the Indian Ocean." For a critique of the regionalization of ocean studies, see Steinberg, "Of Other Seas," 158. On the historicization of ocean divides, see Lewis, "Dividing the Ocean Sea." On oceans and law, see Bishara, "Paper Routes"; Benton, *A Search for Sovereignty*; Ford, "Law"; Mawani and Hussin, "The Travels of Law"; Metcalf, *Imperial Connections*, Ward, *Networks of Empire*.

23. On the *Komagata Maru* in Canada, see Johnston, *The Voyage of the Komagata Maru*; Jensen, *Passage from India*; Kazimi, *Continuous Journey*; Kazimi, *Undesirables*; Macklin, "Historicizing Narratives"; Ward, *White Canada Forever*. In the U.S. context, see Sohi, *Echoes*

of Mutiny. For transnational and global accounts, see Balachandran, "Indefinite Transits"; Mongia, "Race, Nationality, Mobility"; Mawani, "Specters of Indigeneity." In India, see the recent special issue, "The Journey of the Komagata Maru: National, Transnational, Diasporic," *South Asian Diaspora* 8, no. 2 (2016), which was also published as a book, Roy and Sahoo, *Diasporas and Transnationalisms*.

24. Several historians have viewed the Indian Ocean as a useful method of writing history. See Burton, "Sea Tracks and Trails" and Hofmeyr, "The Complicating Sea." I build on and expand their approaches by using microhistory to think through and connect multiple ocean regions.

25. I begin developing this argument on race as a regime of power elsewhere. See Mawani, *Colonial Proximities*, Mawani, "Specters of Indigeneity"; Mawani, "Racial Violence and the Cosmopolitan City."

26. For a discussion of race and jurisdiction, see Ford, "Law's Territory (A History of Jurisdiction)."

27. Marx, "The Future Results of British Rule in India," 660.

28. Barak, *On Time*, 24.

29. To date, the most comprehensive English-language biography of Singh is by Tatla and Tatla, *Sardar Gurdit Singh*. On this point, see p. 2. See also Tatla, "Incorporating Regional Events into the Nationalist Narrative."

30. Key works on Indian radicalism of the time include Grewal, Puri, and Banga, *The Ghadr Movement*, Puri, *Ghadr Movement*. For two recent books that document these anticolonial circuits, see Ramnath, *Haj to Utopia*; Sohi, *Echoes of Mutiny*.

31. "Indians in the Empire," *Register*, 18 January 1915, 4.

32. BL/IOR, L/PJ/6/1338, file 50285028, *'Komagata Maru' Committee of Enquiry: Volume III* (23 October–4 December 1914), exhibit 54: Manuscript giving a history of the voyage of the "S.S. Komagata Maru" written in Gurmukhi, apparently in the handwriting of Daljit Singh, 1914, 112 (my emphasis).

33. See Amrith, *Crossing the Bay of Bengal*; Blythe, *The Empire of the Raj*; Bose, *A Hundred Horizons*; Metcalf, *Imperial Connections*; Aiyar, "Anticolonial Homelands across the Indian Ocean."

34. On the fits and starts of migration and settlement, see Dusinberre and Wenzlhuemer, "Editorial: Being in Transit."

35. I have documented the ship's voyages by consulting the *Lloyd's Weekly Shipping Index* at the Guildhall Library, London, and the Caird Library, National Maritime Museum, Greenwich.

36. Lubbock, *Coolie Ships and Oil Sailors*, 73, 103.

37. Several scholars have made these connections between slavery and indenture. However, the significance of the ship is often forgotten. On Indian indenture and slavery, see Bahadur, *Coolie Woman*; Carter, *Servants, Sirdars, and Settlers*; Kale, *Fragments of Empire*; Mongia, "Impartial Regimes of Truth"; Tinker, *A New System of Slavery*. On Chinese indenture and transatlantic slavery in the U.S. South, see Jung, *Coolies and Cane*; Lowe, *The Intimacies of Four Continents*.

38. On ships and indigenous dispossession, see Russell, "'The Singular Transcultural Space,'" 97. On ships and primitive accumulation, see Sekula, *Fish Story*, 43.

39. It was through a translation error that the ship became the *Komagata Maru*, a point I discuss more fully in chapter 2.

40. These events are detailed in the *Report of the Komagata Maru*. See also Johnston, *Voyage of the Komagata Maru*, esp. chap. 10.

41. Johnston, *The Voyage of the Komagata Maru*; Jensen, *Passage from India*; Kazimi, *Undesirables*; Macklin, "Historicizing Narratives"; Ward, *White Canada Forever*.

42. On 18 May 2016, Prime Minister Justin Trudeau apologized for Canada's exclusion of the ship. Though the apology was the outcome of many community-based struggles, it reinscribed the ship's significance as a Canadian "incident" rather than a global event.

43. In *The Black Atlantic*, Gilroy makes a compelling case for a new method of writing that focuses on the ship. While his interest is in tracing countercultures, mine is in tracking legal contests and counter-histories.

44. This is a vast literature. For recent works, see Ballantyne, *Between Colonialism and Diaspora*; Bashford, *Medicine at the Border*; McKeown, *Melancholy Order*; Ngai, *Impossible Subjects*; Shah, *Stranger Intimacy*.

45. Ballantyne, *Between Colonialism and Diaspora*; Burton, *At the Heart of Empire*; Burton, *Burdens of History*; Ballantyne and Burton, *Empires and the Reach of the Global*; Hall, *Civilizing Subjects*.

46. Ballantyne, "Race and the Webs of Empire." This argument is updated and elaborated in Ballantyne, *Webs of Empire*.

47. Ballantyne, "Race and the Webs of Empire," 39.

48. Metcalf, *Imperial Connections*, 8.

49. Metcalf, *Imperial Connections*, 1.

50. For notable exceptions, see Burton, "Sea Tracks and Ocean Trails"; Dusinberre and Wenzlhuemer, "Editorial: Being in Transit"; Hofmeyr, "The Complicating Sea."

51. Steinberg, "Of Other Seas," 157.

52. Steinberg, "Of Other Seas," 158 (emphasis in original).

53. This is true of many oceanic histories. See Bose, *A Hundred Horizons*; Desai, *Commerce with the Universe*; Gilroy, *The Black Atlantic*.

54. See Hofmeyr, "The Black Atlantic Meets the Indian Ocean," 3. This directionality has started to change with the work of historians tracing South-South relations. See, for example, Burton, *Brown over Black*.

55. Where transnational history and world history have been especially important and influential is in the field of legal pluralism. See Benton, *Law and Colonial Cultures*; Benton and Ross, *Legal Pluralism and Empires*.

56. This is beginning to shift with works that focus on legal travels. See Benton, *A Search for Sovereignty*; Bishara, "Paper Routes"; Mawani and Hussin, "The Travels of Law"; Ward, *Networks of Empire*.

57. Halliday, "Law's Histories," 269.

58. Benton, *Law and Colonial Cultures*, 45.

59. Ward, *Networks of Empire*, 10.

60. Halliday, "Law's Histories," 269. Benton pluralizes imperial geographies in *A Search for Sovereignty*. One could argue, however, that by privileging space at the expense of time, she focuses on two dimensions rather than three.

61. For clear exceptions, see Benton, *A Search for Sovereignty*, chap. 3; Benton and Ford, *Rage for Order*, chap. 5.

62. Armitage, introduction to *The Free Sea*. Though Grotius viewed the sea as a juridical space, as I discuss in the next chapter, he reinforced the land/ sea divide that has since held significant implications for how we think of law, legality, and territoriality.

63. Schmitt, *The Nomos of the Earth*, 42. Vismann also emphasizes the role of the plough, agriculture, and land. See Vismann, *Files*, 15.

64. For a critique of terracentricity, see Rediker, "Toward a Peoples' History of the Sea," 198.

65. On the ship as a cultural technique that produces space, see Siegert, *Cultural Techniques*, 70.

66. See Mawani, "Law, Settler Colonialism, and 'the Forgotten Space' of Maritime Worlds," and Russell, "'The Singular Transcultural Space.'"

67. Mawani, "Law and Migration across the Pacific."

68. "The British Columbia Question," *Indian Opinion*, 26 August 1914, 2.

69. "The British Columbia Question," *Indian Opinion*, 26 August 1914, 2.

70. Borrowing immigration laws from white settler colonies was not uncommon. In 1947, Burma modeled its immigration legislation on policies in the United States and in other white settler colonies. See Amrith, *Crossing the Bay of Bengal*, 216.

71. On Canada, see Ward, *White Canada Forever*. On Australia, see Bashford, "Is White Australia Possible?" For works that draw connections between the white Dominions, see Huttenback, "The British Empire as a 'White Man's Country,'" and Lake and Reynolds, *Drawing the Global Colour Line*.

72. See Bashford, "Immigration Restriction." Bashford's focus is on postcolonial nations. What interests me is how colonial India imposed border restrictions similar to those in Canada and Australia.

73. Marx and Engels, "Review: January–February 1850."

74. Marx and Engels, cited in Mehring, *Karl Marx*, 194.

75. For an account that emphasizes the role of China and the Muslim world in European seafaring, see Chappell, "Ahab's Boat," 76.

76. For a critique of Marx's teleology, see Chakrabarty, *Provincializing Europe*, esp. part 1.

77. See Lewis, "Dividing the Ocean Sea."

78. James Croll, "Letters to the Editor: Ocean Currents," *Nature*, 11 January 1872, 201.

79. A good example of the divided oceans framework that I am critiquing is evidenced in Gabbacia and Hoerder, *Connecting Seas and Connected Ocean Rims*.

80. Gilroy, *The Black Atlantic*, 12.

81. Gilroy, *The Black Atlantic*, 14–15.

82. Linebaugh and Rediker's writings have focused mainly on the Atlantic. See *The Many-Headed Hydra* and also their single-author works: Linebaugh, "All the Atlantic Mountains Shook"; Rediker, *Between the Devil and the Deep Blue Sea*; and Rediker's most recent book, *Outlaws of the Atlantic*.

83. Gilroy, *The Black Atlantic*, 14–15.

84. Isabel Hofmeyr's project has been to connect the Black Atlantic with the Indian Ocean and Africa. See Hofmeyr, "The Black Atlantic Meets the Indian Ocean."

85. Weaver, *The Red Atlantic*.

86. Bishara, *A Sea of Debt*; Bose, *A Hundred Horizons*; Ho, *Graves of Tarim*; Machado, *Ocean of Trade*; Pearson, *The Indian Ocean*. For an interesting account of aboriginal and South Asian seafarers, see Goodhall, Gosh, and Todd, "Jumping Ship—Skirting Empire."

87. Amrith, *Crossing the Bay of Bengal*, 21.

88. Bose, *A Hundred Horizons*, 272.

89. Amrith, *Crossing the Bay of Bengal*, 26.

90. Yu, "The Rhythms of the Transpacific."

91. Diaz, "Voyaging for Anti-colonial Recovery"; Igler, *The Great Ocean*; Hau'ofa, *We Are the Ocean*; Hau'ofa, "Our Sea of Islands"; Mar, *Decolonization and the Pacific*. See also "Pacific Currents," a special issue of *American Quarterly* edited by Paul Lyons and Ty P. Kawika Tengan.

92. Hau'ofa, "Our Sea of Islands," 8.

93. Armitage and Bashford, "Introduction," 9.

94. Armitage and Bashford, "Introduction," 6.

95. Hau'ofa, "Our Sea of Islands," 10.

96. Salesa, "The Pacific in Indigenous Time," 32.

97. Wigen, "Introduction," 2.

98. On the surveillance of ships carrying Indian migrants, see Balachandran, "Indefinite Transits," and Chattopadhyay, "Closely Observed Ships." Both discuss the *Komagata Maru*.

99. The trope of currents has gained momentum in ocean studies. See the recent issue of American Quarterly titled "Pacific Currents," edited by Lyons and Tengan.

100. Croll, "Ocean Currents," *Chambers's Journal of Popular Literature, Science, and the Arts*, 8 July 1893, 422.

101. See Phillips, *The Atlantic Sound*.

102. For a history of the study of ocean currents, see Mills, *The Fluid Envelope of our Planet*.

103. Steinberg, *The Social Construction of the Ocean*, 210.

104. Croll, "Ocean Currents," 422.

105. Hester Blum argues that the sea is not a metaphor. While I agree that the sea has a materiality, I suggest that it cannot be so easily separated from metaphoricity. See Blum, "The Prospect of Ocean Studies." For a response see Steinberg, "Of Other Seas."

106. Some have argued that oceans and ships have different histories that must not be conflated. See Foxhall, *Health, Medicine, and the Sea*, 7. However, as juridical forms, the two are inseparable.

107. Croll, "Ocean Currents," 422. See also Siegert, *Cultural Techniques*, chap. 4.

108. For Braudel, the sixteenth century is a crucial moment in maritime expansion. European ships no longer traveled along coastal lines but increasingly moved to the high seas. See Braudel, *The Mediterranean*, chapter 3.

109. Marx and Engels, "Review: May–October 1850."

110. Marx and Engels, "Review: May–October 1850."

111. For a critique of empty oceans, see Steinberg, *The Social Construction of the Ocean*, 14. A notable exception in the American context is Melville's *Billy Budd, Sailor*.

112. Schmitt, *The Nomos of the Earth*, 42.

113. Ghosh, *Sea of Poppies*, 371.

114. Ghosh, *Sea of Poppies*, 282. Ghosh does a wonderful job of describing these oceanic labor hierarchies through the character of Jodhu, a Muslim boat-hand. In subsequent chapters, I contend that these divisions were absorbed into modern conceptions of race.

115. Several historians of the Black Atlantic have argued that the ship and the plantation were contiguous. See Bolster, *Black Jacks*; Rediker, *The Slave Ship*, 188; Rediker, *Outlaws of the Atlantic*, 139. On ships as colonial legal laboratories, see Heller and Pezzani, "Liquid Traces," 680; Mawani, "Law, Settler Colonialism, and the 'Forgotten Space,'" 123.

116. Yatim, "The Development of the Law of the Sea in Relation to Malaysia," 87–88. Steinberg, *The Social Construction of the Ocean*, 50.

117. Alexandrowicz, *An Introduction to the History of the Law of Nations*, 64. Also cited in Steinberg, *The Social Construction of the Ocean*, 50–51.

118. Benton, *A Search for Sovereignty*, 106. On the importance of national flags at sea, see Van Tilburg, "Vessels of Exchange," 48.

119. Ward is writing of the Dutch, but her analysis is equally applicable to the British Empire. See Ward, *Networks of Empire*, 24.

120. See Chattopadhyay, "Closely Observed Ships."

121. The classic account of the middle passage as a site of revolt is in Gilroy, *The Black Atlantic*. See also McKittrick, *Demonic Grounds*, esp. chap. 1; Rediker, *The Slave Ship*.

122. The term "patchwork" comes from Benton, *Law and Colonial Cultures*, 44–45, 158. For recent scholarship on jurisdiction, see Dorsett and McVeigh, *Jurisdiction*; Ford, "Law's Territory"; McVeigh, *Jurisprudence of Jurisdiction*; Pasternak, "Jurisdiction and Settler Colonialism"; Valverde, "Jurisdiction and Scale"; Valverde, *Chronotopes of Law*.

123. Dorsett and McVeigh, "Questions of Jurisdiction," 3.

124. Dorsett and McVeigh, *Jurisdiction*, 38. On the plurality of the common law, see Halliday, "Law's Histories."

125. Dorsett and McVeigh, "Questions of Jurisdiction," 4–5.

126. Dorsett, "Mapping Territories," 146.

127. The *Santa Catarina* and Grotius's response has been well documented. See Armitage, introduction to *The Free Sea*; Benton, *A Search for Sovereignty*, esp. chap. 3; Borschberg, "Hugo Grotius"; Borschberg, *Hugo Grotius*; Keene, *Beyond the Anarchical Society*; van Ittersum, *Profit and Principle*.

128. Benton, *Law and Colonial Cultures*, 158.

129. On jurisdiction as race and status, see Ford, "Law's Territory," 845.

130. I elaborate this idea of race as jurisdiction in chapters 1 and 3. On slavery, race, and the ship, see Sharpe, *In the Wake*; Smallwood, *Saltwater Slavery*.

131. On the geography of race, see Goldberg, *Racist Culture*, 185. On geographies of blackness, see McKittrick, *Demonic Grounds*.

132. These distinctions of region, religion, and caste are clearly evident in the organization of ship labor. See Ghosh, *Sea of Poppies*.

133. On imperial citizenship, see Banerjee, *Becoming Imperial Citizens*; Mawani, "Specters of Indigeneity."

134. For critiques of the divisions imposed on colonial and racial histories, see Lake and Reynolds, *Drawing the Global Color Line*; Lowe, *The Intimacies of Four Continents*; Mawani, *Colonial Proximities*; Mawani, "Specters of Indigeneity."

135. On this transformation, see Ballantyne and Burton, "Global Empires," 379. Curiously, analyses of imperial mobility and legality commonly engage with questions of space but often at the expense of time. For an account that views migration through time, see Guha, "The Migrant's Time."

136. Benton, *A Search for Sovereignty*, xii.

137. On the quest for longitude and time, see Howse, *Greenwich Time*; Sobel, *Longitude*.

138. On time as the "universalizing will" of imperial rule, see Nanni, *The Colonisation of Time*, 2.

139. See Barak, *On Time*; Barrows, *The Cosmic Time of Empire*; Galison, *Einstein's Clocks*; Nanni, *The Colonisation of Time*; Ogle, *The Global Transformation of Time*.

140. See Barrows, *The Cosmic Time of Empire*; Galison, *Einstein's Clocks*; Ogle, *The Global Transformation of Time*.

141. Galison, *Einstein's Clocks*, 323 (my emphasis).

142. Ogle, *The Global Transformation of Time*, 25.

143. Schivelbusch, *The Railway Journey*, 43.

144. This argument is developed in Howse, *Greenwich Time*, and Sobel, *Longitude*.

145. See Howse, *Greenwich Time*, and Sobel, *Longitude*.

146. The classic account of timekeeping and industrialization is E. P. Thompson, "Time, Work-Discipline and Industrial Capitalism." For elaborations of Thompson that center on naval navigation, see Glennie and Thrift, *Shaping the Day*, esp. chap. 8.

147. These changing forms of timekeeping are set out in Howse, *Greenwich Time*, esp. chap. 3.

148. Sobel, *Longitude*, 168

149. Howse, *Greenwich Time*, 21.

150. Howse, *Greenwich Time*.

151. Harald U. Sverdrup, "The Mystery of Ocean Currents," *Harper's Monthly Magazine*, 1 July 1929, 238.

152. Croll, "Letters to the Editor: Ocean Currents."

153. Galison, *Einstein's Clocks*, 99.

154. Croll, "Letters to the Editor: Ocean Currents."

155. See Nanni, *The Colonisation of Time*.

156. Nanni, *The Colonisation of Time*, 26.

157. On clock time and Britain's claims to cultural supremacy, see Metcalf, "Architecture and the Representation of Empire"; Chakrabarty, *Provincializing Europe*, 74.

158. Chakrabarty, *Provincializing Europe*, 15.

159. See Metcalf, "Architecture and the Representation of Empire."

160. Chatterjee, "Anderson's Utopia," 131.

161. I am thinking through the tension between imposed and lived time in light of the work of Henry Bergson. Bergson describes life in terms of currents. See Bergson, *Creative Evolution*, 26. For an interesting discussion of time and Indian radicalism, see Elam, "Echoes of Ghadr." On time and settler colonialism, see Mawani, "Law as Temporality."

162. The most famous example of time as punishment is the timetable. See Foucault, *Discipline and Punish*. For a discussion of how European chronological time changed public routines and public life in colonial India, see Kalpagam, "Temporalities, Histories, and Routines."

163. The codification debate in India is a good case in point. See Kolsky, "Codification and the Rule of Colonial Difference."

164. On the patchwork of time, see Schivelbusch, *Railway Journey*, 43. On the patchwork of law, see Benton, *Law and Colonial Cultures*, 158.

165. On the temporal disjointedness of the common law, see Parker, *Common Law*, esp. chap. 2.

166. This argument is more fully developed in Mawani, "The Times of Law," which is a comment on Parker's *Common Law*.

167. On Sikh theology, see Mandair, *Religion and the Specter of the West*.

168. The literatures on international law, maritime and admiralty law discuss the juridification of the seas in different ways, and are notable exceptions. However, I would argue that even in these literatures, the sea is not always problematized or discussed as a material space or a site of continual movement. An important exception in world history is Benton, *A Search for Sovereignty*, chap. 3.

169. Armitage, introduction to *The Free Sea*; Schmitt, *The* Nomos *of the Earth*; Schmitt, *Land and Sea*.

170. I am borrowing this term from Chakrabarty's *Provincializing Europe*.

171. Gilroy, *The Black Atlantic*, 4.

172. For a classic account, see Puri, *Ghadr Movement*. For more recent discussions, see Ramnath, *Haj to Utopia*, and Sohi, *Echoes of Mutiny*.

173. For exceptions, see Tatla and Tatla, *Sardar Gurdit Singh*, and Tatla, "Incorporating Regional Events into the Nationalist Narrative."

174. Singh, *Voyage of the Komagatamaru*.

CHAPTER I. The Free Sea

1. Balachandran, *Globalizing Labour;* Fisher, "Working across the Seas"; Tabili, "'A Maritime Race'"; Visram, *Ayahs, Lascars, and Princes*. For a longer historical account of India's maritime activities, see Mookerji, *Indian Shipping.*

2. Balachandran, *Globalizing Labour*, 4.

3. On the ship as productive of space, see Siegert, *Cultural Techniques,* esp. chaps. 4 and 8.

4. Most of those who left the subcontinent during this period were men. There were only two women aboard the *Komagata Maru*.

5. John Cowen, "Race Prejudice," *Indian Opinion*, 23 July 1910, 4. This article was published in the *Westminster Review* and reprinted in *Indian Opinion*. Cowen was a strong supporter of Indian migration to South Africa and condemned anti-immigration arguments, such as the ones he recalled here. For a useful discussion of the perils of imperial mobility, see Ballantyne, "Mobility, Empire, Colonization," 10.

6. For instance, in 1912, authorities alleged that three to four hundred Indian migrants were arriving in British Columbia via the SS *Orterio*. This proved to be unfounded. See Wallace, "Komagata Maru Revisited," 37. The *Panama Maru* arrived in 1913 and was the basis of the *Thirty-Nine Hindus* case. See Johnston, *Voyage of the Komagata Maru,* 44–46.

7. P. K. Ramswamy, a merchant in Seattle, was alleged to be starting a steamship company to bring Indians to Vancouver. See National Archives of India, W. C. Hopkinson to

Immigration Branch Canada, 4 August 1913, Home Department, Political Branch, no. 11, file no. 62–66, November 1913, Part B.

8. For an estimate on the numbers of Indians along the west coast, see Johnston, *Voyage of the Komagata Maru,* esp. introduction; Jensen, *Passage from India.*

9. For a brief discussion of Canada's directives to steamship companies in the case of the *Komagata Maru,* see Johnston, *Voyage of the Komagata Maru,* 17; Macklin, "Historicizing Narratives of Arrival." In the case of Australia, the white Australia policy was applied to both land and sea. See Russell, "'The Singular Transcultural Space,'" 97.

10. I discuss the continuous journey provision in more detail in chapter 3. For a visual account, see Kazimi, *Continuous Journey.*

11. Many of the men who testified at the Komagata Maru Committee of Enquiry's hearings told Indian authorities that they had been awaiting passage some for years, but that no steamers would grant them travel, despite their being British subjects. See British Library, India Office Records (hereafter BL/IOR), 1/PJ6/1338, file 5028, *'Komagata Maru' Committee of Enquiry: Volume III* (23 October–4 December 1914).

12. The legal changes resulted from Husain Rahim's own cases and those of other Indians. See *Re Rahim* (1911) B.C.R. 16, 469; *Re Rahim* (No. 2), (1911) 16 B.C.R., 471; *Re Thirty-Nine Hindus,* (1913), 15, D.L.R. 189. The immigration regime is clearly set out in Macklin, "Historicizing Narratives of Arrival." See also Mawani, "Specters of Indigeneity."

13. Johnston, *Voyage of the Komagata Maru,* 74.

14. Library and Archives Canada (hereafter LAC). Report of J. W. Matoon, Superintendent of Police, Bombay, 20 October 1911, RG7-G-21, vol. 201, file 332, vol. 5a. On Parsis, see Sharafi, *Law and Identity in Colonial South Asia.*

15. LAC, Report of J. W. Matoon, Superintendent of Police, Bombay, 20 October 1911, RG7-G-21, vol. 201, File 332, vol. 5a.

16. Built in 1897, the *Moana* was one of four vessels owned by the Canadian-Australian Steamship Company, each traveling scheduled passages across the Pacific. For a discussion of this "red-route" from Australia to Canada, see Steel, "Lines across the Sea," 315.

17. LAC, W. C. Hopkinson to W. D. Scott, 11 July 1911, RG7-G-21, vol. 201, File 332, 4. On Hopkinson's assassination, see Johnston, *Voyage of the Komagata Maru,* esp. chap. 13.

18. LAC, W. C. Hopkinson to W. D. Scott, 11 July 1911, RG7-G-21, vol. 201, File 332, 4.

19. On Gujarati merchants, see Goswami, *Globalization before Its Time;* Machado, "A Forgotten Corner of the Indian Ocean."

20. LAC, Report of J. W. Matoon, Superintendent of Police, Bombay, 20 October 1911, RG7-G-21, vol. 201, File 332, vol. 5a. Rahim's identity is still very much in dispute. Some speculate that he might have been an Ismaili, from a small Shia sect that follows the Aga Khan. See http://komagatamarujourney.ca/node/14693 (accessed 25 October 2017).

21. LAC, "Note on the Hindu Revolutionary Movement in Canada," March 1919, RG76, vol. 386, file 536999, pt. 11.

22. Johnston, *Voyage of the Komagata Maru,* 25. For a useful biographical account, see Singh, *Canadian Sikhs,* 82–85. For discussion of Rahim as a property owner living in Hawai'i, see *Re Rahim* (1911), B.C.R., p. 471.

23. I am referring here to the *Santa Catarina,* which provided the basis for Hugo Grotius's *Mare Liberum.* See Armitage, *Hugo Grotius.*

24. I am borrowing the term counter-*nomos* from Legg and Vasudevan, "Introduction: Geographies of the Nomos," 11.

25. Singh, *Voyage of the Komagatamaru,* chap. 5, 41.

26. On this point, see Alexandrowicz, *An Introduction to the History of the Law of Nations,* 10. For a classic argument on the colonies as the basis for modern international law, see Anghie, *Imperialism, Sovereignty, and the Making of International Law.*

27. By most accounts, two Dutch ships attacked. According to Borschberg, there were three. See Borschberg, *Hugo Grotius,* 78.

28. Borschberg, "The Seizure of the Sta. Catarina Revisited," 42.

29. Borschberg, "The Seizure of the Sta. Catarina Revisited," 38.

30. Several well-known accounts place the attack in the Straits of Malacca. However, Borschberg argues that the event occurred in the Straits of Singapore. See Borschberg, "Grotius, Maritime Intra-Asian Trade, and the Portuguese Estado da India," 35.

31. Borschberg, *Hugo Grotius,* 42–43.

32. Van Ittersum, "Preparing *Mare Liberum* for the Press," 248.

33. *Mare Liberum* came from the twelfth chapter. For a discussion, see van Ittersum, "Hugo Grotius in Context," 513. See also van Ittersum, "Preparing *Mare Liberum* for the Press," 252.

34. Van Ittersum, "Preparing *Mare Liberum* for the Press," 253.

35. Van Ittersum, "Hugo Grotius in Context," 522.

36. In his introduction to *The Free Sea,* Armitage notes the global consequences of Grotius's text. "It had implications no less for coastal waters than it did for the high seas, for the West Indies as much as for the East Indies, and for intra-European disputes as well as for relations between the European powers and extra-European peoples." Armitage, introduction to *The Free Sea,* xi.

37. Cited in Borschberg, "The Seizure of the Sta. Catarina Revisited," 31.

38. See Chaudhuri, *Trade and Civilization in the Indian Ocean,* especially chapter 3.

39. Borschberg, "Hugo Grotius, East India Trade and the King of Johor," 235.

40. Borschberg, "The Seizure of the Sta. Catarina Revisited." See also Armitage, introduction to *The Free Sea,* xii–xiii.

41. The profits totaled 3.5 million guilders. See Borschberg, "The Seizure of the Sta. Catarina Revisited," 35.

42. Armitage, *Ideological Origins,* 109.

43. For a useful summary, see Armitage's introduction to *The Free Sea,* xi–xx.

44. Van Ittersum, "Hugo Grotius in Context" 513.

45. Anghie's *Imperialism, Sovereignty, and the Making of International Law* is now the classic text on Vitoria. For a very interesting and useful comparison between Gentili and Grotius, see Benton, *A Search for Sovereignty,* 120–37.

46. Chaudhuri, *Trade and Civilization in the Indian Ocean,* 138.

47. Borschberg, *Hugo Grotius,* 164.

48. Grotius, "Defense of Chapter V of the *Mare Liberum*," 111.

49. Grotius, "Defense of Chapter V of the *Mare Liberum*," 112.

50. Grotius, "The Free Sea," 25.

51. On Grotius and Locke, see Armitage, introduction to *The Free Sea,* xvi–xvii.

52. Grotius, "The Free Sea," 25.

53. Grotius, "The Free Sea," 30.

54. Grotius, "The Free Sea," 34 (my emphasis).

55. Armitage, *Ideological Origins,* 109.

56. Another rejoinder came from Portuguese friar Serafim de Freitas. For a discussion of Grotius and his interlocutors, see Vieira, "*Mare Liberum* vs. *Mare Clausum.*"

57. Armitage, *Ideological Origins,* 110–11.

58. Welwod was the only critic who drew a response from Grotius. However, Selden's reply held the greatest scholarly impact. Given the extensive literature on Selden, he is not the focus of my discussion here. See Thornton, "John Selden's Response to Hugo Grotius"; Tuck, "Grotius and Selden"; Ziskind, "International Law and Ancient Sources."

59. Welwod, "Of the Community and Propriety of the Seas," 66.

60. Welwod, "Of the Community and Propriety of the Seas," 67. Here, Welwod is drawing from Baldus.

61. See Selden, *Of the Dominion,* author's preface; see also book 2, chap. 3.

62. Welwod, "Of the Community and Propriety of the Seas," 70.

63. Welwod, "Of the Community and Propriety of the Seas," 71 (my emphasis).

64. Grotius, "Defense of Chapter V of the *Mare Liberum,*" 107.

65. Grotius, "Defense of Chapter V of the *Mare Liberum,*" 108 (my emphasis).

66. Grotius, "Defense of Chapter V of the *Mare Liberum,*" 111 (my emphasis).

67. Grotius, "Defense of Chapter V of the *Mare Liberum,*" 112 (emphasis in original).

68. Grotius, "Defense of Chapter V of the *Mare Liberum,*" 112.

69. Alexandrowicz, *An Introduction to the History of the Law of Nations,* 44. On Alexandrowicz as a controversial figure, see Pitts, "Empire and Legal Universalisms in the Eighteenth Century," 99–104.

70. Alexandrowicz, *An Introduction to the History of the Law of Nations,* 44. Borschberg argues that this was implausible and that Grotius knew little about Asian maritime trade while he was writing *Mare Liberum* and *De Iure Praedae.* See Borschberg, "Grotius, Maritime Intra-Asian Trade," 51.

71. Alexandrowicz, *An Introduction to the History of the Law of Nations,* 229.

72. See van Ittersum, "Hugo Grotius in Context," and Wilson, "The Alexandrowicz Thesis Revisited."

73. Borschberg, "The Seizure of the Sta. Catarina Revisited," 44. See also Borschberg, "Grotius, Maritime Intra-Asian Trade," 38.

74. Borschberg, "Grotius, Maritime Intra-Asian Trade," 37.

75. Borschberg, *Hugo Grotius,* 122.

76. Alexandrowicz, *An Introduction to the History of the Law of Nations,* 45; Borschberg, *Hugo Grotius,* 74; Thumfart, "On Grotius's *Mare Liberum* and Vitoria's *De Indis,*" 68.

77. Borschberg, "The Seizure of the Sta. Catarina Revisited," 44. See also Borschberg, "Grotius, Maritime Intra-Asian Trade," 46.

78. Van Ittersum "Hugo Grotius in Context," 535.

79. Borschberg, "Hugo Grotius, East India Trade and the King of Johor," 246 (my emphasis).

80. Ford, "Law," 219.

81. Van Ittersum, "Hugo Grotius in Context," 535, 540.

82. Borschberg, "Hugo Grotius, East India Trade and the King of Johor," 248.

83. See Ward, *Networks of Empire*, 14. Though Ward does not discuss Grotius, Eric Wilson develops her argument and claims that Ward arrives at conclusions that are very similar to those of Alexandrowicz, as well as his own. See Wilson, "The Alexandrowicz Thesis," 46.

84. For a discussion of this point, see Keene, *Beyond the Anarchical Society*, 44.

85. Wilson makes this argument by drawing very productively from Ward's *Networks of Empire*. See Wilson, "The Alexandrowicz Thesis."

86. Keene, *Beyond the Anarchical Society*, 57.

87. Grotius, "Defense of Chapter V of the *Mare Liberum*," 127.

88. Grotius, "Defense of Chapter V of the *Mare Liberum*," 128.

89. Grotius, "Defense of Chapter V of the *Mare Liberum*," 128.

90. Steinberg, *The Social Construction of the Ocean*, 14, 34–35.

91. Steinberg, *The Social Construction of the Ocean*, 65. See also Borschberg, *Hugo Grotius*, esp. chap. 3.

92. For a useful account of treaties on the high seas, see Crouzet, "A Slave Trade Jurisdiction," 234–49.

93. Benton, *A Search for Sovereignty*, 106.

94. Grotius, "Defense of Chapter V of the *Mare Liberum*," 110.

95. Benton, *A Search for Sovereignty*, 112.

96. Ward, *Networks of Empire*, 16.

97. Mawani, "Law, Settler Colonialism, and 'the Forgotten Space' of Maritime Worlds," 123.

98. See Hussin, "Circulations of Law," 18–32. On the point of international law, see Anghie, *Imperialism, Sovereignty, and the Making of International Law;* Benton and Clulow, "Legal Encounters and the Origins of Global Law"; Benton and Ford, *Rage for Order.*

99. This is Keene's central point in *Beyond the Anarchical Society*. Benton develops this further in *A Search for Sovereignty*, chap. 3.

100. Armitage, *Ideological Origins*, 105.

101. For a brief but very interesting discussion of transatlantic slavery and the role of British Navigation Acts, see Mtubani, "African Slaves and English Law," 72.

102. Schmitt was critical of Grotius and did not necessarily adopt his framework of the free sea. Instead, he was expanding on Hegel's elemental view of land and sea. See Hegel, *The Philosophy of History.*

103. Minca and Rowan, "The Question of Space in Carl Schmitt," 268.

104. Minca and Rowan, "The Question of Space in Carl Schmitt," 268. See Legg, *Spatiality, Sovereignty and Carl Schmitt.*

105. Anghie, "Identifying Regions in the History of International Law," 1074. See also Kalyvas, "Carl Schmitt's Postcolonial Imagination."

106. Schmitt, *Land and Sea*; Schmitt, *The* Nomos *of the Earth.*

107. Schmitt, *Land and Sea*, 6.

108. This is the subtitle to Schmitt's *Land and Sea.*

109. Schmitt, *The* Nomos *of the Earth*, 87.

110. Schmitt, *The* Nomos *of the Earth*, 86.

111. On *nomos* as norm and right see G. L. Ulmen, "Introduction," in Schmitt, *The Nomos of the Earth*, 20. On nomos as "to divide" and "pasture," see Schmitt, *The Nomos of the Earth*, 70.

112. Schmitt, *The Nomos of the Earth*, 49.

113. Schmitt, *The Nomos of the Earth*, 22.

114. On indigenous peoples, see Lipmann, *Saltwater Frontier*. On oceans and the "discovery" of new lands, see Steinberg, "Sovereignty, Territory, and the Mapping of Mobility," 468.

115. Schmitt, *Land and Sea*, 10.

116. Schmitt, *The Nomos of the Earth*, 42.

117. Schmitt, *The Nomos of the Earth*, 45.

118. Schmitt, *The Nomos of the Earth*, 42–43.

119. Schmitt, *The Nomos of the Earth*. The first part of this quote comes from p. 43, the second, after the ellipsis, from 42–43.

120. Schmitt, *The Nomos of the Earth*, 137.

121. Connery, "Ideologies of Land and Sea," 191. See also Legg and Vasudevan, "Introduction: Geographies of the Nomos."

122. Schmitt, *Land and Sea*, 55.

123. Schmitt, *The Nomos of the Earth*, 86.

124. There are, of course, important histories on Arab and Muslim advances in navigation in the Indian Ocean region as well as indigenous histories of navigation on the Pacific. See for example Chappell, "Ahab's Boat"; Diaz, "Voyaging for Anti-colonial Recovery."

125. On the prevalence of shipwrecks, see Hulme, "Cast Away," 187.

126. Schmitt, "The Planetary Tension between Orient and Occident," 10.

127. See, for example, Anderson et al., *Mutiny and Maritime Radicalism in the Age of Revolution*; Grandin, *An Empire of Necessity*.

128. Sobel, *Longitude*, 15. Piracy was important in Schmitt's thinking on international law. See Schmitt, "The Concept of Piracy."

129. See Ballantyne and Burton, *Empires and the Reach of the Global*, 379.

130. Said, *Orientalism*, 49.

131. Mirzoeff, "The Sea and Land," 290.

132. Schmitt, *The Nomos of the Earth*, 94.

133. "America is ancient," Roxanne Dunbar-Oritz reminds us, it "is not a 'new world,'" See Dunbar-Oritz, *An Indigenous Peoples' History*, 15.

134. This is documented succinctly in Dunbar-Oritz, *An Indigenous' Peoples' History*.

135. On Grotius and plural orders, see Keene, *Beyond the Anarchical Society*. See also Benton, *A Search for Sovereignty*, esp. chap. 3.

136. Schmitt, "The Planetary Tension," part 2; See also Schmitt, *The Nomos of the Earth*, 333. The most significant problematization of Orient and Occident is still Said's *Orientalism*.

137. Schmitt, "The Planetary Tension," 11.

138. Schmitt, "The Planetary Tension," 10.

139. For relevant parts of this debate, see Grotius, "Defense of Chapter V of the *Mare Liberum*," 112; Vieira, "*Mare Liberum* vs. *Mare Clausum*," 372.

140. Schmitt, *Land and Sea*, 22.

141. Schmitt, *Land and Sea*, 23.

142. Schmitt makes these observations on the compass in *Land and Sea*, 93.

143. Schmitt, *Land and Sea*, 46.

144. The British Empire produced an enormous amount of paper through correspondence across distance. See Ballantyne, "Archive, Discipline, State"; Burton, *Archive Stories*; Cohn, *Colonialism and Its Forms of Knowledge*.

145. Betts, "John Harrison," 160.

146. Siegel, "Law and Longitude," 7.

147. An Act Providing a Publik Reward for such Person or Persons as Shall Discover the Longitude at Sea (hereafter Longitude Act) (13 Ann.) C.A.P. xv. (14) (emphasis in original).

148. Longitude Act, part 3.

149. For a useful, albeit brief discussion on the free sea and the bonded slave, see Mirzoeff, "The Sea and Land."

150. Sobel, *Longitude*, 4.

151. Glennie and Thrift, *Shaping the Day*, 294.

152. Glennie and Thrift, *Shaping the Day*, 307.

153. Sobel, *Longitude*, 5; Siegel, "Law and Longitude," 10.

154. Howse, *Greenwich Time*, esp. chap. 3.

155. Newton's skepticism was written directly into the opening lines of the Longitude Act. See Howse, *Greenwich Time*, 50–51.

156. Grotius, "Defense of Chapter V of the *Mare Liberum*," 111.

157. Betts, "John Harrison," 166.

158. Fernie, "Finding out the Longitude," 412.

159. Howse, *Greenwich Time*, 71.

160. Schmitt, *The* Nomos *of the Earth*, 88.

161. Schmitt, *The* Nomos *of the Earth*, 88.

162. Galison, *Einstein's Clocks*, 99.

163. Fleming, *Uniform Non-Local Time*, 1.

164. Schmitt, *Land and Sea*, 81.

165. Fleming, *Uniform Non-Local Time*, 3.

166. Fleming, *Uniform Non-Local Time*, 21.

167. On Sanford Fleming, see Barrows, *The Cosmic Time of Empire*, 33. On shipping and GMT, see Galison, *Einstein's Clocks*, 119.

168. Barrows, *The Cosmic Time of Empire*, 8 (emphasis in original).

169. In his magisterial *Fish Story*, Allan Sekula argues that time was extended from land to sea through the railway. Here, I argue for a different chronology, one that places the sea and the ship first. See Sekula, *Fish Story*, 45.

170. Fleming, *Uniform Non-Local Time*, 15 (emphasis in original).

171. Ogle, *The Global Transformation of Time*, 102.

172. Fleming, *Uniform Non-Local Time*, 22.

173. Fleming, *Uniform Non-Local Time*, 31.

174. Cited in Howse, *Greenwich Time*, 114.

175. Statutes, Definition of Time Act, 1880 (43 & 44 Vict.) chap. 9. For a brief discussion, see Ballantyne and Burton, *Empires and the Reach of the Global*, 380–81.

176. Barrows, *The Cosmic Time of Empire*, 19.

177. Fleming, *Uniform Non-Local Time*, 37.

178. In a short but provocative essay on Schmitt, Steinberg argues that "freedom requires policing and mobility requires fixity." In short, the free sea is never free. See Steinberg, "Free Sea," 271.

179. Vieira, "*Mare Liberum* vs. *Mare Clausum*," 370.

180. See Grotius, "The Free Sea."

181. In the 1916 translation of Grotius's *Mare Liberum*, the subtitle reads: "The Right Which Belongs to the Dutch to Take Part in the East Indian Trade." See Grotius, *The Freedom of the Seas*.

182. Balachandran, *Globalizing Labour*, 4. See also Ghosh, *Sea of Poppies*.

183. In addition to transoceanic movements spawned by trade and commerce, the pilgrimage to Mecca to make hajj was a journey that most sects of Islam required their adherents to undertake. See Peters, *The Hajj*; Slight, *The British Empire and the Hajj*.

184. See Mookerji, *Indian Shipping*.

185. Laufer, "Review, Indian Shipping," 76.

186. Mookerji, *Indian Shipping*, 85.

187. Mookerji, *Indian Shipping*, 192, 198.

188. Mookerji, *Indian Shipping*, 254.

189. Mookerji, *Indian Shipping*, 253.

190. From the seventeenth century onward, Surat (Gujarat) was an important site of trade and banking. See Chaudhuri, *Trade and Civilization in the Indian Ocean*, 118.

191. Amrith, *Crossing the Bay of Bengal*, 80. The protagonist of Amitav Ghosh's *River of Smoke* is Bharam Modi, the son-in-law of Rustamji Mistrie, an affluent Parsi shipbuilder from Bombay.

192. Amrith, *Crossing the Bay of Bengal*, 80.

193. Chaudhuri, *Trade and Civilization in the Indian Ocean*, 93.

194. Balachandran, *Globalizing Labour*, 81.

195. Amrith makes this point about Indian boats arriving in Singapore. See Amrith, *Crossing the Bay of Bengal*, 84.

196. Balachandran, *Globalizing Labour*, 128.

197. Mookerji, *Indian Shipping*, 253.

198. Mookerji, *Indian Shipping*, 254.

199. Mookerji, *Indian Shipping*, 256.

200. Amrith, *Migration and Diaspora in Modern Asia*, 1.

201. Chaudhuri, *Trade and Civilization in the Indian Ocean*, 127.

202. The presence of lascars in London was largely due to seasonal restrictions on seaborne travel. See Balachandran, *Globalizing Labour*; Visram, *Ayahs, Lascars, and Princes*.

203. Nicholas Mirzoeff makes a similar point. The sea was "transformed from a commons into the property of the Western state." See Mirzoeff, "The Sea and Land," 292.

204. Desai, *Commerce with the Universe*, 134; Deepak, "Colonial Connections," 147–70.

205. For a discussion of Canada and the United States, see Sohi, *Echoes of Mutiny*. In regard to Calcutta, see Chattopadhyay, "Closely Observed Ships."

206. Sohi, "Race, Surveillance, and Indian Anticolonialism," 423.

207. Rahim, "Canada as a Hindu Saw It," *Hindustanee*, January 1914, 7.

208. Rahim, "Canada as a Hindu Saw It," January 1914, 7. In 1911, Rahim would appear before the British Columbia Court of Appeal to determine whether the continuous journey provision of the Immigration Act, which had been amended after he entered Canada, could be applied retroactively. Ultimately, the court decided that it could not. See *Re Rahim (No.2)*, BCLR, 471.

209. Rahim, "Canada as a Hindu Saw It," January 1914, 7.

210. Rahim, "Canada as a Hindu Saw It," January 1914, 7.

211. Johnston, *Voyage of the Komagata Maru*, 26.

212. *Re Rahim*, (1911), B.C.R. 16, 469; *Re Rahim (No. 2)*, (1911), B.C.R. 16, 471.

213. Rahim put himself on the British Columbia voter's list and was tried for fraud, though not convicted. See Singha, *Canadian Sikhs through a Century*, 119.

214. LAC, "Note on the Hindu Revolutionary Movement in Canada, 20 March 1919, RG 76, vol. 386, File 536999, pt. 11.

215. H. C. Clogston, *Commission to Investigate Hindu Claims following Refusal of Immigration Officials to Allow over 300 Hindus Aboard the S.S. Komagata Maru to Land at Vancouver* (Vancouver, 1914), 4. It is very unlikely that Rahim was Muslim as he was cremated after his death in 1936. See Chand, *Khalsa Diwan Society Diary*, 22. Excerpts of the diary are translated into English and can be found here: http://komagatamarujourney.ca/node/15901 (accessed 30 June 2016).

216. H. C. Clogston was appointed to investigate these matters. See Clogston, *Commission to Investigate Hindu Claims.*

217. Rahim, "Canada as a Hindu Saw It," *Hindustanee*, May 1914, 9.

218. Rahim, "Canada as a Hindu Saw it," *Hindustanee*, April 1914, 11.

219. Rahim was the leader of the "Shore Committee" that assumed the *Komagata Maru*'s charter while it was in Vancouver. See Johnston, *Voyage of the Komagata Maru*, 75.

220. Schmitt, *Land and Sea*, 5.

221. Chaudhuri, *Trade and Civilization in the Indian Ocean*, 143. Schmitt acknowledges the significance of the sea for Pacific peoples, which he describes as "the last-remnants of such fish-humans." See *Land and Sea*, 8.

222. Rahim, "Canada as a Hindu Saw It," *Hindustanee*, May 1914, 9.

223. Rahim, "Canada as a Hindu Saw It," *Hindustanee*, May 1914, 9.

224. Rahim, "Canada as a Hindu Saw It," *Hindustanee*, May 1914, 9.

225. Rahim, "Canada as a Hindu Saw It," *Hindustanee*, May 1914, 10.

226. Rahim, "Canada as a Hindu Saw It," *Hindustanee*, May 1914, 9.

227. Rahim, "Canada as a Hindu Saw It," *Hindustanee*, May 1914, 10.

228. Rahim, "Canada as a Hindu Saw It," *Hindustanee*, May 1914, 10.

229. Rahim, "Canada as a Hindu Saw It," *Hindustanee*, May 1914, 10.

230. The continuous journey law, as Bird argued, was applied largely on the west coast and not to transatlantic crossings, a point I discuss in chapter 3.

231. Rahim, "Canada as a Hindu Saw It," *Hindustanee*, May 1914, 10 (my emphasis).

232. Rahim, "Canada as a Hindu Saw It," *Hindustanee*, June 1914, 11.

233. Rahim, "Canada as a Hindu Saw It," *Hindustanee*, June 1914, 11.

234. Rahim, "Canada as a Hindu Saw It," *Hindustanee*, June 1914, 11.

235. Rahim, "Canada as a Hindu Saw It," *Hindustanee*, June 1914, 12.

236. For a discussion of these ideologies, see Ward, *White Canada Forever*.

237. One of the places that Rahim comments on is Stanley Park. The Squamish who resided on the Peninsula were relocated to the North Shore. For a discussion of this process, see Barman, *Stanley Park's Secret*; Mawani, "Genealogies of the Land."

238. During the recent centenary celebrations marking the *Komagata Maru*'s arrival in Vancouver Harbour, this point was made by Musqueam Elder Larry Grant: "If the boat [the *Komagata Maru*] had come the other way through Indian Arm we would have welcomed the boat as the first peoples" (29 July 2014). http://jccabulletin-geppo.ca/100th-anniversary-of-komagata-maru/ (accessed 5 January 2016).

239. Rahim, "Canada as a Hindu Saw It," *Hindustanee*, June 1914, 11.

240. Ulmen, "Introduction," in Schmitt, *The* Nomos *of the Earth*, 31.

241. On the sea as a connective force, I am drawing from Hau'ofa's *We Are the Ocean*. And on the sea as history, I am drawing from Walcott's famous poem "The Sea Is History."

CHAPTER 2. The Ship as Legal Person

1. British Library, India Office Records (hereafter BL/IOR), 1/PJ/6/1338, file 5028, *'Komagata Maru' Committee of Enquiry: Volume III* (23 October–4 December 1914), exhibit 30: "Notice Dated 21st February 1914, Published by Gurdit Singh," 47.

2. BL/IOR, 1/PJ/6/1338, file 5028, *'Komagata Maru' Committee of Enquiry: Volume III* (23 October–4 December 1914), exhibit 30: "Notice dated 21st February 1914, published by Gurdit Singh," 47.

3. BL/IOR, 1/PJ/6/1338, file 5028, *'Komagata Maru' Committee of Enquiry: Volume III* (23 October–4 December 1914), exhibit 30: "Notice dated 21st February 1914, published by Gurdit Singh," 47.

4. BL/IOR, 1/PJ/6/1338, file 5028, *'Komagata Maru' Committee of Enquiry: Volume III* (23 October–4 December 1914), exhibit 121: "Correspondence between Gurdit Singh and A. W. King, regarding the charter of S.S. Tong-Hong."

5. National Archives of India (hereafter NAI), Proceedings of the Home Department, Political-A, March 1915, nos. 57–82, 28.

6. The two men were introduced by A. Bune, a German shipping agent. NAI, Proceedings of the Home Department, Political-A, March 1915, nos. 57–82, 28.

7. NAI, Proceedings of the Home Department, Political-A, March 1915, nos. 57–82, 28.

8. On shipping regulations and Chinese indentured labor in Hong Kong, see "Ordinance no. 5 of 1876," in A. J. Leach, *The Ordinances of the Legislative Council of the Colony of Hong Kong, the Year 1844*, vol. 3 (Hong Kong: Noronha, 1891), 1423–26.

9. This quote comes from NAI, Proceedings of the Home Department, Political-A, March 1915, nos. 57–82, 28.

10. Britain abolished the slave trade in 1807. But slavery continued throughout the empire and in the United States until much later. If "the sea is slavery," as Fred D'Aguiar argues, then the legal status of the sea remains inseparable from histories of slavery. See D'Aguiar, *Feeding the Ghosts*, 3.

11. In making this argument, many scholars draw from a well-known statement made by Gurdit Singh. This can be found in Johnston, *Voyage of the Komagata Maru*, 72. See also Mongia, "Race, Nationality, Mobility," 549n33.

12. For a very useful biography of Gurdit Singh, see Tatla and Tatla, *Sardar Gurdit Singh;* see also Tatla, "Incorporating Regional Events into the Nationalist Narrative."

13. BL/IOR, 1/PJ/6/1338, file 5028, *'Komagata Maru' Committee of Enquiry: Volume III* (23 October–4 December 1914), exhibit 35: "Translation of Gurmukhi notice issued by Gurdit Singh," 57.

14. BL/IOR, 1/PI/6/1338, file 5028, *'Komagata Maru' Committee of Enquiry: Volume III* (23 October–4 December 1914), exhibit 31: "Translation of Gurmukhi letter sent to Sikhs at Hong Kong, 49.

15. BL/IOR, 1/PJ/6/1338, file 5028, *'Komagata Maru' Committee of Enquiry: Volume III* (23 October–4 December 1914), exhibit 31: "Translation of Gurmukhi letter sent to Sikhs at Hong Kong, 49.

16. BL/IOR, 1/PI/6/1338, file 5028, *'Komagata Maru' Committee of Enquiry: Volume III* (23 October–4 December 1914), exhibit 54. "A Manuscript giving a history of the voyage of the S.S. "Komagata Maru" written in Gurmukhi, apparently in the handwriting of Daljit Singh," 104.

17. BL/IOR, 1/PJ/6/1338, file 5028, *'Komagata Maru' Committee of Enquiry: Volume III* (23 October–4 December 1914), exhibit 85: "Translation of a letter in Gurmukhi from Sardar Singh, Honourary Agent of "Bridh Sewak" (lit., old servant) Bhai Gurdit Singh Contractor, to the Editor, Panth Sewak," 184.

18. For a notable exception, see Dulai's, *Dream/Arteries*. In this book of poetry, Dulai evokes the materiality of the ship through its manifest, previous voyages, and passengers. It is important to note that this problem is not specific to the *Komagata Maru*. Ships have been given little scholarly attention in the literatures on mobility. On this point generally see Anim-Addo, Hasty, and Peters, "The Mobilities of Ships and Shipped Mobilities"; Dusinberre and Wenzlhuemer, "Editorial: Being in Transit."

19. BL/IOR, 1/PJ/6/1338, file 5028, *'Komagata Maru' Committee of Enquiry: Volume III* (23 October–4 December 1914), exhibit 49: "An account in English of the Tyranny over the '*Komagata Maru*' Passengers in Kobe," c. August 1914, p. 98. On the Andamans, *kala pani*, and convict labor, see Anderson, "Convicts and Coolies."

20. I say partial biography because I do not address the ship's life from 1924 to 1926, after it was sold and renamed the *Heian Maru*.

21. Slavery in India and Southeast Asia was never a point of discussion during the ship's journey. On slavery in India and Southeast Asia, see Chatterjee, *Gender, Slavery, and Law in Colonial India*; Chatterjee and Eaton, *Slavery and South Asian History*; Herzog, "Convenient Compromises"; Reid and Brewster, *Slavery, Bondage, and Dependency in Southeast Asia.*

22. Conrad, *The Mirror of the Sea,* 92.

23. For a compelling discussion of the deodand, slavery and "negative personhood," see Dayan, *The Law Is a White Dog,* 42, 127–30. For an account of how land and sea under British law complicated the status of the slave, see Mtubani, "African Slaves and English Law."

24. BL/IOR, I/PJ/6/1338, file 5028, *'Komagata Maru' Committee of Enquiry: Volume III* (23 October–4 December 1914), exhibit 49: "An account in English of the Tyranny over the *'Komagata Maru'* Passengers in Kobe," c. August 1914, 98 (my emphasis).

25. Connections between histories of slavery and histories of the sea have been made by Derek Walcott and Fred D'Aguiar, for example. I build on these thinkers to argue that a *legal* history of the sea cannot be written without slavery. See D'Aguiar, *Feeding the Ghosts;* Walcott, "The Sea Is History."

26. Rediker, Pybus, and Christopher, "Introduction," 2.

27. On legal persons in general, see Dayan, *The Law Is a White Dog.*

28. Van Tilburg, "Vessels of Exchange," 47–48.

29. Lubbock, *The Western Ocean Packets,* xvi.

30. Historically, ship husbands included dockyard workers who oversaw repairs on a specific ship as well as quasi authorities who represented a vessel's owners, traveled aboard, and maintained control over the ship's activities, often under the country of its registration. A "sister" ship was a vessel constructed by the same builder, in the same calendar year, and along a similar design. See Blackmore, *The Seafaring Dictionary,* 289.

31. Conrad makes this point in the epigraph at the start of this chapter, which is from *The Mirror of the Sea,* 92.

32. Brown, "She Was Fine When She Left Here," 96. See also Blackmore, *Seafaring Dictionary,* 289.

33. Mellefont, "Heirlooms and Tea Towels," 7.

34. Mellefont, "Heirlooms and Tea Towels." For a useful discussion of gender and oceans, see Creighton and Norling, *Iron Men, Wooden Women.*

35. Blackmore, *Seafaring Dictionary,* 188. On Guineaman, see Mannix, *Black Cargoes,* 104.

36. See Tabili, "'A Maritime Race,'" 187.

37. Fears of mutiny, lawlessness, and rebellion that were once animated by piracy and slavery were commonly expressed in gendered and racial terms. Herman Melville's novella *Bartleby and Benito Cereno,* which centers on the *Tryal,* is a good example of a slave ship that acquires a gendered and racial reputation. Though Melville does not discuss the ship in these terms, the struggle for power between the slaves and the crew marks the vessel's identity as mutinous, lawless, and male. For an account that situates the ship within transnational histories of slavery, see Grandin, *The Empire of Necessity.* See also the last chapter of Rediker's *Outlaws of the Atlantic,* which discusses the twinned histories of slavery and piracy with reference to the *Amistad.*

38. Schmitt, *The* Nomos *of the Earth,* 98.

39. Importantly, in Schmitt's account the free sea was free of law. See *The* Nomos *of the Earth,* 98.

40. Benton, *A Search for Sovereignty,* chap. 3; Ward, *Networks of Empire,* 15.

41. Armitage, introduction to *The Free Sea,* xxi.

42. Laing, "Historic Origins," 163–82.

43. Vickers, *Young Men and the Sea,* 214.

44. On the presumed cultural superiority of the common law, see Darian-Smith, *Bridging Divides;* Parker, *Common Law, History, and Democracy.*

45. Laing, "Historic Origins," 163.

46. Myburgh, "Arresting the Right Ship," 285.

47. Kercher, "The Limits of Despotic Government at Sea," 40.

48. Fell, *Recent Problems in Admiralty Jurisdiction,* 19.

49. Detsey, *A Manual of the Law Relating to Admiralty and Shipping,* 8.

50. *Tucker v. Alexandroff,* 83 U.S. 424 (1902), cited in Lind, "Pragmatism and Anthropomorphism," 70.

51. *Tucker v. Alexandroff,* in Lind, "Pragmatism and Anthropomorphism," 70.

52. *Tucker v. Alexandroff,* in Lind, "Pragmatism and Anthropomorphism," 70.

53. See Falconer, *A New Universal Dictionary of the Marine.*

54. Scholars argue that vessel personification was drawn from actions *in rem.* While the United States followed vessel personification, Britain followed *in personam* actions that allowed the courts to hold owners rather than ships responsible. See Lind, "Pragmatism and Anthropomorphism," 45.

55. By the late nineteenth century, British courts moved away from vessel personification, and American courts continued to rely on it. See Myburgh, "Arresting the Right Ship," 284. See also "Personification of Vessels," 1124.

56. British ships dominated the slave trade from 1750 to 1807. See Webster, "The *Zong* in the Context of the Eighteenth-Century Slave Trade," 285–98. On American ships, see Johnson, "White Lies," 237–63.

57. Maxwell, *The Spirit of Marine Law,* 323.

58. For the law of deodand and its relation to slavery, see Dayan, *The Law Is a White Dog,* esp. chap. 4.

59. Pietz, "Death of the Deodand," 97. There has been a growing interest of late in the law of deodand. See Bennett, *Vibrant Matter;* Dayan, *The Law Is a White Dog;* Kirton-Darling, "Searching for Pigeons in the Belfry"; Lefebvre, "The Time of Law," 40–41.

60. Pietz, "Death of the Deodand," 97.

61. Pietz, "Death of the Deodand," 97.

62. Pervukhin, "Deodands," 237.

63. Pietz, "Death of the Deodand," 105.

64. Pietz, "Death of the Deodand," 97.

65. "Queer Old Law of the Deodand," *San Francisco Call,* 1 January 1906, 12.

66. Cited in "Queer Old Law of the Deodand," 12.

67. "Deodand," *Chambers's Journal,* 19 October 1889, 672.

68. Pietz, "Death of a Deodand," 102 (my emphasis). Determinations of deodand took place in the Coroner's Office. Decisions were inconsistent and arbitrary, as the article in the *San Francisco Call* pointed out.

69. Slavery was vital to maritime insurance. See Armstrong, "Slavery, Insurance, and Sacrifice in the Black Atlantic." For a discussion of finance capital and transatlantic slavery, see Baucom, *Specters of the Atlantic.*

70. Blackstone is quoted in "Queer Old Law of the Deodand," 12.

71. "Deodand," *Chambers's Journal,* 672.

72. Pietz, "Death of the Deodand," 101.

73. Holmes, *The Common Law,* 24.

74. Holmes, *The Common Law,* 26.

75. Holmes, *The Common Law*, 26–27.

76. On the continuities between the common law and American jurisprudence, see Parker, *Common Law*.

77. In what is known as the "Marshall Trilogy," Chief Justice Marshall would later decide that Indian rights were occupancy rights. See Darian-Smith, *Religion, Race, Rights*, 203–5.

78. Lind, "Pragmatism and Anthropomorphism," 52–56.

79. Lind, "Pragmatism and Anthropomorphism," 53.

80. Quoted in "Personification of Vessels," 1126.

81. Lind, "Pragmatism and Anthropomorphism," 40.

82. Cited in Lind, "Pragmatism and Anthropomorphism," 53.

83. Johnson argues that following the abolition of slavery, the U.S. flag became a flag of convenience for slavers across the globe. See Johnson, "White Lies." 240.

84. On "maritime metaphysics" and Marshall, see Lind, "Pragmatism and Anthropomorphism," 53. Under forfeiture, the state was allegedly acting against the property as opposed to its owner. For connections between forfeiture and deodand, see Berman, "An Anthropological Approach to Modern Forfeiture Law," 2.

85. On Marshall, see Lind, "Pragmatism and Anthropomorphism," 53. Lind says nothing of slavery. This is an argument that I am making.

86. This is most evident in maritime insurance. See Philip, *Zong!*, 196. See also Mtubani, "African Slaves and English Law," 73.

87. Benton, "The Melancholy Labyrinth," 95.

88. For slaves who committed crimes on land, see Dayan, *The Law Is a White Dog*. For a brief discussion of slaves as cargo and the personhood/property divide in maritime insurance, see Webster, "The *Zong* in the Case of the Eighteenth-Century Slave Trade," 296.

89. On negative personhood, see Dayan, *The Law Is a White Dog*, 42.

90. Dayan develops this point in chapter 4 of *The Law Is a White Dog*.

91. Baucom, *Specters of the Atlantic*; Gilroy, *The Black Atlantic*; Hartman, *Scenes of Subjection*; Sharpe, *In the Wake*.

92. Best, *The Fugitive's Properties*, 39.

93. The point about the law of deodand and slavery is developed in Dayan, *The Law Is a White Dog*, 129.

94. On slaves, ships, and capital, see De Lombard, "Salvaging Legal Personhood," 35–64.

95. On slaves as persons and property see Kawash, "Fugitive Properties," 277–90.

96. Smallwood, *Saltwater Slavery*, 30.

97. Smallwood, *Saltwater Slavery*. On the links between the slave ship and plantation, see Rediker, *The Slave Ship*.

98. Baucom, *Specters of the Atlantic*, 11. See also Philip, *Zong!*

99. On the unfreedom of slaves and the freedom of the seas, see Mirzoeff, "The Sea and Land," 293.

100. Kercher, "The Limits of Despotic Government at Sea," 41.

101. Walvin, *The Zong*, 43.

102. I am drawing here from Smallwood in order to expand Baucom's arguments. See Smallwood, *Saltwater Slavery*, 35.

103. BL, IOR, 1/PJ/6/1338, file 5028, 'Komagata Maru' Committee of Enquiry: Volume III (23 October–4 December 1914), exhibit 43: "Telegrams to Governor General, Canada," Sunday 28th June 1914, Translation of Pages 67 and 68, 86.

104. Connell apprenticed for Robert Steele of Greenock and was later employed as a yard manager at Alexander Stephens and Sons in Kelvinhaugh. See Walker, *Song of the Clyde*, 82. For a discussion of Clyde shipbuilders including Connell see Robbins, *Scotland and the Sea*, esp. chap. 7.

105. Ritchie, *The Shipbuilding Industry*, 171.

106. Ritchie, *The Shipbuilding Industry*, 8.

107. I have compiled this number from the records of Charles Connell and Co., held at the Glasgow City Archives (hereafter GCA), GB243/T-CO. From 1931 to 1937, during the Great Depression, the yard was closed, and there was no production for these years.

108. Lubbock, *Coolie Ships and Oil Sailors*, 76.

109. On the relationship between British maritime power and naval mastery, see Armitage, *Ideological Origins*, esp. chap. 4.

110. Paine makes this point about Europe in general. See Paine, *The Sea and Civilization*, 5.

111. Paine, *The Sea and Civilization*, 4. Paine is referring here to Britain and other European powers. On the Portuguese, see Law, "On the Methods of Long-Distance Control."

112. Rasor, "Shipping and Seamen," 716.

113. The company is also referred to as Dampfschiff Rederei Hansa. See Johnston, *Voyage of the Komagata Maru*, 57.

114. "Stubbenhuk," *Lloyd's Register of Ships* (London, 1891).

115. *Importers' Directory*, 14.

116. *Importers Directory*, 15.

117. GCA, GB243/T-CO10/6, Connell, timber accounts, 368.

118. GCA, GB243/T-CO10/6, Connell, timber accounts, 368.

119. On the Suez Canal and globalization see Huber, *Channeling Mobilities;* Benians, "The Suez Canal, Coaling Stations," 200.

120. *Tucker v. Alexandroff*, 83 U.S. 424 (1902), quoted in Lind, "Pragmatism and Anthropomorphism," 70.

121. GCA, GB243/T-CO1/5, Connell, Letter Book 22, 829.

122. Sekula, *Fish Story*, 12. On race and maritime power, see Paine, *The Sea and Civilization*, 4.

123. Van Tilburg, "Vessels of Exchange," 47.

124. Van Tilburg describes flagged ships as "elements of sovereign territory." See "Vessels of Exchange," 47.

125. This is most evident in "flags of convenience." Since the 1940s, American ship owners have promoted use of the flag of convenience as a way to deregulate maritime labor markets. See Sekula, *Fish Story*, 50. For an account that locates flags of convenience in transatlantic slavery, see Johnson, "White Lies," 240.

126. GCA, GB243/T-CO1/5, Connell Letter Book 21, 8 July 1890, 594.

127. On its three passages to Ellis Island, the *Stubbenhuk* carried a total of 723 passengers. The breakdown is as follows: 12 September 1892: 232 passengers; 5 January 1893:

139 passengers; 19 April 1894: 352 passengers. Many of these passengers were from Russia and Prussia; others were from Austria and Hungary. The manifests are at http://www.libertyellisfoundation.org/ship (accessed May 2015). For a poetic account of the *Stubbenhuk*, see Dulai, *Dream/Arteries*.

128. LAC, From P. Doyle to H. B. Small, Secretary, Department of Agriculture, Ottawa, 26 August 1891, R194–40–3-E, file 80009, vol. 698.

129. LAC, From P. Doyle to H. B. Small, Secretary, Department of Agriculture, Ottawa, 26 August 1891, R194–40–3-E, file 80009, vol. 698.

130. LAC, From P. Doyle to H. B. Small, Secretary, Department of Agriculture, Ottawa, 26 August 1891, R194–40–3-E, file 80009, vol. 698.

131. The *Sicilia*'s voyages and its passenger lists are available on the Ellis Island website at: http://www.libertyellisfoundation.org/ship (accessed May 2015).

132. The Ellis Island memorial has acknowledged the need to expand its history to include Indigenous peoples and African American communities. See http://www.libertyellisfoundation.org (accessed May 2015).

133. Kupperberg, *A Primary Source History of the Colony of New York*, 5.

134. Harris, *In the Shadow of Slavery*.

135. Harris, *In the Shadow of Slavery*, 3.

136. Bahadur, *Coolie Woman*, 22.

137. On Mauritius, see Allen, *Slaves, Freedmen, and Indentured Laborers in Colonial Mauritius*; Carter, *Servants, Sirdars, and Settlers*. The British indenture trade was one-third the size of the African slave trades. See Bahadur, *Coolie Woman*, 22.

138. Lubbock, *Coolie Ships*, 108.

139. Lubbock, *Coolie Ships*, 103. On Nourse's involvement in the West Indian indenture trade, see Hollett, *Passage from India*, 201.

140. Hollett, *Passage from India*, 238.

141. Bahadur, *Coolie Woman*, 76.

142. Lubbock, *Coolie Ships*, 70.

143. Hudson, "Slavery, the Slave Trade, and Economic Growth," 50.

144. Gikandi, *Slavery and the Culture of Taste*, 109. By the early twentieth century, some of the largest sugar exports from Sandbach's plantations were bound for Canadian markets. See Hollett, *Passage from India*, 236.

145. See Beckert, *Empire of Cotton*; Johnson, *River of Dark Dreams*; Tomlins, *Freedom Bound*. For a discussion of Guyana, see Jackson, *Creole Indigeneity*.

146. In the U.S. context, see Johnson, *River of Dark Dreams*.

147. Hollett, *Passage from India*, 18.

148. Beckert, *Empire of Cotton*, 88.

149. Hudson, "Slavery, the Slave Trade," 50.

150. Bahadur, *Coolie Woman*, 79; Jung, *Coolies and Cane*; Kale, *Fragments of Empire*; Look Lai, *Indentured Labor, Caribbean Sugar*; Lowe, *The Intimacies of Four Continents*. On slavery as part of a continuum of unfreedom, see Anderson, "After Emancipation."

151. Hall et al., *Legacies of British Slave Ownership*, 87.

152. See Hollett, *Passage from India*. For a useful discussion of records surrounding Sandbach and Tinne, see Clover, "Exploring Caribbean Shipping Company Records." On the

reinvestment of slave earnings in indenture ships, see McClelland, "Redefining the West Indian Interest."

153. Angel, *The Clipper Ship*, 201.

154. Angel, *The Clipper Ship*, 202.

155. Angel, *The Clipper Ship* 202.

156. Hollett, *Passage from India*, 171.

157. Angel, *The Clipper Ship*, 11.

158. Angel, *The Clipper Ship* 14–15.

159. Angel, *The Clipper Ship*, 143.

160. Angel, *The Clipper Ship*, 11.

161. Lubbock, *Coolie Ships*, 1 (my emphasis).

162. See, for example, Bahadur, *Coolie Woman*; Lowe, *The Intimacies of Four Continents*; Tinker, *A New System of Slavery*.

163. Cateau, "Re-examining the Labour Matrix," 101–8.

164. Roopnarine, "The Indian Sea Voyage," 70. The most vivid description of death aboard indenture ships is in the well-known diary of Captain Swinton's wife. Captain and Mrs. Swinton, *Journal of a Voyage with Coolie Emigrants*.

165. Angel, *The Clipper Ship*, 204–5.

166. Angel, *The Clipper Ship*, 150.

167. Angel, *The Clipper Ship*, 264.

168. On the hold, see Harney and Moten, *The Undercommons*, esp. chap. six; Sharpe, *In the Wake*, chap. three. On resistance and mutiny aboard the indenture ship, see Ghosh, *Sea of Poppies*.

169. Little is known of the company. In some records, the firm is made up of four or five people. In others, it consists of three, including A. Nagata from Moji, S. Momosaki, and Kuga of Kobe. See *Report on the Komagata Maru Committee of Inquiry*, 3. NAI, Proceedings of the Home Department, Political-A, March 1915, Nos. 57–82, 28.

170. For a useful history of Dalian's transformation, see Hess, "From Colonial Port to Socialist Metropolis."

171. See *Lloyd's Register* (London, 1914–15).

172. Some of the other ships that carried Indian migrants to British Columbia include the *Panama Maru* and *Tosha Maru*. The *Panama Maru* was the basis of the *Thirty-Nine Hindus* Case. See Johnston, *Voyage of the Komagata Maru*, 44–46.

173. Mellefont, "Heirlooms and Tea Towels," 6.

174. The Charter-Party was dated 24 March 1914 but signed the previous day. "Government Form of the Charter-Party," in Singh, *Voyage of the Komagatamaru*, chap. 3.

175. Singh, *Voyage of the Komagatamaru*, "Government Form of the Charter-Party," p. 1, s. 1.

176. For a discussion of the captain's unlimited authority over the slave ship, see Rediker, *The Slave Ship*, 157.

177. Singh, *Voyage of the Komagatamaru*, "Government Form of the Charter-Party," p. 2, s. 12.

178. Singh, *Voyage of the Komagatamaru*, "Government Form of the Charter-Party," 24 March 1914 p. 3, s. 32.

179. Singh, *Voyage of the Komagatamaru*, "Government Form of the Charter-Party," 24 March 1914, p. 3, s. 32.

180. Singh, *Voyage of the Komagatamaru*, chap. 2, 20.

181. BL/IOR, 1/PJ/6/1338, file 5028, *'Komagata Maru' Committee of Enquiry: Volume III* (23 October–4 December 1914), exhibit 54: "A Manuscript giving a history of the voyage of the S.S. 'Komagata Maru' written in Gurmukhi, apparently in the handwriting of Daljit Singh," 105.

182. BL/IOR, 1/PJ/6/1338, file 5028, *'Komagata Maru' Committee of Enquiry: Volume III* (23 October–4 December 1914), "Testimony of Bhan Singh," 485.

183. BL/IOR, 1/PJ/6/1338, file 5028, *'Komagata Maru' Committee of Enquiry: Volume III* (23 October–4 December 1914), "Translation of Gurmukhi Letter sent by Gurdit Singh to the Sikhs at Hong Kong, 5 February 1914," 50.

184. BL/IOR, 1/PJ/6/1338, file 5028, *'Komagata Maru' Committee of Enquiry: Volume III* (23 October–4 December 1914), exhibit 54: "A Manuscript giving a history of the voyage of the S.S. 'Komagata Maru' written in Gurmukhi, apparently in the handwriting of Daljit Singh," 105.

185. *Report of the Komagata Maru Committee of Inquiry: Volume I* (Calcutta, 1914) (hereafter *Report*), 6.

186. *Report*, 6.

187. Johnston, *Voyage of the Komagata Maru*, 27.

188. NAI, Proceedings of the Home Department, Political-A, November 1914, nos. 97–177, D. Petrie, "Note on the Budge Budge Riot," 8 October 1914, 27.

189. Clogston, *Commission to Investigate Hindu Claims*, 13.

190. Hong Kong, Ordinance No. 1 of 1889, 2. In Leach, *The Ordinances of the Legislative Council of the Colony of Hong Kong* (hereafter Hong Kong, Ordinance No. 1 of 1889), 1062

191. The ordinance defined a "colony" to include "all her majesty's Possessions abroad, not being under the Government of the Viceroy of India." Hong Kong, Ordinance No. 1 of 1889, 2, 1063.

192. Hong Kong, Ordinance No. 1 of 1889, 21, 1068.

193. Hong Kong, Ordinance No. 1 of 1889, 54, 1074.

194. Hong Kong, Ordinance No. 1 of 1889, s. 40(1), 1071.

195. If a person was found "unlawfully, either by force or fraud," detaining a man or boy against his will "with intent to put him on board a Chinese passenger ship," the punishment was imprisonment "for any term not exceeding seven years, with or without hard labour." Hong Kong, Ordinance No. 1 of 1889, 55, 1074.

196. Hong Kong, Ordinance No. 1 of 1889, 42, 1072.

197. Hong Kong, Ordinance No. 1 of 1889, 65, 1076.

198. See McClelland, "Redefining the West Indian Interest."

199. BL/IOR, 1/PJ/6/1338, file 5028, *'Komagata Maru' Committee of Enquiry: Volume III* (23 October–4 December 1914), exhibit 33: Blue Tickets of the Sri Guru Nanak Steamship Company, 53.

200. BL/IOR, 1/PJ/6/1338, file 5028, *'Komagata Maru' Committee of Enquiry: Volume III* (23 October–4 December 1914), exhibit 32: A Roll of White Tickets, signed Geo. Grimble, 52.

201. The passenger listed on the ticket reproduced here, Surjan Singh (Naba), was one of fifty-nine men who willingly boarded a train to Punjab following the ship's arrival at Budge Budge.

202. BL/IOR, 1/PJ/6/1338, '*Komagata Maru' Committee of Enquiry: Volume III* (23 October–4 December 1914), file 5028, exhibit 32: A Roll of White Tickets, signed Geo. Grimble, 52.

203. Hong Kong, Ordinance No. 1 of 1889, 31, 1069.

204. Hong Kong, Ordinance No. 1 of 1889, 34, 1070.

205. Singh, *Voyage of the Komagatamaru*, chap. 4, 35.

206. See Sheridan, "The Commercial and Financial Organization of the Slave Trade," 253; Baucom, *Specters of the Atlantic*; Morgan, *Slavery, Atlantic Trade, and the British Economy*, 78; Walvin, *Crossings*, 77–78.

207. Beckert, *Empire of Cotton*, 30.

208. Baucom, *Specters of the Atlantic*, 15.

209. Baucom, *Specters of the Atlantic*, 64 (emphasis in original).

210. Baucom, *Specters of the Atlantic*, 64.

211. Baucom, *Specters of the Atlantic*, 64. "Mendacity" was a commonly used term in characterizations of Indians. See for example Ahuja, "Mendacity in our Midst."

212. For a useful analysis of "indigenous" forms of capital that focus on the Marwaris, see Birla, *Stages of Capital*.

213. BL/IOR, 1/PJ/6/1338, file 5028, '*Komagata Maru' Committee of Enquiry: Volume III* (23 October–4 December 1914), Reexamination of Bhan Singh, 481.

214. BL/IOR, 1/PJ/6/1338, file 5028, '*Komagata Maru' Committee of Enquiry: Volume III* (23 October–4 December 1914), Testimony of Kirpa Singh, 530.

215. BL/IOR, 1/PJ/6/1338, file 5028, '*Komagata Maru' Committee of Enquiry: Volume III* (23 October–4 December 1914), Testimony of Pohlo Ram, 470.

216. BL/IOR, 1/PJ/6/1338, file 5028, '*Komagata Maru' Committee of Enquiry: Volume III* (23 October–4 December 1914), exhibit 41: An Agreement Signed by Certain Passengers, 83 (my emphasis).

217. BL/IOR, 1/PJ/6/1338, file 5028, '*Komagata Maru' Committee of Enquiry: Volume III* (23 October–4 December 1914), exhibit 41: An Agreement Signed by Certain Passengers, 83.

218. BL/IOR, 1/PJ/6/1338, file 5028, '*Komagata Maru' Committee of Enquiry: Volume III* (23 October–4 December 1914), exhibit 100: Memorandum on the voyage of the Komagata Maru and on the incidents which led to the riot at Budge Budge, based chiefly on information of the Director of Criminal Intelligence, 202.

219. Grandin, *The Empire of Necessity*, 99.

220. Grandin, *The Empire of Necessity*, 99; Philip, *Zong!*; Sharpe, *In the Wake*, 52.

221. Philip, *Zong!*, 194.

222. BL/IOR, 1/PJ/6/1338, file 5028, '*Komagata Maru' Committee of Enquiry: Volume III* (23 October–4 December 1914), Testimony of Kirpa Singh, 530. It is not entirely clear whether Gurdit Singh or his comrades penned the agreement. The handwriting is inconsistent and reflects more than one author. As the charterer of the ship, the passenger list would come under his jurisdiction.

223. NAI, Private Collection, "Summary of Freight List," 2.

224. BL/IOR, 1/PJ/6/1338, file 5028, *'Komagata Maru' Committee of Enquiry: Volume III* (23 October–4 December 1914), exhibit 48: Papers relating to the receipt of 9,000 yen from the British Consul, Kobe, and departure of the S.S. Komagata Maru from Kobe, 97.

225. BL/IOR, 1/PJ/6/1338, file 5028, *'Komagata Maru' Committee of Enquiry: Volume III* (23 October–4 December 1914), exhibit 49: An account in English of the Tyranny over "Komagata Maru" Passengers in Kobe, 98.

226. BL/IOR, 1/PJ/6/1338, file 5028, *'Komagata Maru' Committee of Enquiry: Volume III* (23 October–4 December 1914), exhibit 54: A manuscript giving a history of the voyage of the S.S. Komagata Maru written in Gurmukhi, apparently in the handwriting of Daljit Singh, 106–7 (emphasis in original). The term "feranghi" is derived from Arabic and means "foreigner." In colonial India, it was used disparagingly to describe the British.

227. The slave ship *Brookes* served to popularize the horrific conditions of the slave ship and, thus, was one catalyst for the abolition movement in Britain. See Rediker, *The Slave Ship*, esp. chap. 10.

228. Clogston, *Commission to Investigate Hindu Claims*, 10.

229. BL/IOR, 1/PJ/6/1338, file 5028, *'Komagata Maru' Committee of Enquiry: Volume III* (23 October–4 December 1914), exhibit 45: An Appeal for Money, printed in Gurmukhi, 93.

230. According to Clogston, the Khalsa Diwan Society raised $5,000 in cash and $66,000 in land titles "in and around Vancouver." See Clogston, *Commission to Investigate Hindu Claims*, 5.

231. The shore committee of fifteen, including Bhag Singh and Husain Rahim, tried to recover $14,791.85 from the Dominion Government—funds used to assume the Charter-Party—but they were unsuccessful. See Clogston *Commission to Investigate Hindu Claims*, 8.

CHAPTER 3. Land, Sea, and Subjecthood

1. "When Is a British Subject?," *New York Times*, 20 July 1914, 6 (my emphasis).

2. "When Is a British Subject?," *New York Times*, 20 July 1914, 6.

3. "When Is a British Subject?," *New York Times*, 20 July 1914, 6.

4. "When Is a British Subject?," *New York Times*, 20 July 1914, 6.

5. "When Is a British Subject?," *New York Times*, 20 July 1914, 6.

6. I discuss South Africa at the end of this chapter and more fully in the following one.

7. For restrictions on Indian migration to the white settler colonies, see Jensen, *Passage from India;* Huttenback, *Racism and Empire;* Lake and Reynolds, *Drawing the Global Color Line,* esp. part 3.

8. "When Is a British Subject?," *New York Times*, 20 July 1914, 6.

9. A number of scholars have challenged this directionality. See Benton, "Empires of Exception;" Benton, *A Search for Sovereignty;* Benton and Ford, *A Rage for Order;* Metcalf, *Imperial Connections;* Ward, *Networks of Empire.* For a book that challenges the certainty of British imperial rule, see Burton, *The Trouble with Empire.*

10. On the composite of imperial worlds, see Benton, *Law and Colonial Cultures,* 44–45. On the uneven political organization of the British Empire, see Burbank and Cooper, *Empires in World History,* 7.

11. Benton, *A Search for Sovereignty*, 2.

12. Benton makes this point about the multiple and uneven spaces of imperial rule in *A Search for Sovereignty*. On islands, and to a lesser extent oceans, as specific juridical formations, see Jones and Motha, "A New Nomos Offshore and Bodies as Their Own Signs."

13. Hy S. L. Polak, "The Dominions and India," *Living Age*, 17 March 1917, 293.

14. "Indians and Canada," *Leader*, 26 June 1914, 5.

15. Dorsett and McVeigh, "Questions of Jurisdiction," 3–4; Dorsett and McVeigh, *Jurisdiction*, 3.

16. On layered sovereignty, see Bose, *A Hundred Horizons*, 25. On degrees of sovereignty, see Stoler, "Degrees of Imperial Sovereignty."

17. Dorsett and McVeigh, *Jurisdiction*, 32; Ford, "Law's Territory"; Valverde, "Jurisdiction and Scale;" Dorsett and McVeigh, *Jurisdiction*.

18. For a useful recent collection that examines legal plurality, see Benton and Ross, *Legal Pluralism and Empires*. On legal pluralism in India, see Kolsky, "Forum"; Parmar, *Indigeneity and Legal Pluralism in India*.

19. Dorsett and McVeigh, "Questions of Jurisdiction," 11–12.

20. On the shift in jurisdiction from status to territory, see Ford, "Law's Territory," 843; Dorsett, "Mapping Territories."

21. On jurisdiction as government, see Ford, "Law's Territory," 851.

22. On medieval maps and temporality, see Elden, *The Birth of Territory*, 149. On premodern and early modern maps, see Ford, "Law's Territory," 875. Time as mobility is a phrase I have drawn from the philosophy of Henri Bergson. See Bergson, *The Creative Mind*, 2.

23. On law and the inauguration of a new temporal order, see Douzinas, "The Metaphysics of Jurisdiction," 39. In the U.S. context, see Tomlins, "The Threepenny Constitution."

24. Schmitt, *The Nomos of the Earth*, 48.

25. I develop the point on the continuous journey regulation below. On the white Australia policy and oceans, see Russell, "'The Singular Transcultural Space,'" 108.

26. On colonial subjects being out of time, see McClintock, *Imperial Leather*, 16. On indigenous peoples and temporality as a form of governance, see Povinelli, "The Governance of the Prior."

27. I develop this argument further in Mawani, "Law as Temporality."

28. In my discussion of the case, I am drawing from the court's judgment and from the court transcripts. Library and Archives Canada (hereafter LAC), "In the Matter of the Immigration Act and in the Matter of Munshi Singh, Court of Appeal Transcripts," 29–30, June 1914, Victoria, Immigration File 879545(3), vol. 601, RG 76, Microfilm reel B-3097 (hereafter Munshi Singh Court of Appeal Transcripts).

29. The first order-in-council was passed in 1908 but was deemed ultra vires and struck down. As I discuss briefly in chapter 1, there were three preceding legal cases that addressed these restrictions: *Re Rahim* (1911) 16 B.C.R. 469; *Re Rahim* (No. 2) (1911), 16 B.C.R. 471; and *Re Thirty-Nine Hindus* (1913) 15 D.L.R. 189. The constitutionality of the most recent orders-in-council were determined in *Re Munshi Singh* (1914) 20 B.C.R. 243 (hereafter *Re Munshi Singh*).

30. For a useful discussion of "Caucasian," see Baum, *The Rise and Fall of the Caucasian Race*; Haney-Lopez, *White by Law*, esp. chap. 4.

31. As I note in the introduction, there are conflicting claims about the number of passengers who were allowed to disembark. By some accounts, it was twenty; by others, twenty-one; and by still others, twenty-two.

32. Singh, *Voyage of the Komagatamaru*, 90.

33. This is one of the arguments made by Gurdit Singh in *Voyage of the Komagatamaru*, which I discuss in chapter 5.

34. City of Vancouver Archives (hereafter CVA), Copy of letter from Gurdit Singh to Immigration Agent re Calling Before the Board of Inquiry, 24 June 1914, H. H. Stevens Fonds (1878–1973), AM69, p. 354.

35. CVA, From Daljit Singh to Malcolm Reid, 17 June 1914, H. H. Stevens Fonds (1878–1973), AM69, p.180.

36. LAC, From Malcolm Reid to Daljit Singh, 17 June 1914, Department of Immigration, RG 76, vol. 601, File 879545, part 3.

37. An Act for Regulating the Production of Manifests, and for More effectually Preventing Fraudulent Practices in Obtaining Bounties and Drawbacks, and in the Clandestine Relanding of Goods, 1786. In Raithby, *The Statutes Relating to the Admiralty*, 421.

38. Waterson, *A Cyclopedia of Commerce*, 232.

39. Raithby, *The Statutes Relating to the Admiralty*, 424–26.

40. *Re Munshi Singh*, 274 (my emphasis).

41. Macklin, "Historicizing Narratives of Arrival," 48.

42. Munshi Singh Court of Appeal Transcripts, 59.

43. Thampi, "The Indian Community in China and Sino-Indian Relations," 73.

44. Deol, *Gadar Party Ate Bharat Da Kaumi Andolan*, 102–3.

45. LAC, Minutes of a Board of Inquiry held in the Dominion Immigration Office, Vancouver, 28 June 1914, RG 76, Immigration File 879545(3), vol. 601, reel C-10669, 13 (hereafter Board of Inquiry Minutes).

46. Board of Inquiry Minutes, 13.

47. Board of Inquiry Minutes, 15.

48. Board of Inquiry Minutes, 14.

49. Board of Inquiry Minutes, 18.

50. National Archives of India (hereafter NAI), Home Department, Political, No. 4465-A, From the Honorable Sir William Vincent and the Members of the "Komagata Maru" Committee of Enquiry to the Secretary of the Government of India, 3 December 1914, 7.

51. Board of Inquiry Minutes, 2.

52. Board of Inquiry, Minutes, 2.

53. Waterson, *A Cyclopedia of Commerce*, 232.

54. The documentation of slaves aboard the *Zong* is a case in point. See Walvin, *The Zong*, esp. chap. 8. Though Walvin does not discuss the manifest directly, he does address the various forms of enumeration and documentation aboard the ship. On the slave manifest, see also Sharpe, *In the Wake*, 52, 94. For a wonderful account of the captain's ledger and its authority aboard the ship, see D'Aguiar, *Feeding the Ghosts*.

55. Slave manifests have been discussed mainly in terms of archival sources and genealogical research. For an interesting discussion of the slave manifest as an expression of "Black Atlantic politics," see Johnson, "White Lies," 253.

56. Philip, *Zong!*, 194.

57. On the passengers as "undesirables," see Kazimi, *Undesirables*.

58. Poovey, *A History of the Modern Fact*, 29.

59. Lee, "The Oldest European Account Book," 28–60.

60. Carruthers and Espeland, "Accounting for Rationality," 45.

61. Thring and Farrer, *Memorandum on the Merchant Shipping Law Consolidation Bill*, xxix.

62. Thring and Farrer, *Memorandum on the Merchant Shipping Law Consolidation Bill*, xxix.

63. Poovey, *A History of the Modern Fact*, xviii.

64. Poovey, *A History of the Modern Fact*, 41.

65. Piggott, *Nationality*, 45.

66. Piggott, *Nationality*, 14.

67. Piggott, *Nationality*, 14.

68. Jones, *Commentaries of the Law of Evidence in Civil Cases*, 459.

69. Board of Inquiry Minutes, 3.

70. Board of Inquiry Minutes, 4.

71. Board of Inquiry Minutes, 4.

72. Board of Inquiry Minutes, 4.

73. Board of Inquiry Minutes, 4.

74. NAI, Home Department, Political-A, Secret Notes, no. 211, From R. E. Enthoven to Commerce and Industry Department, 17 August 1914, 2.

75. Board of Inquiry Minutes, 6.

76. For a brief biography of Cassidy, see Johnston, *The Voyage of the Komagata Maru*, 99.

77. Munshi Singh Court of Appeal transcripts, 40.

78. Munshi Singh Court of Appeal transcripts, 36.

79. Munshi Singh Court of Appeal transcripts, 37.

80. *Re Munshi Singh*, 250.

81. *Re Munshi Singh*, 250.

82. Munshi Singh Court of Appeal transcripts, 42.

83. Munshi Singh Court of Appeal transcripts, 93.

84. Munshi Singh Court of Appeal transcripts, 97.

85. Munshi Singh Court of Appeal transcripts, 97–98.

86. Munshi Singh Court of Appeal transcripts, 99–100 (my emphasis).

87. Munshi Singh Court of Appeal transcripts, 99–100.

88. Munshi Singh Court of Appeal transcripts, 96. For an intestate case that deals with jurisdiction in a territorial sense, see Stephens, "An Uncertain Inheritance."

89. Munshi Singh Court of Appeal transcripts, 94.

90. Munshi Singh Court of Appeal transcripts, 96.

91. *Re Munshi Singh*, 266.

92. *Re Munshi Singh*, 266.

93. *Re Munshi Singh*, 266.

94. *Re Munshi Singh*, 258.

95. *Re Munshi Singh*, 259.

96. *Re Munshi Singh*, 261.

97. *Re Munshi Singh*, 280.

98. *Re Munshi Singh*, 275.

99. The historical literature on race and Asian immigration is vast. See, for example, Ballantyne, *Orientalism and Race;* Lake and Reynolds *Drawing the Global Color Line;* Ngai, *Impossible Subjects;* Shah, *Contagious Divides;* Shah, *Stranger Intimacy;* Yu, *Thinking Orientals.*

100. Huttenback, "The British Empire as a 'White Man's Country,'" 110.

101. This is the argument made by Lake and Reynolds in *Drawing the Global Color Line.*

102. For a critique of race as ideology, see Hesse, "Im/Plausible Deniability."

103. This argument is more fully developed in Mawani, "Specters of Indigeneity," and Mawani, "Racial Violence and the Cosmopolitan City."

104. I am building here on the argument made by Stoler that race was interwoven into the tissues of colonial society. See Stoler, *Race and the Education of Desire,* esp. chap. 2.

105. The territorial demarcations of race can be traced to Montesquieu's *The Spirit of the Laws* and to Kant, "Of the Different Human Races."

106. This is evident in the writings of a range of European thinkers from English Utilitarians, including James and John Stuart Mill, to Marx. For a discussion of the English Utilitarians, see Mehta, *Liberalism and Empire.* On Marx, see Anderson, *Marx at the Margins.* The quotes are from Hy S. L. Polak, "The Dominions and Canada," *Living Age,* 17 March 1917, 293.

107. *Leader,* 7 July 1914, 3.

108. *Leader,* 7 July 1914, 3.

109. "East and West," *Indian Opinion,* 21 September 1907, 1.

110. *Leader,* 7 July 1914, 3

111. Polak, "The Dominions and India," *Living Age,* 17 March 1917, 293.

112. Polak, "The Dominions and India," *Living Age,* 17 March 1917, 293.

113. These arguments are developed in Mamdani, *Citizen and Subject,* and Mamdani, *Define and Rule.* Unlike Mamdani, I see the distinctions between natives, migrants, and settlers as juridical-racial lines. See Mawani, "Law as Temporality."

114. Maine, *Village-Communities in the East and West,* 237.

115. Mamdani, *Citizen and Subject,* 17.

116. *Re Munshi Singh,* 245.

117. *Re Munshi Singh,* 272.

118. Munshi Singh Court of Appeal Transcripts, 52.

119. Munshi Singh Court of Appeal Transcripts, 51.

120. Munshi Singh Court of Appeal Transcripts, 52.

121. Munshi Singh Court of Appeal Transcripts, 54.

122. *Re Munshi Singh,* 289–90.

123. CVA, In the Court of Appeal in the matter of Munshi Singh, Unpublished Judgment of Chief Justice MacDonald, July 1914, 509-D-7, File 3 (hereafter Munshi Singh unpublished judgment), 488.

124. Munshi Singh unpublished judgment, 488.

125. Munshi Singh unpublished judgment, 488 (my emphasis).

126. *Re Munshi Singh,* 286. On the powers of peace, order, and good government, see Valverde "'Peace, Order, and Good Government.'"

127. *Re Munshi Singh,* 290.

128. *Re Munshi Singh,* 290 (my emphasis).

129. *Re Munshi Singh,* 290. On climate, see Mongia, "Race, Nationality, Mobility," 527.

130. *Re Munshi Singh,* 291.

131. Cited in *Re Munshi Singh,* 291.

132. *Re Munshi Singh,* 291–92.

133. Chakrabarty, *Provincializing Europe,* 8.

134. *Re Munshi Singh,* 259.

135. *Re Munshi Singh,* 256–57 (emphasis in original).

136. *Re Munshi Singh,* 275.

137. *Re Munshi Singh:* 275 (my emphasis).

138. British North America Act, 1867, 30 and 31 Vict. 3.

139. Schmitt, *The* Nomos *of the Earth,* 80.

140. I am reading race into Derrida's arguments about law's violence in "Force of Law." For an elaboration of this reading, see Mawani, "Law's Archive." For a useful account of law's racial violence that excavates the domain of legal and political philosophy, see Da Silva, "No Bodies."

141. Schmitt, *The* Nomos *of the Earth,* 45.

142. British Library, India Office Records (hereafter BL/IOR), 1/PJ/6/1335, *Proceedings of the Komagata Maru Committee of Enquiry, Vol. II,* file 3601, Maxwell Smith, "An Open Letter to the Editor of the London Statist," *Vancouver Sun,* 16 June 1914, n.p.

143. Povinelli, "The Governance of the Prior," 22. See also Byrd, *The Transit of Empire.*

144. Borrows, *Recovering Canada;* Perrin, "Approaching Anxiety," 25.

145. On the significance of priorness, see Povinelli, "The Governance of the Prior."

146. On heterotemporality, see Chakrabarty, *Provincializing Europe,* 239. On a critique of indigenous peoples as the past, see Povinelli, The *Cunning of Recognition,* 48.

147. Byrd, *The Transit of Empire,* xx (my emphasis). Spectrality, as I suggest elsewhere, intimates a dynamic simultaneity of past and future compressed in the present. Its oscillation productively disrupts linear chronologies without necessarily situating indigenous peoples in the past or out of time. See Mawani, "Specters of Indigeneity." For Derrida, spectrality is a recursive force, one that places time "out of joint." Specters, as apparitions, phantoms, ghosts, he argues, are always of time and its interruption and thus can never be of the past alone. Rather, the specter "is the future, it is always to come, it presents itself only as that which could come or come back." See Derrida, *Specters of Marx,* 34.

148. Perrin argues that indigenous peoples are placed in a "time immemorial," which is nonhistorical and which contests rather than confirms a temporal narrative of modernity. See Perrin, "Approaching Anxiety," 27.

149. Munshi Singh Court of Appeal transcript, 71.

150. Munshi Singh Court of Appeal transcript, 71.

151. Munshi Singh Court of Appeal transcript, 71.

152. Munshi Singh Court of Appeal transcript, 71.

153. On the putative lawlessness of indigenous peoples, see Fitzpatrick, *Modernism and the Grounds of Law,* 125. On aboriginal law as the oldest source of law in Canada, see Borrows, *Recovering Canada.*

154. Borrows, "Wampum at Niagara."

155. Borrows, "Wampum at Niagara," 162.

156. Borrows, "Wampum at Niagara," 165–66.

157. Borrows, "Wampum at Niagara," 166.

158. Munshi Singh Court of Appeal transcript, 71.

159. *Re Munshi Singh,* 275.

160. *Re Munshi Singh,* 275 (my emphasis).

161. *Re Munshi Singh,* 276.

162. For a comprehensive discussion of indigenous dispossession in British Columbia, see Harris, *Making Native Space;* Harris, *The Resettlement of British Columbia.*

163. The Indian Act had devastating gendered effects. See Monture-Angus, *Thunder in My Soul.* For a comparison between Canada and the United States, see Bonita Lawrence, "Gender, Race, and the Regulation of Native Identity."

164. Munshi Singh Court of Appeal transcript, 71.

165. Munshi Singh unpublished judgment, 488.

166. See Mamdani, *Define and Rule,* 28. In the Canadian context, see Mawani, *Colonial Proximities.*

167. "A Visitor's Impression of South Africa," *Indian Opinion,* 27 May 1911, 4 (my emphasis). For a biographical sketch of Webb, see Riddick, *The History of British India,* 324.

168. "A Visitor's Impression," *Indian Opinion,* 27 May 1911, 3.

169. NAI, Proceedings of the Home Department, no. 158, From E. Blake Robertson to Sir Robert Borden, 20 July 1914, November 1914, 162.

170. BL/ IOR, 1/PJ/6/1325, file 3601, *Proceedings of the Komagata Maru Committee of Enquiry, Vol. II,* Maxwell Smith, "An Open Letter to the Editor of the London Statist," *Vancouver Sun,* 16 June 1914, n.p.

171. NAI, Proceedings of the Home Department, no. 158, From E. Blake Robertson to Sir Robert Borden, 20 July 1914, 163.

CHAPTER 4. Anticolonial Vernaculars of Indigeneity

1. "Lecture on the Future Prospects of India, by Baboo Gyanendra Mohun Tagore, Barrister-at-Law" *Pioneer* (Allahabad), June 6, 1866, 6 (hereafter, "Lecture").

2. "Lecture" (my emphasis).

3. Marx, "The Future Results of British Rule in India," 659.

4. Marx, "The Future Results of British Rule in India, 659.

5. "Lecture." Tagore's chronology is a very contentious one, especially in contemporary India where many claim that India has no "original inhabitants." For a useful sketch of these debates, see Karlsson and Subba, *Indigeneity in India;* Parmar, "Undoing Historical Wrongs"; Parmar, *Indigeneity and Legal Pluralism;* Skaria, *Hybrid Histories.* For an account of the origins of aboriginal in India, see Guha, "Lower Strata, Older Races, and Aboriginal Peoples."

6. "Lecture."

7. "Lecture."

8. It is important to note that "aboriginal" and "native" as signifiers of original peoples were regularly conflated in the history of settler colonial contexts, as I discuss below.

9. "Lecture." This was not Tagore's only engagement with the question of indigeneity in India. Sumit Guha notes that "Professor Tagore" remarked to the Anthropological Society in 1863 that the aborigines in India were flesh eating. See Guha, "Lower Strata, Older Races, and Aboriginal Peoples," 428.

10. Marx, "The Future Results of British Rule in India," 659.

11. Writing of the U.S. context, Jodi Byrd argues that "indigenous peoples are located outside temporality and presence, even in the face of the very present and ongoing colonization of indigenous lands, resources, and lives." See Byrd, *The Transit of Empire,* 6. For a wonderful account of the conflicting temporalities of indigeneity, see King, *The Inconvenient Indian.*

12. Interestingly, there was little discussion of Adivasis in India. See n. 16 below.

13. Canadian Gentleman, "Re: Exclusion of the Hindus," *Hindustanee,* 1 June 1914, 12.

14. This argument is further developed in Mawani, "Specters of Indigeneity."

15. I am using indigeneity as a method to trace the inconsistencies and intensities of colonial power. For a useful discussion of "indigeneity as method" that resonates with and informs what I am doing here, see Byrd, "A Return to the South," 615.

16. Indigeneity is highly contested in India. Many argue that India is home to "tribal peoples," known as "Adivasis," but that these people are distinct from indigenous peoples. Others vehemently disagree. In the post–World War II period, Adivasis have increasingly identified themselves as indigenous. For a fuller account of these debates, see Skaria, *Hybrid Histories.*

17. On New Zealand colonial history that centers the Maori, see Ballantyne, *Webs of Empire.* For a discussion of New Zealand and colonial Punjab, see Ballantyne's pathbreaking *Orientalism and Race.*

18. "Papers from Sydney New South Wales," *Pioneer,* 8 June 1866, 2.

19. On problems with the idea of legal transplant, see Mawani and Hussin, "The Travels of Law," 13.

20. This is more fully elaborated in Mawani, "Law as Temporality."

21. "Lecture," *Pioneer,* June 6, 1866, 6.

22. "Time out of joint" comes from Shakespeare's *Hamlet* and is cited by Derrida in *Specters of Marx,* 21.

23. For a discussion of indigeneity as a "traveling discourse," to and from India, see Karlsson, "Anthropology and the 'Indigenous Slot,'" 414. As I read it, Karlsson's essay offers an important critique of indigeneity as a white settler construct.

24. Marx, "The Future Results of British Rule in India," 659.

25. This is a voluminous literature. See Bhana, *Indentured Indian Emigrants to Natal;* Dhupelia-Mestrie, *From Cane Fields to Freedom;* Huttenback, *Gandhi in South Africa;* Huttenback, *Racism and Empire;* Mongia, "Gender and the Historiography of Gandhian Satyagraha"; Tinker, *A New System of Slavery.*

26. On colonial categories, see Mamdani, *Citizen and Subject;* Mamdani *Define and Rule;* Mawani, *Colonial Proximities;* Stoler, *Carnal Knowledge and Imperial Power.*

27. This was not specific to the southern regions of Africa. See Mamdani, *Define and Rule,* 30.

28. Though not writing of indigenous peoples directly, Kerry Ward argues that Britain did not eschew Dutch legalities or claims to sovereignty but absorbed these into its own repertoire of colonial rule. See Ward, *Networks of Empire,* esp. chap. 1.

29. Sir Montague de Pomeroy Webb, "A Visitor's Impression of South Africa," *Indian Opinion,* 27 May 1911, 4.

30. "Seeds of Disruption," *Indian Opinion,* 13 June 1908, 11–12.

31. "A Visitor's Impression of South Africa," *Indian Opinion,* 27 May 1911, 4.

32. South Africa has recently been seen as crucial to the politics of white superiority and to Indian anticolonialism and radicalism. On the former, see Chang, *Pacific Connections.* On the latter, see Banerjee, *Becoming Imperial Citizens.*

33. For a discussion of slavery under Dutch rule, see Shell, *Children of Bondage.*

34. On the connections between indenture and slavery in the Caribbean, see Bahadur, *Coolie Woman,* especially 22 and 26. On the Indian Ocean, see Anderson, "After Emancipation." With regard to Indians in South Africa, see Dhupelia-Mesthrie, "The Place of India in South African History," 12–14.

35. Dhupelia-Mesthrie, "The Place of India in South African History," 13.

36. Bhana and Brain, *Setting Down Roots;* Tinker, *A New System of Slavery.*

37. See Dhupelia-Mesthrie, *From Cane Fields to Freedom,* 27.

38. Lake and Reynolds, *Drawing the Global Color Line,* 118.

39. Dhupelia-Mesthrie, *From Cane Fields to Freedom,* 14.

40. John Cowen, "Race Prejudice," *Indian Opinion,* 16 July 1910, 1.

41. John Cowen, "Race Prejudice," *Indian Opinion,* 16 July 1910, 1.

42. Sir Montague de Pomeroy Webb, "A Visitor's Impression of South Africa," *Indian Opinion,* 27 May 1911, 3–4

43. C. F. Andrews, "The Danger in East Africa: Economic Commission Report," *Indian Opinion,* 20 February 1920, 6.

44. C. F. Andrews, "The Danger in East Africa: Economic Commission Report," *Indian Opinion,* 20 February 1920, 6.

45. C. F. Andrews, "The Danger in East Africa: Economic Commission Report," *Indian Opinion,* 20 February 1920, 6.

46. C. F. Andrews, "The Danger in East Africa: Economic Commission Report," *Indian Opinion,* 20 February 1920, 6.

47. "Mr. Churchill on the Racial Problems," *Indian Opinion,* 22 July 1921, 2.

48. On this point, see Mongia, "Gender and the Historiography of Gandhian Satyagraha," 132.

49. There is a large scholarship on the legal and political contests over what is now Natal, the Cape Colony, Transvaal, and Orange Free State. For a general overview of these developments and of Dutch and British conflicts see Beck, *History of South Africa.*

50. "Seeds of Disruption," *Indian Opinion,* 13 July 1908, 11.

51. "Seeds of Disruption," *Indian Opinion,* 13 July 1908, 11.

52. Some have argued that immigration restrictions against Indians in South Africa figured prominently as a key example for the other Dominions. See Huttenback, *Racism and Empire.* See also Johnston, *The Voyage of the Komagata Maru,* 6.

53. Dhupelia-Mesthrie, *From Cane Fields to Freedom.*

54. Dhupelia-Mesthrie, *From Cane Fields to Freedom*, 22; Huttenback, *Gandhi in South Africa*, 279–80.

55. Huttenback, *Gandhi in South Africa*, 279.

56. Deborah Posel argues that after the 1910 union of South Africa under British rule, as racially specific laws increased in number and intensity, there remained "no general constitutional definition of racial categories, which meant that each statute concerned with race produced its own rendition." See Posel, "Race as Common Sense," 89–90.

57. "What Is a Native?" *Rhodesia Herald*, 30 March 1905, 5. For an account of the "native question" as considered by this commission and others, see Ashforth, *The Politics of Official Discourse in Twentieth-Century South Africa*.

58. Bhattacharjea, "Gandhi and the Chinese Community in South Africa," 151.

59. "British Indian Association and Constitution Committee," *Indian Opinion*, 21 June 1906, 12.

60. Huttenback, *Ghandi in South Africa*, 286.

61. "The British Indian Problem," *Indian Opinion*, 27 October 1906, 12.

62. "Transvaal Indian Mass Meeting: Anti-Asiatic Bill Denounced," *Indian Opinion*, 6 April 1907, 9.

63. "Transvaal Indians' Predicament," *Indian Opinion*, 12 October 1907, 13.

64. "British Indian Association and Constitution Committee," *Indian Opinion*, 21 June 1906, 12.

65. "The Coloured Vote," *Indian Opinion*, 4 August 1906, 13.

66. "The Coloured Vote," *Indian Opinion*, 4 August 1906, 13.

67. "The Transvaal Constitution," *Indian Opinion*, 6 October 1906, 12.

68. "The Transvaal Constitution," *Indian Opinion*, 6 October 1906, 12.

69. "What Is a Native?" *Indian Opinion*, 1 September 1906, 2.

70. "What Is a Native?" *Indian Opinion*, 1 September 1906, 2.

71. Isabel Hofmeyr argues that Indian periodicals and Indian diasporic newspapers including the *Modern Review* and to a lesser extent *Indian Opinion*, created a "textual circuit" and "a diasporic public forum of debate." See Hofmeyr, "The Idea of 'Africa' in Indian Nationalism," 72. For a discussion of Gandhi's *Indian Opinion*, see Hofmeyr, "Violent Texts, Vulnerable Readers"; Hofmeyr, *Gandhi's Printing Press*.

72. "The Transvaal Struggle: Letters to the British Press," *Indian Opinion*, 30 July 1910, 5.

73. "Race Prejudice," *Indian Opinion*, 23 July 1910, 4.

74. "Coloured Persons in South Africa," *Indian Opinion*, 8 July 1905, 12.

75. "Coloured Persons in South Africa," *Indian Opinion*, 8 July 1905, 12.

76. C. F. Andrews, "The Asiatic Question: Analysis of a Vital Problem," *Indian Opinion*, 11 June 1920, 5.

77. C. F. Andrews, "The Asiatic Question: Analysis of Vital Problem," *Indian Opinion*, 11 June 1920, 5. On race and caste, see Ghurye, *Caste and Race in India*; Loomba, "Race and the Possibilities of Comparative Critique"; Immerwahr, "Caste or Colony?"

78. C. F. Andrews, "The Asiatic Question: Analysis of Vital Problem," *Indian Opinion*, 11 June 1920, 5.

79. C. F. Andrews, "The Asiatic Question: Analysis of Vital Problem," *Indian Opinion*, 18 June 1920, 5.

80. C. F. Andrews, "The Asiatic Question: Analysis of Vital Problem," *Indian Opinion*, 11 June 1920, 5.

81. C. F. Andrews, "The Asiatic Question: Analysis of Vital Problem," *Indian Opinion*, 18 June 1920, 5.

82. C. F. Andrews, "The Asiatic Question: Analysis of Vital Problem," *Indian Opinion*, 11 June 1920, 5.

83. "'The White Man's Title Deeds,' *The Canadian Courier*," quoted in the *Aryan*, 2, no. 2 (February 1912): 5.

84. On the "vanishing Indian" see King, *The Inconvenient Indian*, 36.

85. "Time out of joint" is from Derrida, *Specters of Marx*, 21.

86. Mitter, *Art and Nationalism in Colonial India*, 138.

87. Khanduri, "Vernacular Punches," 461.

88. On Parsis and legal culture in India, see Sharafi, *Law and Identity in Colonial South Asia*.

89. For a discussion of the *Hindi Punch*, see Harder and Mittler, *Asian Punches*, especially part 2, "Punch in South Asia"; Khanduri, "Vernacular Punches"; Mitter, *Art and Nationalism in Colonial India*, 138, 155.

90. Mitter, *Art and Nationalism*, 155.

91. Khanduri, "Vernacular Punches," 478.

92. The classic account of "playing Indian" comes from Deloria, *Playing Indian*. For a version that centers on the Pacific Northwest, see Raibmon, *Authentic Indians*.

93. On the globalizing force of the telegraph more generally, see Wenzlhuemer, *Connecting the Nineteenth-Century World*.

94. *Hindi Punch*, 3 May 1913, 16.

95. This argument about Canada defending its sovereignty as a "white man's country" is a common one. See Johnston, *The Voyage of the Komagata Maru*; Ward, *White Canada Forever*.

96. On *terra nullius* and indigenous dispossession, see Banner, *How the Indians Lost Their Land*; Banner, *Possessing the Pacific*.

97. Jebb, *Studies in Colonial Nationalism*. For a detailed discussion of Jebb and his politics, see Gorman, *Imperial Citizenship*, esp. chap. 5.

98. Gorman, *Imperial Citizenship*, 152.

99. Jebb, *Studies in Colonial Nationalism*, vii.

100. "Jingoism in Excess: Mr. Richard Jebb on British Indians," *Indian Opinion*, 19 January 1907, 14.

101. "Jingoism in Excess," *Indian Opinion*, 19 January 1907, 14 (my emphasis).

102. "Jingoism in Excess," *Indian Opinion*, 19 January 1907, 14 (my emphasis).

103. "Imperial Insularity," *Indian Opinion*, 19 January 1907, 8.

104. "Imperial Insularity," *Indian Opinion*, 19 January 1907, 8.

105. Farred, "The Unsettler," 797.

106. Farred, "The Unsettler," 798.

107. On this point, see Simpson, "Settlement's Secret."

108. In early twentieth-century Canada, totem poles became important markers of "ancient aboriginal culture" in the emerging Canadian nation. See Mawani, "From Colonialism to Multiculturalism?"

109. Borrows, "Wampum at Niagara," 161.

110. On the recognition and disavowal of indigenous peoples, see Byrd, *Transit of Empire*; Simpson, *Mohawk Interruptus*, esp. the introduction.

111. For a discussion of racial taxonomies that divided indigenous people from Chinese migrants, see Mawani, *Colonial Proximities*, 10–16.

112. Povinelli, "The Governance of the Prior," 19.

113. Distinguishing the specter from Hegel's Spirit, Derrida argues that "for there to be a ghost, there must be a return to the body, but to a body that is more abstract than ever." That is certainly the case with Miss Columbia. See Derrida, *Specters of Marx*, 157.

114. On the effects of gendered violence under the Indian Act, see Lawrence, "Gender, Race, and the Regulation of Native Identity in Canada and the United States"; Lawrence, *"Real" Indians and Others*, especially chapters 1 and 2; Monture-Angus, *Thunder in My Soul*.

115. For a discussion of the *Modern Review*, see Hofmeyr, "The Idea of 'Africa.'"

116. *Modern Review*, July 1914, 19 (my emphasis).

117. British Library, India Office Records (hereafter BL/IOR) 1/PJ/6), *Proceedings of the Komagata Maru Committee of Enquiry, vol. II*, file 3601, Maxwell Smith, "An Open Letter to the Editor of the London Statist," *Vancouver Sun*, 16 June 1914, n.p.

118. "Re Exclusion of Hindoos," *Hindustanee*, 1 June 1914, 13.

119. "Re Exclusion of Hindoos," *Hindustanee*, 1 June 1914, 13.

120. "Re Exclusion of Hindoos," *Hindustanee*, 1 June 1914, 13.

121. On "imperial citizenship," see Banerjee, *Becoming Imperial Citizens*; Gorman, *Imperial Citizenship*; Mawani, "Specters of Indigeneity."

122. On race as a modern form of governance, see Hesse, "Racialized Modernity"; Da Silva, *Toward a Global Idea of Race*.

123. On the effects of racial categories, see Mawani, *Colonial Proximities*; Stoler, *Carnal Knowledge and Imperial Power*.

124. See, for example, Da Silva, *Toward a Global Idea of Race*; Stoler, *Race and the Education of Desire*.

125. Foucault, *Discipline and Punish*, 201.

126. On the importance of effect over intention, see Foucault, *The History of Sexuality*, 94–95.

127. "Excerpt from a Speech by Mr. Nanak Chand at a Meeting in Lahore," *Khalsa Advocate*, 11 July 1914, 4.

128. "Excerpt from a Speech by Mr. Nanak Chand at a Meeting in Lahore," *Khalsa Advocate*, 11 July 1914, 4.

129. "Excerpt from a Speech by Mr. Nanak Chand at a Meeting in Lahore," *Khalsa Advocate*, 11 July 1914, 4.

130. "Excerpt from a Speech by Mr. Nanak Chand at a Meeting in Lahore," *Khalsa Advocate*, 11 July 1914, 4.

131. Burton, "The Pain of Racism," 214.

132. See Burton "The Pain of Racism," 214. See also Burton, *Brown over Black*.

133. Burton, "'Every Secret Thing'?" 63.

134. Burton, "'Every Secret Thing'?" 63.

135. Burton, "'Every Secret Thing'?" 63.

136. "Indian Affairs in the Natal Parliament," *Indian Opinion*, 20 July 1907, 9.

137. "Indian Affairs in the Natal Parliament," *Indian Opinion*, 20 July 1907, 10 (my emphasis).

138. "The Indians in Africa," *Indian Opinion*, 23 July 1920, 4.

139. Banerjee, *Becoming Imperial Citizens*, 100–101.

140. Banerjee, *Becoming Imperial Citizens*, 107.

141. "Indians and the Dominions," *Civil and Military Gazette* Lahore, 17 June 1914, XXXVIII, 10.

142. Chakrabarty, *Provincializing Europe*, 8.

143. "Indians and the Dominions," *Civil and Military Gazette*, 17 June 1914, 10.

144. "Indians and the Dominions," *Civil and Military Gazette*, 17 June 1914, 10.

145. "Hubshi" is a term derived from the Arabic word "Habshi" and used disparagingly to describe Indians of African origin. See Prashad, *Everybody Was Kung Fu Fighting*, 8.

146. "Rights of British Indian Subjects," *Tribune*, 18 June 1914, 2 (my emphasis).

147. On the exclusionary impulses of British liberal thought, see Mehta, *Liberalism and Empire*.

148. Marx, "The Future Results of British Rule in India," 659.

149. Several scholars have made the argument that South Asians, Africans, and African Americans developed solidarities through their subjected positions. See Bald, *Bengali Harlem*; Prashad, *Everybody Was Kung Fu Fighting*; Shah, *Stranger Intimacy*. On solidarities between Chinese and Indians in South Africa, see Bhattacharjea, "Gandhi and the Chinese Community." For accounts that focus on the antinomies between Indians and Africans, see Burton, *Brown over Black*; Hughes, "The Coolies Will Elbow Us out of the Country"; Soske, "'Wash Me Black Again.'" For a critique of the argument that Indians are "settlers," see Mawani, "Law as Temporality."

150. "Re: Exclusion of the Hindus," *Hindustanee*, 1 June 1914, 12.

151. "East and West," *Indian Opinion*, 21 September 1907, 1.

CHAPTER 5. The Fugitive Sojourns of Gurdit Singh

1. Singh initiated a series of lawsuits in Malaya. In a judgment passed against him in the Straits Settlements, the judge described him to be "guilty of very great deceit and impropriety." British Library, India Office Records (hereafter BL/IOR), 1/PJ/6/1338, file 5028, *'Komagata Maru' Committee of Enquiry: Volume III* (23 October–4 December 1914), exhibit 53: Copy of a Judgment in a Civil Suit containing Reflections on the Character of Gurdit Singh, 103. On Singh as "litigious," see Johnston, *The Voyage of the Komagata Maru*, 54.

2. These descriptions of Singh come from the *Komagata Maru* Committee of Enquiry, BL/IOR, 1/PJ/6/1325, file 3601, *Proceedings of the Komagata Maru Committee of Enquiry, vol. II,* Canadian Immigration: The Komagata Maru Incident, 26 June 1914–14 April 1916, enclosure 5, no date, 21.

3. "Gurdit Singh" in India, Intelligence Bureau, *The Ghadr Directory*, 92. Punjab is a region well known for agriculture and not for seafaring.

4. For a contemporary discussion of the sea as a white male space, see Perera, "Oceanic Corpo-Graphies."

5. The sea was a site of hostility and of freedom for lascars and fugitive/freed slaves. The classic writing on lascars is Visram, *Ayahs, Lascars, and Princes.* See also Jaffer, *Lascars and Indian Ocean Seafaring.* Slaves, both the bonded and the newly freed, often turned to the sea as a site of escape and opportunity. Two famous examples are Frederick Douglass and Olaudah Equiano. See Bolster, *Black Jacks;* Carretta, *Equiano, the African;* Douglass, *Narrative of the Life of Frederick Douglass;* Wong, *Neither Fugitive nor Free.*

6. Douglass, *Narrative of the Life of Frederick Douglass,* 60–61.

7. Douglass was a caulker in the Baltimore shipyards and escaped slavery after borrowing a seaman's protection certificate. See Bolster, *Black Jacks,* 1–2.

8. Oceans have a long history of revolt and mutiny. Some of this history is captured in Linebaugh and Rediker, *The Many Headed Hydra.* On the seabound travel of Indians via steamers, see Chanderbali, *Indian Indenture in the Straits Settlements,* 67. See also Amrith, *Crossing the Bay of Bengal.*

9. "Gurdit Singh," *Vancouver Sun,* 13 June 1914, 7.

10. India, Intelligence Bureau, *The Ghadr Directory,* 93.

11. India, Intelligence Bureau, *The Ghadr Directory,* 93.

12. National Archives India (hereafter NAI), Home Department, Political-A, "Report of the Committee Appointed to Inquire into Circumstances Connected with the Voyage of the Komagata Maru," March 1915, 65.

13. India, Intelligence Bureau, *The Ghadr Directory,* 92. Some of the passengers aboard the ship were known Ghadrites, but Singh was not one of them.

14. I make this argument more fully in Mawani, "Circuits of Law."

15. Suchetana Chattopadhyay has been documenting the ways in which the returning passengers connected with working-class revolutionary activities already under way in Calcutta. See Chattopadhyay, "The Last Stretch of the Journey."

16. On India and World War I, see Pati, *India and the First World War;* Singha, "Front Lines and Status Lines."

17. Ordinance III of 1914; Ordinance no. V of 1914, 5 September 1914, 24 & 25 Vict. C. 58.

18. The classic text on emergency in colonial India is Hussain, *The Jurisprudence of Emergency.* Though Hussain covers the period in question, he does not reference the Foreigners Act or the Ingress into India Ordinance. On the ordinances, see Pati, *India and the First World War,* 117; Sohi, *Echoes of Mutiny,* esp. chap. 5. For a discussion of these ordinances and others enacted during the First World War, see Dam, *Presidential Legislation in India,* 42.

19. The most authoritative account of the ship's arrival in Calcutta is still Johnston, *Voyage of the Komagata Maru.* He covers Budge Budge and Singh's escape in chapters 10 and 11 and Singh's surrender in chapter 12. An English account of Gurdit Singh's life is written by Tatla and Tatla, *Sardar Gurdit Singh;* see also Tatla, "Incorporating Regional Events into the Nationalist Narrative."

20. *Zulmi Katha* was published in 1921 and *Voyage of the Komagatamaru, or India's Slavery Abroad* (hereafter Singh, *Voyage*) in 1928.

21. Hartman argues that movement was central to the resistance of slaves but that "stealing away" demonstrated the limits of emancipation. See Hartman, *Scenes of Subjection,* 13–14. For an argument that opposes any direct line between fugitivity and resistance, see Kawash, "Fugitive Properties."

22. For a useful discussion of "stealing away," see Hartman, *Scenes of Subjection,* chap. 2.

23. On the beauty and creativity of fugitivity, see Harney and Moten, *The Undercommons,* 97. Carter makes a similar point about the middle passage as "sheer possibility and potentiality." See Carter, "Paratheological Blackness," 593.

24. For a general discussion of slavery and maritime worlds, see Bolster, *Black Jacks.* On the Merchant Seaman's Act (1790) and the Fugitive Slave Act (1793) in the United States, see Guttoff, "Fugitive Slaves and Ship-Jumping Sailors." On the connections between fugitivity and maroon communities, see Linebaugh and Rediker, *Many Headed Hydra;* Roberts, *Freedom as Marronage.*

25. This is captured in the quote from Douglass. See also Wong, *Neither Fugitive nor Free,* esp. chap. 4.

26. "Government Form of the Charter-Party," in Singh, *Voyage,* chaps. 3, 4.

27. NAI, Proceedings of Home Department, no. 158, November 1914, Telegram from the Secretary of State for the Colonies to the Governor-General of Canada, 29 July 1914, 171.

28. NAI, Home Department, Political-A, Report of the Committee Appointed to Inquire into Circumstances Connected with the Voyage of the Komagata Maru, March 1915, 15.

29. On the expansive use of vagrancy laws, see Lowe, *The Intimacies of Four Continents,* 132.

30. "An Ordinance entitled The Vagrancy Ordinance, 1888" (3 March 1888), in Leach, *The Ordinances of the Legislative Council of the Colony of Hong Kong,* 1023. The Chinese were governed by a different law. See "The Regulation of Chinese Ordinance, 1888," 1028.

31. "An Ordinance entitled The Vagrancy Ordinance, 1888." See also Johnston, *Voyage of the Komagata Maru,* 144.

32. BL/IOR, 1/PJ/6/1325, file 3601, Canadian Immigration: The Komagata Maru Incident, 26 June 1914–14 April 1916, Telegram: Governor of Hong Kong to the Secretary of State for the Colonies, 23 July 1914.

33. Johnston, *Voyage of the Komagata Maru,* 151; Sohi, *Echoes of Mutiny,* 58.

34. BL/IOR, 1/PJ/6 1338, file 5028, *'Komagata Maru' Committee of Enquiry: Volume III* (23 October–4 December 1914), Testimony of Captain Yamamoto, 12.

35. NAI, Home Department, Political-A, Report of the Committee Appointed to Inquire into Circumstances Connected with the Voyage of the Komagata Maru, March 1915, 17.

36. Singh, *Voyage,* part 2, 29.

37. NAI, Home Department, Political-A, Report of the Committee Appointed to Inquire into Circumstances Connected with the Voyage of the Komagata Maru, March 1915, 17.

38. NAI, Home Department, Political-A, Report of the Committee Appointed to Inquire into Circumstances Connected with the Voyage of the Komagata Maru, March 1915, 51.

39. Ordinance no. V of 1914, 5 September 1914, 24 & 25 Vict. C. 58.

40. To maintain the quasi autonomy of the Princely states, the ordinance could not be used against persons who entered there, unless they were arriving from a foreign country.

41. BL/IOR, 1/PJ/6 1330, file 4312, The Ingress into India Ordinance: 10 September 1914–6 October 1914, Minute Paper, September 1914 (my emphasis).

42. BL/IOR, 1/PJ /6 1338, file 5028, *'Komagata Maru' Committee of Enquiry: Volume III* (23 October–4 December 1914), Testimony of Mr. McDonald, 404.

43. For a brief discussion, see Sohi, "Race, Surveillance, and Indian Anticolonialism," 423.

44. BL/IOR, 1/PJ /6 1330, file 4312, The Ingress into India Ordinance: 10 September 1914–6 October 1914. Minute Paper, September 1914.

45. BL/IOR, 1/PJ /6 1330, file 4312, The Ingress into India Ordinance: 10 September 1914–6 October 1914, *Gazette of India,* 19 October 1914.

46. NAI, Home Department, Political-A, no. 216, Summary of Ordinance, 3 September 1914, 9.

47. BL/IOR, 1/PJ /6 1338, file 5028, *'Komagata Maru' Committee of Enquiry: Volume III* (23 October–4 December 1914), Confidential Memorandum on Foreigners in India, India Office, 30 September 1914, 7.

48. BL/IOR, 1/PJ /6 1338, file 5028, *'Komagata Maru' Committee of Enquiry: Volume III* (23 October–4 December 1914), Confidential Memorandum on Foreigners in India, India Office, 30 September 1914, 7.

49. NAI, Home Department Notes, no. 148, December 1914, From Presbyterian Church in Canada to Robert Borden, 13 October 1914, 4.

50. NAI, Home Department Notes, no. 148, December 1914, From Seton to the Under Secretary of State Colonial Office, 16 November 1914, 10.

51. NAI, Home Department Notes, no. 148, December 1914, From Secretary of State to Viceroy, Home Department, 12 November 1914, 11.

52. On whiteness and oceans in the Australian context, see Perera, *Australia and the Insular Imagination;* Russell, "'The Singular Transcultural Space.'"

53. NAI, Home Department, Political, no. 132, From Members of the Komagata Maru Committee to the Secretary of the Government of India, 3 December 1914, 18.

54. NAI, Home Department, Political, no. 132, From Members of the Komagata Maru Committee to the Secretary of the Government of India, 3 December 1914, 18.

55. BL/IOR, 1/PJ /6 1338, file 5028, *'Komagata Maru' Committee of Enquiry: Volume III* (23 October–4 December 1914), Testimony of Mir Muhammed Khan, 111.

56. NAI, Home Department, Political, no. 132, From Members of the Komagata Maru Committee to the Secretary of the Government of India, 3 December 1914, 18.

57. NAI, Home Department, Political, no. 132, From Members of the Komagata Maru Committee to the Secretary of the Government of India, 3 December 1914, 18.

58. "Condemnation of Reporting on Budge Budge," *Leader,* 3 October 1914, 3.

59. "Budge Budge Riot," *Tribune,* 16 October 1914, 3.

60. BL/IOR, 1/PJ/6 1338, file 5028, *'Komagata Maru' Committee of Enquiry: Volume III* (23 October–4 December 1914), Reexamination of Bhan Singh, 482.

61. BL/IOR, 1/PJ/6 1338, file 5028, *'Komagata Maru' Committee of Enquiry: Volume III* (23 October–4 December 1914), Reexamination of Bhan Singh, 482.

62. Singh, *Voyage,* chap. 4, 127.

63. NAI, Home Department, Political-A, nos. 1–13. R. H. Raddock to H. Wheeler, 21 December 1914, 4.

64. BL/IOR, 1/PJ/6 1338, file 5028, *'Komagata Maru' Committee of Enquiry: Volume III* (23 October–4 December 1914), Testimony of Surain Singh, 213.

65. BL/IOR, 1/PJ/6 1338, file 5028, *'Komagata Maru' Committee of Enquiry: Volume III* (23 October–4 December 1914), Testimony of D. Petrie, Delhi Police and CID, 500.

66. BL/IOR, I/PJ/6 1338, file 5028, 'Komagata Maru' Committee of Enquiry: Volume III (23 October–4 December 1914), Testimony of D. Petrie, Delhi Police and CID, 500.

67. BL/IOR, I/PJ/6 1338, file 5028, 'Komagata Maru' Committee of Enquiry: Volume III (23 October–4 December 1914), Testimony of D. Petrie, Delhi Police and CID, 500.

68. See Chattopadhyay, "Last Stretch of the Journey."

69. BL/IOR, I/PJ/6 1338, file 5028, 'Komagata Maru' Committee of Enquiry: Volume III (23 October–4 December 1914), Testimony of D. Petrie, Delhi Police and CID, 500.

70. NAI, Home Department, Political-A, nos. 1–13. Demi-official letter from Vincent to Wheeler, 6 January 1915, 13. The paragraph was removed from the *Komagata Maru* Enquiry's Final Report.

71. NAI, Home Department, Political, no. 132. From Members of the Komagata Maru Committee to the Secretary of the Government of India, 3 December 1914, 18.

72. BL/IOR, I/PJ/6 1338, file 5028, 'Komagata Maru' Committee of Enquiry: Volume III (23 October–4 December 1914), Testimony of Jawahir Mal, 97. For a discussion of the Andaman Islands and convict labor, see Anderson, "Convicts and Coolies"; Sen, *Disciplining Punishment.*

73. *Report of the Komagata Maru Committee of Inquiry* (Calcutta 1914) (hereafter *Report*), 15.

74. BL/IOR, I/PJ/6 1338, file 5028, 'Komagata Maru' Committee of Enquiry: Volume III (23 October–4 December 1914), Testimony of Hazarah Singh, 334.

75. BL/IOR, I/PJ/6 1338, file 5028, 'Komagata Maru' Committee of Enquiry: Volume III (23 October–4 December 1914), Testimony of Bhan Singh, 542.

76. BL/IOR, I/PJ/6 1338, file 5028, 'Komagata Maru' Committee of Enquiry: Volume III (23 October–4 December 1914), Testimony of Baru, 136.

77. NAI, Home Department, Political, no. 132. From Members of the Komagata Maru Committee to the Secretary of the Government of India, 3 December 1914, 18.

78. Still others tailed the procession to Howrah, insisting that they were entitled to a portion of the $9,000 (Hong Kong dollars) that the British Consul paid to Gurdit Singh when the ship anchored at Kobe. BL/IOR, I/PJ/6 1338, file 5028, 'Komagata Maru' Committee of Enquiry: Volume III (23 October–4 December 1914), Reexamination of Bhan Singh, 483.

79. BL/IOR, I/PJ/6 1338, file 5028, 'Komagata Maru' Committee of Enquiry: Volume III (23 October–4 December 1914), Testimony of Pohlo Ram, 476.

80. "Recent Events in India: The Outbreak of War: India's Loyalty," *Leader,* 22 July 1918, 8.

81. BL/IOR, I/PJ/6 1338, file 5028, 'Komagata Maru' Committee of Enquiry: Volume III (23 October–4 December 1914), Testimony of Bishen Singh, 547.

82. BL/IOR, I/PJ/6 1338, file 5028, 'Komagata Maru' Committee of Enquiry: Volume III (23 October–4 December 1914), Testimony of Harnam Singh, 311.

83. The numbers of those killed range from twenty-six to forty. The *Report of the Komagata Maru Committee* estimated on the lower end. Of the twenty-six people killed, twenty were Sikhs, two Europeans, two police officers from Punjab, and two residents from Budge Budge. See *Report,* 17.

84. It is important to note that the events at Budge Budge were described by anticolonials as a "massacre" and by Indian authorities as a "riot." See *Report,* 17.

85. BL/IOR, 1/PJ/6 1338, file 5028, *'Komagata Maru' Committee of Enquiry: Volume III* (23 October–4 December 1914), Testimony of F. Slocock, 3 November 1914, 208.

86. NAI, Home Department, Political, no. 1, From the Chairman of the Members of the Komagata Maru Committee of Enquiry, 3 December 1914, 2.

87. NAI, Home Department, Political, no. 132, From Members of the Komagata Maru Committee to the Secretary of the Government of India, 3 December 1914, 10.

88. *Report,* 1. See also Johnston, *Voyage of the Komagata Maru,* 166.

89. NAI, Home Department, Political, no. 132, From the Chairman of the Members of the Komagata Maru Committee of Enquiry, 3 December 1914, 16.

90. NAI, Home Department, Political-A. no. 57, From the Honorable J. G. Cumming to the Honorable C. A. Barron, 3 November 1914, 3.

91. NAI, Home Department, Political-A, no. 57, The Chief Secretary (Punjab) from the Secretary to the Government of Bengal, 8 October 1914, 2.

92. NAI, Home Department, Political-A. no. 57, From Sardar Daljit Singh and the Maharaja of Burdwan to Sir James DuBoulay, 30 November 1914, 4.

93. NAI, Home Department, Political-A, no. 57, From the Honorable J. G. Cumming to the Honorable C. A. Barron, 3 November 1914, 3.

94. NAI, Home Department, Political-A, no. 57, From Lieutenant Governor of Punjab to the Viceroy, 24 November 1914, 5.

95. NAI, Home Department, Political-A, no. 57, From Lieutenant Governor of Punjab to the Viceroy, 24 November 1914, 5.

96. NAI, Home Department, Political-A, no. 57, Extract from a letter from His Excellency the Viceroy, to His Excellency the Lord Carmichael of Skirling, Governor of Bengal, 27 November 1914, 5.

97. BL/IOR, 1/PJ/6 1338, file 5028, *'Komagata Maru' Committee of Enquiry: Volume III* (23 October–4 December 1914), exhibit 74: From Mir Muhammad Khan to the Editor of the Loyal Gazette, Lahore, 169.

98. BL/IOR, 1/PJ/6 1338, file 5028, *'Komagata Maru' Committee of Enquiry: Volume III* (23 October–4 December 1914), exhibit 74: From Mir Muhammad Khan to the Editor of the Loyal Gazette, Lahore, 169.

99. See, for example, the Case of Sidi Cassim. BL/IOR, R/2/747/331, file R/C 574, C/44, 1917.

100. "Punjab Legislative Council," *Tribune,* 11 January 1918, 5.

101. BL/IOR, 1/PJ/6 1338, file 5028, *'Komagata Maru' Committee of Enquiry: Volume III* (23 October–4 December 1914), Parliamentary Notice, 8 February 1915.

102. Singh, *Voyage,* 51.

103. Singh, *Voyage,* 125.

104. Singh, *Voyage,* 54.

105. Singh, *Voyage,* 59. It appears that the reference is to the Jagannath Temple, in Puri, Orissa.

106. Singh, *Voyage,* 59.

107. Singh, *Voyage,* 71.

108. Singh, *Voyage,* 156.

109. Singh, *Voyage,* 156.

110. Singh, *Voyage*, 105.

111. Singh, *Voyage*, 81.

112. Singh, *Voyage*, 125.

113. Singh, Voyage, 125. For a discussion of the Jallianwalla Bhag Massacre see Fein, *Imperial Crime and Punishment.*

114. Singh, *Voyage*, 125.

115. Singh, *Voyage*, 126.

116. NAI, Political Department Notes, Pros. "B," nos. 206–38, October 1915. "Translation of the selected articles from the Hindustan Ghadr of 4ᵗʰ April 1915." "Dacoit" was a term used by colonial officials in India for an armed bandit or a robber.

117. NAI, Political Department Notes, Pros. "B," nos. 206–38, October 1915. "Translation of the selected articles from the Hindustan Ghadr of 4ᵗʰ April 1915."

118. Singh, *Voyage*, 131.

119. Singh, *Voyage*, 145.

120. Singh, *Voyage*, 146.

121. Singh, *Voyage*, 146.

122. Singh, *Voyage*, 146.

123. Johnston, *Voyage of the Komagata Maru,* 170.

124. Singh, *Voyage*, 147.

125. Singh, *Voyage*, 147.

126. Singh, *Voyage*, 147. See Guha, *Gandhi before India.* For a more recent and controversial account, see Desai and Vahed, *The South African Gandhi.*

127. Singh, *Voyage*, 147.

128. Singh, *Voyage*, 147.

129. Singh, *Voyage*, 35.

130. "Komagata Maru Recalled: Dramatic Appearance of Absconder," *Leader,* 19 November 1921, 8. "Panth" refers to the spiritual path of Sikhism. "Swaraj" means "home rule" or "self-rule" and was used by Gandhi to signal Indian independence.

131. "Komagata Maru Recalled: Dramatic Appearance of Absconder," *Leader,* 19 November 1921, 8.

132. Singh, *Voyage*, 35.

133. *Report,* 2.

134. *Report,* 2.

135. *Report,* 2.

136. NAI, Home Department, Political, no. 132, From Members of the Komagata Maru Committee to the Secretary of the Government of India, 3 December 1914, 8.

137. "Komagata Enquiry: Report of the Committee," Supplement to *The Tribune,* 19 January 1915, 2.

138. *Report,* 2

139. *Report,* 8.

140. BL/IOR, 1/PJ/6 1338, file 5028, *'Komagata Maru' Committee of Enquiry: Volume III* (23 October–4 December 1914), Testimony of Pal Singh, 217.

141. BL/IOR, 1/PJ/6 1338, file 5028, *'Komagata Maru' Committee of Enquiry: Volume III* (23 October–4 December 1914), Testimony of Jagat Singh, 220.

142. *Lahore Conspiracy Case,* Judgment, In re King Emperor versus Anand Kishore and Others, Part II, 1915, 75. Simon Fraser Special Collections and Rare Books, Komagata Maru—Continuing the Journey Collection.

143. *Report,* 22.

144. NAI, Home Department, Political-A, Note on the Budge Budge Riot, 17 October 1914, 28.

145. NAI, Home Department, Political-A, no. 219, From D. D. Phillott September 1914, 13.

146. NAI, Home Department, Political-A, no. 219, From D. D. Phillott September 1914, 13.

147. NAI, Home Department, Political, no. 132, From the Komagata Maru Committee of Enquiry to the Secretary to the Government of India, 3 December 1914, 10.

148. NAI, Home Department, Notes, Political, no. 430, 1924, "Notice of the institution of a civil suit against the Secretary of State for compensation in connection with the 'Komagata Maru' Affair," 3 and 6.

149. NAI, Home Department, Notes, Political, no. 419, no.106, From Home Department to the Director, Intelligence Bureau, 30 November 1921, 2.

150. NAI, Home Department, Notes, Political, no. 419, no. 106, From Craik to Director, Intelligence Bureau, 3 December 1921, 2.

151. NAI, Home Department, Notes, Political, no. 419, no. 106, Draft Summary, 30 December 1921, 4.

152. "Baba Gurdit Singh in Amritsar," *Tribune,* 9 March 1922, 5.

153. "Baba Gurdit Singh in Amritsar," *Tribune,* 9 March 1922, 5.

154. Baba Gurdit Sinch's [*sic*] Case: Text of Judgment," *The Tribune* (hereafter "Text of Judgment"), 3.

155. "Text of Judgment," 3.

156. India, The Prevention of Seditious Meetings Act, 1911.

157. Tatla and Tatla, *Sardar Gurdit Singh,* 25

158. "Text of Judgment," 3.

159. "Text of Judgment," 3.

160. "Text of Judgment," 3.

161. Singh, *Voyage,* 160.

162. I am drawing here from Derrida's remarks on Mandela where he describes him as a man of law (as a lawyer) and an outlaw. See Derrida, "The Laws of Reflection," 73.

163. "Text of Judgment," 3.

164. For a discussion of the legal archive as a site of destruction/production, see Mawani, "Law's Archive."

165. Derrida, "Laws of Reflection," 82.

166. "Text of Judgment," 3.

167. "Crown v. Baba Gurdit Singh: Written Statement Filed," *Tribune,* 29 June 1922, 4.

168. "Text of Judgment," 3 (my emphasis).

169. "Text of Judgment," 3

170. "Baba Gurdit Singh's Case," *Tribune,* 17 August 1922, 1.

171. "Text of Judgment," 3

172. "Text of Judgment," 3

173. "Text of Judgment," 3

174. On the taboos of seaborne journeys, see Anderson, *Convicts in the Indian Ocean;* Ghosh, *Sea of Poppies;* Yang, "Indian Convict Workers in Southeast Asia in the Late Eighteenth and Early Nineteenth Centuries."

175. These prohibitions on seafaring are in the Laws of Manu. See Paine, *The Sea and Civilization,* 140.

176. "Baba Gurdit Singh's Case," *Tribune,* 17 August 1922, 1.

177. Kawash, "Fugitive Properties," 247 (my emphasis).

178. Kawash, "Fugitive Properties," 247 (my emphasis).

179. Singh, *Voyage,* 156.

180. Singh, *Voyage,* 1.

181. A few Indian scholars have linked the *Komagata Maru* to struggles for Indian independence. For a brief discussion, see Waraich and Sidhu, *Komagata Maru: A Challenge to Colonialism, Key Documents,* 338.

182. Tatla, preface to Tatla, *Voyage of the Komagata Maru.*

183. Singh, *Voyage,* 128.

184. Singh, *Voyage,* chap. 4, 44.

185. Two pages from Singh's diary (251–53) were submitted as evidence to the Komagata Maru Committee of Enquiry. See BL/IOR, 1/PJ/6/1338, file 5032, *'Komagata Maru' Committee of Enquiry: Volume III* (23 October–4 December 1914), exhibit 52, 101.

186. Singh, *Voyage,* 163.

187. Singh, *Voyage,* foreword.

188. Singh, *Voyage,* foreword.

189. Singh, *Voyage,* chap. 1, 17.

190. Singh, *Voyage,* 57,

191. Singh, *Voyage,* chap. 4, 100.

192. Singh, *Voyage,* 55.

193. Singh, *Voyage,* 53.

194. Singh, *Voyage,* 59.

195. Singh, *Voyage,* chap. 1, 17.

196. In my reading, Singh was not saying that indenture was a new system of slavery but that the two were linked through abolition. Several scholars have made the argument about indenture as slavery. See Tinker, *A New System of Slavery.* Chanderbali argues that many reformers and advocates made similar arguments. See Chanderbali, *Indian Indenture,* 48–51.

197. These distinctions are examined by Herzog in "Convenient Compromises."

198. Herzog, "Convenient Compromises," vi.

199. See Parmer, "Colonial Labor Policy and Administration."

200. Parmer, "Colonial Labor Policy and Administration," 7.

201. Drabble, "The Plantation Rubber Industry in Malaya up to 1922," 53.

202. For an overview of this, see Das, *The Torrens System in Malaya.*

203. Torrens draws the link between shipping and land reform in *The South Australia System of Conveyancing,* vi. Although the Torrens system is frequently cited, few have drawn connections to imperial shipping. For a notable exception, see Bhandar, "Title by

Registration," 258. I develop this point on Torrens registration as a land reform system that emerged from the sea in "Law, Settler Colonialism, and 'the Forgotten Space' of Maritime Worlds," 119–22.

204. Bhandar, "Title by Registration," 59.

205. Taylor, *The Law of the Land*, 65.

206. Bhandar, "Title by Registration," 258. For the commodification of village lands and new land holdings in Malaya, see Ong, *Spirits of Resistance and Capitalist Discipline*, 18.

207. On the abstraction of the slave manifest, see Philip, *Zong!*, 185, 194; Sharpe, *In the Wake*, 94.

208. Bhandar, "Title by Registration," 256; see also Keenan, "Smoke, Curtains, and Mirrors." In the context of Malaya, see Hagan and Wells, "The British and Rubber in Malaya, c1890–1940," 143.

209. Bhandar, "Title by Registration," 256.

210. Taylor, *The Law of the Land*, 6.

211. See Bhandar, "Title by Registration," 274.

212. Hagan and Wells, "The British and Rubber in Malaya, c1890–1940." For a discussion of Torrens and Islamic law, see Hussin, *The Politics of Islamic Law*, 91.

213. Milner, *The Invention of Politics in Colonial Malaya*, 117.

214. Ong, *Spirits of Resistance and Capitalist Discipline*, 19–21. For a classic account of representations of indigenous Malays, see Alatas, *The Myth of the Lazy Native*.

215. Ong, *Spirits of Resistance and Capitalist Discipline*, 20–21.

216. See Thomas, *Violence and Colonial Order*, 183; Hagan and Wells, "The British and Rubber, c1890–1940," 143.

217. On Singh in Selangor, see Johnston, *Voyage of the Komagata Maru*, 53.

218. On the infrastructure that connected plantations to ports, see McKittrick, "Plantation Futures," 8. It is important to note that McKittrick is discussing the Caribbean, but one could make the same argument for plantations elsewhere, including in the Straits Settlements.

219. The quote comes from McKittrick, "Plantation Futures," 8. Changes in land reforms generated profits that were used to build infrastructure, including roads and railways. See Chanderbali, *Indian Indenture in the Straits Settlements*, 18

220. Singh, *Voyage*, chap. 1, 4.

221. Singh, *Voyage*, chap. 1, 3.

222. On the relation between indenture and slavery in the U.S. context, see Jung, *Coolies and Cane;* in the Caribbean, see Kale, *Fragments of Empire*. On the role of sugar in British imperial culture, see Gikandi, *Slavery and the Culture of Taste*, 109–10.

223. Singh, *Voyage*, 4.

224. Singh, *Voyage*, 4.

225. Singh was not alone. C. F. Andrews and Gopal Krishna Gokhale also drew connections between indenture and transatlantic slavery. See Chandarbali, *Indian Indenture in the Straits Settlements*, 48–49.

226. Mongia, "Impartial Regimes of Truth," 752.

227. Lowe, *The Intimacies of Four Continents*, 38.

228. Singh, *Voyage*, 2.

229. Singh, *Voyage*, 4. For a very useful discussion of slavery, indenture, and convict labor as a "continuum of labour exploitation" and unfreedom, see Anderson, "After Emancipation," 121.

230. Singh, *Voyage*, chap. 1, 3.

231. Singh, *Voyage*, 3.

232. Singh, *Voyage*, 3

233. Singh *Voyage*, 1.

234. Singh, *Voyage*, 14. Singh was likely referring to the continuous journey regulation.

235. Singh, *Voyage*, 15.

236. Singh, *Voyage*, 15.

237. Singh, *Voyage*, 15.

238. Singh, *Voyage*, 199.

239. Singh, *Voyage*, 188.

240. Singh, *Voyage*, 199.

241. Singh, *Voyage*, 200.

242. Best and Hartman, "Fugitive Justice," 3.

243. Neil Roberts argues that "freedom is a process of flight." See Roberts, *Freedom as Marronage*, 13.

244. Singh, *Voyage*, 159.

245. Singh, *Voyage*, 159.

246. Singh, *Voyage*, foreword, 1–2.

247. Singh, *Voyage*, foreword, 1.

248. This last page is missing from Singh's *Voyage*. I am drawing from Tatla, *Voyage of the Komagata Maru*, 235.

249. Singh, *Voyage*, 195 (my emphasis).

250. Singh, *Voyage*, 195.

251. Singh, *Voyage*, 197.

252. Singh, *Voyage*, 196.

253. Singh's name was spelled "Giani" and "Gyani." NAI, Home Department, Intelligence Bureau, no. 200, "Report Re: Giani Harnam Singh of the Khalsa Diwan Society, Vancouver, B.C., 30 September 1926.

254. On partition see Zamindar, *The Long Partition and the Making of Modern South Asia*.

255. Wong, *Neither Fugitive nor Free*, esp. chap. 4. See also Bolster, *Black Jacks;* Visram, *Ayahs, Princes, and Lascars*.

EPILOGUE

1. Armitage, "The Elephant and the Whale," 27.

2. On the relation between ships and the production of space, see Siegert, *Cultural Techniques*, 70.

3. Heller and Pezzani, "Liquid Traces," 662. See also *United Nations Convention on the Law of the Sea*.

4. James Muldoon notes that *Mare Liberum* did not establish freedom of travel and trade for everyone. Rather, it ensured "the freedom of every European Maritime nation

to trade with any other nation." See Muldoon, "Who Owns the Sea?" 24. Scholars have argued that Grotius gave Locke the architecture to develop his argument about labor and property in the *Second Treatise of Government*. See Armitage, introduction to *The Free Sea*, xvi–xvii.

5. For Schmitt, land and sea was an opposition of East/West and Orient/Occident. See Schmitt, "The Planetary Tension between Orient and Occident," 3. On Orient/Occident as a colonial and civilizational distinction, see Said, *Orientalism*. On the ideological aspects of the elementary, see Connery, "Ideologies of Land and Sea."

6. See Hegel, *The Philosophy of History*, 90. For a useful discussion of Hegel, Europe, and the sea, see Wick, *The Red Sea*, 57–63.

7. Schmitt, *Land and Sea*, 74. The opposition of land and sea was, of course, materialized in the distinction between the common law (land) and admiralty law (sea).

8. Schmitt, *Land and Sea*, 93.

9. Schmitt, *Land and Sea*, 93.

10. Schmitt, *Land and Sea*, 93.

11. Schmitt, *Land and Sea*, 93. Schmitt argued that the decline of the sea and of Britain as a maritime empire was the result of another element: air. On Schmitt and the rise of German air power, see Hussain, "Air Power."

12. Mirzoeff, "The Sea and the Land," 291.

13. For a classic argument against empty oceans, see Steinberg, *The Social Construction of the Ocean*.

14. Recall that for Schmitt "on the waves there is nothing but waves." See *The* Nomos *of the Earth*, 42–43.

15. On the Pacific, see Hau'ofa, *We Are the Ocean;* Igler, *The Great Ocean*. On the Atlantic, see Lipmann, *Saltwater Frontier;* Weaver, *The Red Atlantic*.

16. James Croll, "Letters to the Editor: Ocean Currents," *Nature*, 11 January 1872, 201.

17. Indigenous and Indian travelers continued to traverse ocean regions, despite the lines of the cartographer's map. See Chappell, "Ahab's Boat," 76. For later periods, see Amrith, *Crossing the Bay of Bengal*. On indigenous-European struggles over the Pacific, see Diaz, "Voyaging for Anti-colonial Recovery; Hau'ofa, *We Are the Ocean*. See also Lyons and Tengan, "Pacific Currents"; Mar, *Decolonization and the Pacific*. On the Atlantic in this regard, see Lipmann, *Saltwater Frontier;* Weaver, *The Red Atlantic*.

18. On this point about the separation of settler colonialism from slavery and indenture, see Lowe, *The Intimacies of Four Continents*, esp. the introduction.

19. Oceans have been described by some as a "patchy legal space," see Heller and Pezzani, "Liquid Traces," 663. See also Benton, *A Search for Sovereignty*, esp. chap. 3.

20. Alexis Wick notes that a "thalassological genealogy of the Western tradition," brings us back to Europe's primeval sea as "the cradle of European civilization." See Wick, *The Red Sea*, 61. The key text is still Braudel's *The Mediterranean*.

21. Heller and Pezzani, "Liquid Traces," 657.

22. International Organization for Migration, "UN Migration Agency: Mediterranean Migrant Deaths Top 3,000 for 4th Straight Year," 28 November 2017. https://reliefweb .int/report/world/un-migration-agency-mediterranean-migrant-deaths-top-3000-4th -straight-year (accessed 29 November 2017).

23. On the "Black Mediterranean," see Sharpe, *In the Wake,* 58–59. On the Mediterranean and slavery, see Ungerer, *The Mediterranean Apprenticeship of British Slavery.*

24. "Man accused of being captain of capsized migrant ship on trial in Italy," *The Guardian,* 12 January 2016. https://www.theguardian.com/world/2016/jan/12/man-accused-of
-being-captain-of-capsized-migrant-ship-on-trial-in-italy (accessed 30 January 2016).

25. I develop this point about the archive of the sea further in Mawani, "Archival Legal History." On the Indian Ocean as legal archive, see Motha, *Archiving Sovereignty.* For an account of how the sea has become an archive for remembering slavery, see Hameed, "Black Atlantis," and Philip, *Zong!*

26. Eric Reguly, "Captain in Mediterranean Migrant Disaster Charged with Manslaughter," *Globe and Mail,* 21 April 2015. http://www.theglobeandmail.com/news/world/italian
-prosecutors-charge-tunisian-captain-with-reckless-homicide-in-mediterranean-migrant
-disaster/article24041402/ (accessed 14 February 2016).

27. Heller and Pezzani, "Liquid Traces," 670.

ARCHIVES AND LIBRARIES

British Library, India Office Records and Private Papers (BL/ IOR)
    Public and Judicial Department, 1792–1955
    Western India States Agency, 1802–1947
Caird Library and Archive
    Lloyd's Weekly Shipping Index
City of Vancouver Archives
    Henry Herbert Stevens Fonds, 1878—1935
Glasgow City Archives
    Charles Connell and Co. Ltd.
    Day book, 1886–1895
    Journal, 1884–1892
    Ledger, 1886–1893
    Ship Accounts, 1889–1890 (Ship Numbers 165–169)
Guildhall Library
    Lloyd's Register of Ships
    Lloyd's Weekly Shipping Index, 1880–1917
Library and Archives Canada
    RG 7—Governor General's Office
    RG 76—Records of the Immigration Branch
    R 194—Department of Agriculture
National Archives of India
    Home Department, Political
    Home Department, Intelligence Bureau
    Private Collections
Simon Fraser University Special Collections and Rare Books
    Kohaly Collection
    Komagata Maru—Continuing the Journey Collection
The Statue of Liberty—Ellis Island Foundation, Inc.
University of British Columbia Rare Books and Special Collections
    SPAM Periodical Collection
Vancouver Public Library Special Collections
    Leonard Frank Collection
    Dominion Photo Company Collection

LEGAL CASES

Abd-ul-Messih v. Chukri Farra (1888) Privy Council 13 App Case 431
Re Rahim (1911) B.C.R. 16, 469
Re Rahim (No. 2) (1911) 16 B.C.R. 471
Re Thirty-Nine Hindus (1913) 15 D.L.R. 189
Re Munshi Singh (1914) 20 B.C.R. 243

NEWSPAPERS AND PERIODICALS

Chambers's Journal (London)
Civil and Military Gazette (Lahore)
Harper's Monthly Magazine (New York)
Hindi Punch (Bombay)
Hindustanee (Vancouver)
Indian Opinion (Natal/ Phoenix)
Khalsa Advocate (Amritsar)
Leader (Allahabad)
Modern Review (Calcutta)
Nature (London)
New York Times (New York)
Pioneer (Allahabad)
Register (Adelaide)
Rhodesia Herald (Harare)
San Francisco Call (San Francisco)
Tribune (Chandigarh)
Vancouver Sun (Vancouver)

PUBLISHED PRIMARY SOURCES

Angel, Captain W. H. *The Clipper Ship 'Sheila.'* London: Heath Cranton, 1919.
Chand, Arjan Singh. *Khalsa Diwan Society Diary.* Vancouver, 1959. http:// komagatamarujourney.ca/node/15901 (accessed 30 June 2016).
Clogston, H. C. *Commission to Investigate Hindu Claims following Refusal of Immigration Officials to Allow over 300 Hindus Aboard the S.S. Komagata Maru to Land at Vancouver.* Vancouver, 1914.
Detsey, Robert. *A Manual of the Law Relating to Shipping and Admiralty.* San Francisco: Sumner Whitney, 1879.
Douglass, Frederick. *Narrative of the Life of Frederick Douglass, an American Slave, Written by Himself.* 6th ed. London: H. G. Collins, 1851.
Fell, Edgar Tremlett. *Recent Problems in Admiralty Jurisdiction.* Baltimore: Johns Hopkins Press, 1922.
Fleming, Sanford. *Uniform Non-Local Time (Terrestrial Time).* Ottawa, 1876.

Grotius, Hugo. "Defense of Chapter V of the *Mare Liberum*." In *The Free Sea* by Hugo Grotius, translated by Richard Hakluyt, edited by David Armitage, 77–130. Indianapolis: Liberty Fund, 2004.

Grotius, Hugo. *The Freedom of the Seas, or, The Right Which Belongs to the Dutch to Take Part in the East Indian Trade.* Translated by Ralph Van Deman Magoffin. New York: Oxford University Press, 1916.

Grotius, Hugo. *The Free Sea.* Translated by Richard Hakluyt. Edited, with an introduction, by David Armitage. Indianapolis, IN: Liberty Fund, 2004.

Grotius, Hugo. "The Free Sea: A Disputation Concerning the Right Which the Hollanders Ought to Have to the Indian Merchandise for Trading." In *The Free Sea* by Hugo Grotius, translated by Richard Hakluyt, edited by David Armitage, 5–62. Indianapolis: Liberty Fund, 2004.

Importers' Directory: Compiled for the Use of Livestock Importers. U.S. Consuls Banks, 1891.

India, Intelligence Bureau. *The Ghadr Directory: Containing the Names of Persons Who Have Taken Part in the Ghadr Movement in America, Europe, Africa and Afghanistan, as well as India.* Patiala: Punjabi University, 1934.

Jebb, Richard. *Studies in Colonial Nationalism.* London: Edward Arnold, 1905.

Jones, Burr W. *Commentaries on the Law of Evidence in Civil Cases.* San Francisco: Bancroft-Whitney, 1908.

Laufer, B. "Indian Shipping: A History of the Sea-Borne Trade and Maritime Activity of the Indians from the Earliest Times." *American Anthropologist* 19, no. , no. 1 (1917): 75–78.

Leach, A. J., comp. *The Ordinances of the Legislative Council of the Colony of Hong Kong From the Year 1844 to the Year 1890.* Volume II. Hong Kong: Norhona & Government Printers, 1892.

Lubbock, Basil. *Coolie Ships and Oil Sailors.* Glasgow: Brown, Son, and Ferguson, 1935.

Lubbock, Basil. *The Western Ocean Packets.* New York: Dover, 1925.

Maine, Henry Sumner. *Village-Communities in the East and West: Six Lectures Delivered at Oxford.* London: John Murray, Albemarle Street, 1871.

Maxwell, John Irving. *The Spirit of Marine Law or Compendium of the Statutes Relating to the Admiralty.* London: Printed by Bunny and Gold, 1800.

Mookerji, Radhakumud. *Indian Shipping: A History of the Sea-borne Trade and Activity of the Indians from Earliest Times.* London: Longmans, Green, 1912.

Piggott, Francis Taylor. *Nationality: Naturalization and English Law on the High Seas and Beyond the Realm.* Part 1. London: William Clowes and Sons, 1907.

Raithby, John, ed. *The Statutes Relating to the Admiralty, Navy, Shipping, and Navigation of the United Kingdom: From 9 Hen III. To 5 Geo. IV, Inclusive.* London: George Eyre and Andrew Strahan, Printers to the King's Most Excellent Majesty, 1823.

Report of the Komagata Maru Committee of Inquiry. Calcutta: Superintendent Government Printing, India 1914.

Selden, John. *Of the Dominion or Ownership of the Sea: Two Books.* London: Printed by William Du-Guard, 1652.

Singh, Baba Gurdit. *Voyage of the Komagatamaru, or India's Slavery Abroad.* Calcutta, 1928.

Singh, Gurdit. *Zulmi Katha.* 1921. Repr., Chandigarh: Unistar, 2007.

Swinton, Captain, and Mrs. Swinton. *Journal of a Voyage with Coolie Emigrants from Calcutta to Trinidad.* London, Alfred W. Bennett, 1859.

Thring, Henry, and Thomas Henry Farrer. *Memorandum on the Merchant Shipping Law Consolidation Bill.* London: Printed by George E. Eyre and William Spottiswoode, 1854.

Torrens, Sir Robert Richard. *The South Australia System of Conveyancing by Registration of Title.* Adelaide: Observer General Printing Offices, 1859.

Waterson, William. *A Cyclopaedia of Commerce, Mercantile Law, Finance, Commercial Geography, and Navigation.* With John Ramsay McCulloch. London: H. G. Bohn, 1847.

Welwod, William. "Of the Community and Propriety of the Seas." In *The Free Sea* by Hugo Grotius, translated by Richard Hakluyt, edited by David Armitage, 65–74. Indianapolis: Liberty Fund, 2004.

SECONDARY SOURCES

Ahuja, Dilip. "Mendacity in Our Midst: Treatments in Ramanujan, Max Muller, and in Ancient Indian Behaviour Codes." *Economic and Political Weekly* 38, no. 18 (2003): 1795–99.

Aiyar, Sana. "Anticolonial Homelands across the Indian Ocean: The Politics of the Indian Diaspora in Kenya, c. 1930–1950." *American Historical Review* 111, no. 6 (2011): 987–1013.

Alatas, Syed Hussein. *The Myth of the Lazy Native.* Abingdon, Oxon: Routledge, 2006.

Alexandrowicz, Charles Henry. *An Introduction to the History of the Law of Nations in the East Indies (16th, 17th, and 18th Centuries).* Oxford: Oxford University Press, 1967.

Allen, Richard B. *Slaves, Freedmen, and Indentured Laborers in Colonial Mauritius.* Cambridge: Cambridge University Press, 1999.

Amrith, Sunil. *Crossing the Bay of Bengal: The Furies of Nature and the Fortunes of Migrants.* Cambridge, MA: Harvard University Press, 2013.

Amrith, Sunil. *Migration and Diaspora in Modern Asia.* Cambridge: Cambridge University Press, 2011.

Anderson, Clare. "After Emancipation: Empires and Imperial Formations." In *Emancipation and the Remaking of the British Imperial World,* edited by Catherine Hall, Nicholas Draper, and Keith McClelland, 113–27. Manchester: University of Manchester Press, 2014.

Anderson, Clare. "Convicts and Coolies: Rethinking Indentured Labour in the Nineteenth Century." *Slavery and Abolition* 30, no. 1 (2009): 93–109.

Anderson, Clare. *Convicts in the Indian Ocean: Transportation from South Asia to Mauritius.* London: Palgrave-MacMillan, 2000.

Anderson, Clare, Niklas Frykman, Lex Heerma van Voss, and Markus Rediker, eds. *Mutiny and Maritime Radicalism in the Age of Revolution: A Global Survey.* Special issue, *International Review of Social History* 21 (December 2013).

Anderson, Kevin B. *Marx at the Margins: On Nationalism, Ethnicity, and Non-Western Societies.* Chicago: University of Chicago Press, 2010.

Anghie, Antony. "Identifying Regions in the History of International Law." In *The Oxford Handbook of the History of International Law,* edited by Bardo Fassbender and Anne Peters, 1058–80. Oxford: Oxford University Press 2012.

Anghie, Antony. *Imperialism, Sovereignty, and the Making of International Law.* Cambridge: Cambridge University Press, 2007.

Anim-Addo, Anya, William Hasty, and Kimberley Peters. "The Mobilities of Ships and Shipped Mobilities." *Mobilities* 9, no. 3 (2014): 337–49.

Armitage, David. "The Elephant and the Whale: Empires of Land and Sea." *Journal for Maritime Research* 9, no. 1 (2007): 23–36.

Armitage, David. *The Ideological Origins of the British Empire.* Cambridge: Cambridge University Press, 2000.

Armitage, David. Introduction to *The Free Sea,* by Hugo Grotius, translated by Richard Hakluyt, edited by David Armitage, xi–xx. Indianapolis: Liberty Fund, 2004.

Armitage, David, and Alison Bashford. "Introduction: The Pacific and Its Histories." In *Pacific Histories: Ocean, Land, People,* edited by David Armitage and Alison Bashford, 1–28. Palgrave-Macmillan, 2014.

Armstrong, Tim. "Slavery, Insurance, and Sacrifice in the Black Atlantic." In, *Sea Changes: Historicizing the Ocean,* edited by Bernard Klein and Gesa Mackenthun, 167–85. New York: Routledge, 2004.

Ashforth, Adam. *The Politics of Official Discourse in Twentieth-Century South Africa.* Oxford: Clarendon Press, 1990.

Bahadur, Gaitura. *Coolie Woman: The Odyssey of Indenture.* Chicago: University of Chicago Press, 2013.

Balachandran, G. *Globalizing Labour: Indian Seafarers and World Shipping, c. 1870–1945.* Oxford: Oxford University Press, 2012.

Balachandran, G. "Indefinite Transits: Mobility and Confinement in the Age of Steam." *Journal of Global History* 11, no. 2 (2016): 187–208.

Bald, Vivek. *Bengali Harlem and the Lost Histories of South Asian America.* Cambridge, MA: Harvard University Press, 2013.

Ballantyne, Tony. "Archive, Discipline, State: Power and Knowledge in South Asian Historiography." *Asian Studies* 3, no. 1 (2001): 87–105.

Ballantyne, Tony. *Between Colonialism and Diaspora: Sikh Cultural Formations in an Imperial World.* Durham, NC: Duke University Press, 2006.

Ballantyne, Tony. "Mobility, Empire, Colonization." *History Australia* 11, no. 2 (2014): 7–37.

Ballantyne, Tony. *Orientalism and Race: Aryanism in the British Empire.* London: Palgrave-Macmillan, 2001.

Ballantyne, Tony. "Race and the Webs of Empire: Aryanism from India to the Pacific." *Journal of Colonialism and Colonial History* 2, no. 3 (2001).

Ballantyne, Tony. *Webs of Empire: Locating New Zealand's Colonial Past.* Vancouver: University of British Columbia Press, 2012.

Ballantyne, Tony, and Antoinette Burton. *Empires and the Reach of the Global, 1870–1945.* Cambridge, MA: Harvard University Press, 2014.

Ballantyne, Tony, and Antoinette Burton. "Global Empires, Transnational Connections." In *A World Connecting, 1870–1945,* edited by Emily S. Rosenberg, 285–431. Cambridge, MA: Harvard University Press, 2012.

Banerjee, Sukanya. *Becoming Imperial Citizens: Indians in the Late Victorian Empire.* Durham, NC: Duke University Press, 2010.

Banner, Stuart. *How the Indians Lost Their Land: Law and Power on the Frontier.* Cambridge, MA: Harvard University Press, 2007.

Banner, Stuart. *Possessing the Pacific: Land, Settlers, and Indigenous Peoples from Australia to Alaska.* Cambridge, MA: Harvard University Press, 2007.

Barak, On. *On Time: Technology and Temporality in Modern Egypt.* Berkeley: University of California Press, 2013.

Barman, Jean. *Stanley Park's Secret: The Forgotten Families of Whoi Whoi, Kanaka Ranch, and Brockton Point.* Vancouver: Harbour Publishing, 2007.

Barrows, Adam. *The Cosmic Time of Empire: Modern Britain and World Literature.* Berkeley: University of California Press, 2010.

Bashford, Alison. "Immigration Restriction: Rethinking Period and Place from Settler Colonies to Postcolonial Nations." *Journal of Global History* 9, no. 1 (2014): 26–48.

Bashford, Alison. "Is White Australia Possible? Race, Colonialism, and Tropical Medicine." *Ethnic and Racial Studies* 23, no. 2 (2000): 248–71.

Bashford, Alison. *Medicine at the Border: Disease, Globalization and Security, 1850 to the Present.* New York: Palgrave, 2007.

Baucom, Ian. *Specters of the Atlantic: Finance Capital, Slavery, and the Philosophy of History.* Durham, NC: Duke University Press, 2005.

Baum, Bruce. *The Rise and Fall of the Caucasian Race: A Political History of Racial Identity.* New York: New York University Press, 2006.

Beck, Roger S. *History of South Africa.* Westport, CT: Greenwood Press, 2000.

Beckert, Sven. *Empire of Cotton: A Global History.* New York: Knopf, 2014.

Benians, E. A. "The Suez Canal, Coaling Stations." In *The Cambridge History of the British Empire,* vol. 3, edited by John Holland Rose, 200–202. Cambridge: Cambridge University Press, 1929.

Bennett, Jane. *Vibrant Matter: A Political Ecology of Things.* Durham, NC: Duke University Press, 2009.

Benton, Lauren. "Empires of Exception: History, Law, and the Problem of Imperial Sovereignty." *Quaderni di Relazioni Internazionali* 6, (2007): 54–67.

Benton, Lauren. *Law and Colonial Cultures: Legal Regimes in World History, 1400–1900.* Cambridge: Cambridge University Press, 2002.

Benton, Lauren. "The Melancholy Labyrinth: The Trial of Arthur Hodge and the Boundaries of Imperial Law." *Alabama Law Review* 64, no. 1 (2009): 91–122.

Benton, Lauren. *A Search for Sovereignty: Law and Geography in European Empires, 1400–1900.* Cambridge: Cambridge University Press, 2009.

Benton, Lauren, and Adam Clulow. "Legal Encounters and the Origins of Global Law." In *The Cambridge World History,* edited by Jerry J. Bentley, Sanjay Subrahmanyan, Merry E. Weisner-Hanks, 50–79. Cambridge: Cambridge University Press, 2015.

Benton, Lauren, and Lisa Ford. *Rage for Order: The British Empire and the Origins of International Law, 1800–1850.* Cambridge, MA: Harvard University Press, 2016.

Benton, Lauren, and Richard Ross, eds. *Legal Pluralism and Empires, 1500–1850.* New York: New York University Press, 2013.

Bergson, Henri. *Creative Evolution.* Translated by Arthur Mitchell. New York: Dover, 1998.

Bergson, Henri. *The Creative Mind: An Introduction to Metaphysics.* Translated by Mabelle L. Andison. Mineola, NY: Dover, 2007.

Berman, Paul Schiff. "An Anthropological Approach to Modern Forfeiture Law: The Symbolic Function of Legal Actions Against Objects." *Yale Journal of Law and the Humanities* 11, no. 1 (1999): 1–45.

Best, Stephen M. *The Fugitive's Properties: Law and the Poetics of Possession.* Chicago: University of Chicago Press, 2004.

Best, Stephen M., and Saidiya Hartman. "Fugitive Justice." *Representations* 92, no. 1 (2005): 1–15.

Betts, Jonathan. "John Harrison: Inventor of the Precision Timekeeper." *Endeavor* 17, no. 4 (1993): 160–167.

Bhana, Surendra. *Indentured Indian Emigrants to Natal, 1860–1902.* New Delhi: Promilla, 1991.

Bhana, Surendra, and Joy B. Brain. *Setting Down Roots: Indian Migrants in South Africa, 1860–1911.* Johannesburg: Witwatersrand University Press, 1990.

Bhandar, Brenna. "Title by Registration: Instituting Modern Property Law and Creating Racial Value in the Settler Colony." *Journal of Legal History* 42, no. 2 (2015): 253–82.

Bhattacharjea, Mira Sinha. "Gandhi and the Chinese Community in South Africa." In *India and China in the Colonial World,* edited by Madhavi Thampi, 150–66. Delhi: Social Science Press, 2005.

Birla, Ritu. *Stages of Capital: Law, Culture, and Market Governance in Late Colonial India.* Durham, NC: Duke University Press, 2009.

Bishara, Fahad. "Paper Routes: Inscribing Islamic Law across the Nineteenth Century Western Indian Ocean." *Law and History Review* 32, no. 4 (2014): 797–820.

Bishara, Fahad. *A Sea of Debt: Law and Economic Life in the Western Indian Ocean, 1780–1950.* Cambridge: Cambridge University Press, 2017.

Blackmore, David S. T. *The Seafaring Dictionary: Terms, Idioms, and Legends of the Past and Present.* Jefferson, NC: McFarland, 2009.

Blum, Hester. "The Prospect of Ocean Studies." *PMLA* 125, no. 3 (2010): 670–77.

Blythe, Robert J. *The Empire of the Raj: India, East Africa, and the Middle East, 1858–1947.* New York: Palgrave, 2003.

Bolster, Jeffrey. *Black Jacks: African Seamen in the Age of Sail.* Cambridge, MA: Harvard University Press, 1998.

Borrows, John. *Recovering Canada: The Resurgence of Indigenous Law.* Toronto: University of Toronto Press, 2002.

Borrows, John. "Wampum at Niagara: The Royal Proclamation, Canadian Legal History, and Self Government." In *Aboriginal and Treaty Rights in Canada: Essays* on *Law, Equality, and Respect for Difference,* edited by Michael Asch, 155–72. Vancouver: University of British Columbia Press, 1997.

Borschberg, Peter. "Grotius, Maritime Intra-Asian Trade, and the Portuguese Estado da India: Problems, Perspectives and Insights from *De Iure Praedae.*" *Grotiana* 26, no. 1 (2007): 31–60.

Borschberg, Peter. "Hugo Grotius, East India Trade and the King of Johor." *Journal of Southeast Asian Studies* 30, no. 2 (1999): 225–48.

Borschberg, Peter. *Hugo Grotius, the Portuguese, and Free Trade in the East Indies.* Singapore: National University of Singapore Press, 2011.

Borschberg, Peter. "Hugo Grotius' Theory of Trans-Oceanic Trade Regulation: Revisiting Mare Liberum (1609)." *Itinererio* 29, no. 3 (2005): 31–53.

Borschberg, Peter. "The Seizure of the Sta. Catarina Revisited: The Portuguese Empire in Asia, VOC Politics and the Origins of the Dutch-Johor Alliance (1602–c. 1616)." *Journal of Southeast Asian Studies* 33, no. 1 (2002): 31–62.

Bose, Sugata. *A Hundred Horizons: The Indian Ocean in the Age of Global Empire.* Cambridge, MA: Harvard University Press, 2009.

Braudel, Fernand. *The Mediterranean and the Mediterranean World in the Age of Philip II.* Vol. 1. Berkeley: University of California Press, 1996.

Brown, Stephen. "She Was Fine When She Left Here: Polysemy, Patriarchy, and Personification in Brand *Titanic*'s Birthplace." *Psychology and Marketing* 31, no. 1 (2014): 93–102.

Burbank, Jane, and Frederick Cooper. *Empires in World History: Power and the Politics of Difference.* Princeton, NJ: Princeton University Press, 2011.

Burton, Antoinette, ed. *Archive Stories: Facts, Fictions and the Writing of History.* Durham, NC: Duke University Press, 2005.

Burton, Antoinette. *At the Heart of Empire: Indians and the Colonial Encounter in Late Victorian Britain.* Berkeley: University of California Press, 1998.

Burton, Antoinette. *Brown over Black: Race and the Politics of Postcolonial Citation.* Gurgaon, India: Three Essays Collective, 2012.

Burton, Antoinette. *Burdens of History: British Feminists, Indian Women, and Imperial Culture, 1865–1915.* Durham, NC: Duke University Press, 2002.

Burton, Antoinette. "'Every Secret Thing'? Racial Politics in Ansuyah R. Singh's Behold the Earth Mourns." *Journal of Colonialism and Colonial History* 46, no. 1 (2011): 63–81.

Burton, Antoinette. "The Pain of Racism in the Making of a 'Coolie Doctor.'" *Interventions: A Journal of Postcolonial Studies* 13 (2011): 212–35.

Burton, Antoinette. "Sea Tracks and Trails: Indian Ocean Worlds as Method." *History Compass* 11, no. 7 (2013): 497–502.

Burton, Antoinette. *The Trouble with Empire: Challenges to Modern British Imperialism.* Oxford: Oxford University Press, 2015.

Byrd, Jodi. "A Return to the South." *American Quarterly* 66, no. 3 (2014): 609–20.

Byrd, Jodi. *The Transit of Empire: Indigenous Critiques of Colonialism.* Minneapolis: University of Minnesota Press, 2011.

Carretta, Vincent. *Equiano, the African: Biography of a Self-Made Man.* Athens: University of Georgia Press, 2005.

Carruthers, Bruce, and Wendy Nelson Espeland. "Accounting for Rationality: Double-Entry Bookkeeping and the Rhetoric of Economic Rationality." *American Journal of Sociology* 97, no. 1 (1991): 31–69.

Carter, J. Kameron. "Paratheological Blackness." *South Atlantic Quarterly* 112, no. 4 (2013): 589–611.

Carter, Marina. *Servants, Sirdars, and Settlers: Indians in Mauritius, 1834–1874.* Delhi: Oxford University Press, 1995.

Cateau, Heather. "Re-examining the Labour Matrix in the British Caribbean, 1750 to 1850." In *Emancipation and the Remaking of the Imperial World,* edited by Catherine Hall, Nicholas Draper, and Keith McClelland, 98–112. Manchester: University of Manchester Press, 2014.

Chakrabarty, Dipesh. *Provincializing Europe: Postcolonial Thought and Historical Difference.* Princeton, NJ: Princeton University Press, 2000.

Chanderbali, David. *Indian Indenture in the Straits Settlements: The Politics of Policy and Practice in the Straits Settlements.* Leeds, UK: Peepal Tree Press, 2008.

Chang, Kornel. *Pacific Connections: The Making of the US-Canada Borderlands.* Berkeley: University of California Press, 2012.

Chappell, David. "Ahab's Boat: Non-European Seamen in Western Ships of Exploration and Commerce." In *Sea Changes: Historicizing the Ocean,* edited by Bernard Klein and Gesa Mackenthun, 75–89. New York: Routledge, 2004.

Chatterjee, Indrani. *Gender, Slavery, and Law in Colonial India.* Oxford: Oxford University Press, 2002.

Chatterjee, Indrani, and Richard M. Eaton, eds. *Slavery and South Asian History.* Bloomington: Indiana University Press, 2006.

Chatterjee, Partha. "Anderson's Utopia." *Diacritics,* 29, no. 4 (1999): 128–134.

Chattopadhyay, Suchetana. "Closely Observed Ships." *South Asian Diaspora* 8, no. 2 (2016): 203–22.

Chattopadhyay, Suchetana. "The Last Stretch of the Journey: Komagata Maru, War-Time Political Radicalism and Migrant Workers from Punjab in Calcutta." In *Charting Imperial Itineraries: Unmooring the Komagata Maru,* edited by Rita Dhamoon, Davina Bhandar, Renisa Mawani, and Satwinder Bains. Vancouver: University of British Columbia Press: forthcoming.

Chaudhuri, Kriti N. *Trade and Civilization in the Indian Ocean: An Economic History from the Rise of Islam to 1750.* Cambridge: Cambridge University Press, 1985.

Christopher, Emma, Cassandra Pybus, and Marcus Rediker, eds. *Many Middle Passages: Forced Migration and the Making of the Modern World.* Berkeley: University of California Press, 2007.

Clover, David. "Exploring Caribbean Shipping Company Records: The Case of Sandbach, Tinne, and Co." http://sas-space.sas.ac.uk/5169/1/SCS2011_Sandbach_Tinne_and_Co.pdf (accessed 20 August 2015).

Cohn, Bernard S. *Colonialism and Its Forms of Knowledge: The British in India.* Princeton, NJ: Princeton University Press, 1996.

Connery, Christopher L. "Ideologies of Land and Sea: Alfred Thayer Mahan, Carl Schmitt, and the Shaping of Global Myth Elements." *boundary 2* 28, no. 2 (2001): 173–201.

Conrad, Joseph. *The Mirror of the Sea.* New York: Harper and Brothers, 1906.

Convention on the Law of the Sea. December 10, 1982. Enacted as "United Nations Convention on the Law of the Sea," on November 1, 1994.

Creighton, Margaret S., and Lisa Norling, eds. *Iron Men, Wooden Women: Gender and Seafaring in the Atlantic World, 1700–1920.* Baltimore: Johns Hopkins University Press, 1996.

Crouzet, Guillemette. "A Slave Trade Jurisdiction: Attempts against the Slave Trade and the Making of a Space of Law (Arabo-Persian Gulf, Indian Ocean, Red Sea, circa 1820–1900)." In *Legal Histories of the British Empire: Law, Engagements, Legacies,* edited by Shannaugh Dorsett and John McLaren, 234–49. Abingdon, Oxon: Routledge, 2014.

D'Aguiar, Fred. *Feeding the Ghosts: A Novel.* New York: HarperCollins, 1997.

Dam, Shubhankar. *Presidential Legislation in India: The Law and Practice of Ordinances.* New York: Cambridge University Press, 2014.

Darian-Smith, Eve. *Bridging Divides: The Channel Tunnel and English Legal Identity in Europe.* Berkeley: University of California Press, 1999.

Darian-Smith, Eve. *Religion, Race, Rights: Landmarks in the History of Modern Anglo-American Law.* Oxford: Hart Publishing, 2010.

Das, S. K. *The Torrens System in Malaya.* Singapore: Malaya Law Journal, 1963.

Da Silva, Denise Ferreira. "No Bodies: Law, Raciality, and Violence." *Griffith Law Review* 18, no. 2 (2009): 212–36.

Da Silva, Denise Ferreira. *Toward a Global Idea of Race.* Minneapolis: University of Minnesota Press, 2007.

Dayan, Colin. *The Law Is a White Dog: How Legal Rituals Make and Unmake Persons.* Princeton, NJ: Princeton University Press, 2013.

Deepak, B. R. "Colonial Connections: Indian and Chinese Nationalists in Japan and China." *China Report* 48, nos. 1–2 (2012): 147–70.

De Lombard, Jeannine Marie. "Salvaging Legal Personhood: Melville's Benito Cereno." *American Literature* 81, no. 1 (2009): 35–64.

Deloria, Phillip J. *Playing Indian.* New Haven, CT: Yale University Press, 1998.

Deol, Gurdev Singh. *Gadar Party Ate Bharat Da Kaumi Andolan.* Amritsar: Sikh Itihas Research Board, 1970.

Derrida, Jacques. "Force of Law." In *Acts of Religion,* edited by Gil Anidjar, 230–98. New York: Routledge, 2002.

Derrida, Jacques. "The Laws of Reflection: Nelson Mandela in Admiration." In *Psyche: Interventions of the Other,* vol. 2. Stanford: Stanford University Press, 2008.

Derrida, Jacques. *Specters of Marx: The State of Debt, the Work of Mourning, and the New International.* New York: Routledge, 1994.

Desai, Ashwin, and Goolem Vahed. *The South African Gandhi: Stretcher-Bearer of Empire.* Stanford: Stanford University Press, 2016.

Desai, Gaurav. *Commerce with the Universe: Africa, India, and the Afrasian Imagination.* New York: Columbia University Press, 2013.

Dhupelia-Mestrie, Uma. *From Cane Fields to Freedom: A Chronicle of South African Life.* Cape Town: NB Publishers, 2010.

Dhupelia-Mesthrie, Uma. "The Place of India in South African History: Academic Scholarship, Past, Present, and Future." *South African Historical Journal*, 57 (2007): 12–34.

Diaz, Vincent M. "Voyaging for Anti-colonial Recovery: Austronesian Seafaring, Archipelagic Rethinking, and the Re-Mapping of Indigeneity." *Pacific Asia Inquiry* 2, no. 1 (2011): 21–32.

Dorsett, Shaunnagh. "Mapping Territories." In *Jurisprudence of Jurisdiction*, edited by Shaun McVeigh, 137–58. Abingdon, Oxon: Routledge, 2007.

Dorsett, Shaunnagh, and Shaun McVeigh. *Jurisdiction*. Abingdon, Oxon: Routledge-Cavendish, 2012.

Dorsett, Shaunnagh, and Shaun McVeigh. "Questions of Jurisdiction." In *Jurisprudence of Jurisdiction*, edited by Shaun McVeigh, 1–18. Abingdon, Oxon: Routledge, 2007.

Douzinas, Costas. "The Metaphysics of Jurisdiction." In *Jurisprudence of Jurisdiction*, edited by Shaun McVeigh, 29–32. Abingdon, Oxon: Routledge, 2007.

Drabble, John H. "The Plantation Rubber Industry in Malaya up to 1922." *Journal of Malaysian Branch of the Royal Asiatic Society* 40, no. 1 (1967): 52–77.

Dulai, Phinder. *Dream/Arteries*. Vancouver: Talon Books, 2014.

Dunbar-Ortiz, Roxanne. *An Indigenous Peoples' History of the United States*. Boston: Beacon Press, 2015.

Dusinberre, Martin, and Roland Wenzlhuemer. "Editorial: Being in Transit: Ships and Global Incompatibilities." *Journal of Global History* 11, no. 2 (2016): 155–62.

Elam, J. Daniel. "Echoes of Ghadr: Lala Hayar Dal and the Time of Anticolonialism." *Comparative Studies of South Asia, Africa, and the Middle East* 34, no. 1 (2014): 9–23.

Elden, Stuart. *The Birth of Territory*. Chicago: University of Chicago Press, 2013.

Falconer, William. *A New Universal Dictionary of the Marine*. Edited by William Burney. Cambridge: Cambridge University Press, 2011.

Farred, Grant. "The Unsettler." *South Atlantic Quarterly* 107, no. 4 (2008): 791–808.

Fein, Helen. *Imperial Crime and Punishment: The Massacre at Jallianwalla Bhag and British Judgment, 1919–1920*. Honolulu: University of Hawai'i Press, 1977.

Fernie, J. Donald. "Finding Out the Longitude." *American Scientist* 90, no. 1 (2002): 412.

Fisher, Michael. "Working across the Seas: Indian Maritime Labourers in India, Britain, and in Between, 1600–1857." *International Review of Indian History*, 51 (2006): 21–45.

Fitzpatrick, Peter. *Modernism and the Grounds of Law*. Cambridge: Cambridge University Press, 2001.

Ford, Lisa. "Law." In *Pacific Histories: Land, Ocean, Peoples*, edited by David Armitage and Alison Bashford, 216–36. London: Palgrave, 2014.

Ford, Richard. "Law's Territory (A History of Jurisdiction)." *Michigan Law Review* 97, no. 4 (1999): 843–930.

Foucault, Michel. *Discipline and Punish: The Birth of the Prison*. New York: Pantheon Books, 1977.

Foucault, Michel. *The History of Sexuality: An Introduction*. Vol. 1. New York: Vintage, 1990.

Foxhall, Katherine. *Health, Medicine, and the Sea: Australian Voyages, c. 1815–60*. Manchester: Manchester University Press, 2012.

Gabbacia, Donna, and Dirk Hoerder, eds. *Connecting Seas and Connected Ocean Rims: Indian, Atlantic, and Pacific Oceans and China Seas Migrations from the 1830s to the 1930s*. Leiden: Brill, 2011.

Galison, Peter. *Einstein's Clocks and Poincaré's Maps: Empires of Time*. New York: W. W. Norton, 2004.

Ghosh, Amitav. *River of Smoke: A Novel*. New York: Farrar, Strauss, and Giroux, 2011.

Ghosh, Amitav. *Sea of Poppies*. Toronto: Penguin Group, 2009.

Ghuyre, Govind Sadish. *Caste and Race in India*. Mumbai: Popular Praxshan Private Limited, 2008.

Gikandi, Simon. *Slavery and the Culture of Taste*. Princeton, NJ: Princeton University Press, 2014.

Gilroy, Paul. *The Black Atlantic*. Cambridge, MA: Harvard University Press, 1993.

Glennie, Paul, and Nigel Thrift. *Shaping the Day: A History of Time-Keeping in England and Wales, 1300–1800*. Oxford: Oxford University Press, 2009.

Goldberg, David T. *Racist Culture: Philosophy and the Politics of Meaning*. Malden: Blackwell, 1993.

Goodhall, Heather, Devleena Gosh, and Lindi R. Todd. "Jumping Ship—Skirting Empire: Indians, Aborigines, and Australians across the Indian Ocean." *Transforming Cultures* 3, no. 1 (2008): 44–74.

Gorman, Daniel. *Imperial Citizenship: Empire and the Question of Belonging*. Manchester: University of Manchester Press, 2006.

Goswami, Chhaya. *Globalization before Its Time: Gujarati Traders in the Indian Ocean*. Gurgaon: Penguin Books India, 2016.

Grandin, Greg. *The Empire of Necessity: Slavery, Freedom, and Deception in the New World*. New York: Metropolitan Books, 2014.

Grewal, J. S., Harish K. Puri, and Indu Banga, eds. *The Ghadr Movement: Background, Ideology, Action and Legacies*. Patiala: Publication Bureau, Punjabi University, 2013.

Guha, Ramchandra. *Gandhi before India*. New York: Vintage, 2015.

Guha, Ranajit. "The Migrant's Time." *Postcolonial Studies* 1, no. 2 (2010): 155–60.

Guha, Sumit. "Lower Strata, Older Races, and Aboriginal Peoples: Racial Anthropology and Mythical History Past and Present. *Journal of Asian Studies* 57, no. 2 (1998): 423–41.

Guttoff, Jonathan M. "Fugitive Slaves and Ship-Jumping Sailors: The Enforcement and Survival of Coerced Labor." *U. Pa. Journal of Labor and Employment Law* 9, no. 1 (2006): 87–116.

Hagan, James, and Andrew Wells. "The British and Rubber in Malaya, c1890–1940." In *The Past Is before Us: Proceedings of the Ninth National Labour History Conference, ASSLH, Business and Labour History Group*, edited by G. Patmore, J. Shields, and N. Balnave, 143–50. Sydney: Australian Society for the Study of Labour History and Business and Labour History Group, 2005.

Hall, Catherine. *Civilizing Subjects: Metropole and Colony in the English Imagination, 1830–1867*. Chicago: University of Chicago Press, 2002.

Hall, Catherine, Nicholas Draper, Keith McClelland, Katie Donington, and Rachel Lang. *Legacies of British Slave Ownership*. Cambridge: Cambridge University Press, 2014.

Halliday, Paul D. "Law's Histories: Pluralisms, Pluralities, Diversity." In *Legal Pluralism and Empires, 1500–1850*, edited by Lauren Benton and Richard Ross, 261–78. New York: New York University Press, 2013.

Hameed, S. Ayesha. "Black Atlantis: Three Songs." In *Forensis: The Architecture of Public Truth*, edited by Forensic Architecture, 712–19. Berlin: Sternberg Press, 2014.

Haney-Lopez, Ian. *White by Law: The Legal Construction of Race*. New York: New York University Press, 2006.

Harder, Hans, and Barbara Mittler, eds. *Asian Punches: A Transcultural Affair*. New York: Springer, 2013.

Harney, Stefano, and Fred Moten. *The Undercommons*. New York: Autonomedia, 2013.

Harris, Cole. *Making Native Space: Colonialism, Resistance, and Reserves in British Columbia*. Vancouver: UBC Press, 2002.

Harris, Cole. *The Resettlement of British Columbia: Essays on Colonialism and Geographical Change*. Vancouver: UBC Press, 1997.

Harris, Leslie M. *In the Shadow of Slavery: African Americans in New York City, 1626–1863*. Chicago: University of Chicago Press, 2002.

Hartman, Saidiya. *Scenes of Subjection: Terror, Slavery, and Self-Making in Nineteenth-Century America*. Oxford: Oxford University Press, 1997.

Hau'ofa, Epeli. "Our Sea of Islands." In *A New Oceania: Rediscovering our Sea of Islands*, edited by Eric Waddell, Vijay Naidu, Epeli Hau'ofa, 2–16. Suva: University of the South Pacific School of Social and Economic Development and Beake House, 1993.

Hau'ofa, Epeli. *We Are the Ocean: Selected Works*. Honolulu: University of Hawai'i Press, 2008.

Hegel, Georg W. F. *Lectures on the Philosophy of World History: Introduction, Reason in History*. Translated by H. B. Nisbet. Cambridge: Cambridge University Press, 1975.

Hegel, Georg W. F. *The Philosophy of History*. Translated by J. Sibree. New York: Dover, 1956.

Heller, Charles, and Lorenzo Pezzani. "Liquid Traces: Investigating the Deaths of Migrants at the EU's Maritime Frontier." In *Forensis: The Architecture of Public Truth*, edited by Forensic Architecture, 657–84. Berlin: Sternberg Press, 2014.

Herzog, Shawna. "Convenient Compromises: A History of Slavery and Abolition in the British East Indies, 1795–1841." PhD diss., Washington State University, 2013.

Hess, Christian. "From Colonial Port to Socialist Metropolis: Imperialist Legacies and the Making of 'New Dalian.'" *Urban History* 38, no. 3 (2011): 373–90.

Hesse, Barnor. "Im/Plausible Deniability: Racism's Conceptual Bind. *Social Identities* 10, no. 1 (2004): 9–29.

Hesse, Barnor. "Racialized Modernity: An Analytics of White Mythologies." *Racial and Ethnic Studies* 30, no. 4 (2007): 643–66.

Ho, Engseng. *The Graves of Tarim: Genealogy and Mobility across the Indian Ocean.* Berkeley: University of California Press, 2006.

Hofmeyr, Isabel. "The Black Atlantic Meets the Indian Ocean: Forging New Paradigms of Transnationalism for the Global South—Literature and Cultural Perspectives." *Social Dynamics* 33, no. 2 (2007): 3–32.

Hofmeyr, Isabel. "The Complicating Sea: The Indian Ocean as Method." *Comparative Studies of South Asia, Africa, and the Middle East* 32, no. 3 (2012), 584–90.

Hofmeyr, Isabel. *Gandhi's Printing Press: Experiments in Slow Reading.* Cambridge, MA: Harvard University Press, 2013.

Hofmeyr, Isabel. "The Idea of 'Africa' in Indian Nationalism: Reporting the Diaspora in the Modern Review, 1907–1929." *South African Historical Journal* 57 (2007): 60–81.

Hofmeyr, Isabel. "Violent Texts, Vulnerable Readers: *Hind Swaraj* and its South African Audiences." *Public Culture* 23, no. 2 (2011): 285–97.

Hollett, David. *Passage from India to El Dorado: Guyana and the Great Migration.* Madison, NJ: Fairleigh Dickinson University Press, 1999.

Holmes, Oliver Wendell, Jr. *The Common Law.* 1881. Reprint, New York: Dover, 1991.

Howse, David. *Greenwich Time and the Discovery of the Longitude.* Oxford: Oxford University Press, 1980.

Huber, Valeska. *Channeling Mobilities: Migration and Globalization in the Suez Canal Region and Beyond, 1869–1914.* Cambridge: Cambridge University Press, 2015.

Hudson, Pat. "Slavery, the Slave Trade, and Economic Growth: A Contribution to the Debate." In *Emancipation and the Remaking of the British Imperial World,* edited by Catherine Hall, Nicholas Draper, and Keith McClelland, 36–59. Manchester: Manchester University Press, 2014.

Hughes, Heather. "The Coolies Will Elbow Us out of the Country." *Labour History Review* 72, no. 2 (2007): 155–68.

Hulme, Peter. "Cast Away: The Uttermost Parts of the Earth." In *Sea Changes: Historicizing the Ocean,* edited by Bernard Klein and Gesa Mackenthun, 187–201. New York: Routledge, 2004.

Hussain, Nasser. "Air Power." In *Spatiality, Sovereignty, and Carl Schmitt: Geographies of the Nomos,* edited by Stephen Legg, 244–50. Abingdon, Oxon: Routledge, 2011.

Hussain, Nasser. *The Jurisprudence of Emergency: Colonialism and the Rule of Law.* Ann Arbor: University of Michigan Press, 2003.

Hussin, Iza. "Circulations of Law: Colonial Precedents, Contemporary Questions." *Onati Socio-Legal Series* 2, no. 7 (2012): 18–32.

Hussin, Iza. *The Politics of Islamic Law: Local Elites, Colonial Authority, and the Making of the Muslim State.* Chicago: University of Chicago Press, 2016.

Huttenback, Robert A. "The British Empire as a 'White Man's Country'—Racial Attitudes and Immigration Legislation in the Colonies of White Settlement." *Journal of British Studies* 13, no. 1 (1973): 108–37.

Huttenback, Robert A. *Gandhi in South Africa: British Imperialism and the Indian Question, 1860–1914.* Ithaca, NY: Cornell, 1971.

Huttenback, Robert A. *Racism and Empire: White Settlers and Colored Immigrants in the Self-Governing Colonies.* Ithaca, NY: Cornell University Press, 1976.

Igler, David. *The Great Ocean: Pacific Worlds from Captain Cook to the Gold Rush.* Oxford: Oxford University Press, 2013.

Immerwahr, Daniel. "Caste or Colony? Indianizing Race in the United States." *Modern Intellectual History* 4, no. 2 (2007): 275–301.

Jackson, Shona. *Creole Indigeneity: Between Myth and Nation in the Caribbean.* Minneapolis: University of Minnesota Press, 2012.

Jaffer, Aaron. *Lascars and Indian Ocean Seafaring, 1780–1860: Shipboard Life, Unrest, and Mutiny.* Suffolk, UK: Boydell Press, 2015.

Jensen, Joan. *Passage from India: Asian Indian Immigrants in North America.* New Haven, CT: Yale University Press, 1988.

Johnson, Walter. *River of Dark Dreams: Slavery and Empire in the Cotton Kingdom.* Cambridge, MA: Harvard University Press, 2013.

Johnson, Walter. "White Lies: Human Property and Domestic Slavery aboard the Slave Ship Creole." *Atlantic Studies* 5, no. 2 (2008): 237–63.

Johnston, Hugh. *The Voyage of the Komagata Maru: The Sikh Challenge to Canada's Colour Bar.* Rev. ed. Vancouver: University of British Columbia Press, 2014.

Jones, Stephanie, and Stewart Motha. "A New Nomos Offshore and Bodies as Their Own Signs." *Law and Literature* 27, no. 2 (2015): 253–78.

Jung, Moon-Ho. *Coolies and Cane: Race, Labor, and Sugar in the Age of Emancipation.* Baltimore: Johns Hopkins University Press, 2006.

Kale, Madhavi. *Fragments of Empire: Capital, Slavery, and Indian Indentured Labor in the Caribbean.* Cambridge: Cambridge University Press, 2010.

Kalpagam, U. "Temporalities, Histories, and Routines of Rule in Colonial India." *Time and Society* 8, no. 1 (1999): 141–59.

Kalyvas, Andreas. "Carl Schmitt's Postcolonial Imagination." *Constellations,* forthcoming 2017. http://wiser.wits.ac.za/content/carl-schmitts-postcolonial-imagination-12704 (accessed December 2016).

Kant, Immanuel. "Of the Different Human Races." In *The Idea of Race,* edited by Robert Bernasconi and Tommy L. Lott, 8–22. Indianapolis: Hackett Publishing, 2000.

Karlsson, Bengt G. "Anthropology and the 'Indigenous Slot': Claims to and Debates about Indigenous Peoples' Status in India." *Critique of Anthropology* 23, no. 4 (2003): 403–23.

Karlsson, Bengt T., and Tanka Bahudur Subba, eds. *Indigeneity in India.* London: Kegan Paul, 2006.

Kawash, Samira. "Fugitive Properties." In *The New Economic Criticism: Studies at the Intersection of Literature and Economics,* edited by Martha Woodmansee and Mark Osteen, 277–90. London: Routledge, 1999.

Kazimi, Ali. *Continuous Journey.* Toronto: TV Ontario, 2004.

Kazimi, Ali. *Undesirables: White Canada and the Komagata Maru: An Illustrated History.* Toronto: Douglas and McIntyre, 2012.

Keenan, Sarah. "Smoke, Curtains, and Mirrors: The Production of Race through Time and Title Registration." *Law and Critique* 28, no. 1 (2016): 87–108.

Keene, Edward. *Beyond the Anarchical Society: Grotius, Colonialism, and Order in World Politics.* Cambridge: Cambridge University Press, 2002.

Kercher, Bruce. "The Limits of Despotic Government at Sea." In *The Grand Experiment: Law and Legal Culture in British Settler Societies,* edited by Hamar Foster, Benjamin Berger, and Andrew R. Buck, 38–54. Vancouver: University of British Columbia Press, 2008.

Khanduri, Ritu G. "Vernacular Punches: Cartoons and Politics in Colonial India." *History and Anthropology* 20, no. 4 (2009): 459–86.

King, Thomas. *The Inconvenient Indian: A Curious Account of Native People in North America.* Toronto: Doubleday Canada, 2012.

Kirton-Darling, Edward. "Searching for Pigeons in the Belfry: The Inquest, the Abolition of the Deodand and the Rise of the Family." *Law, Culture, and Humanities* (2014): 1–23.

Kolsky, Elizabeth. "Codification and the Rule of Colonial Difference." *Law and History Review* 23, no. 3 (2005): 631–83.

Kolsky, Elizabeth. "Forum: Maneuvering the Personal Law System in Colonial India." *Law and History Review* 28, no. 4 (2010): 973–1071.

Kupperberg, Paul. *A Primary Source History of the Colony of New York.* New York: Rosen Publishing, 2006.

Laing, Lionel H. "Historic Origins of Admiralty Jurisdiction in England." *Michigan Law Review* 45, no. 2 (1946): 163–82.

Lake, Marilyn, and Henry Reynolds. *Drawing the Global Color Line: White Men's Countries and the International Challenge of Racial Equality.* Cambridge: Cambridge University Press, 2008.

Law, John. "On the Methods of Long-Distance Control: Vessels, Navigation, and the Portuguese Route to India." *Sociological Review* 32 (1984): 234–63.

Lawrence, Bonita. "Gender, Race, and the Regulation of Native Identity in Canada and the United States: An Overview." *Hypatia* 18, no. 2 (2003): 3–31.

Lawrence, Bonita. *"Real" Indians and Others: Mixed-Blood Urban Native Peoples and Indigenous Nationhood.* Lincoln: University of Nebraska Press, 2004.

Lee, Geoffrey. "The Oldest European Account Book: A Florentine Bank Ledger of 1211." *Nottingham Medieval Studies* 16, no. 2 (1972): 28–60.

Lefebvre, Alexandre. "The Time of Law: Evolution in Holmes and Bergson." In *Deleuze and Law: Forensic Futures,* edited by Rosi Braidotti, Claire Colebrook, and Patrick Hanafin, 24–46. New York: Palgrave-MacMillan, 2009.

Legg, Stephen, and Alexander Vasudevan. "Introduction: Geographies of the Nomos." In *Spatiality, Sovereignty, and Carl Schmitt: Geographies of the Nomos,* edited by Stephen Legg, 1–23. Abingdon, Oxon: Routledge, 2011.

Lewis, Martin W. "Dividing the Ocean Sea." *Geographical Review* 8, no. 2 (1999): 188–214.

Lind, Douglas. "Pragmatism and Anthropomorphism: Reconceiving the Doctrine of the Personality of the Ship." *U.S.F. Maritime Law Journal* 22, no. 1 (2009–2010): 42–121.

Linebaugh, Peter. "All the Atlantic Mountains Shook." *Labour/ Le Travail* 10 (1982): 87–121.

Linebaugh, Peter, and Marcus Rediker. *The Many-Headed Hydra: Sailors, Slaves, Commoners, and the Hidden History of the Revolutionary Atlantic.* Boston: Beacon Press, 2001.

Lipmann, Andrew. *Saltwater Frontier: Indians and the Contest for the American Coast.* New Haven, CT: Yale University Press, 2015.

Look Lai, Walton. *Indentured Labor, Caribbean Sugar: Chinese and Indian Migrants to the British West Indies.* Baltimore: Johns Hopkins University Press, 1993.

Loomba, Ania. "Race and the Possibilities of Comparative Critique." *New Literary History* 40, (2009): 501–22.

Lowe, Lisa. *The Intimacies of Four Continents.* Durham, NC: Duke University Press, 2015.

Lyons, Paul, and Ty P. Kawika Tengan, eds. "Pacific Currents." Special issue, *American Quarterly* 67, no. 3 (September 2015).

Machado, Pedro. "A Forgotten Corner of the Indian Ocean: Gujarati Merchants, Portuguese India, and the Mozambique Slave Trade, c. 1730–1830." *Slavery and Abolition* 24, no. 2 (2003): 17–32.

Machado, Pedro. *Ocean of Trade: South Asian Merchants, Africa and the Indian Ocean, c. 1750–1850.* Cambridge: Cambridge University Press, 2014.

Macklin, Audrey. "Historicizing Narratives of Arrival: The Other Indian Other." In *Storied Communities: Narratives of Contact and Arrival in Constituting Political Community,* edited by Hester Lessard, Rebecca Johnson, and Jeremy Webber, 40–67. Vancouver: University of British Columbia Press.

Mamdani, Mahmood. *Citizen and Subject: Contemporary Africa and the Legacy of Late Colonialism.* Princeton, NJ: Princeton University Press, 1996.

Mamdani, Mahmood. *Define and Rule: Native as Political Identity.* Cambridge, MA: Harvard University Press, 2012.

Mandair, Arvind. *Religion and the Specter of the West: Sikhism, India, Postcoloniality, and the Politics of Translation.* New York: Columbia University Press, 2009.

Mannix, Daniel P. *Black Cargoes: A History of the Transatlantic Slave Trade.* New York: Viking, 1962.

Mar, Tracey Banivanua. *Decolonization and the Pacific: Indigenous Globalization and the Ends of Empire.* Cambridge: Cambridge University Press, 2016.

Marx, Karl. "The Future Results of British Rule in India." In *The Marx-Engels Reader,* edited by Robert C. Tucker, 659–64. 2nd ed. New York: W. W. Norton, 1978.

Marx, Karl, and Friedrich Engels. "Review: January–February 1850." *Neue Rheinische Zeitung Revue.* https://www.marxists.org/archive/marx/works/1850/01/31.htm (accessed July 2015).

Marx, Karl, and Friedrich Engels. "Review: May–October 1850." *Neue Rheinische Zeitung Revue.* https://www.marxists.org/archive/marx/works/1850/11/01.htm (accessed July 2015).

Mawani, Renisa. "Circuits of Law: The *Komagata Maru* and the Heterogeneous Lineages of Anticoloniality." In *Komagata Maru: Context, Significance, and Legacy,* edited by Jaspal Grewal and Indu Bhanga. Patiala: Punjab University Press, forthcoming.

Mawani, Renisa. *Colonial Proximities: Crossracial Encounters and Juridical Truths in British Columbia, 1871–1921.* Vancouver: University of British Columbia Press, 2009.

Mawani, Renisa. "From Colonialism to Multiculturalism? Totem Poles, Tourism, and National Identity in Vancouver's Stanley Park." *ARIEL: A Review of International English Literature* 35, nos. 1–2 (2004): 31–57.

Mawani, Renisa. "Genealogies of the Land: Aboriginality, Law, and Territory in Vancouver's Stanley Park." *Social and Legal Studies* 14, no. 3 (2005): 315–39.

Mawani, Renisa. "Law, Settler Colonialism, and 'the Forgotten Space' of Maritime Worlds." *Annual Review of Law and Social Science* 12 (2016): 107–31.

Mawani, Renisa. "Law and Migration across the Pacific: Narrating the *Komagata Maru* Outside and Beyond the Nation." In *Within and Without the Nation: Canadian History as Transnational History,* edited by Adele Perry, Karen Dubinsky, and Henry Yu, 253–75. Toronto: University of Toronto Press, 2015.

Mawani, Renisa. "Law as Temporality: Colonial Politics and Indian Settlers." *UC Irvine Law Review* 4, (2014): 64–95.

Mawani, Renisa. "Law's Archive." *Annual Review of Law and Social Science* 8 (2012): 337–65.

Mawani, Renisa. "Racial Violence and the Cosmopolitan City." *Environment and Planning D* 30 (2012): 1083–102.

Mawani, Renisa. "Specters of Indigeneity in British Indian Migration." *Law and Society Review* 46, no. 2 (2012): 369–403.

Mawani, Renisa. "The Times of Law." *Law and Social Inquiry* 40, no. 1 (2015): 253–63.

Mawani, Renisa, and Iza Hussin. "The Travels of Law: Indian Ocean Itineraries." *Law and History Review* 32, no. 4 (2014): 733–47.

McClelland, Keith. "Redefining the West Indian Interest: Politics and the Legacies of Slave-Ownership." In *Legacies of British Slave-Ownership,* edited by Catherine Hall, Nicholas Draper, Keith McClelland, Katie Donington, and Rachel Lang, 127–62. Cambridge: Cambridge University Press, 2014.

McClintock, Anne. *Imperial Leather: Race, Gender, and Sexuality in the Colonial Contest.* New York: Routledge, 1995.

McKeown, Adam. *Melancholy Order: Asian Migration and the Globalization of Borders, 1834–1929.* New York: Columbia University Press, 2008.

McKittrick, Katherine. *Demonic Grounds: Black Women and the Cartography of Struggle.* Minneapolis: University of Minnesota Press, 2006.

McKittrick, Katherine. "Plantation Futures." *Small Axe* 17, no. 3 (2013): 1–15.

McVeigh, Shaun, ed. *Jurisprudence of Jurisdiction.* Abingdon, Oxon: Routledge, 2007.

Mehring, Franz. *Karl Marx: The Story of His Life.* Oxford: Routledge, 2003.

Mehta, Uday Singh. *Liberalism and Empire: A Study in Nineteenth-Century British Liberal Thought.* Chicago: University of Chicago Press, 1999.

Mellefont, Jeffrey. "Heirlooms and Tea Towels: Views of Ships' Gender in the Modern Maritime Museum." *Journal of the Australian Association for Maritime History* 22, no. 1 (2000): 5–16.

Melville, Herman. *Bartelby and Benito Cereno.* New York: Dover, 2012.

Melville, Herman. *Billy Budd, Sailor.* Chicago: University of Chicago Press, 1962.

Metcalf, Thomas. "Architecture and the Representation of Empire, 1860–1910." *Representations* 6 (spring 1984): 37–65.

Metcalf, Thomas R. *Imperial Connections: India in the Indian Ocean Arena, 1860–1920.* Berkeley: University of California Press, 2008.

Mills, Eric L. *The Fluid Envelope of Our Planet: How the Study of Ocean Currents Became a Science.* Toronto: University of Toronto Press, 2009.

Milner, Anthony. *The Invention of Politics in Colonial Malaya.* Cambridge: Cambridge University Press, 2002.

Minca, Claudio, and Rory Rowan. "The Question of Space in Carl Schmitt." *Progress in Human Geography* 39, no. 3 (2015): 268–89.

Mirzoeff, Nicholas. "The Sea and Land: Biopower and Visuality from Slavery to Katrina." *Culture, Theory, and Critique* 50, no. 2 (2009): 289–305.

Mishra, Sudesh. "The Leonidas Fijians: A Minor History." *Journal of Pacific History* 49, no. 3 (2014): 283–300.

Mitter, Partha. *Art and Nationalism in Colonial India, 1850–1922.* Cambridge: Cambridge University Press, 1995.

Mongia, Radhika. "Gender and the Historiography of Gandhian Satyagraha." *Gender and History* 18, no. 1 (2006): 130–49.

Mongia, Radhika. "Impartial Regimes of Truth: Indentured Indian Labor and the Status of the Inquiry." *Cultural Studies* 18, no. 5 (2004): 749–68.

Mongia, Radhika. "The *Komagata Maru* as Event: Legal Transformations in Migration Regimes." In *Charting Imperial Itineraries: Unmooring the Komagata Maru,* edited by Rita Dhamoon, Davina Bhandar, Renisa Mawani, and Satwinder Bains. Vancouver: University of British Columbia Press, forthcoming.

Mongia, Radhika. "Race, Nationality, Mobility: A History of the Passport." *Public Culture* 11, no. 3 (1999): 527–55.

Monture-Angus, Patricia. *Thunder in My Soul: A Mohawk Woman Speaks.* Halifax, NS: Fernwood, 1995.

Morgan, Kenneth. *Slavery, Atlantic Trade, and the British Economy, 1660–1800.* Cambridge: Cambridge University Press, 2001.

Motha, Stewart. *Archiving Sovereignty.* Ann Arbor: University of Michigan Press, forthcoming.

Mtubani, V. C. D. "African Slaves and English Law." *Botswana Journal of African Studies* 3, no. 2 (1981): 71–75.

Muldoon, James. "Who Owns the Sea?" In *Fictions of the Sea: Critical Perspectives on the Ocean in English Literature and Culture,* edited by Bernhard Klein, 13–27. Aldershot, UK: Ashgate, 2002.

Myburgh, Paul. "Arresting the Right Ship: Procedural Theory, the in Personam Link and Conflict of Laws." In *Jurisdiction and Forum Selection in International Maritime Law: Essays in Honor of Robert Force,* edited by M. Davies, 283–320. The Hague: Kluwer Law International, 2005.

Nanni, Giordanno. *The Colonisation of Time: Ritual, Routine and Resistance in the British Empire.* Manchester: Manchester University Press, 2013.

Ngai, Mae. *Impossible Subjects: Illegal Aliens and the Making of Modern America.* Princeton, NJ: Princeton University Press, 2004.

Ogle, Vanessa. *The Global Transformation of Time, 1870–1950.* Cambridge, MA: Harvard University Press, 2015.

Ong, Aihwa. *Spirits of Resistance and Capitalist Discipline: Factory Women in Malaysia.* Albany: SUNY Press, 1987.

Paine, Lincoln. *The Sea and Civilization: A Maritime History of the World.* New York: Alfred A. Knopf, 2013.

Parker, Kunal. *Common Law, History, and Democracy in America, 1790–1900.* Cambridge: Cambridge University Press, 2013.

Parmar, Pooja. *Indigeneity and Legal Pluralism in India: Claims, Histories, Meanings.* New York: Cambridge University Press, 2015.

Parmar, Pooja. "Undoing Historical Wrongs: Law and Indigeneity in India." *Osgoode Hall Law Journal* 49, (2011–12): 491–526.

Parmer, J. Norman. "Colonial Labor Policy and Administration: A History of Labor in the Rubber Plantation Industry in Malaya, 1910–1941." PhD diss., Cornell University, 1957.

Pasternak, Shiri. "Jurisdiction and Settler Colonialism: Where Do Laws Meet?" *Canadian Journal of Law and Society* 29, no. 2 (2014): 145–61.

Pati, Budheswar. *India and the First World War.* New Delhi: Atlantic Publishers, 1996.

Pearson, Michael. *The Indian Ocean.* London: Routledge, 2003.

Perera, Suvendrini. *Australia and the Insular Imagination: Beaches, Borders, Boats, and Bodies.* New York: Palgrave, 2009.

Perera, Suvendrini. "Oceanic Corpo-Graphies, Refugee Bodies and the Making and Unmaking of Waters." *Feminist Review,* no. 103 (2013): 58–79.

Perrin, Colin. "Approaching Anxiety: The Insistence of the Postcolonial in the Rights of Indigenous Peoples." In *Laws of the Postcolonial,* edited by Eve Darian-Smith and Peter Fitzpatrick, 19–38. Ann Arbor: University of Michigan Press, 1999.

"Personification of Vessels." *Harvard Law Review* 77, no. 6 (1964): 1122–32.

Pervukhin, Anna. "Deodands: A Study in the Creation of Common Law Rules." *American Journal of Legal History* 47, no. 3 (2005): 237–56.

Peters, F. E. *The Hajj: The Muslim Pilgrimage to Mecca and the Holy Places.* Princeton, NJ: Princeton University Press, 1994.

Philip, M. NourbeSe. *Zong!: As Told to the Author by Setaey Adamu Boateng.* Middletown, CT: Wesleyan University Press, 2008.

Phillips, Caryl. *The Atlantic Sound.* New York: Vintage, 2001.

Pietz, William. "Death of the Deodand: Accursed Objects and the Money Value of Human Life." *RES: Anthropology and Aesthetics* 31, (1997): 97–108.

Pitts, Jennifer. "Empire and Legal Universalisms in the Eighteenth Century." *American Historical Review* 117, no. 1 (2012): 99–104.

Poovey, Mary. *A History of the Modern Fact: Problems of Knowledge in the Sciences of Wealth and Society.* Chicago: University of Chicago Press, 1998.

Posel, Deborah. "Race as Common Sense: Racial Classification in Twentieth-Century South Africa." *African Studies Review* 44, no. 2 (2001): 87–113.

Povinelli, Elizabeth. *The Cunning of Recognition: Indigenous Alterities and the Making of Australian Multiculturalism.* Durham, NC: Duke University Press, 2002.

Povinelli, Elizabeth. "The Governance of the Prior." *Interventions: International Journal of Postcolonial Studies* 13, no. 1 (2011): 13–30.

Prashad, Vijay. *Everybody Was Kung Fu Fighting: Afro-Asian Connections and the Myth of Cultural Purity.* Boston: Beacon Press, 2001.

Puri, Harish K. *Ghadr Movement: Ideology, Organization, Strategy.* Amritsar: Guru Nanak Dev University, 1993.

Raibmon, Paige. *Authentic Indians: Episodes of Encounter from the Late-Nineteenth Century Northwest Coast.* Durham, NC: Duke University Press, 2005.

Ramnath, Maia. *Haj to Utopia: How the Ghadr Movement Charted Global Radicalism and Attempted to Overthrow the British Empire.* Berkeley: University of California Press, 2011.

Rasor, Eugene L. "Shipping and Seamen." In *Victorian Britain: An Encyclopedia,* edited by Sally Mitchell, 716–17. New York: Garland Publishing, 1988.

Rediker, Marcus. *Between the Devil and the Deep Blue Sea: Merchant Seamen, Pirates, and the Anglo-American Maritime World, 1700–1750.* Cambridge: Cambridge University Press, 1987.

Rediker, Markus. *Outlaws of the Atlantic: Sailors, Pirates, and Motley Crews in the Age of Sail.* Boston: Beacon Press, 2014.

Rediker, Markus. *The Slave Ship: A Human History.* New York: Viking, 2007.

Rediker, Marcus. "Toward a Peoples' History of the Sea." In *Maritime Empires: British Imperial Maritime Trade in the Nineteenth Century,* edited by David Killingray, Margarette Lincoln, and Nigel Rigby, 195–206. Woodbridge, Suffolk, UK: Boydell and Brewer, 2004.

Rediker, Markus, Cassandra Pybus, and Emma Christopher. "Introduction." In *Many Middle Passages: Forced Migration and the Making of the Modern World,* edited by Emma Christopher, Cassandra Pybus, and Marcus Rediker, 1–19. Berkeley: University of California Press.

Reid, Anthony, and Jennifer Brewster, *Slavery, Bondage, and Dependency in Southeast Asia.* New York: St. Martin's Press, 1983.

Riddick, John F. *The History of British India.* Westport, CT: Praeger Publishers, 2006.

Ritchie, L. A., ed. *The Shipbuilding Industry: A Guide to Historical Records.* Manchester: Manchester University Press, 1992.

Robbins, Nick. *Scotland and the Sea: The Scottish Dimension in Maritime History.* Barnsley, UK: Seaforth, 2014.

Roberts, Neil. *Freedom as Marronage.* Chicago: University of Chicago Press, 2015.

Roopnarine, Lomarsh. "The Indian Sea Voyage between India and the Caribbean during the Second Half of the Nineteenth Century." *Journal of Caribbean History* 44, no. 1 (2010): 48–74.

Roy, Anjali Gera, and Ajaya Kumar Sahoo, eds. *Diasporas and Transnationalisms: The Journey of the* Komagata Maru. New York: Routledge, 2017.

Russell, Lynette. "'The Singular Transcultural Space': Networks of Ships, Mariners, Voyagers, and 'Native' Men at Sea, 1790–1870." In *Indigenous Networks: Mobility, Networks, and Exchange,* edited by Jane Carey and Jane Lydon, 97–113. New York: Routledge, 2014.

Said, Edward W. *Orientalism.* New York: Vintage, 1975.

Salesa, Damon. "The Pacific in Indigenous Time." In *Pacific Histories: Ocean, Land, People*, edited by David Armitage and Alison Bashford, 31–52. Palgrave-Macmillan, 2014.

Schivelbusch, Wolfgang. *The Railway Journey*. Berkeley: University of California Press, 2014.

Schmitt, Carl. "The Concept of Piracy (1937)." *Humanity: An International Journal of Human Rights, Humanitarianism, and Development* 2, no. 1 (2011): 27–29.

Schmitt, Carl. *Land and Sea: A World-Historical Meditation*. Translated by Samuel Garrett Zeitlin. Candor, NY: Telos Press, 2015.

Schmitt, Carl. *The* Nomos *of the Earth: In the International Law of the Jus Publicum Europeaeum*. Translated by G. L. Ulmen. Candor, NY: Telos Press, 2003.

Schmitt, Carl. "The Planetary Tension between Orient and Occident and the Opposition between Land and Sea." *Politica Comun* 5 (2014): 1–19. http://dx.doi.org/10.3998/pc.12322227.0005.011

Sekula, Allan. *Fish Story*. Dusseldorf: Richter Verlag, 1995.

Sekula, Allan, and Noël Burch. *The Forgotten Space*. Amsterdam/Vienna: Doc.Eye Film, in collaboration with WILDart Film, 2010.

Sen, Satadru. *Disciplining Punishment: Colonialism and Convict Society in the Andaman Islands*. Oxford: Oxford University Press, 2000.

Shah, Nayan. *Contagious Divides: Epidemics and Race in San Francisco's Chinatown*. Berkeley: University of California Press, 2001.

Shah, Nayan. *Stranger Intimacy: Contesting Race, Sexuality, and the Law in the North American West*. Berkeley: University of California Press, 2012.

Sharafi, Mitra. *Law and Identity in Colonial South Asia: Parsi Legal Culture, 1772–1947*. New York: Cambridge University Press, 2014.

Sharpe, Christina. *In the Wake: On Blackness and Being*. Durham, NC: Duke University Press, 2016.

Shell, Robert. *Children of Bondage: A Social History of the Slave Society at the Cape of Good Hope, 1652–1858*. Johannesburg: Witwatersrand University Press, 1994.

Sheridan, R. B. "The Commercial and Financial Organization of the Slave Trade, 1750–1807." *Economic History Review* 11, no. 2 (1958): 249–63.

Siegel, Jonathan. "Law and Longitude." *Tulane Law Review* 84, no. 1 (2009): 1–66.

Siegert, Bernhard. *Cultural Techniques: Grids, Filters, Doors, and Other Articulations of the Real*. New York: Fordham University Press, 2015.

Simpson, Audra. *Mohawk Interruptus: Life across the Border of Settler States*. Durham, NC: Duke University Press, 2014.

Simpson, Audra. "Settlement's Secret." *Cultural Anthropology* 26, no. 2 (2011): 205–17.

Singh, Narindar. *Canadian Sikhs: History, Religion, and Culture of Sikhs in North America*. Ottawa: Canadian Sikh Studies Institute, 1994.

Singha, Bhagata. *Canadian Sikhs through a Century, 1897–1997*. Delhi: Gyan Sagar Publications, 2001.

Singha, Radhika. "Front Lines and Status Lines: Sepoy and 'Menial' in the Great War, 1916–1920." In *The World in World Wars: Experiences, Perceptions and Perspectives from Africa and Asia,* edited by Heike Liebau, Katrin Bromber, Katharina Lange, Dyala Hamzah, and Ravi Ahuja, 55–106. Leiden: Brill, 2010.

Singha, Radhika. "Settle, Mobilise, and Verify: Identification Practices in Colonial India." *Studies in History* 16, no. 2 (2000): 151–98.

Skaria, Ajay. *Hybrid Histories: Forests, Frontiers and Wildness in Western India.* New Delhi: Oxford University Press, 1999.

Slight, John. *The British Empire and the Hajj, 1865–1956.* Cambridge, MA: Harvard University Press, 2015.

Smallwood, Stephanie E. *Saltwater Slavery: A Middle Passage from Africa to American Diaspora.* Cambridge, MA: Harvard University Press, 2008.

Smith, Vanessa. "Costume Changes: Passing at Sea and on the Beach." In *Sea Changes: Historicizing the Ocean,* edited by Bernhard Klein and Gesa Mackenthun, 37–53. New York: Routledge, 2004.

Sobel, Dava. *Longitude: The Story of a Genius Who Solved the Greatest Scientific Problem of His Time.* New York: Bloomsbury, 2007.

Sohi, Seema. *Echoes of Mutiny: Race, Surveillance, and Indian Anticolonialism in North America.* New York: Oxford University Press, 2014.

Sohi, Seema. "Race, Surveillance, and Indian Anticolonialism in the Transnational Western U.S.-Canadian Borderlands." *Journal of American History* 98, no. 2 (2011): 420–36.

Soske, Jon. "'Wash Me Black Again': African Nationalism, the Indian Diaspora, and Kwa-Zulu Natal, 1944–1960." PhD diss., University of Toronto, 2009.

Steel, Frances. "Lines across the Sea: Trans-Pacific Shipping in the Age of Steam." In *The Routledge History of Western Empires,* edited by Robert Aldrich and Kirsten McKenzie, 315–29. London: Routledge, 2013.

Steinberg, Philip. "Free Sea." In *Spatiality, Sovereignty and Carl Schmitt,* edited by Stephen Legg, 268–75. Abingdon, Oxon: Routledge, 2011.

Steinberg, Philip. "Of Other Seas: Metaphors and Materialities in Maritime Regions." *Atlantic Studies: Global Currents* 10, no. 2 (2013): 156–69.

Steinberg, Philip. *The Social Construction of the Ocean.* Cambridge: Cambridge University Press, 2001.

Steinberg, Philip. "Sovereignty, Territory, and the Mapping of Mobility: A View from the Outside." *Annals of the Association of American Geographers* 99, no. 3 (2009): 467–95.

Stephens, Julia. "An Uncertain Inheritance: The Imperial Travels of Legal Migrants, from British India to Ottoman Iraq. *Law and History Review* 32, no. 4 (2014): 749–72.

Stoler, Ann Laura. *Carnal Knowledge and Imperial Power: Race and the Intimate in Colonial Rule.* Berkeley: University of California Press, 2002.

Stoler, Ann Laura. "Degrees of Imperial Sovereignty." *Public Culture* 18, no. 1 (2006): 125–46.

Stoler, Ann Laura. *Race and the Education of Desire: Foucault's History of Sexuality and the Colonial Order of Things.* Durham, NC: Duke University Press, 1995.

Tabili, Laura. "'A Maritime Race': Masculinity and the Racial Division of Labor in British Merchant Ships, 1900–1939." In *Iron Men, Wooden Women: Gender and Seafaring in the Atlantic World, 1700–1920,* edited by Margaret S. Creighton and Lisa Norling, 169–88. Baltimore: Johns Hopkins University Press, 1996.

Tatla, Darshan Singh. "Incorporating Regional Events into the Nationalist Narrative: The Life of Gurdit Singh and the *Komagata Maru* Episode in Postcolonial India." *South Asian Diaspora* 8, no. 2 (2016): 1–22.

Tatla, Darshan Singh, ed. *Voyage of the Komagata Maru or India's Slavery Abroad by Baba Gurdit Singh.* Chandigarh: Unistar Books and Punjab Center for Migration Studies, 2007.

Tatla, Darshan Singh, and Mandeep K. Tatla. *Sardar Gurdit Singh: Komagata Maru: A Short Biography.* Chandigarh: Unistar Books and Punjab Center for Migration Studies, 2007.

Taylor, Greg. *The Law of the Land: The Advent of the Torrens System in Canada.* Osgoode Society for Legal History. Toronto: University of Toronto Press, 2008.

Thampi, Madhavi. "The Indian Community in China and Sino-Indian Relations." In *India and China in the Colonial World,* edited by Madhavi Thampi, 66–82. Delhi: Social Science Press, 2005.

Thomas, Martin. *Violence and Colonial Order: Police, Workers, and Protest in the European Colonial Empires, 1918–1940.* Cambridge: Cambridge University Press, 2012.

Thompson, E. P. "Time, Work-Discipline and Industrial Capitalism." *Past and Present* 38, (1967): 56–97.

Thornton, Helen. "John Selden's Response to Hugo Grotius: The Argument for Closed Seas." *International Journal of Maritime History* 18, no. 2 (2006): 105–28.

Thumfart, Johannes. "On Grotius's *Mare Liberum* and Vitoria's *De Indis,* Following Agamben and Schmitt." *Grotiana,* 30, no. 1 (2009): 65–87.

Tinker, Hugh. *A New System of Slavery: The Export of Indian Labour Overseas, 1830–1920.* London: Oxford University Press, 1974.

Tomlins, Christopher. *Freedom Bound: Law, Labor, and Civic Identity in Colonizing English America, 1580–865.* New York: Cambridge University Press, 2010.

Tomlins, Christopher. "The Threepenny Constitution (and the Question of Justice)." *Alabama Law Review* 58, (2007): 979–1008.

Tuck, Richard. "Grotius and Selden." *The Cambridge History of Political Thought, 1450–1700,* edited by H. J. Burns, 499–529. Cambridge: Cambridge University Press, 1991.

Ungerer, Gustav. *The Mediterranean Apprenticeship of British Slavery.* Madrid: Editorial Verbum, 2008.

Valverde, Mariana. *Chronotopes of Law: Jurisdiction, Scale, and Governance.* Abingdon, Oxon: Routledge, 2015.

Valverde, Mariana. "Jurisdiction and Scale: Legal 'Technicalities' as Resources for Theory." *Social and Legal Studies* 18, no. 2 (2009): 139–57.

Valverde, Mariana. "'Peace, Order, and Good Government': Policelike Powers in Postcolonial Perspective." In *The New Police Science: The Police Power in Domestic and International Governance,* edited by Marcus Dubber and Mariana Valverde, 73–106. Stanford: Stanford University Press, 2006.

Van Ittersum, Martine Julia. "Hugo Grotius in Context: Van Heemskerck's Capture of the "Santa Catarina" and Its Justification in "De Jure Praedae" (1604–1606)." *Asian Journal of Social Science* 31, no. 3 (2003): 511–48.

Van Ittersum, Martine Julia. "Preparing *Mare Liberum* for the Press: Hugo Grotius's Rewriting of Chapter 12 of *De iure praedae* in November–December 1608." In *Property, Piracy and Punishment: Hugo Grotius on War and Booty in* De Iure Praedae, edited by Hans Blom, 246–80. Leiden: Brill, 2009.

Van Ittersum, Martine Julia. *Profit and Principle: Hugo Grotius, Natural Rights Theories and the Rise of Dutch Power in the East Indies.* Leiden: Brill, 2006.

Van Tilburg, Hans Konrad. "Vessels of Exchange: The Global Shipwright in the Pacific." In *Seascapes: Maritime Histories, Littoral Cultures, and Transoceanic Exchanges,* edited by Jerry Bentley, Renate Bidenthal, and Karen Wigen, 38–52. Honolulu: University of Hawai'i Press, 2007.

Vickers, Daniel. *Young Men and the Sea: Yankee Seafarers in the Age of Sail.* New Haven, CT: Yale University Press, 2007.

Vieira, Monica Brito. "*Mare Liberum* vs. *Mare Clausum:* Grotius, Freitas, and Selden's Debate on Dominion over the Seas." *Journal of the History of Ideas* 64, no. 3 (2003): 361–77.

Vismann, Cornelia. *Files: Law and Media Technology.* Translated by Geoffrey Winthrop-Young. Stanford: Stanford University Press, 2008.

Visram, Rozina. *Ayahs, Lascars, and Princes: Indians in Britain, 1700–1947.* London: Pluto Press, 1986.

Walcott, Derek. "The Sea Is History." In *Collected Poems, 1948–1984,* 364–67. New York: Farrar, Straus and Giroux, 1986.

Walker, Fred M. *Song of the Clyde: A History of Clyde Shipbuilding.* Somerset, UK: Patrick Stephens, 1984.

Wallace, Isabel. "Komagata Maru Revisited: 'Hindus,' Hookworm, and the Guise of Public Health Protection." *BC Studies* 178, (2013): 33–50.

Walvin, James. *Crossings: Africa, the Americas, and the Transatlantic Slave Trade.* Chicago: University of Chicago Press, 2013.

Walvin, James. *The Zong: A Massacre, the Law and the End of Slavery.* New Haven, CT: Yale University Press, 2011.

Waraich, Malwinder Singh, and Gurdev Singh Sidhu, eds. *Komagata Maru: A Challenge to Colonialism, Key Documents.* Chandigarh: Unistar, 2014.

Ward, Kerry. *Networks of Empire: Forced Migration in the Dutch East India Company.* Cambridge: Cambridge University Press, 2009.

Ward, W. Peter. *White Canada Forever: Popular Attitudes and Public Policy toward Orientals in British Columbia.* 3rd ed. Montreal: McGill-Queen's University Press, 2002.

Weaver, Jace. *The Red Atlantic: American Indigenes and the Making of the Modern World, 1000–1927.* Chapel Hill: University of North Carolina Press, 2014.

Webster, Jane. "The *Zong* in the Context of the Eighteenth-Century Slave Trade." *Journal of Legal History* 28, no. 3 (2007): 285–98.

Wenzlhuemer, Roland. *Connecting the Nineteenth-Century World: The Telegraph and Globalization.* Cambridge: Cambridge University Press, 2012.

Wick, Alexis. *The Red Sea: A Search for Lost Space.* Berkeley: University of California Press, 2016.

Wigen, Karen. "Introduction." In *Seascapes: Maritime Histories, Littoral Cultures, and Transoceanic Exchanges,* edited by Jerry Bentley, Renate Bidenthal, and Karen Wigen, 1–18. Honolulu: University of Hawai'i Press, 2007.

Wilson, Eric. "The Alexandrowicz Thesis Revisited: Hugo Grotius, Divisible Sovereignty, and Private Avengers within the Indian Ocean World System." In *Early Modern Southeast Asia, 1350–1800,* edited by Ooi Keat Gin and Hoang Ahn Tuan, 28–54. Abingdon, Oxon: Routledge, 2016.

Wong, Edlie. *Neither Fugitive nor Free: Atlantic Slavery, Freedom Suits, and the Legal Culture of Travel.* New York: New York University Press, 2009.

Yang, Anand. "Indian Convict Workers in Southeast Asia in the Late Eighteenth and Early Nineteenth Centuries." *Journal of World History* 14, no. 2 (2003): 179–208.

Yatim, Zakaria M. "The Development of the Law of the Sea in Relation to Malaysia." *Malaysian Management Journal* 1, no. 1 (1992): 87–98.

Yu, Henry. "The Rhythms of the Transpacific." In *Connecting Seas and Connected Ocean Rims: Indian, Atlantic, and Pacific Oceans and China Seas Migrations from the 1830s to the 1930s,* edited by Donna Gabbaccia and Dirk Hoerder, 389–92. Leiden: Brill, 2011.

Yu, Henry. *Thinking Orientals: Migration, Contact, and Exoticism in Modern America.* Oxford: Oxford University Press, 2002.

Zamindar, Vazira Fazila-Yacoobali. *The Long Partition and the Making of Modern South Asia: Refugees, Boundaries, Histories.* New York: Columbia University Press, 2007.

Ziskind, Jonthan. "International Law and Ancient Sources: Grotius and Selden." *Review of Politics* 35, no. 4 (1973): 537–59.

Index

Page references in italics refer to illustrations

Best, Stephen, 227

Bikhit, Mahmud, 238

Bird, J. Edward, 64, 67, 177, 257n230; on continuous journey regulation, 124; on indigenous peoples, 144; questioning of Munshi Singh, 125; in *Re Munshi* case, 131, 132, 133, 134, 139; representation of shore committee, 122

Blackstone, William: *Commentaries on the Laws of England*, 83; on deodand, 83, 84

Bodin, Jean, 48

bookkeeping: as mode of governing, 128; objective truth in, 127

Borges, Jorge Luis: *Labyrinths,* xi

Borrows, John, 145, 146, 175

Borschberg, Peter, 47, 251nn27, 30, 252n70

Bose, Sugata, 19

boundaries, imperial: around Oceania, 20; fluidity of, 124; role of race in, 14. *See also* territoriality

boundaries, maritime: European imposition of, 18; ships inside, 128–29, 133

Braudel, Fernand: on maritime expansion, 246n108; *The Mediterranean,* 291n20

Brazil, immigration regulations of, 229

British Columbia Court of Appeal, 149; authority of, 135; on Canadian sovereignty, 131–32; on continuous journey regulation, 4; on indigenous peoples, 154; *Komagata Maru* deliberations before, 114, 120, 131, 169, 242n11; Salish people and, 147. *See also* Immigration Board of Inquiry (British Columbia); *Re Munshi Singh*

British Empire: absorption of Dutch, 276n28; citizenship in, 33, 117; competing legalities of, 187; direct/indirect rule in, 138; display of time in, 29; freedom from, 2, 217; Gurdit Singh's critique of, 193; horizontal connections within, 12; Indians' standing in, 178, 185, 226; interconnected spaces of, 8; juridical violence in, 230; land/sea divisions of, 35, 80, 84; legal authority of, 115; long-distance correspondence of, 255n144; necessity of free migration for, 186; print media of, 154, 156, 172–78; race-mixing in, 178, 182; racial asymmetries in, 118, 137–42, 147, 150, 159, 167, 169, 174, 182–85; racial coercion in, 155; racial structuring of, 25, 60, 158; racial vernaculars

of, 165; racial violence in, 157, 220, 221, 225, 228; railway networks of, 8; sites of opposition to, 6; slave trade in, 96–98, 258n10, 261n56; spatio-temporality of, 6–7, 25–26, 69; temporal divisions in, 137–42, 169–70; temporalities of, 220; timekeeping in, 56–59; use of global time, 28–29; vagrancy laws of, 195. *See also* imperialism, British; maritime power, British; subjecthood, British

British Empire, maritime, 5; control of, 40; economic instruments of, 107; jurisdictional spaces of, 117; open/closed sea and, 50; shipbuilding dominance of, 89; sources of authority, 122; steamships of, 8; subjecthood in, 134; technology of, 15, 49–50, 83; vulnerabilities of, 190. *See also* maritime power, British

British North America Act, 135; Dominion authority in, 136; financial requirements of, 140; indigenous dispossession in, 150; *Komagata Maru* detention and, 142–43; "priorness" in, 144; in *Re Munshi Singh*, 143, 150

Brookes (slave ship), 268n227

Brown, Henry Billings, 81

Budge Budge: Gurdit Singh's flight from, 194, 206; *Komagata Maru* passengers at, 196, 199–200, 201; map of, *203. See also* Calcutta

Budge Budge massacre, 11, 12, 15, 194–206, 210, 238, 284nn83–84; arrests following, 204; fugitives from, 206; Ingress into India Ordinance and, 204; *Komagata Maru* passengers in, 202–4; leaders of, 204; in Singh's sedition trial, 216

Burma, immigration legislation of, 245n70

Burton, Antoinette, 182

Byrd, Jodi, 144, 275n11

Calcutta: Asiatic Society of, 140; *Komagata Maru* in, 196, 199–200, 281n19; radicalism in, 196. *See also* Budge Budge

Canada: border fluidity of, 124; Citizenship Act (1947), 241n9; Immigration Act, 141–42; Indian Act, 147; Indian migrants to, 36, 139–41, 148; jurisdiction over harbors, 134; racial exclusion in, 11, 115, 155; Rahim on, 66; Royal Proclamation (1763), 145–46; territorial authority of, 65, 131, 136, 143, 155, 173,

"coolie ships." *See* indenture ships

cosmologies, indigenous: land/sea distinction in, 19

Cowen, John, 249n5; on "Asiatics," 166; on Indian migration, 160, 161

Craddock, R. H., 200

crews, ships': racial governance of, 22. *See also* mariners

crime, maritime: punishment of, 48

Croll, James, 18, 28; on contiguity of oceans, 30; on earth's atmosphere, 235

currents, ocean: connectivity of, 25; global time and, 27–28; influence on commerce, 20; multidirectional, 20; in ocean studies, 246n99; space-time coordinates of, 21

D'Aguiar, Fred, 258n10, 260n25

Dayan, Colin, 262n90

Definition of Time Act (Great Britain, 1880), 59–60

Demerara: Indian indentured labor of, 96, 98; indigenous inhabitants of, 97

deodand, law of, 82–85, 261n59; abolition of, 83, 84; Biblical derivation of, 83; Coroner's Office on, 261n68; forfeiture under, 82, 83–84, 262n84; ownership and, 85; slavery and, 83, 262n93

Derrida, Jacques, 275n22; on Mandela, 287n162; on spectrality, 144, 273n147, 279n113; on violence of law, 273n140

dispossession, indigenous, 33, 94–95; in British North America Act, 150; in British subject-hood, 144; British violence in, 157; under Canadian Indian Act, 147; Connell's ships in, 78; in Dominions, 115–16, 155–56; on free sea, 99, 234; global circuits of, 11; *Hindi Punch* on, 174–76; in Indian migration, 156; in South Africa, 168–69. *See also* indigenous peoples

distance, spatio-temporal: compression of, 9

Dominions, British: under British North America Act, 136; colonial historiographies of, 181; versus colonies, 118, 137–42; denial of entry into, 68–69; immigration regulations of, 16; indigenous dispossession in, 115–16, 155–56; mobility of Asiatics in, 117; open/closed sea of, 63; oppression in, 193; racial hierarchies of, 117, 158, 174, 182; racial laws of, 78; racial power of, 178; subjects versus citizens in, 135, 138–39, 146, 173–74, 179; travel restrictions of, 63; vertical hierarchies of, 30, 120; as young spaces, 29

dominium (property), etymology of, 54

Donald, Mr. (British Indian magistrate), 197, 201; and *Komagata Maru* passengers, 199

Dorsett, Shaunnagh, 24

Douglass, Frederick, 217, 281n5; escape from slavery, 281n7; sea imagery of, 190

Drawing the Global Color Line (Lake and Reynolds), 272n101

DuBoulay, James, 204

Dulai, Phinder: *Dream/Arteries,* 259n18

Dunbar-Ortiz, Roxanne, 254n133

Dutch: capture of *Santa Catarina,* 41–43, 51, 53, 54, 247n127, 251n27; slavery under, 160, 276n33. *See also* East India Company, Dutch

Dutch Admiralty Board, on *Santa Catarina,* 41–42

Dyer, Reginald, 208

earth: counter-*nomos* of, 60–72, 235; as property, 9, 115; spatial order of, 52. *See also* land

East, land-based countries of, 54

East India, parallels with New World, 47

East India Company, British, 42; government of Malaya, 222; lascar employees of, 35

East India Company, Dutch: Grotius's work for, 41; indigenous rulers and, 47; right of free trade, 232

Ellis Island, 93; dispossession at, 94; memorial, 264n132; *Sicilia's* voyage to, 264n131; *Stubbenhuk's* voyage to, 263n127

Engels, Friedrich: on colonial expansion, 5; on contiguity of oceans, 30; on steam travel, 22

Enthoven, R. E., 130

Equiano, Olaudah, 281n5

"The Exclusion of Hindoos" *(Hindustanee),* 177

expansion, European: history of, 18; Marx and Engels on, 5

Farred, Grant, 174

Federated Malay States, 222

feranghis (foreigners), 112, 268n226

figureheads, female, 79, 98

flags, ships,' 91–92, 247n118, 263nn124–25; of convenience, 262n83, 263n125; decision process for, 92; information conveyed by, 23

challenges to, 171. *See also* British Empire; maritime power, British; subjecthood, British

indenture: Caribbean, 224; consent in, 99; forcible, 266n195; maritime relations and, 98–99; outlawing of, 222; racial exploitation of, 95; in Straits Settlements, 224; transatlantic slavery and, 98–99, 101, 104, 109, 113, 114, 186, 221–22, 225, 227, 243n37, 288n196, 289n225; West Indian, 77. *See also* contract labor

indenture, Indian, 11, 243n37; Connell's ships in, 78; contract tickets for, 106; of Demerara, 96, 98; on free sea, 99; of Guiana, 96; Gurdit Singh on, 224–26; juridical forms of, 225; in Malaya, 222; on plantations, 222; in South Africa, 160, 162; in Straits Settlements, 225; in sugar trade, 97–98

indenture ships, 74–75; architecture of, 95; British, 89, 95–97, 264n137; conditions aboard, 99; inspection of, 104; licenses for, 103; paper currency of, 106; regulation of, 98–99; seasonal restrictions on, 103–4; in sugar trade, 96–97

India: caste system, 167–68; civilizational superiority of, 179–80, 186; conquests of, 153, 167; temporal registers of, 153–54

India, British: border regulations, 189; codification debate in, 249n163; competing jurisdictions of, 29; equality in, 117; Home Department, 198; immigration restrictions of, 245n72; in imperial itineraries, 10; *Komagata Maru* supporters in, 154; oppression in, 193; Penal Code of, 214–15, 217; permission to enter, 198; print media of, 154, 156, 172–78; role of empire in, 137–38; seaborne threats to, 198; security regime of, 191, 192, 197; Seditious Meetings Act, 214; slavery in, 259n21; travel restrictions of, 63. *See also* Foreigners Ordinance; Ingress into India Ordinance

Indian Act (Canada), 147, 176, 274n163

Indian National Congress, Gurdit Singh and, 209, 210

Indian Ocean: Black Atlantic and, 245n84; Dutch claims in, 47, 48; global nature of, 19; historiography of, 243n23; legal regimes of, 22–23; outward radiation from, 13; restrictions on, 63; scholarship on, 18

Indian Opinion (newspaper): on Dominion-colony difference, 138; on European indigeneity, 174; on racial classification, 163, 165; on white colonization, 186

Indians: as "Asiatics," 139–41; mendacity charges against, 267n211; spectrality of, 144. *See also* migrants, Indian; travelers, Indian

Indians, South Africa, 157, 158–68; versus aboriginal peoples, 164, 175; Africans and, 159, 182–83, 185; claims to the soil, 165; competition from, 174; disruption of indigenous peoples, 161; "free," 161, 167; immigration restrictions on, 157–69, 276n53; indentured, 160, 162; protests by, 164; racial taxonomies for, 164–67; subjecthood of, 181; taxation of, 162; as threat to British rule, 160–61

indigeneity: anticolonialism and, 154–58, 176; challenges to sovereignty, 168–69; in contemporary India, 274n5, 275n16; in Dominion sovereignty, 33, 143, 150; European claims to, 173–74; global politics of, 151; in Indian print media, 174–78; in *Komagata Maru* deliberations, 148–49, 179; lines drawn over, 53; mobility of, 154; multiple figures of, 154–55, 158, 168; present and future, 157; racial power and, 157; in *Re Munshi Singh*, 143–47, 151; South African struggles over, 158–68; as temporal figure, 144; as territorial challenge, 168; transoceanic vernacular of, 150

indigenous peoples: anticolonial vernaculars and, 186; autonomy of, 175; capital of, 267n212; effect of land registration on, 223; global time and, 28; Malay, 223–24; putative lawlessness of, 273n153; of South Africa, 148; temporality of, 154, 273n148, 275n11; in U.S. imperialism, 144; violence against, 157, 187. *See also* aboriginal peoples; dispossession, indigenous; "natives"

indigenous peoples, Canada, 33, 142–49, 258nn237–38; autonomy of, 155; under Dominion control, 147–48; Indian migrants and, 148; internal migrations of, 146; in peace conference of 1764, 145–46; in *Re Munshi Singh*, 143–47; resistance to authority, 169; sovereignty of, 33, 143, 150, 168–69; subordinate status of, 144–45; temporality of, 169; territorial claims of, 155; use of wampum, 145, 146; as wards of Crown, 145, 147–48, 150. *See also* Salish peoples

coverage of, 9, 15, 116, 177, 183; racial impact of, 15, 76, 78; radicalism inspired by, 5, 16, 23; refitting of, 103; scholarship on, xii, 7, 76, in Singh's sedition trial, 216; sovereignty and, 7; spatio-temporality of, 30, 233; supporters of, 154, 166, 178, 185; supporters' rhetoric, 186; symbolism of, 6; territoriality and, 7, 120, 135; voyages, *4*, 34, 36, 72, *100;* voyage to Vancouver, 2–3; worship aboard, 6. See also *Heian Maru; Sicilia; Stubbenhuk*

Komagata Maru Committee of Inquiry (British India), 203–4; on emigrants from America, 201; on Gurdit Singh's criminality, 212; on Guru Nanak Steamship Company, 213; on *Komagata Maru* passengers, 212; *Report of,* 211, 241n6; testimony before, 250n11

Komagata Maru deliberations (British Columbia): admiralty law in, 118–19, 120–31; anticolonialism in, 64–65, 144; before Court of Appeal, 114, 120, 131, 169, 242n11; and Dominion authority, 168; global interest in, 116, 172; immigration regulations affecting, 118; imperial responsibilities in, 179; Indian exclusion following, 120; Indian mobility and, 3–4; indigeneity in, 148–49, 179; political implications of, 116; press coverage of, 9, 15, 116, 177, 183; race in, 120, 184; ships' manifest in, 129–30; territory in, 120, 135; time in, 120. *See also* British Columbia Court of Appeal; Immigration Board of Inquiry; *Re Munshi Singh*

Komagata Maru deportation, 11, 120, 154, 190–91, 192; to Calcutta, 196, 199–200, 281n19; under continuous journey regulation, 190; cost of, 196; destinations for, 194, 195; Indian independence and, 202–3, 218, 288n181; in Kobe, 196; negotiations over, 195–96; responsibility for, 194; in Yokohama, 195–96

Komagata Maru detention (Vancouver), *3,* 5, 7, 11, 32, 33, *66, 68, 133;* authority over, 131–32, 142; delays affecting, 121; Indian mobility and, 115

Komagata Maru manifest, 118–19, *127;* Board of Inquiry on, 122, 126–27, 129–30, 150; as legal decree, 126; legitimacy of, 130; passenger information in, 126, 149; preparation of, 125; in *Re Munshi Singh,* 133; signers of, 126

Komagata Maru passengers, 2–7, 36, 242n11; appeal to governor-general, 149; authorities' searching of, 205; British subjecthood of, 116–17, 120; at Budge Budge, 196, 199–200, 201; as Caucasians, 121, 179; civil rights of, 132, 134; demands for inclusion, 25; departure at Yokohama, 195–96; deprivations suffered by, 202, 204; disaffection among, 200; disembarked, 4, 241n10, 270n31; financial losses of, 194; as foreigners in India, 197; free migrants, 101, 109; Ghadrites, 281n13; Hindu, 3, 33; as illegals, 126–27; immigration law and, 118, 149–50; Indian officials' threat to, 201; Indian press on, 177; under Ingress into India Ordinance, 197, 199, 204–5; invocation of admiralty law, 149; jailing at Alipore, 204, 238; jurisdiction over, 133–34; legal status of, 129; lists of, *110–11;* loans to Singh, 107–8, 112, 199, 213, 284n78; march toward Howrah, 201–2, 284n78; Muslim, 3, 6, 107; number of, 102–3; racial violence against, 112; radicalization allegations against, 195, 196, 200–201, 205, 281n15; Rahim and, 39, 201; references to indigeneity, 148–49; relationship with Gurdit Singh, 212–13; Sikhs, 6, 205, 226; as slaves, 87; test-case for, 120, 121; tickets issued to, 104–5, *105,* 106, 125; train to Punjab for, 200–201; women, 241n8, 249n4

Komagata Maru shore committee (Vancouver): Bird's representation of, 122; financial losses of, 113; fund raising by, 109; losses of, 268n231; Rahim on, 38, 64, 67, 257n219

labor markets, maritime, 263n125. *See also* indenture

Ladner, H. W. D.: questioning of Munshi Singh, 124–25

Laeisz, Ferdinand, 90

land: biopolitical struggles over, 234; commodification of, 223; European appropriation of, 52; immovability of, 44. *See also* earth

land reform, profit from, 289n219

land registration: effect on indigenous peoples, 223; Torrens system of, 222–24, 288n203

land/sea divisions: of British Empire, 35, 80, 84; freedom in, 239; historiography of, 231; of imperialism, 70; in indigenous cosmologies,

19; inequality in, 233–34; in international law, 19; juridico-political aspects of, 231; in *Mare Liberum,* 40, 43, 45–46, 48, 50; moving ships in, 232

lascars, Indian, 39, 230; on European ships, 62; in London, 256n202; in maritime commerce, 35; mobility of, 62; shipbound lives of, 22

latitude: division of earth through, 69; in new global order, 26; record-keeping for, 128

law: as cultural process, 14; fugitive slave, 193–94; movement across oceans, 23; terra-centric borders in, 15; violence of, 273n140. *See also* admiralty law; common law, British; immigration laws, Canadian

law, colonial: circulation of, 20, 26; currents in, 21; mythical origins of, 119–20; oceans in, 15, 25

law, international: land-based foundation of, 51; land/sea distinction in, 19; myth of, 49; piracy in, 254n128; temporal grids of, 119

lawlessness, gendered terms for, 260n37

Leader (Allahabad), on *Komagata Maru* passengers, 199, 202

legal personhood, 236; denial of, 86; Justice Marshall on, 85; positive and negative, 77, 86–87; slaves', 86–88, 113, 194

legal personhood, ships', 32, 72, 76–77, 78–88, 194; actions against, 85–86; in admiralty law, 80, 82; baptism in, 81; British departure from, 261n56; civilizational properties of, 91; in commerce, 82; in common law, 80; family terms in, 79, 260n30; feminine, 78–79, 87; origins of, 90; personality in, 85; protection of imperialism, 85; slavery in, 82; Supreme Court on, 81, 85–86; and transatlantic slavery, 82, 86–88, 113, 114

Lenape people (Algonquians), of New York, 94

linearity, in imperial history, 12

Linebaugh, Peter, 18, 281n8

lines, global: atop indigenous sovereignties, 53. *See also* latitude; longitude

liquids, possession of, 46

Little Charles case, ships' legal standing in, 86

Locke, John: *Second Treatise of Government,* 291n4

longitude: determination of, 55–59; division of earth through, 69; Greenwich Mean Time and, 57; as measure of time, 27, 29; in new

global order, 26, 27; record-keeping for, 128. *See also* navigation; timekeeping

Lubbock, Basil: *The Coolie Ships and Oil Sailors,* 98

MacDonald, J. A., 131; on jurisdictional divides, 134, 135; on racial status, 142

Maine, Henry Sumner, 138

Malaya: British ties to, 222; Gurdit Singh in, 218, 223, 225; Indian indentured labor in, 222; Singh's lawsuits in, 280n1

Malay Reservation Enactment, 223

Malay States, expatriation of Sikhs from, 226

Malek, Ali, 238

Mamdani, Mahmood, 138, 272n113

Mandela, Nelson, 287n162

Manu, Laws of, 288n175

The Many Headed Hydra (Linebaugh and Rediker), 281n8

maps: racial representations of, 119; representations of time, 119; uniform time and, 26. *See also* cartography

mare clausum, 44–46, 190. *See also* sea, open/closed

mariners: free black, 99; fugitive laws concerning, 193–94; non-Western, 46; ship sense of, 78–79. *See also* lascars, Indian

maritime law: competing histories of, 32; effect of *Komagata Maru* on, 9, 12; emerging from seafaring life, 49; international, 44; natural law and, 41; origins of, 40. *See also* admiralty law

maritime power: gendered, 79–80; inaccessibility for Indians, 88

maritime power, British: decline of, 291n11; German airpower and, 71, 233, 291n11; Indian commerce and, 62; law of sea in, 80; Schmitt on, 55; ships symbolizing, 8–9; Suez Canal in, 89–90; technology in, 83. *See also* British Empire, maritime

maritime travel: from Asia, 60; "Asiatics'" access to, 235; dangers of, 53; East-West connection in, 20; effect on travelers' perspectives, 24; freedom of, 2; in imperialism, 5, 52; new global order of, 26; potential of, 9; racial power in, 25; right to, 5, 115, 116, 134, 183, 186, 211; timekeeping for, 27. *See also* travel maritime travel, Indian, 35; radicalism in, 9, 23; revival of, 5, 76, 229; Singh's appeal for, 1–2. *See also* travelers, Indian

Marshall, John: on Indian rights, 262n77; on legal personhood, 85, 92; in *Little Charles* case, 86

Martin, A., 131; on "Asiatics," 179; on indigeneity, 144, 145, 147–48, 176; on three-mile territorial border, 135

Marwaris, indigenous capital of, 267n212

Marx, Karl: on colonial expansion, 5; on contiguity of oceans, 30; "The Future Results of British Rule in India," 152, 153–54; on steam travel, 1, 8, 9, 22

masculinity, maritime, 79–80

Mattoon, J. W., 39

Maxwell, John Irving, 82

McKittrick, Katherine, 289n218

McPhillips, A. E., 131; on British subjecthood, 135; on immigrant exclusion, 132; on Indian law, 141; on indigeneity, 144–45, 148; on jurisdiction, 136; on undesirables, 140–41; use of *Encyclopedia Britannica*, 142; views on race, 139–41

Mecca, pilgrimage to, 256n183

Mediterranean: control over, 48; maritime disputes of, 230; migrant crises in, 236–38; militarization of, 237; racial struggle in, 34; triumphalist history of, 70; Western power on, 238

Melaka, Maritime Code of, 22

Melville, Herman: *Benito Cereno*, 260n37; *Billy Budd, Sailor*, 246n111

merchants, Indian: competition in South Africa, 174; Gujarati, 39. *See also* commerce, maritime

Metcalf, Thomas, 13

middle passage, 235; of *Komagata Maru*'s journey, 78, 100–13

middle passage, Atlantic: as site of revolt, 247n121; spatio-temporal dangers of, 23

migrants: aboard open boats, 10; juridical distinctions concerning, 272n113

migrants, Indian: achievements of, 227; versus Britons, 117; to Canada, 36, 139–41, 148; colonizing role of, 185; imperial jurisdiction over, 145; on indigenous dispossession, 157; and indigenous peoples, 148; as

non-assimilative, 141–42; as pioneers, 186; Rahim's advice for, 67–68; rail travel for, 68–69; ships carrying, 265n172; to South Africa, 156–57, 158–68; as undesirables, 140–41; use of indigeneity, 158; on U.S. west coast, 250n8; violence against, 181, 182

migration: territoriality and, 13; twenty-first century crises of, 10, 34, 236–38; unidirectional, 13

migration, forced, 160; historiography of, 78; racial violence in, 193

migration, free: British law and, 114; Connell's ships in, 78; Gurdit Singh's account of, 220; on *Komagata Maru*, 101, 109; necessity for British Empire, 186; overlap with slavery, 230. *See also* freedom of travel

migration, Indian: Bombay-to-Brazil route, 229; Calcutta-Vancouver route, 36, 123–24; forced, 160; indigenous dispossession and, 156; maritime mobility and, 63; within maritime worlds, 6; radicalism concerning, 6; restrictions on, 157–78, 172, 276n53; transoceanic contests over, 156. *See also* mobility, Indian; travelers, Indian

Milner, Lord (governor of the Transvaal), 164–65, 167

Mirzoeff, Nicholas, 233–34

missionaries, Canadian: under Foreigners Ordinance (India), 198

Moana (steamship), 40; Pacific crossings of, 250n16; Rahim's journey aboard, 38, 64, 71

mobility: in fugitivity, 193; horizontal-vertical, 14; of indigeneity, 154; north-south, 13; of race, 180–81

mobility, imperial: cartography and, 119; perils of, 249n5; spatio-temporality of, 248n135

mobility, Indian: under Ingress into India Ordinance, 197; and *Komagata Maru* deliberations, 3–4; *Komagata Maru* detention and, 115; restrictions on, 2–3, 63–64, 68, 102, 190, 193, 226, 236; right of, 36; violent constraints on, 7. *See also* migration, Indian; travelers, Indian

Modern Review (Calcutta weekly), on *Komagata Maru*, 177

Mookerji, Radhakumud: *Indian Shipping*, 61–62, 70

motion, in imperial politics, 8

Muldoon, James, 290n4

"Reward for the Discovery of Longitude" (Great Britain, 1714), 55–56

Rhodes, Cecil, 167

rights, Indian, 262n77; as British subjects, 183; to travel, 115, 116, 134, 183, 186, 211

Ritchie, L. W., 164, 166

Ritchie, W. A. B., 144

Roberts, Neil, 290n243

Royal Observatory (Greenwich), founding of, 27. *See also* Greenwich Mean Time

rubber plantations: indenture on, 222, 225; Torrens registration system and, 223, 224

Said, Edward: *Orientalism,* 254n136

sailing ships: effect of currents on, 20; Indian travelers on, 18–19; navigation of, 20–21

Salamanca, School of, 47

Salesa, Damon, 20

Salish peoples, 67, 224; and British Columbia Court of Appeal, 147; in Canadian autonomy, 116; incorporation into Vancouver, 70. *See also* indigenous peoples, Canadian

Sandbach, Tinne, and Co., 95; indenture fleet of, 96–97, 98

Santa Catarina (carrack), 119; cargo of, 41, 42; Dutch capture of, 41–43, 51, 53, 54, 196, 232, 247n127, 251n27; Indian seamen aboard, 61; profits from, 251n41

Sardar Gurdit Singh (Tatla and Tatla), 243n29

Schmitt, Carl: on British Empire, 50, 55; and British North America Act, 143; on the compass, 255n142; on East-West Divide, 56; Eurocentrism of, 234; on free sea, 52, 260n39; geographical thought of, 52; on Grotius, 253n102; on imperial expansion, 51; on indigenous sovereignty, 53; on land/sea divide, 232, 291n5; on maritime technology, 233; under Nazi regime, 50; on ocean as void, 22, 291n14; on Pacific peoples, 257n221; and rise of free trade, 31; on spatiality, 119; spatial *nomos* of, 40; terracentrism of, 51, 52–53, 234; on terrestrial time, 59. Works: *Land and Sea,* 31, 67; *The* Nomos *of the Earth,* 15, 31, 51, 71 143

sea: as archive, 292n25; ceaseless mobility of, 8; colonial history of, 25, 31; as connective force, 258n241; contested spaces of, 12, 34; as cradle of European civilization, 291n20;

in domination of earth, 43; empty, 52; as European, 242n15; feminist scholarship on, 242n15; global legality of, 14; incommensurability of, 81–82; incomprehensibility of, 44, 46; in international order, 49, 57; juridification of, 5, 32, 35, 113, 149, 249n168; jurisdiction over, 24, 48; legal status of, 5, 14, 33, 36, 40–42, 49, 291n22; materiality of, 234, 246n105; measurement of, 46, 48; metaphoricity of, 234, 246n105; open/closed, 44–46, 49–50, 63, 190; physico-material properties of, 232; primordial quality of, 234; as property, 46, 60, 115; as racial form, 113, 235; racial rule of, 190, 233; as site of imagination, 233; as site of resistance, 190; spatial representations of, 14, 244n60; technological mastery of, 57; in terrestrial order, 51; ungovernability of, 30; as unlimited liquid, 46; as Western commons, 256n202. *See also* free sea; oceans

seafarers, non-Western: influence on Grotius, 46. *See also* mariners; travelers, Indian

Sekula, Alan: *Fish Story,* 91, 255n169

Selden, John: on *mare clausum,* 44, 45; response to Grotius, 252n58

self-government, power of, 180

Shakespeare, William: *Hamlet,* 275n22

Sheila (iron clipper), 98; free black sailors of, 99

Shinyei Sisen Goshi Kaisha (firm), 100, 211, 265n169

ship husbands, 79, 260n30

shipping: and Ingress into India Ordinance, 198; and land reform, 288n203. *See also* commerce; indenture ships

shipping, Indian, 5, 62, 63; anticolonialism in, 71, 235

ships: anthropomorphized, 78–79; in antiquity, 79; in common law, 71–72; effect on global time, 29; enabling of radicalism, 14; feminized, 78–79; as floating islands, 129; free/slave distinctions aboard, 25; inside territorial borders, 128–29, 133; as juridical forms, 32, 49, 71–72, 127; legal standing of, 8, 22–23, 71, 81, 244n43; as legal symbols, 23; legal violence on, 88; materiality of, 259n18; in mobility literature, 259n18; *in personam* actions for, 261n54; production of free sea,

30, 54; as quasi-territory, 23; racial standing
of, 71, 72, 260n37; in resource extraction,
15; role in imperialism, 77, 85; "sister," 79,
260n30; timetables of, 22. *See also* indenture
ships; legal personhood, ships'; sailing ships;
steamships
ships' manifests, 109; accounts in, 126; accuracy of, 129; under admiralty law, 122;
authority of, 129–30; enumeration in, 130;
functions of, 122–23, 125–26; governing
of mobility, 126; and imperial administration, 122; power of detention through, 130;
seaborne knowledge in, 128; slaves' status
in, 109, 126, 270n55; submission to port
authorities, 123, 128
Shovell, Cloudsley: wreck of, 55
Sicilia (steamship), 90; European immigrants
aboard, 93, 264n131; owners of, 100; renaming of, 11, 91; voyages of, 34, 72, 78, 93–94,
94, 236–37, 264n131. See also *Komagata
Maru*
Sikhism: British authority and, 30; "Panth" of,
210, 286n130
Sikhs: among *Komagata Maru* passengers, 6,
205, 226; freedom of travel for, 2; murder
at Jallianwalla Bagh, 208, 209, 214; Singh's
appeal to, 1–2; support for Singh, 102
Singapore: Gurdit Singh in, 224; Indian boats
in, 256n195
Singh, Balwant, 3, *220*, 229
Singh, Bhag, 4; appeal for financing, 38, 112–13;
on *Komagata Maru* detainees, 5–6; on
passenger solidarity, 201
Singh, Bhan, 199
Singh, Daljit (secretary of Gurdit Singh), 9;
history of *Komagata Maru*, 268n226; and
Komagata Maru manifest, 122, 125; rhetoric
of slavery, 112
Singh, Daljit Sardar, 204
Singh, Gurdit, *189;* aboard *Komagata Maru, 3,
220;* on abolition, 193; accounting systems
of, 107; advertisements of, 1, 73–74, 241n6;
allegations of criminality against, 191, 192,
194–95, 199, 212, 216; anticolonialism of, 30,
32, 34, 40, 113–14, 186, 191, 194, 208, 224;
arrests of, 214; association with Odagiri,
74, 100, 103, 104, 258n6; authorities'
monitoring of, 102, 188–89, 191, 202–3,

208; and Board of Inquiry hearing, 122; at
Budge Budge, 199–200; and Budge Budge
Massacre, 194, 204, 206; capital problems
of, 74; challenge to continuous journey
regulation, 50; challenge to racial divisions,
60; chartering of *Komagata Maru*, 2, 74,
100–101, 149; civil case (Bengal), 226–27;
contracts with passengers, 107–8, 267n222;
critique of empire, 187, 189; debts to
passengers, 107–8, 112, 199, 213, 284n78;
encouragement of immigration, 141;
financial difficulties of, 107–8, 112, 211–12;
as follower of satyagraha, 208; fraud charges
against, 104, 106–7, 108–9, 211–12, 221; free
sea and, 31, 34, 213, 236; fugitivity of, 11, 33,
113, 186, 192, 194, 204–11, *207*, 230; Gandhi
and, 208–10; geographic imaginary in, 34,
224; and global time, 30; herbal studies
of, 208; imprisonments of, 113, 214–15,
217; and Indian independence, 227; and
Indian National Congress, 209, 210; under
Indian Penal Code, 214–15, 217; under
Ingress into India Ordinance, 192, 199, 211,
217; interest-bearing certificate of, 107–8,
108; itinerary of, 194, 219; journal of, 219,
288n185; juridical forces opposing, 217;
lawsuits in Malaya, 280n1; Malaya residence
of, 218, 223; maritime ambitions of, 9, 37,
46, 73–76, 102, 108, 189, 229, 230; maritime
experience of, 9, 206; and maritime trade,
62–63; on passenger solidarity, 201; "Proclamation to Indians," 1–2, 4, 34; radicalism
of, 39; as railway contractor, 218, 223–24;
relationship with passengers, 212–13; release
from prison, 219; repudiation of British
authority, 34; reputation in Punjab, 190;
reward for, 213; right to travel, 5; in Savli,
207–8; on seaborne travel, 40; as security
threat, 213; sedition trial (1922), 192, 212,
215–17; seizure of property from, 219, 227;
sentencing of, 216–17; shipboard authority
of, 101, 122, 212, 267n222; Sikh identity of,
191, 206, 217; Sikh support for, 102; in Singapore, 224; speeches of, 214, 215; surrender
at Sheikhupura, 191, 192, 205–6, 209–11,
213, 216; temporality in writings, 34; tickets
issued by, 104–5, *105,* 106, 125; voyages of,
186; writings of, 34, 65

Singh, Gurdit (*continued*)
—*Voyage of the Komagatamaru,* 33–34, 192–93, 270n33; on abolition, 224; on British justice, 219, 227–28; Budge Budge in, 215; composition of, 193, 218; continuous journey regulation in, 290n234; as counter-history, 221; critique of British rule, 218, 221, 227–28; draft of, 215; on free migration, 220; fugitivity in, 219; on immigration law, 226; incompletion of, 226, 230; on indentured labor, 221–22, 224–26, 288n196; indigeneity in, 224; itinerancy in, 219; on land/sea divide, 238; maritime imaginary of, 228–29; oceans in, 228; publication of, 281n19; Punjabi version of, 218; purpose of, 218–19; Singh's defense in, 219, 220–21; temporalities of, 193, 219–20; on transatlantic slavery, 193; writing styles of, 219

Singh, Gyani Hanam, 229, 290n253

Singh, Hazarah, 201

Singh, Kirpa, 107

Singh, Munshi: choice for test case, 122; questioning of, 123; refusal of passage for, 124–25; rejection as immigrant, 132; ticket of, 125; transit through Hong Kong, 124, 125. See also *Re Munshi Singh*

Singh, Pal, 212

Singh, Raghunanth, 126

Singh, Surain, 200

slavery: abolition of, 95, 96–98, 113, 224, 258n10; under Dutch rule, 160, 276n32; fugitivity of, 193; in India, 259n21; law of deodand and, 83, 262n93; modernity and, 260n25; negative personhood of, 77, 86–88; overlap with free migration, 230; resistance to, 281n21; in Southeast Asia, 259n21

slavery, transatlantic, 11; anticolonial rhetoric of, 75; Connell's ships in, 78; economic practice and, 87; free sea and, 50, 86–88, 99, 258n10; Gurdit Singh on, 193; indenture and, 98–99, 101, 104, 109, 113, 114, 186, 221–22, 225, 227, 243n37, 288n196, 289n225; legal personhood and, 82, 86–88, 113, 114; living conditions in, 268n227; manifests of, 109, 126, 270n55; maritime jurisdiction of, 24–25; modes of enumeration for, 126; and ships' corporeality, 88; and ships' personhood, 82; ships' status in, 78; under U.S. flag, 262n83

Smith, Maxwell, 116, 143, 147

South Africa: anti-Asiatic attitude in, 159; British Indian Committee, 164; colonial bureaucracy of, 158; Dutch-British conflicts in, 276n49; immigrations restrictions of, 157–59, 276n53; indenture in, 160, 162; Indian anticolonialism and, 276n32; Indian migrants in, 116, 156, 158–68; Indian/native distinction in, 158, 181; *Komagata Maru* supporters in, 154; native administration in, 159; Native Affairs Commission, 163, 165; New Immigration Act, 148; racial classification in, 163, 164–67, 277n56; racial labor in, 160; sovereignty of, 160. See also aboriginal peoples, South African; Indians, South African; indigenous peoples, South African

South China Sea, maritime disputes of, 230

Southeast Asia: British interest in, 42; European commerce in, 42; slavery in, 259n21; waterways of, 40–41

sovereignty: Grotius on, 48; indivisible, 48; versus jurisdiction, 24; *Komagata Maru* and, 7

sovereignty, Canadian, 32, 116, 117, 119; challenges to, 154, 168–69; defense of, 278n95; in *Re Munshi Singh,* 131–32, 150; territorial, 136, 143, 155

sovereignty, indigenous, 61; Canadian, 33, 143, 150, 168–69; global lines atop, 53

spectrality, 273n147; of Indian people, 144

steamships: in "awakening" of Asia, 68; of British Empire, 8; coordination with railways, 68–69; expansion of global law, 22; Indian, 63; revival of Indian trade, 5, 76; transformation of circulation, 21–22

steam technology: opportunities for "Asiatics," 35–36; rise of, 10. See also technology, maritime

steam travel, Marx on, 1, 8, 9

Steinberg, Philip, 13; on free sea, 256n178

Straits of Singapore, 39, 40; imperial expansion in, 42; indigenous rulers of, 42, 47; *Komagata Maru* in, 196. See also *Santa Catarina*

Straits Settlements, 222; indenture in, 224; Indian labor in, 225; oppression in, 193; plantations of, 289n218

Stubbenhuk (steamship), 89–93, *91;* Atlantic crossings of, 92–93, *93;* as cargo ship,

89; construction of, 11, 77, 88, 89, 90–91; European immigrants aboard, 92, 263n127; furnishings of, 89; under German flag, 92; launch of, 91; legal personhood of, 91; renaming of, 93; sale of, 93; technology of, 89; transatlantic documentation of, 89; voyages of, 72, 78, *93;* voyage to Ellis Island, 263n127. See also *Komagata Maru*

subjecthood, British: among *Komagata Maru* passengers, 116–17, 120; asymmetries of, 167; citizenship and, 135, 138–39, 146, 173–74, 179; class in, 138; constraints on, 117; definition of, 116; disenfranchisement from, 144; hierarchy in, 172, 174; indigenous peoples and, 144, 147–48, 159, 178; jurisdiction in, 117, 119, 138; *Komagata Maru* and, 116; maritime, 134; racial distinctions in, 145, 167, 169–70, 172, 180, 184, 236; racial struggles over, 120; in *Re Munshi* case, 133–35; of South African Indians, 181; temporal distinctions in, 167, 172, 236; territorial disputes over, 236

subject peoples, solidarities among, 280n149

subjects, British Indian: equality of, 186; silencing of, 216; travel rights of, 115, 116, 134, 183, 186

Suez Canal, in British maritime power, 89–90

sugar production and trade: and abolition of slavery, 97; Indian labor in, 97–98; shipping for, 96, 264n144; South African Indians in, 160, 161

Supreme Court, U.S.: on ships' personhood, 81–82

Surat (Gujarat), commercial importance of, 256n190

Swaraj (home rule), 210, 286n130

Tagore, Gyanendra Mohun, 157; on aboriginals, 162, 275n9; chronology of, 154, 274n5; "Future of India," 152–54, 155; on white colonization, 186

Tatla, Darshan Singh: *Sardar Gurdit Singh,* 243n29; *Voyage of the Komagata Maru,* 290n248

tea plantations, indenture on, 222

technology, maritime, 43, 57; Asian, 17; of British Empire, 15, 49–50, 83; compass, 45; mastery over nature, 233; power in, 232. *See also* steam technology

telegraph, uniform time of, 26

temporality: of anticolonialism, 217; of British Empire, 137–42, 169–70, 220; in British jurisdiction, 150; in British subjecthood, 167, 172, 236; discrepant, 29–30; in Gurdit Singh's writings, 34, 193, 219–20; in immigration, 16; Indian registers of, 153–54; of indigenous peoples, 144, 154, 169, 273n148, 275n11; of international law, 119; in jurisdictional disputes, 236; of *nomos,* 56; of ocean divisions, 28; racial, 172

territoriality: in British subjecthood, 236; in Canadian sovereignty, 65, 131, 136, 143, 155, 173, 177; and global migration, 13; Grotius's influence on, 245n62; imperial, 119; indigenous peoples and, 155, 168; *Komagata Maru* and, 7, 120, 135; migration and, 13; in *Re Munshi Singh,* 133–35. *See also* boundaries, imperial

Thirty-Nine Hindus case: *Panama Maru* in, 249n6, 265n175; Rahim in, 64, 67

time: as conceptual device, 16–17; display of, 29; heterogeneity of, 58; in imperial control, 235; imposed and lived, 248n161; legal, 59–60; as punishment, 29, 248n162; as racial civility, 28; as register of colonialism, 28; as site of struggle, 30; terrestrial, 59; twelve-hour days, 60

time, global, 6, 40, 50–60; British use of, 28–29; effect of ships on, 29; Greenwich Mean Time and, 60; imposition of order, 28; imposition on indigenous populations, 28; versus lived time, 29; in maritime supremacy, 56–57; ocean currents and, 27–28; steamships' expansion of, 22

time, nautical, 26–31; rise of, 27

time, uniform: in spatial/juridical order, 59; standardization of, 26; in transoceanic travel, 27

timekeeping: in British Empire, 56–59; changing forms of, 248n147; industrialization and, 248n146; for maritime travel, 27; in settler colonialism, 28. *See also* chronometer; clocks; longitude

Tinne, Mrs. J. E., 98

Tong-Hong (steamship), 74, 102

Torrens, Robert Richard: land registration system of, 222–24, 288n203

Tosha Maru, Indian migrants aboard, 265n171
totem poles, 145, 278n108
transnationalism, movements across, 13
Transvaal: Asiatic Restriction Act, 164;
    British Indian Association, 164; "natives"
    of, 163–64; restrictions on Indians in, 160,
    163–64
travel, accidental death in, 83. *See also* maritime
    travel; migration
travelers, Indian: achievements of, 227; antico-
    lonialism of, 25; as cargo, 25; in era of sail,
    18–19; escape from British imperialism, 36,
    112; European cartography and, 291n17; im-
    perial concern over, 23, 38; itineraries of, 10;
    land/sea divide and, 235; restrictions on, 2–3,
    63–64, 68, 102; spatio-temporal challenges
    of, 40; surveillance of, 69; transoceanic
    mobility of, 181. *See also* migrants, Indian
Tribune (Chandigarh), on Asian-African
    distinction, 185

unidirectionality: of colonial migration, 13; in
    imperial history, 12
United Nations High Commission for Refu-
    gees, 238

Vancouver: Asian population of, 66; Indian
    community of, 65, 67, 120; indigenous peo-
    ples in, 70, 258n237; Stanley Park, 258n237;
    as white city, 70. See also *Komagata Maru*
    detention
Vancouver Sun, Indian migrant cartoon in,
    135–36, *136,* 142, 143, 169
van Heemskerk, Jakob, 41, 47, 196; privateering
    by, 42
van Ittersum, Martine, 43
Van Tilburg, Hans Konrad, 78–79
Vereeniging, Treaty of (South Africa), 164

violence: gendered, 176; against Indian mi-
    grants, 181, 182; of white resettlement, 176.
    See also racial violence
violence, maritime, 76, 88, 233; in commerce,
    13, 113; contemporary forms of, 232; against
    Komagata Maru passengers, 112
Vitoria, Francisco de, 47; and Alberico Gentili,
    43
Vosper, Frank L.: *Gurdit Singh,* 188, 189,
    190–91, 210, 230

Wadia, Lowji Nuserwanji, 62
Walcott, Derek, 234, 237, 260n25; "The Sea Is
    History," 231, 258n241
Walvin, James, 270n54
Ward, Kerry, 14, 23, 49, 253n83; on Dutch
    legality, 276n28
Watson, Lord, 141
Weaver, Jace: *The Red Atlantic,* 18
Webb, Montagu de Pomeroy, 148; on South
    African aboriginals, 159
Welwod, William: Grotius's response to,
    44–46, 48, 54, 252n58; on *mare clausum,*
    44–46
West, association with sea, 54
"What Is a Native?" *(Indian Opinion),* 163
"*When* Is a British Subject?" *(New York Times),*
    116
Wick, Alexis, 291n20
Wigen, Karen, 20
Williams, A. W., 140
Wilson, Eric, 253nn83,85
World War I, 213; commencement of, 192

Yamamoto (captain of *Komagata Maru*), 126
Yokohama, *Komagata Maru* at, 195–96

Zong (slave ship), documentation of, 270n54